Understanding Consumer Choice

Understanding Consumer Choice

By Gordon R. Foxall

First published 2005 by
PALGRAVE MACMILLAN
Houndmills, Basingstoke, Hampshire RG21 6XS and
175 Fifth Avenue, New York, N. Y. 10010
Companies and representatives throughout the world

PALGRAVE MACMILLAN is the global academic imprint of the Palgrave Macmillan division of St. Martin's Press, LLC and of Palgrave Macmillan Ltd. Macmillan® is a registered trademark in the United States, United Kingdom and other countries. Palgrave is a registered trademark in the European Union and other countries.

ISBN-13: 978–1–4039–1492–7   hardback
ISBN-10: 1–4039–1492–3   hardback

This book is printed on paper suitable for recycling and made from fully managed and sustained forest sources.

A catalogue record for this book is available from the British Library.

Library of Congress Cataloging-in-Publication Data
Foxall, G. R.
  Understanding consumer choice / by Gordon R. Foxall.
    p. cm.
  Includes bibliographical references and index.
  ISBN 1–4039–1492–3 (cloth)
    1. Consumer behavior. 2. Consumers' preferences.
3. Consumers–Attitudes. 4. Marketing–Psychological aspects. I. Title.

HF5415.32.F688 2005
658.8'342–dc22   2004060623

10   9   8   7   6   5   4   3   2   1
14   13   12   11   10   09   08   07   06   05

Printed and bound in Great Britain by
Antony Rowe Ltd, Chippenham and Eastbourne

To Jean
sine qua non

Contents

Acknowledgements

A predecessor of this book is my *Marketing Psychology* (Macmillan, 1997) and a predecessor of that was my *Consumer Choice* (Macmillan, 1983). The present work is new and its analyses and conclusions far transcend those of the earlier books, but I have retained some original portions of those works. With the permission of the publishers, I have also drawn upon extracts from the following:

Foxall, G. R. (1997). The explanation of consumer behavior: from social cognition to environmental control, *International Review of Industrial and Organizational Psychology*, Eds. Cooper, C. L. & Robertson, I. Chichester: John Wiley and Sons. Pp. 229–287.

Foxall, G. R. (1998). Intention versus context in consumer psychology, *Journal of Marketing Management*, 14, 29–62.

Foxall, G. R. (1999). The substitutability of brands, *Managerial and Decision Economics*, 20, 241–57.

Foxall, G. R. (1999). The contextual stance. *Philosophical Psychology*, 12, 25–52.

Foxall, G. R. (2002). Marketing's attitude problem – and how to solve it, *Journal of Customer Behaviour*, 1, 19–48.

Foxall, G. R. & Yani-de-Soriano, M. M. (2005). Situational influences on consumers' attitudes and behavior, *Journal of Business Research*, in press.

Foxall, G. R., Oliveira-Castro, J. M. & Schrezenmaier, T. C. (2004). The behavioral economics of consumer brand choice: Patterns of reinforcement and utility maximization, *Behavioural Processes*, 66, 235–260.

I am grateful to the publishers for permission to reproduce this material, and to my co-authors who have permitted me to use extracts from joint works.

In addition, I am particularly indebted for comments on all or part of the manuscript, sometimes detailed and painstaking, to Drs. Teresa Schrezenmaier, Mirella Yani-de-Soriano, and Sajid Kahn, and to Professors Jorge Oliveira – Castro, Leonard Minkes, and John O'Shaughnessy. I retain responsibility, however, for the present exposition.

List of Figures

List of Tables

Preface

> Our theories are our inventions: but they may be merely ill-reasoned guesses, bold conjectures, *hypotheses*. Out of these we create a world: not the real world, but our own nets in which we try to catch the real world.
>
> (Popper, 1992, p. 60).

> [O]ne cannot expect the question as to the scientific status of psychology to be settled by empirical research in psychology itself. To achieve this is rather an undertaking in epistemology.
>
> (Hempel, 1980, p. 16).[1]

The research program on which this book is based had its origins in a critique of cognitive models of consumer choice and, especially, their somewhat unsearching acceptance that consumers' beliefs and attitudes would unfailingly predict, prefigure and even cause their behaviors. This criticism stemmed from the failure of such models actually to predict consumer behavior and, in particular, their reluctance to take sufficient account of situational influences on consumer behavior. In order to comprehend more fully the effects of situations on consumer choice, the program turned to behavioral psychology which has made the influence of the social and physical environment on individual behavior its central theme.

This research program stems from an interest in the role of attitude in consumer research which led to the realization that the empirical evidence on attitudinal – behavioral consistency is such that it can support either a cognitive or a behavior analytic methodology. As I pursued the theme of how to explain attitude-behavior relations and their relationships to our understanding of consumer behavior and marketing management, two papers appeared in the marketing literature that were concerned with the relevance of behavioral perspectives in psychology to marketing management, especially in retail contexts (Nord & Peter, 1980; Rothschild & Gaidis, 1981). Admittedly, their authors pointed out that they were not seeking an explanatory model of consumer choice based on radical behaviorism but rather an understanding of the managerial implications of the social learning theories of Bandura and Staats, but they were welcome insofar as they encouraged my fledgling explorations of the possibility that behavior analysis had a role in consumer research. They nevertheless presented a somewhat unelaborated idea of how that discipline might translate into the basis of a fresh understanding of marketing. In short, they subscribed to the notion that the principles of behavior gained in the animal laboratory could be extrapolated without further analysis to the marketplaces of advanced economies marked by severe competition among providers and all the complexities of purchase and consumption among buyers. Since these articles appeared, consumer behavior texts have carried an apparently mandatory chapter on the application of learning principles to aspects of retail and marketing management, based for the most part on an extension of the findings of animal research to the complex world of the human consumer.

Such extrapolation had long been noted as absurd by cognitivists and other post-behavioristic psychologists but also by behavior analysts themselves. The recent history of behavior analysis is actually dominated by three trends that make it highly relevant to understanding consumer research and marketing management as environmentally-shaped behaviors. These trends are, first, the behavior analysis of economic choice; second, the analysis of verbal behavior in humans which renders the causation of their actions quite separate and subject to disparate principles from those of non-humans; and, third, the problems associated with the need to interpret much complex human behavior which is so complex that it cannot be subjected to a direct experimental analysis. Perhaps because these factors have not been taken on board in the marketing context and despite the occasional mention of operant conditioning as a peripheral component of models of consumer behavior, radical behaviorism has failed to find a settled, argued position within consumer research from which standpoint its unique contribution can be gained. This volume is a part of a long-standing exploration of the implications of these factors for a behavior analytic understanding of consumer behavior and marketing management. In the process, the role of social cognitive psychology in consumer research requires attention. The preeminence of cognitive psychology here has never been conceptually addressed by consumer researchers: it has rested, by contrast, on the preeminence of this perspective in psychology and social science generally and on the pragmatic success of cognitive consumer psychology, the reasons for which have gone largely unexamined.

A central aim of *consumer behavior analysis* has been to ascertain whether a model of consumer behavior based on the principles of behavior analysis can be constructed and, if so, the epistemological status of such a model.[2] The strategy from the beginning was to employ the most parsimonious of models derived from the experimental analysis of behavior, which eschewed unobservables, and to incorporate intervening variables and hypothetical constructs only as they might become necessary to enhance the model's explicatory and predictive capabilities (Foxall, 1988). In other words, the strategy involved "testing to destruction" the idea of a behaviorist approach to consumer research. That a social cognitive model would emerge as a superior explicator of consumer choice was thus from the start a serious possibility. Bandura's (1986) social cognitive theory was particularly considered, and the first book-length treatment of the Behavioral Perspective Model (Foxall, 1990), incorporated several of Bandura's criticisms of radical behaviorism. Indeed, from the earliest stages of the research program, the aim has not been to replace one paradigm with another (though it was early recognized that the relatively low level of understanding of the behavior analytic approach to the study of consumption meant that this approach would require serious attention). Rather, it was to establish a frame of reference in which each of the relevant paradigms could act as a standpoint from which to criticize the other on the Feyerabendian understanding that the "active interplay of competing theories" was essential to the growth of knowledge (Foxall, 1986, 1988.)

That model has proved successful in offering a viable operant interpretation of such aspects of consumer behavior as purchasing, consumption, saving, the adoption and diffusion of innovations, attitudinal – behavioral relationships, the marketing firm, and environmental conservation (Foxall, 1996, 2002a). It has also given rise to a program of empirical and applied work that has shown its relevance to the role of situational factors in attitude formation and attitudinal – behavioral consistency, brand choice, and marketing management. Recent theoretical work, based on the empirical findings of some of this research, has again considered the inclusion of mediating stimuli and responses as explicators of affective – behavioral responses (Foxall & Greenley, 2000). However, although the original model has been gradually refined, it has remained broadly, though not uncritically, within the bounds of behavior analysis. In other words, its underlying orientation has been that of the "contextual stance" (Foxall, 1999b) which interprets behavior by reference to the actor's learning history and the behavior setting in which he or she is currently located. The model has been shown by a growing cadre of scholars to generate empirical research which elucidates both practical and theoretical facets of consumer and marketer behavior.[3]

It has now become necessary, partly in order to probe the richness of the interpretation of the empirical findings generated in the course of evaluating the model, partly as a result of continuing conceptual refinement, to transcend that initial position. As a result of my interests in the contextual components of marketing and consumer theory, and because the theoretical issues are so fascinating in themselves, the original intended scope of the program has broadened as it has become necessary to delineate and critique the nature of behavioral explanation itself. This has culminated in a thorough examination of behavior theory and the empirical results to which it has given rise (Foxall, 2004b), which in this book are deployed toward the explanation and interpretation of consumer choice. The model developed in the course of the last two decades remains the centerpiece. It has proved a valuable predictive device, at least as useful in this regard as the cognitive models – and possibly more useful from a practical viewpoint – and, within the methodological limits of behavior analysis it has proved also to be a valuable explanatory system. But the theoretical understanding of consumer behavior has become more sophisticated, not yielding uncritically to a social learning theory approach, which has problems of its own, but reaching toward a more subtle framework of conceptualization and analysis that incorporates both behaviorist and cognitive viewpoints.

Chapter 1 sets the scene by considering a central question in both academic and practical marketing: how far are cognitive factors (exemplified by attitudes and intentions) implicated in shaping behavior? "Marketing's attitude problem" consists in part in the expectation, common to social scientists in general, that attitudes can be relied on to predict and explain behavior. Chapter 2 emphasizes that there is no simple answer given the competing research perspectives of cognitive psychology and behavior analysis which supply rather different answers to this difficulty. Adherents of the cognitive approach are likely to pursue more refined conceptualizations of cognitive and behavioral variables and, in particular, to seek more elaborate and precise measures; behavior analysts are likely, however, to minimize the problem insofar as they see it as an empirical question concerning the consistency of verbal and nonverbal behaviors rather than as a methodological difficulty. Chapters 3 and 4 deal with recent trends in attitude theory and research in the cognitive tradition. They argue that what recent success there has been in predicting behavior from attitudinal measures has resulted from recognizing that both cognition and choice are influenced by their situational contexts.

Attempts to formalize this situational influence by means of both theoretical reasoning and empirical research are described in Chapters 5, 6 and 7. The first two of these endeavor to show that attitudes, behavior and their consistency are systematically related by means of a functional categorization of situational influence derived from behavior analysis. In Chapter 7, an alternative approach to the conceptualization and measurement of consumer choice is discussed, one that sees choice as a sequence of behavior in the context of alternative behaviors. Insights are sought from behavioral economics and marketing science to demonstrate the viability of an understanding of consumer choice as influenced by the pattern of rewards to which it leads. Finally, in an attempt to marry up the variety of themes pursued in the book, Chapters 8 and 9 advance a general framework that retains both the emphasis on environmental influences in predicting choice, which is the hallmark of behavior analysis, and the possibility of employing intentionalistic language, which is that of cognitive psychology, in explaining why patterns of choice are maintained. These concluding chapters deal with the adequacy of a cognitive or behavior analytical framework of conceptualization and analysis to account for attitudinal – behavioral consistency (such as it is) in a way that is useful for marketing theory. It is apparent that each has its place in the explanation of consumer choice but attempts by psychologists to "combine" them into a single framework have tended to be reductionistic with the result that the unique contribution of one or other is lost. Finally, the Notes section contains material that is integral to the argument of the foregoing chapters.

There is good reason for the quotation from Hempel at the beginning of this preface. My earliest expectations as a consumer researcher favored the development of a technology of consumer marketing that was not simply the offspring of the underling disciplines, predominantly psychology and economics, on which marketing science is built, but a scientific entity in its own right. I am still critical of the tendency for some social scientists to use the consumer arena as merely a testing ground for the theories of the "parent" disciplines in which they remain embedded. The academic subject area of marketing and consumer research must always, I believe, be constrained by the activities of marketing managers, consumers and other parties to the transactions that we study. This does not necessarily entail our taking a managerialist or consumerist viewpoint, but it binds and gives coherence to our activities, and prevents them straying too far. But, having said that, it is not my opinion that marketing is a discipline in its own right: it is an application area over which the technical perspectives that are disciplines shed their lights. When it comes to *explaining* – as opposed to describing or predicting – the behaviors of marketers and consumers, therefore, the imperatives arise not just from the empirical findings of marketing and consumer research, but from the epistemological capacities of the underlying disciplines in terms of which the required explanations must ultimately be construed. If the text and Notes that follow seem to deviate at times, therefore, from the everyday ins and outs of consumer research and managerial marketing, if the conclusions seem to be framed in the languages of psychology and philosophy rather than marketing, I hope the reason will be clear and that readers will have no difficulty in translating from one kind of disciplinary analysis to its related sphere of application.

There is equally good reason for the quotation from Popper. The development of marketing and consumer research as a field of intellectual endeavor has often been stymied by a concentration on so-called practical matters, ad hoc empiricism and grand theory-building. If these subjects are to deserve a place in the academy, then more sustained intellectual work must be conducted at the theoretical and empirical levels and these levels must be clearly related on to the other. The book treats philosophical and psychological issues because the solutions to the theoretical problems the research program has posed lie in those directions. "The foundations of consumer behavior analysis" (Foxall, 2001) describes the theoretical and empirical context of this program. This book evaluates the kinds of explanations produced by cognitive and behavioral accounts of choice, and aims to show where both sources of explanation fit into the expanding explanatory base of consumer behavior analysis. A commentator on theories in marketing remarked some years ago that, like other marketing generalizations, Reilly's law of retail gravitation "hardly has the force of a Federal enactment." Nor does what follows. Any genuine contribution to marketing theory is bound by its very nature to be both partial and incomplete: inquiry of this kind is always tentative: the expectation that it be final is itself a misunderstanding of the nature of the quest.

Gordon Foxall
Penarth
September 2004

1

Marketing's Attitude Problem

Marketing's attitude problem stems from the expectation that consumer behavior can be predicted from measures of beliefs, attitudes, and intentions regardless of situational factors.This expectation, which has underlain research in social psychology and sociology as well as marketing for decades, is problematic for two reasons. The first is that it is often not borne out by empirical evidence (Davies, et al. 2002; Foxall, 1983, 1997a, b). The second is that although attitude research has improved dramatically in predictive power in recent years, notably through the incorporation of cognitive measures that attempt to capture situational effects, there is no systematic account in marketing thought or practice to show how situations are implicated in the formation of attitudes and how attitudes can predict and explain actions. There is not even a generally held view of how the word itself should be used.

If this appears remote from everyday marketing experience, something that can be safely left to psychologists while practical people get on with the business of life, consider how pervasive is marketing's dependency on the concept of attitude. Persuasive marketing communications are everywhere aimed toward changing or strengthening people's evaluations of the brands they have bought or are likely to buy. Distribution strategies are directed toward the creation of retail images that are similarly based on ambient responses to stores, restaurants, airport lounges, and other channels that deliver not just goods but life-enhancing consumption experiences. In affluent, consumer-orientated economies, price is widely employed as a creative marketing variable: no longer communicating simply the financial burden that consumers will have to bear but augmenting the impression of quality provided by an integrated marketing mix. And the product or service itself, of course, is a skillfully-constructed bundle of attributes that seeks to elicit the "emotionally colored points of view" as Katona (1960, p. 55) described consumers' attitudes.

The fact is that there is scarcely any element of either academic or practical marketing that is not closely bound up with the concept of attitude and, in particular, with the expectation that attitudes prefigure, predict and cause consumer behaviors. The challenge for marketing research is to show how, in the face of so much contradictory empirical evidence, this foundational assumption of marketing thought and practice can still be relied upon. Answering this challenge is not merely an intellectual exercise: it is one on which the credibility and practicality of managerial marketing vitally depends. It requires not just a series of isolated empirical results but an integrated framework that makes sound prediction possible and, through it, reliable managerial prescription. The suspicion that marketing research must systematically incorporate situational variables in order to predict behavior (Foxall, 1984) inaugurated a research program, described in a later chapter, that is now bearing fruit for marketing theory and potential insights for managerial practice. That chapter addresses the question of how these factors be incorporated into a model of consumers' attitudes and behavior that takes situational influences properly into consideration.

From behavior to attitude

The notion that attitudes provide straightforward explanations and predictions of behavior is beguiling. After all, attitudes are generally defined as predispositions to behave in particular pro or contrary ways to given objects (Foxall et al., 1998) – the task seems only to find a means of measuring attitudes sensitively in order to have no difficulty in forecasting behavioral outcomes. That task preoccupied social psychologists in particular for many decades, beginning in the 1920s, and marketing researchers for almost as long. And not surprisingly, for attitude theory and research promise not only a ready-made explanation why human behavior takes the forms it does but also a practical technology by which consumers' attitudes can be tracked over time and perhaps shaped by marketing managers and other change agents.

Unfortunately for this approach, a whole host of research evidence had accumulated by the end of the 1960s showing that, at best, attitudes and behavior were only weakly related (Wicker, 1969). This may come as a surprise to consumer and other applied social researchers who have trained since then. Surely, in the Theories of Reasoned Action (Ajzen & Fishbein, 1980) and Planned Behavior (Ajzen, 1985) we have clear demonstrations that attitudes do after all prefigure behavior and that it is perfectly legitimate to seek both explanatory models and research techniques in the prevailing social cognition paradigm that underlies almost every consumer behavior textbook? There is a lot riding on this view. Countless dissertations, theses, and journal articles rely on the supposition of an attitude → intention → behavior sequence; and a whole host of commercial studies rest no less surely though perhaps less formally on the same underlying assumption. It works to some extent – students get their degrees and marketing mangers find empirical bases for advertising campaigns and new product development programs. But our systematic knowledge of how attitudes are related to behavior is nowhere as certain as these pragmatic dependencies suggest (Foxall, 1983).

To the extent that progress has been made since then in accurately predicting consumer behavior from these and other cognitive measures, it has come through the incorporation of direct and indirect measures of situational influence on consumer choice (Foxall, 1997a, 1997b, 2002a). Yet there is no generally-accepted model of consumer behavior that relates it to the situational influences that shape it. There is no systematic understanding of how attitudinal – behavioral consistency is related to these situational pressures, nor any methodological basis for understanding consumer choice as situationally determined or marketing management as dependent upon such understanding.

This book explores the expectation that attitudes would be related to behavior and shows why it was thwarted. It goes on to show how recent attempts to relate attitudes and actions have implicitly incorporated measures of the two situational variables on which a situationally-based model of consumer choice must be based: the consumption history of the buyer and the elements of the physical and social setting in which consumer behavior takes place. These variables are combined into a model of the consumer situation from which a typology of consumer situations is derived. The model has been tested in England and Venezuela in terms of its capacity to predict attitudes known to relate to consumer behaviors in a variety of situational contexts. Beyond that, however, the book proposes a novel integration of the cognitive and behavioral perspectives, an overarching research philosophy for consumer research.

Let us remind ourselves what we mean by attitude. While there are numerous concepts and definitions of *attitude*, they have in common the *affective* side of human reactions, how people feel about a particular object, person or other entity, their favorable or unfavorable emotional or evaluative response to it. Although individuals' physiological responses can sometimes be measured to gain some idea of their attitudinal feelings, the usual way of assessing attitudes is to ask people for their feelings and to record their verbal responses. The pencil and paper tests that are at the heart of attitude research are therefore an attempt to gauge people's underlying attitudes, evaluations, emotional reactions second hand from what they are able to say about their feelings. Straightforward as that seems, there lurk behind it numerous theoretical interpretations of how saying and doing are linked, and how attitudes ought to be conceptualized, measured, and related to behavior. We might, for instance, think of attitudes – at least as they are expressed and made available to others – simply as "evaluative verbal behavior" (Lalljee et al., 1984) rather than as an underlying mental entity that undergirds such behavior. It is easy to overlook the array of alternatives before us, especially when we are engaged in applied research, looking for quick, uncomplicated answers. But this may be counter-productive even for the projects in which we are immediately engaged, and certainly for the development of theory in marketing.

"Just the facts, ma'am!"

For there is another attitude problem in marketing, one that stems from its origins and its continuing practical emphases. Marketing, much like engineering, medicine, and law, did not begin as an academic subject or a body of knowledge taught and learned for its own sake. Rather, its origins are linked to the practical concerns of business management and, in particular, with the establishment of regular, formalized patterns of economic exchange in order to make possible higher material standards of living. In spite of great increases in the complexity of social and economic life, the aims of marketing management remain largely unchanged. Indeed, while all of these disciplines are now institutionalized within the established frameworks of education and research, they can still be legitimately regarded as technologies, as well as areas of scholarship. They are technologies firmly based upon bodies of systematic or scientific knowledge and enquiry or are in the process of becoming so. All, including marketing, have developed sophisticated technical analyses and theories, but marketing alone is without a philosophical approach to its subject matter. Marketing equally lacks a scientifically plausible means of determining how far academic work assists or inhibits the practical marketing task. And, despite its technical successes, marketing research, too, lacks an overall understanding of what it is trying to accomplish and how well it does so.

Consonant with marketing's practical origins, business men and women usually avoid referring to the theories and academic disciplines which allegedly underpin their work and achievements. However it is highly probable that their success depends largely upon the accuracy of their beliefs about the economic and business relationships which are implicit in their activities. Keynes (1936, p. 383) went as far as to say that, "Practical men, who believe themselves to be quite exempt from intellectual influences, are usually the slaves of some defunct economist." Staddon (1997, p. 108) puts it equally graphically: "No matter how much they scorn theory ('Just the facts, ma'am!'), by ignoring theory in general, their servitude to some particular theory is ensured." Although this may be an overstatement, it is true that human behavior, including marketing, is generally founded upon commonly held views about the salient components of social and economic situations, opinions about what can safely be ignored and the ways in which the individuals in these situations are likely to make decisions and choices. Without such notions, consistent interaction with other members of society would be impossible, as would the interventions in the physical and social worlds made possible by the various forms of technology.

But these assumptions, the *methodological* postulations we are obliged to rely on, need to be critically examined if we are to draw the appropriate conclusions from our real-world observations of marketer and consumer behavior. In particular, consumer and marketing researchers need to be aware of how alternative theoretical assumptions might lead to interpretations of those observations that would have quite different implications for both marketing theory and marketing practice. It is not just the practical marketing managers who overlook the methodological basis of the concepts they use. Marketing professors in need of a quick fix to make their research results, lecture notes or consultancy recommendations intelligible to a general audience all too often grab in passing at whatever intellectual framework is currently fashionable. But the uncritically accepted concept may not be worth having.

Marketing management as a day-to-day activity relies upon commonly held generalizations about the nature of consumer behavior and the effect upon it of intervening in markets by means of the marketing mix (broadly speaking, the four instruments – product, price, promotion and place – by which managers may seek to influence demand). Recent progress in the introduction of marketing education to universities and colleges and its establishment as an integral part of management studies have hastened the systematic search for such generalizations. Special attention has been given to the exploration of consumers' decision making processes as manifested in the choice of particular brands and the consequent rejection of others and in loyalty to specific retail outlets. The existence of consumer choice – or at least the inability of marketers to know in advance the selections made by customers – lies at the heart of marketing oriented management itself. High levels of competition among companies, accompanied by the large amounts of discretionary income available to buyers, were the key structural factors in the development and adoption of the marketing concept as a contemporary business philosophy. This was because businessmen and women discovered that in order to achieve their own financial objectives they needed to fulfill the requirements of potential customers far more precisely than had previously been the case. And, ever since this discovery began to influence the actions of businessmen and women in the economic conditions of twentieth century America, there has been a diversity of views about how marketing works, the extent to which marketers are able to analyze and understand consumers' wants and needs, and make use of their knowledge of consumers' psychological processes in order to persuade them to buy Brand *A* or to shop at Store *X*.

In a volume of the *Library of Business Practice* concerned with advertising and published nearly a century ago a perspective is found which is frequently encountered today to the effect that:

> Advertising would be a simple proposition if the advertising man had ability to read the individual human mind. Unhappily – or perhaps happily – the advertising man has no supernatural power to scan a crowd and determine what each individual wants, or what argument would avail in a particular case ... Here lies the art of advertising – to find the point of contact between the goods and the consumer. It is indeed an art that has had much to do with mind reading, not of individuals, but of classes. It is the art of knowing the weak spots of self-interest in any group of mankind – of knowing the psychological operation of advertising arguments. (Woolley, 1914, pp. 25–26).

This quotation doubtless reflects the emerging sales orientation of the day. Its emphasis on advertising as a persuasive force rather than on integrated marketing is characteristic of a determination to sell rather than to market, a managerial style which is still encountered all too often in the twenty-first century. Advertising and marketing are still seen in terms of persuading, of building the conviction which leads to purchases that favor a particular brand or store. But more significant is the continuing belief that marketing research must continue to "probe the consumer's psyche" in the hope that the mental processes which are the antecedents of choice will be discovered and, perhaps, made subject to managerial control.

A rather different emphasis, yet one which is built upon the same assumptions, occurs in another chapter of the same volume and nicely illustrates the diversity of variations on the traditional and prevailing theme of consumer choice and marketing action:

> Underneath the changing forms of business stand the fixed motives of men. From the time of stone axes, when men bartered necessities one for the other, the reasons behind the bargaining have always been the same. The man who knows how to sell or advertise today does not need to invent novel arguments or create new demands. Instead, he builds his appeal upon the foundation motives of hunger, cold, self-preservation, pride, love, enjoyment, gain. The man who plumbs the spirit and attitude of the buyer, who frames the right appeal in kind and aim, succeeds whether he does business by stagecoach or limited train. The problem, then, is: can these various appeals – these vital motives of the buying public – be analyzed and charted? Keen businessmen have demonstrated the answer beyond doubt or question. They have been and can be so charted and so used every day (Murphy, 1914, p. 9)

These sentiments are over-generalized and dogmatic perhaps, but does any of this sound so far removed from current marketing practice and consumer research, from the simplifications and nostrums of marketing and consumer behavior textbooks? The widespread view of the role of marketing, then as now, was based upon the belief that human choice is the outcome of mental deliberation or cognitive processes and that persuasion means influencing or manipulating those internal events. The purpose of this book is to demonstrate that there is an alternative viable framework within which consumer choice may be conceptualized and analyzed. This approach is not entirely new to marketing but has received far less attention than that which stresses the need to delve profoundly into consumers' cognitive processes. In contrast to that idea, the alternative framework focuses upon the behavior of consumers in itself and the environment within which it takes place. The book is concerned with the extent to which a consumer's choices are influenced by his or her mind, or by factors external to the individual.

Take the concept of *choice*, a word that is in prolific current use not only among marketing managers and educators but by politicians and journalists, as though it referred simply and unambiguously to something that is both generally understood without undue need for deliberation and manipulable by members of the political and economic systems. But even the notion of choice is surrounded by continuing conceptual ingenuity and debate. Inevitably, the acceptance of one or other of the sets of psychological assumptions on which the idea of choice may be posited strongly influences the direction and content of consumer research programs, the ways in which marketing mangers seek to create and influence markets, and the ways in which politicians are tempted to intervene in their working.

Perspectives on choice

Defining choice appears initially to be a straightforward, commonsense task. From this viewpoint, it is difficult to improve on the description suggested by Hansen (1976, p. 117) at the beginning of the present era in consumer research:

> We all intuitively understand what a choice is. It is classically illustrated by the person walking down a road who hesitates at a fork in the road before choosing which route to take. We all agree that he is faced with a choice. If, however, the example is changed slightly, it is more doubtful whether we are still talking about a choice. The person walking on a sidewalk, when confronted with a puddle, changes his direction slightly and continues. In this case, few people would say that a choice is involved.

Hansen makes it clearer still by distinguishing choice from other forms of behavior, pointing out that choice involves a multiplicity of possible outcomes, the arousal of conflict as a result of the individual's perception that mutually exclusive outcomes are open to him, and an attempt to reduce this conflict by means of cognitive activity. Thus when an individual is faced with the selection of a single course of action from among several ostensible options,

> a particular pattern of reactions can be observed: hesitation, inspection of alternatives, uncertainty ... [C]onscious and unconscious brain processes occur, processes that may possibly be observed directly and are reflected in measurements such as electrocardiograms and galvanic skin response. These suggest that a conflict is present and that cognitive activities occur (Hansen, 1976, p. 117)

Few would disagree with the proposition that the first example given by Hansen involves choice while the second does not and, as the word "choice" is employed in everyday discourse, the distinction is clear enough. But scientists and philosophers have developed systems of thought which do not distinguish between these two examples. Sartre (1973) would argue, for instance that the individual confronted with the puddle did have a choice and that it is "bad faith" to claim that he could not have stepped into the water had he so decided. More relevant to the framework of conceptualization and analysis advanced in the present work is the proposition that the person in the first example had as little freedom of choice as the one in the second: both, on the basis of previous identical or similar experience and the consequences of previous behavior in similar situations, would be capable of only one course of action, that which was taken. In the words of B. F. Skinner (1974, p. 113), the psychologist most frequently associated with this approach, "To exercise choice is simply to act, and the choice a person is capable of making is the act itself. The person requires freedom to make it simply in the sense that he can make it only if there are no restraints – either in the physical situation or in other conditions affecting his behavior." The first explanation, that of the individual faced with a puddle, places the locus of control entirely within the individual; the second, that which focuses on the act itself as the only choice available, places the locus of control ultimately outside the person.

The differences between these accounts stem largely from the different frameworks of conceptualization and analysis which investigators bring to the study of their subject matter. Appreciation of the role of such frameworks in scientific progress has recently increased substantially in a wide range of fields of research. This development has followed the publication by Kuhn (1970) of the view that scientific development advances more significantly as a result of the revolutionary substitution of an innovatory framework or *paradigm* for the existing framework than by the evolutionary accumulation of knowledge. The idea of paradigmatic scientific progress is rather more complicated than this but the following brief account cannot be improved upon as a concise description of what is involved in Kuhn's thesis. Social psychologists, Jones and Gerard (1967, p. 46) refer to a paradigm as:

> essentially a model for asking research questions. Paradigms are partly a matter of broad theoretical outlook or perspective, partly a matter of pre-ferred methods of obtaining evidence, and partly a matter of the standard by which such evidence is to be evaluated. In the developmental history of a particular discipline, a certain paradigm may characterize the outlook of one or more generations of scientists. Eventually, certain anomalous findings may force a shift to a new paradigm, bringing about radical changes in perspective, new suggestions about where to look for evidence, and new standards of evaluation. The change from Aristotelian to Galilean physics represents a very broad paradigm shift. The shift from Newtonian mechanics to Einsteinian relativity provides a more recent example. The point is that these shifts are more than changes in theories appropriate to account for a particular set of phenomena. They are shifts that revolutionize our entire scientific stance and radically change the way in which investigators view their subject matter.

In contrast to the popular view that scientific progress is the straightforward result of the continual accumulation of facts within a given framework of conception and analysis, Kuhn hypothesizes that 'mature' sciences, notably physics, develop by means of dramatic paradigmatic supersession. The revolutionary replacement of a previously productive paradigm has profound implications for the concepts that are deemed relevant, the canons of theoretical judgment which are applicable and the appropriate practical methods of data collection, techniques of analysis and procedures of interpretation. Such revolution is, Kuhn argues, a periodic necessity of advance.

How does he account for the occurrence of these revolutions? Because of the essentially ideological nature of scientific paradigms, they are not themselves amenable to direct empirical test. A paradigm consists, after all, of the most general, albeit highly influential, beliefs of a scientific community with respect to the investigation of reality. Kuhn (1970, p. 230) defines a paradigm as, "what the members of a scientific community share ... some implicit body of intertwined theoretical and methodological belief that permits selection. evaluation and criticism." This resembles to some extent (though without capturing the political and institutional concomitants) what Thelen and Withal (1949) long before called simply a "frame of reference", a device by which the researcher, "perceives and interprets events by means of a conceptual structure of generalizations or contexts, postulates about what is essential, assumptions as to what is valuable, attitudes about what is possible, and ideas about what will work effectively." It is more frequently called today a *methodology*, denoting not just a series of techniques but a body of knowledge that links a rationale of how theory and the findings of empirical research are linked in a consensually acceptable framework of explanation. For our purposes, the term *perspective* will suffice.

Fundamental to Kuhn's thesis is the observation that such is the nature of paradigm based "normal" science that its exponents act very conservatively, rejecting initially any subversive philosophy which threatens the tenets of the paradigm within which they are working. The first cracks in the scientific community's acceptance of the prevailing paradigm appear only as a result of the clear inability of theories devised within it to account for new findings. Repeated theoretical failure often results in a scientific crisis, the proliferation of theories to account for the new evidence. The crisis ends with the general acceptance of a novel paradigm that accommodates both those new theories which are deemed valid and those elements of the older body of knowledge which are held to be worthy of retention. Thus while paradigms cannot be subjected to direct testing as can hypotheses, they give rise to the theories, models and hypotheses whose empirical verification or refutation eventually confirm or disconfirm the prevailing conventional wisdom.

Kuhn's hypothesis was developed in the course of his studies of historical developments in the physical sciences. The social sciences may well prove to be an exception to the pattern of progress he identified. In the physical sciences, for example, a single paradigm usually dominates the entire scientific community most of the time. Multiple paradigms and the division of the scientific community along fundamental lines occurs, by and large, only during critical phases of development. This is manifestly not the case in the social sciences where a plurality of competing paradigms is usually apparent. The possibility of paradigmatic supersession is a constant fact of life for the social scientist, even though it is unlikely that displaced frames of reference ever completely disappear. None of these viewpoints is entirely new; nor has their acceptance been total, nor have they provided an enduring general theoretical framework.

Social science disciplines are usually characterized by the simultaneous flourishing of more than one paradigm and drawn out debates between their exponents rather than by conformity to a single, general philosophy, of the nature of the discipline. Consequently when change does occur it is usually less dramatic and less obviously revolutionary than in the mature sciences. Feyerabend (1970) argues that competing theories proliferate not intermittently, during the periods of crisis that precede the revolutionary overthrow of one paradigm by another, but all the time as a constant feature of scientific investigation and discovery. He writes that, "Science as we know it is not a temporal succession of normal periods and periods of proliferation; it is their *juxtaposition*. Science has its normal and proliferative modes but their relationship is accurately described as one of simultaneity and interaction" (p. 209). The deliberate proliferation of competing theories, "methodological pluralism," produces an active interplay of various tenaciously held views which is necessary to scientific progress or, more accurately, the growth of knowledge (Feyerabend, 1975). Having more than one theoretical perspective enables the results produced by any one to be criticized from the standpoint of the other, and promotes the generation of knowledge that would not be sought if only one theory were universally embraced (Valentine, 1992). Far from being finally settled, scientific knowledge is always open to debate: something that is borne out by the relatively long period that ensued before Crick and Watson's model of the structure of DNA was generally accepted by biologists and the continuance until at least recently of scientific attempts to discredit it (Crick, 1988).

That the social sciences do not precisely correspond to Kuhn's model of scientific progress ought not, however, to obscure the value of conceiving of the development of these disciplines in terms derived from it. Psychology – and the study of consumer behavior conceived in psychological terms – contains two broad meta-theoretical stances, two broad paradigms: that which casts behavior as the result of intrapersonal, cognitive information processing, which explains choice as the outcome of deliberation and decision making; and that which interprets behavior in terms of the consequences of previous behavior, which describes choice in terms of determined responses to environmental (and, less significantly) in the present context, inherited) stimuli. The description and analysis of consumer behavior in ways which are both intellectually and commercially valid and reliable require a more detailed understanding of these paradigmatic stances.

Two broad conceptions of *attitude*

In order to remain close to the theme of this chapter, the relevance of measures of consumers' attitudes to the prediction and explanation of consumer behavior, it would be useful in this discussion to have a basic understanding of the ways in which the idea of *attitude* has been used in social psychology. Fortunately, a classic paper by DeFleur and Westie (1963) simplifies greatly the task before us. Their classification of attitude constructs as either "probability conceptions" or "latent process conceptions" is an invaluable first approximation in determining the essential differences between cognitive and behavioral notions of attitudes and their relationships to behavior. This division does not correspond to that between the cognitive and behaviorist psychologies mentioned in the previous paragraph since latent process notions of attitude can be found in both systems, while probability conceptions belong only to the behaviorist camp. However, while Chapter 8 will take the argument beyond these authors' basic dichotomy of attitude constructs, for now it provides a means by which to approach the issue of how far different schools of psychological thought account for the empirical evidence for attitudinal-behavioral consistency.

A probability conception is concerned with the consistency of behavioral responses and derives from the observation that a set of responses to a particular object exhibits a degree of consistency and thus predictability. The term "attitude" in this case refers simply to the probability that a particular behavioral response will recur in reaction to a given object or stimulus and this probability is inferred directly from observations of previous behavior in similar circumstances. As these authors point out, any definition based upon a probability conception, "*anchors the attitude concept* firmly to observable events ... The attitude, then is an inferred property of the responses, namely their consistency. Stated in another way, attitude is equated with the probability of recurrence of behavior forms of a given type or direction" (DeFleur and Westie, 1963, p. 21). Use of the word "attitude" is consequently confined to the description of observable behavior in terms of the extent to which it shows consistency over time.

The latent process conception goes beyond the observation of response consistency by positing an intrapersonal function or process which intervenes between the stimulus object and the responsive behavior, causing or at least acting upon it, shaping and guiding it. In the words of DeFleur and Westie (1963, p. 21):

> the observable organization of behavior is said to be "due to" or can be "explained by" the action of some mediating latent variable. The attitude, then, is not the manifest responses themselves, or their probability, but an intervening variable operating between stimulus and response and inferred from the overt behavior. This inner process is seen as giving both direction and consistency to the person's response.

This is the most widely encountered understanding of attitude in social psychology where "The implicit assumption has usually been of a simple, causal relationship between a multidimensional conception of attitude toward a social object and specific behavior toward the object, irrespective of situation" (Thomas, 1971, p. 9). Like the paradigm to which it belongs, this is now the conventional wisdom, for "Most psychologists take the view that a concept such as attitude is best viewed as an 'intervening' or 'mediating' variable. By this is meant that we have to posit a construct which we assume to exist but which is not directly observable" (Reich and Adcock, 1976, pp. 12–13).

Nevertheless, inferences about the nature of attitude must eventually be related to the observable responses which are assumed to be caused by attitude and to be consistent with it over a range of situations. A similar remark with respect to the non-observability of attitudes is made in the context of consumer behavior by Walters (1978, p. 226) who nevertheless claims that "we must make the attempt to understand attitudes because they guide everyday consumer actions. People seldom act in opposition to their attitudes, just as they seldom go against their motives." And, again in the realm of consumer research, Day (1973, pp. 188–209) endorses the conception of attitude as an unobservable mediating or intervening construct which is linked to two forms of observable factors, "One link is with the *antecedent* conditions which lead to it; these might be the stimulus of an advertisement, a move to a new house, and so forth. The second link is with the *consequents* that follow from the attitude, including search and purchase behavior." All of these statements are in alignment with the definition of attitude devised by Allport (1935, p. 810) which has had a profound effect upon both social psychology and marketing, "An attitude is a mental and neural state of readiness, organized through experience, exerting a directive or dynamic influence upon the individual's response to all objects and situations with which it is related."

Each of these conceptions has direct and specific implications for attitudinal-behavioral consistency. The latent process conception leads logically to the expectation of consistency between "verbal" behavior (the responses made to attitude measuring devices such as questionnaires) and "overt" behavior, both of which are responses which, if directed toward the same object, ought to be consistent since the identical latent process mediates both. The stable, underlying mechanisms of behavior postulated by latent process theorists who depict attitude change as a slow, resistant procedure, cause all classes of response to the objects they govern regardless of whether those responses are verbal or active. The consistency which is the hallmark of the latent process approach should be manifest in both types of *behavior*.

The verbal responses which are usually taken to be measures of underlying attitudes ought to correlate highly with and predict accurately the active responses which are also the result of the attitude. The underlying, unobservable mental mechanism or process which comprises the individual's attitude (sometimes called his 'true' attitude) is, according to the latent process conception, equally causative of the various behaviors of that individual with respect to the referent object. In the case of probability conceptions of attitude, however, consistency is simply a question of empirical observation, a matter of determining by relatively straightforward recording the probabilities of the occurrence of various classes of response in given circumstances. Observed inconsistency between what an individual says and what he does about an object would pose no problem of theory, concept, or method since the verbal and overt responses belong to different classes of behavior, each occurring in accord with its peculiar set of situational contingencies. Thus DeFleur and Westie (1963, p. 30) describe attitudes as "specific *probabilities* of specific forms of response to specific social objects".

The terms "latent process conception" and "probability conception" do not in themselves denote specific definitions of attitude but refer to conceptual categories from which definitions and operational categories derive. These conceptual categories derive, in turn, from paradigms. The latent process view has its origins in some behaviorisms and cognitive psychology, the psychology of internal information processing which asserts that behavior results and is predictable from knowledge of antecedent, intrapersonal states. The probability conception makes no such attribution of pre-behavioral, intervening processes. It belongs to the broad paradigm of behaviorism. It is placed there in a review of DeFleur and Westie's paper by Alexander (1966, pp. 278–281) who states that their definition:

anchors attitude to the specific, external stimulus situations in which the individual responds. Attitude has been regarded as an inner-state variable that exists dispositionally, but the authors are denying its independence of the specific stimulus situations in which responses are observed. Consequently, as Skinner (1953) observed long ago, an inner-state directly expressed and totally exhausted by the probability of a class of responses is conceptually superfluous; it is necessary only to deal directly with the response probabilities.

Neither does the probability conception lead to inferences of a simple, causal relationship between attitudes and behavior or between different classes of behavioral response regardless of contextual differences which arise from situational factors and contingencies of reinforcement. The closer the correspondence between the situations within which verbal and overt responses to a stimulus object occur, however, the greater is the probability of response similarity and consistency. While, in the latent process conception of attitude, attitudinal change is causative and a necessary antecedent of behavioral change, probability conception theorists assume that behavioral change occurs as a result of the patterns of reward and sanction encountered in consequence of past behavior or as a result of changes in reinforcement contingencies. The latent process conception of attitude is found in both cognitive and some behaviorist perspectives on behavior, while the probability conception is exclusively found in the more extreme behaviorist programs. It is time to examine these in greater detail in the context of consumer behavior.

2
Consumer Behavior

Consumer behavior includes all of the activities of buyers, ex-buyers and potential buyers from prepurchase deliberation to postpurchase evaluation, and from continued consumption to discontinuance. It extends from the awareness of a want, through the search for and evaluation of possible means of satisfying it, and the act of purchase itself, to the evaluation of the purchased item in use, which directly impacts upon the probability of repurchase (Alba et al., 1991). The models of consumer behavior that emerged in the mid- to late-1960s on which the central theoretical perspective for academic consumer research has since relied almost exclusively, provided a distinctive meld of cognitive and social psychologies. Fundamental components of this paradigm include the goal-oriented reception, encoding, representation and processes of information; but equally determining was the way in which this cognitive procedure was linked to behavior in the sequence of belief–, attitude–, and intention–formation. The initial emphasis was upon high involvement processing but, by successive elaborations, several of the models have gradually acceded to and accommodated low involvement processing (Engel et al., 1995; Howard, 1989) which may influence capacity for recall without requiring prior evaluation (Hawkins & Hoch, 1992).

An outline of consumer behavior

Consumer behavior is most frequently modeled as a cognitive process, an intellectual sequence of thinking, evaluating, and deciding. These information processing activities are believed to shape the more overt aspects of choice: acquiring information, perhaps from an advertisement or salesperson, placing an order, using the product selected, and so on. The inputs to the process are the most basic bits of data available to the consumer, stimuli from the environment in the form of marketing messages and conversations with friends and relatives. The processing itself consists in the mental treatment of these data as the consumer stores them, links them with existing ideas and memories, and evaluates their relevance to his or her personal goals. The outputs are the attitudes the consumer forms toward say an advertised brand, an intention to buy or postpone buying, and – if attitude and intention are positive – the act of purchase. A similar sequence characterizes the use of the purchased item: it is evaluated again in use and a decision is reached about its suitability for repurchase.[1]

Awareness

Figure 2.1 summarizes the process of consumer decision making, while Table 2.1 outlines the sub-processes involved in it. Consumer awareness is not spontaneous: it is actually the endpoint of a highly selective procedure. Consumers are bombarded daily by thousands of messages that seek to persuade them – from advertisers, political organizations, religious groups, employers, government, and numerous other sources. All of these compete for the attention and understanding of citizens, none of whom can cope with the cumulative effect of so great a mass of information on the nervous system. As a result, the majority of these social, economic and marketing stimuli in the environment are filtered out by the individual's attentional and perceptual processes and have no effect on the decision process.

To be efficient, consumer decision making relies on these processes being selective. What we might look upon as a kind of "perceptual defense mechanism" screens out all but those messages that are most familiar, consistent with the consumer's current beliefs and prejudices, motives, expectations and wants. Perception is evidently more than a matter of stimuli impinging on the sense organs: it is the starting point of information processing itself, the initial interpretation of those stimuli to which the consumer does pay attention according to his or her existing attitudes, experiences, and motivations. Not until an advertising message has penetrated this filtering mechanism, and this preliminary processing activity is underway, can the consumer be said to be aware of a problem (dandruff, for instance), its potential consequences (for their health and social activity), and the salience of the proffered means of overcoming it (the advertised brand of medicated shampoo).

Search and evaluation

Such awareness of a problem is no guarantee that the process of decision making will continue. Only if the problem is sufficiently important to the consumer amid all the other imperatives of life, and he or she comes to believe that a viable solution is attainable, does it become likely. If a high enough level of involvement or engagement with the problem is present, the consumer is likely to seek further information to evaluate the claims of the advertiser. First, internal search takes place within the consumer's memory system, an attempt to locate relevant pre-existing knowledge, notably beliefs and attitudes about the problem, current practices, the

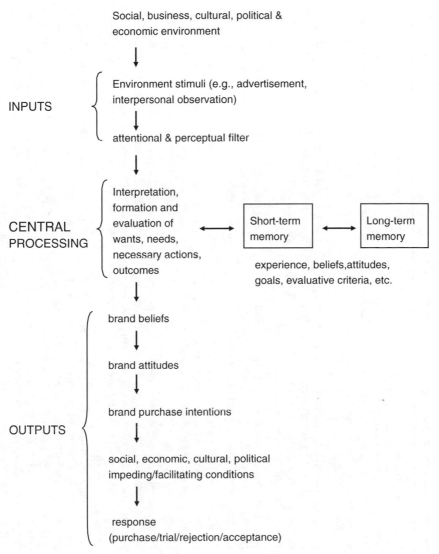

Figure 2.1 A Model of Consumer Choice as a Cognitive Process

likely solutions, and remedies that are already in use. Should the advertiser's proffered solution be radically new to the customer, internal search may prove inadequate, in which case an external search may be necessary, including perhaps an active seeking of information from neighbors or colleagues, salespersons, advertisements for competing brands, newspapers or magazines, even *Which?* or *Consumer Reports*.

Table 2.1 Elements of the Information Processing Perspective in Consumer Research

Process components	Typical research issues	Typical managerial concerns
Attention	Arousal, interest, exposure patterns, sensory reception, social and personality contexts, avoidance of discrepant information, information search pre-attentive delay, attentive screening.	Segmentation of markets, media selection, use of fear or humor, packaging, sensory stimuli.
Perception	Perceptual selectivity, sensory-overload and filtering of information, post attentive delay, perceptual shift, stimulus intensity, reinforcement history, needs states, values, expectation, perception by exception.	Dimensional factors, packaging size and shape, repetition, stimulus intensity, sensory stimulation.
Comprehension	Short and long term memory, interpretation and meaning, abstraction, verbal and visual encoding research, initial processing of information.	Use of linguistic and visual explanation, stimulation of information seeking, repetition of message.
Acceptance	Agreement, persuasion, belief formation, attitude change, personal and social characteristics, message discrepancy, credulity, receptivity to emotional appeals, attribution of motives.	Source credibility, media selection and copywriting, structure of appeals (one sided/two sided appeals), proximity and recency, emotional appeals, reference groups.
Information storage and retrieval	Retention, memory and memory decay, forgetting, recall, retrieval, decoding, temporal effects, delayed processing, personal and social influences or remembering and forgetting, short term and long term memory interactions, information search.	Evocative advertising, emotional appeals (e.g., to nostalgia), provision of information, stimulation to information seeking, stimulation of interpersonal communication.
Establishment of preferences	Choice strategies, decision making processes, risk and uncertainty, elimination of options, evaluation, use of information, evaluative criteria, goals and expectations.	Comparative advertising, reinforcement, point of sale communication, sales promotions.
Behavior	Attitudinal-behavioral consistency, behavioral intentions and their correlation with behavior and its outcomes, unconscious motivation, dissonance reduction, purchase and consumption.	Manipulation of purchase and consumption situations, product availability, pricing, repeat buying, reduction of post-decisional dissonance.

These activities take the form of mental processing of the advertising message in the consumer's short term and long term memory stores. Much of the information that targets the consumer fails to get this far, and even that which reaches short term memory is there only briefly. If it is not effectively transferred to the long term store, where it is poised to be effective in this and subsequent decisions, it may be lost within about a minute. Several operations may occur in the consumer's memory to ensure that information can be retained and retrieved: *rehearsal* – the mental repetition of information which links it to informational already stored; *encoding* – the symbolic representation of information which permits its long-term association with other stored information; *storage* – the elaboration of information in which it is organized into structures, and *retrieval* – its return from long term to short term memory for use in making a choice.

The outputs of this information processing are the beliefs and attitudes that shape decisions, and the intentions that predispose the consumer to activate them through such actions as purchasing, consuming, and saving. Beliefs are statements about the product or brand that the consumer assumes to be factual; attitudes are evaluations of the product or brand; and intentions are strong motivations to act in accordance with beliefs and attitudes. Together they form the cognitive (intellectual), affective (evaluative) and conative (action-oriented) components of the consumer's decision activity.

Post-decisional evaluation

Another filtering device determines the speed with which consumers put their intentions into practice, shown in Figure 2.1 as "impeding and facilitating conditions." These situational variables include access to funds or credit, the availability of brands that seem likely to fulfill the consumer's goals, and the social acceptability of buying and using the product, especially in an environmentally-aware world, all of which determine whether a particular purchase will take place. Even the strongest of consumer intentions cannot guarantee that a purchase will take place in the absence of these and a hundred other facilitating conditions. In addition, purchasing reflects on past behavior and its outcomes. Post-purchase evaluation is important, above all, because of its implications for future purchase patterns.[2]

Hence the consumer decision process does not end once a purchase has been made. The first purchase of a brand – perhaps the first of several purchases – can be considered no more than a trial by the consumer. The clearest indication of whether it is worth buying again comes from its evaluation in use (Ehrenberg, 1988/1972). Something that may need to be resolved in the case of expensive, infrequently bought items such as consumer durables is the "cognitive dissonance" or feeling of mental unease that follows their purchase. Cognitive dissonance arises when two contradictory beliefs are held simultaneously: "Yesterday I spent so much on this car and now my neighbor tells me his gets from 0–60 mph a second faster!" Consumers reduce dissonance by dropping one or other of the opposing beliefs or by emphasizing one or the other. The car purchaser might conclude, therefore, that his car was more prestigious since it had cost more or had a more auspicious marque. Or that his car was guaranteed for longer, or ran on unleaded fuel, or needed less frequent service. Some advertising is geared especially to the dissonant consumer who has recently purchased; although they are less obvious than they used to be, ads for cars still sometimes stress the performance characteristics of the advertized and competing makes.[3]

It is important to remember that the process of consumer decision making is not in practice the dry, mechanistic procedure that this kind of model may suggest. The evaluative component of both pre-purchase and post-purchase consumer behavior gives rise to emotional reactions as well as cognitive judgments. Indeed, the entire decision process is permeated by affective responses. As O'Shaughnessy and O'Shaughnessy (2003, p. 3) put it, "Marketing folklore suggests that emotion can stimulate buying interest, guide choices, arouse buying intentions, and influence future buying decisions. All these popular beliefs about the power of emotion have received research support."

This outline of the consumer decision process includes the consumer in both cognitive and behavioral procedures: thinking, evaluating, decision-making on the one hand, using experience and its outcomes to guide present behavioral choices on the other. In practice, models of consumer choice have tended to emphasize the former at the expense of the latter. The distinction this chapter makes between cognitive and behavioral models of consumer choice depends in some degree on where one places the emphasis within this process of consumer behavior. However, far-reaching theoretical and epistemological consequences follow from this apparently simple demarcation. Appreciation of this requires an apparent detour into some of the historical landmarks in the development of cognitive psychology as it has come to influence consumer research, followed by a treatment of the behaviorist perspective and how it elucidates aspects of consumer choice.

Cognitive information processing

The popular view of psychology as the formal study of mind, mental phenomena and processes, or of internal, subjective or covert experience, was, until recently, not shared by the majority of psychologists. From the early years of the twentieth century until the mid to late 1950s, most psychologists adhered to the belief propounded by Watson (1914, 1924), "the father of behaviorism," that so-called mental phenomena were beyond the scope of a science of behavior. During those years, the behaviorist framework of analysis characterized the normal science of psychology and, although there was some work done outside of this paradigm throughout the period, the shift which enthroned cognitive psychology as the prevailing conventional wisdom is a fairly recent occurrence. Members of a symposium convened to identify and discuss contemporary issues in cognition psychology clearly understood the emergence (or re-emergence) of the cognitive paradigm in terms of Kuhn's ideas of the nature of scientific progress (Solso, 1973; cf. Baars, 1986; Gardner, 1985).

That cognitive phenomena provide the basis of psychology's prevailing paradigm is evident from the observation that, while psychologists increasingly recognize situational and other external environmental factors as influences upon behavior, their definitions of psychology and, especially significant, the way they demarcate it from other social, behavioral and physiological sciences are expressed predominantly in terms of perception, memory, thought and emotions. This is also evident from the stress they place upon the mediating roles of cognitive factors even when tracing, analyzing and interpreting the effects of extrapersonal influences on behavior. In an address to the American Psychological Association in 1973, Hebb asked "What is psychology about?" and answered that, "Psychology is about the mind: the central issue, the great mystery, the toughest problem of all." He went on to define mind as "the capacity for thought" and thought as "the integrative activity of the brain – that activity up in the control tower that, during waking hours, overrides reflex response and frees behavior from sense dominance" (quoted by Blumenthal, 1977, p. iv).

The peculiar focus of the *social* psychologist, within whose bailiwick attitudinal–behavioral relationships naturally fall, has been stated by Tajfel and Fraser (1978, pp. 25–26) as consisting in an interest in information about how the various social structures, social systems or groups affect an individual's way of viewing the world in which he lives and of acting in it; and about how his or her "nature", i.e., motives, perceptions and interpretations will in turn affect his functioning in groups and the relationships between groups. Thus, while social psychology shares the field of intergroup relations with numerous other professional investigators, the focus consists uniquely "in establishing links between an individual's interpretation or perception of social situations and his behavior and attitudes toward the groups to which he belongs and other groups; in the ways in which various kinds of intergroup situations may affect an individual's motives ... and in the ways in which certain motives may affect, in turn, the nature of these intergroup relations: in analyzing the process of communication which help or hinder the diffusion of certain modes of behavior and attitudes toward in-groups and outgroups."

The essential theme of psychological study is, according to this, the prevailing perspective, not only individual and group behavior of itself but the mental antecedents which are assumed to determine it. The description of cognitive psychology offered by Moore (1981, p. 62) summarizes well its dominant character: "Mentalism may be considered as a particular orientation to the explanation of behavior, involving the following implicit or explicit features: (a) the bifurcation of human experience into a behavioral and a pre-behavioral dimension (b) the use of psychological terms to refer to organo-centric entities from the pre-behavioral dimension, and (c) the use of organo-centric entities as causally effective antecedents in explaining behavior."

Intervening variables

Some of the earliest challenges to the rigid stimulus-response paradigm (which approached behavior solely in terms of the physical stimuli, S, such as heat and light, which act upon a subject, and the response, R, in terms of movement elicited) originated in the work of behaviorists. For example, an interesting expression of the view that behavior can be accurately understood, predicted and controlled only when intrapersonal mediating processes are considered occurs in the writings of Tolman (e.g., 1932). Not content to study behavior exclusively in terms of S-R mechanisms, Tolman hypothesized "intervening variables" which summarized the effects on behavior of previous experience or learning and inherited influences; these mediating factors were assumed to modify the effects of stimuli in individual cases, accounting for variations in response. Tolman's central interests remained in the sphere of investigations of the relationships between stimuli and the responses they evoke and he attributed his work to the behaviorist paradigm since he ascribed the intrapersonal variables upon which his theories depended to reflex, physiological factors rather than mental events. His work had a profound influence upon later behaviorists but in paradigmatic terms it encouraged the progress of cognitive psychology since many subsequent researchers comprehended the organo-centric intervening variables as psychological or mental processes.

The growth of Gestalt psychology (e.g., Koffka, 1935) which influenced Tolman through the tenet that intervening factors constituted the psychological pattern through which stimuli received subjective meaning, also facilitated the diffusion of the non-behaviorist paradigm. Such variables as beliefs, attitudes, personality traits, motives and values were assumed to mediate stimuli and responses by psychologists who adopted the stimulus $\rightarrow$ organism $\rightarrow$ response or $S \rightarrow [O] \rightarrow R$ model. Within this perspective, the classification and measurement of stimuli and responses allow inferences to be drawn with respect to the nature of the "black box" of internal, psychological processes which are not available for direct investigation. (The model of consumer choice depicted in Figure 2.1 follows this $S \rightarrow [O] \rightarrow R$ logic).

George Miller has drawn attention to "one day in September 1956 as a significant date in the emergence of cognitive psychology." In describing it further, he draws attention to some of the key actors in the socalled cognitive revolution: "It was a meeting of the Special Group on Information Theory of the IEEE at MIT, where we actually had Noam Chomsky's preliminary paper, before *Syntactic Structures* (1957) came out; my first publication on the magical number seven [Miller, 1956]; one of the first publications of the General Problem Solver by Newell and Simon [1956]. All of that happened in 1956. That rather unusual meeting seemed to me to signal something interesting" (quoted in Baars, 1986, p. 211). Other significant influences on the cognitive revolution were Chomsky's (1959) critique of Skinner's (1957) book, *Verbal Behavior*, and the publication in 1960 of *Plans and the Structure of Behavior* (Miller, et al., 1960).[4]

Adherents of the cognitive viewpoint differ in that some make the assumption that the inferred processes correspond in some way to actual inner states while others argue that the posited intervening variables are of an entirely hypothetical character. The operative point is, however, that real or hypothetical intra-organismic variables now play a crucial role in the explanation of overt action which is no longer understood to be the simple result of stimulus inputs and conditioned reflexes. Indeed once the intervening variables are taken to correspond to actual or hypothetical mental processes, it is natural to enquire further into the nature and properties of these processes. Their capacity to act upon and transform informational inputs has become a preoccupation of social psychologists. Thus Newcomb et al. (1965, p. 27) asserted with confidence that "Man's most distinctive physiological equipment is the mind itself – an unparalleled tool for processing and storing great quantities of information. The complexity of his behavior is dependent not only on his capacity to retain much information in his memory, but also on the fact that this stored information is organized in useful ways." In these two sentences they summarize succinctly the rationale of cognitive psychology as it had developed by the mid-1960s.

In the consumer research domain, this viewpoint has been put forcibly by Paul Albanese (2002, p. 8) albeit with respect to personality rather than cognitive psychology: "The intrapsychic structure of the personality organization constitutes the psychological foundation for the exploration of consumer behavior. When we ask the basic question, 'Why do consumers behave as they do?' the answer lies within, with the intrapsychic structure of the personality, the part of the personality structure that is inside the person's head."

Cognitive psychology

The contemporary psychological study of cognitive information processing is, however, immensely more sophisticated than either the basic $S \to [O] \to R$ model or any short quotation can convey. Cognitive psychology tends to de-emphasize the role of the environment as a source of stimuli of behavior. Whilst not denying the environment as the inevitable source of external stimuli, cognitive psychologists place more stress on and devote a greater proportion of their effort to the investigation of internal stimuli, i.e. those intrapersonal, mental events and processes which are consequent upon environmental inputs, through which the recipient individual's experience is constructed and by which contingent responses are initiated. Neisser (1967) illustrates this general proposition in the statement that the study of visual cognition, "deals with the process by which a perceived, remembered and thought-about world is brought into being from as unpromising a beginning as the retinal patterns." The investigation of cognition is not, of course, confined to the consequences of visual stimulation but "refers to all the processes by which the sensory input is transformed, reduced, elaborated, stored, recovered, and used. It is concerned with these processes even when they operate in the absence of relevant stimulation, as in images and hallucinations. Such terms as sensation, perception, imagery, retention, recall, problem-solving, and thinking, among many others, refer to hypothetical stages or aspects of cognition" (p. 4).

Specifically, cognitive psychology focuses upon the reception by the organism of inputs which take the form of stimuli having their origin in the environment. The capacity of organisms to recognize information via the senses is generally greater than their capacity to process internalized information effectively. Consequently, this process of reception avoids sensory overload by incorporating a highly selective form of attention. Some of the information which impinges upon the individual's sensory registers nevertheless passes through the attentive and perceptual filters by which cognitive overload is avoided, into short term (or temporary, working) memory which interacts with the long term memory (or permanent memory store). All of these activities involve cognitive processes which place the environmental inputs into the context of the individual's remembered and recalled experience, motives, goals, and other constructs which facilitate the comprehension, interpretation and positioning of the novel stimulus. The endpoint of the stimulus induced information processing is a response output which often takes the form of verbal or overt behavior.

Atkinson and Shiffrin (1971) attached pivotal significance within the entire cognitive process to the role of temporary, working memory "because the processes carried out in the short-term store are under the immediate control of the subject and govern the flow of information in the memory system; they can be called into play at the subject's discretion, with enormous consequences for performance." Short term memory holds the key to the control of the entire information processing sequence precisely because it mediates, co-ordinates and integrates immediate environmental inputs with the permanent memory store which encapsulates past experience in subjective form. Short term memory processes carry out these functions while editing and giving a subjective meaning to the information received by the sensory registers so that subsequent processing or use of the data can take place. Short term memory shapes cognitive, information processing in the individual and, thereby, his or her output responses through such operations as rehearsal (the repetition of information until it can be recalled at will or written down for more permanent storage), coding (linking the novel information with other, retrievable data), imaging (storage of verbal information in visual form) and decision and retrieval strategy making. Short term memory thus has particular implications for exposure to new information, the precise operation of selective attention and perception, forgetting and the modification and effect of attitudes and behavioral intentions. (For an account of recent research on learning and memory and, in particular, an appraisal of the Shiffrin and Atkinson approach, see Gordon, 1989).

The parallel between the human cognitive transformation of information and the information processing functions of computers was drawn from the earliest days of the cognitive revolution (e.g., Newell et al., 1958). However, the early enthusiasms of advocates of the view that digital computers simulated human information processing has given way to the idea that computer programming is analogous to the way in which the human mind or brain operates. The simulation concept ignores the limitations of computers to represent human mental processes. For example, computers lack the capacity to be distracted or emotional. The requisite role of the cognitive psychologist is therefore "analogous to that of a man trying to discover how a computer has been programmed" (Neisser, 1967, p. 6). Neither is concerned more than superficially with the composition of the entity controlled by the information processing in question (the nature of the physical computing machinery or the physiology of the living organism) but each is vitally interested in unraveling the procedural rules and routines which govern the information processing itself. There is always the danger, well recognized by cognitivists, of employing the analogy of computer programming too rigidly and thereby presenting as naive a view of "man the machine" as the crudest forms of behaviorism. What distinguishes the psychology of cognitive information processing from the more mechanistic approaches of the behaviorists is, according to Bower (1972, p. 108), the assumption by the former that the ego or self acts as an "executive monitor" which can intervene in the situations in which human problems arise in order to permit the selection of appropriate responses from the available options: "the self thus acts as an overseer or monitor controlling mental processes."

The fundamental tenets of the cognitive information processing paradigm have pervaded textbooks of consumer behavior ever since they first appeared in the late 1960s. Such concepts as perception, cognition, learning memory, personality, belief, attitudes, and purchase intentions have served well the attempt to describe and explain consumers' pre-behavioral "decision processes" and their behavioral outcomes. Like the business writers of the early twentieth century quoted earlier, modern prescriptive accounts of consumer research and marketing management (particularly those concerned with the administration of marketing communications and the evaluation of the effects of advertising) emphasize strongly the need to identify and measure consumers' pre-purchase cognitive processes. These prescriptions rest upon the argument that in effective persuasion the buyer's pre-purchase processing of information, gained significantly though not exclusively through advertising, strengthens or modifies his attitudes and purchase intentions which in turn maintain or cause changes in his buying behavior, particularly with respect to brand choice. Studies of the "communications process" and its elements – *the message source* (analyzed in such terms as credibility, likeability and status), *the message* itself (ordering of arguments, one sided and two sided appeals, and message contents) and *the audience* (persuasibility, self-esteem, attitudinal position) – such as those conducted by Hovland and colleagues (e.g., Hovland et al., 1953) in the famed Yale University Communications Research Program are expected to lead to its control.[5]

This approach figures strongly in the widely known marketing models of consumer behavior. All of these models are based on the logical sequence of the computer flow chart and all espouse the view that pre-purchase mental events and processes, notably *attitude*, are proximally causative of consumer choice behavior and that behavioral change is a function of the antecedent modification of attitudes.

The cognitive consumer: "hierarchies of effect"

In the course of the last seven decades a range of "hierarchy of effects" models have developed, some of them reminiscent in their simplicity of the businessmen's nostrums from 1914 quoted in Chapter 1. In fact, these models vary considerably in their sophistication but they all suggest an essentially similar pre-purchase process comprising a sequence of psychological states of increasing comprehension and desire and culminating in the "strong conviction" which determines purchase and its outcome. They are all predominantly cognitive in their exposition of consumer choice. A selection of these models of consumer information processing is shown in Table 2.2 which also presents outline summaries of some of the models which have been described.

Examples of the manner in which the general cognitive information processing model of consumer choice has been incorporated into the marketing literature are so widely available as to require no corresponding, detailed exposition here. Briefly the assumed pattern of cognitive processing follows the scheme employed in mainstream psychology with the added emphasis of certain managerially relevant components of the overall process. The

Table 2.2 Some Information Processing Depictions of Consumer Choice

Author(s)	Year	Sequence
Starch	1925	Seeing → Reading → Believing → Remembering → Acting
Strong	1925	Awareness → Interest → Desire → Action
Lionberger, Rogers	1960 1962	Awareness → Interest → Evaluation → Trial → Adoption
Colley	1961	Unawareness → Awareness → Comprehension → Conviction → Action
Lavidge and Steiner	1961	Awareness → Knowledge → Liking → Preference → Conviction → Purchase (i.e. cognition → affect → conation)
McGuire	1969	Exposure → Attention → Comprehension → Yielding → Retention → behavior
Howard and Sheth	1969	Attention → Brand Comprehension → Attitude → Intention → Purchase
Rogers and Shoemaker	1971	Knowledge → Persuasion → Decision → Confirmation
McGuire	1976	Exposure → Perception → Comprehension → Agreement → Retention → Retrieval → Decision making → Action
Engel, Blackwell and Kollat	1978	Perceived information → Problem recognition → Search Evaluation of Alternatives → Beliefs → Attitudes → Intentions → Choice
Britt	1978	Exposing → Attending → Perceiving → Learning and Remembering → Motivating → Persuading → Desired Action
Foxall and Goldsmith	1994	Environment → Attentional and perceptual filter → Interpretation (involving experiences, beliefs, attitudes and goals held in short and long term memory) → Brand beliefs → Brand attitudes → Brand purchase intentions → Response
Rossiter and Percy	1997	Need arousal → Information search and evaluation → Purchase → Usage

contribution of attitudes to behavioral (purchase) intentions and the assumption that behavioral intentions correlate highly with manifest behavioral choice looms especially large in the marketing based study and depiction of consumer behavior. The information processing approaches of Howard and Sheth and of Engel, Blackwell and Kollat draw particular attention to the attitude → intention → purchase sequence although it is taken for granted throughout the consumer behavior literature.

An additional component of the prevailing paradigm of both cognitive psychology and consumer research is the assignment to individuals of a framework of motivation which adds a dynamic aspect to the behavior under investigation. So important has the psychology of motivation become, especially in the wake of the psychoanalytical revolution, that dynamic psychology could well be considered here a third paradigm were it not so well integrated in consumer research with the information processing perspective. Once again, the points of contact between dynamic psychology and consumer research – from Maslow's "hierarchy of needs" to Freudian suppression and repression and beyond – are well covered in consumer behavior texts (e.g., Foxall et al., 1998) and there is no need for elaboration here.

Managerial implications of consumer research are not a concern of the present volume but, in view of use of the information processing paradigm for the analysis of both consumer behavior and the response of marketing management (they almost seem made for each other), it is worth noting briefly the consequences of cognitive information processing for the prescribed marketing action for each stage of the cognitive continuum of consumer behavior. Ehrenberg and Goodhardt (1979–81) present the general implications of cognitively based models in terms of marketing communications. In doing this they provide a useful summary of the conclusions of an information processing analysis for the use by marketing managers of the entire marketing mix as a persuasive device by marketing managers. These authors use the phrase "the strong theory of advertising" to identify that view of marketing communications which depicts it as very persuasive, moving the customer along a "hierarchy of effects" sequence until his or her conviction of the merits of a given brand and consequent desire to own and use it compel the appropriate purchase and sustained brand loyalty. Thus the consumer information processing perspective accords well with the predominant idea of the use of advertising in marketing and, indeed, the persuasive use of the entire marketing mix by attributing to marketing considerable power to determine purchase and consumption behavior via the influence of pre-behavioral mental processes.

Texts on consumer behavior, marketing management and advertising typically advocate this approach in order to ensure managerial manipulation of those aspects of the source–message–audience continuum which are believed to be within their control (Zimbardo & Ebbesen, 1970, pp. 20–21; for a critical review see Fishbein & Ajzen, 1975, pp. 451–457). In particular, in modern accounts of the contributions of consumer research to managerial decision making, consumers' attitudes and the purchase intentions derived from them take precedence over other mental constructs and, on occasion, subsume the effects of social and environmental stimuli. Since attitudes are cast in this approach as the primal causative antecedents of behavior, the primary task of consumer research is held to be the identification and validation of more sensitive and powerful means of defining and measuring them. The effect of this approach on marketing research and managerial planning has been immense: from the "perceptual mapping" which underpins brand "positioning" to the measurement of consumers' sensitivity to price, from the measurement of store "images" to the motivation of consumers to ascend a hierarchy of behavioral effects, the academic and professional marketing literatures are replete with synonyms for "attitude" and "attitudinal change." Marketing managers and commercial consumer researchers, as well as marketing academics, evince strong acceptance of the relationship between attitudes and behavior posited by cognitive psychology and of the derivative argument that behavioral change necessarily requires antecedent attitudinal change induced primarily by persuasive marketing communications, notably advertising.

The elaboration-likelihood model of persuasion

Not all consumer choices seem to entail all of these procedures and cognitive models of consumer choice have come to make allowance for the tendency of consumer behavior over time to look habitual, routine, and relatively uninvolving. While formal decision making may sometimes be necessary, such as the first time a purchase of a new brand in a new product category is considered, the frequent purchase of established brands seems to require far less commitment to a detailed sequence of information search, evaluation, and problem solving. The first time one encounters an advertisement for a novel item, especially if it belongs to a product category that is infrequently purchased and which is expensive, one may attend closely to what is claims, examining its arguments, and making comparisons between the brand offered and existing means of solving the problem of consumption it addresses. On subsequent occasions, this need for close scrutiny diminishes as one acquires personal knowledge of the item, expertise in its use, and familiarity with the trustworthiness of the advertiser's claims. As one moves, in other words, from high involvement with the purchase to low involvement.

Petty and Cacioppo (1986a, 1986b; see also Petty et al., 1991, 1994; recent work is covered by Briñol et al., 2004; Tormala & Petty, 2004) are concerned to understand under what circumstances individuals yield to a persuasive message such as an advertising appeal. They posit two routes to persuasion, the central and the peripheral which differ in the extent to which context and personality influence the probability that the individual will elaborate the message by means of conscious information processing. The central route extends from the individual's first exposure to a persuasive message and progresses, much as do the hierarchy of effect models, through preattention, focal attention, comprehension and elaboration to the reception of information in memory and its subsequent processing there to produce beliefs, feelings, associations, schema and scripts. The peripheral route short circuits at either exposure or preattention and delivers the information directly to the memory. (For accounts of elaboration likelihood theory in its marketing applications, see *inter alia* Foxall et al., 1998; Greenwald & Levitt, 1984.)

When elaboration likelihood is high, the central route is brought into play; when it is low, the peripheral. Central route processing is an effortful endeavor to uncover any worth in the message. It requires mental exertion in which previous experience is examined along with relevant knowledge in the process of evaluating the usefulness and validity of the message. This is an active procedure in which the information provided by the would-be persuader is carefully inspected. As a result of this active information processing, the individual forms an attitude that is both clear and supported by evidence. By contrast, the peripheral route to persuasion recognizes the limitations of human cognitive capacity, the impossibility of devoting substantial mental effort to the evaluation of all messages. It leads to attitude change that is far from being based on extensive thinking about the claims made about the attitude object. The individual does not allocate costly resources of time and cognitive effort to evaluating the claims of the message but employs accumulated knowledge of the rewards, punishments and affective responses that have followed previous experience with the attitude object. Classical and operant conditioning may provide such rapid appraisals of the object which are expressed in terms of inferences drawn from self-observation (as in Bem's 1972 example: "I must like brown bread; I'm always eating it") or heuristics grounded in abundant practice ("You get what you pay for") or stereotyped reactions ("He's a karate black belt: I'll steer clear of him.")

This leads appropriately to the prediction and explanation of consumer behavior based on the ways that it is shaped by the situation in which it occurs and the direct experience of the consumer rather than through cognitive information processing.

The situated consumer: The continuing influence of behaviorism

In place of the comprehensive hierarchy of effects models of consumer behavior, Ehrenberg and Goodhardt (1979–81) present a model which is consistent with a "weak theory of advertising" in which marketing communications work primarily through suggestion and reinforcement. The descriptive model of consumer choice which they advocate is based upon a three-stage sequence of buying: awareness → trial → reinforcement (or ATR). Advertising which is aimed at establishing awareness of a new product or brand often relies upon obtrusive effects and repetition in order to overcome the discrimination (or, in the terminology of cognitive psychology, the perceptual selectivity) by which consumers avoid messages concerned with unknown or currently unused brands. Awareness is, nevertheless, created or rekindled by advertising only with difficulty: there are no strongly persuasive marketing techniques even at this inaugural phase of the consumer choice sequence. Some consumers who nevertheless notice such advertising try the brand, albeit in an atmosphere of ignorance and uncertainty, for no amount of informative advertising or interpersonal communication can provide the experiential knowledge which only a product trial can supply.

The key role of advertising in this scheme is the reinforcement of whatever satisfaction the customer feels as a result of buying and using the product. It is not, however, the sole source of reinforcement: word of mouth communication and the purchaser's direct, comparative observation also fulfill this role. If continued purchase of the brand results from this reinforcement, advertising continues to perform the function of reminding the consumer of the benefits of the brand in question.

The primary role of competitive brand advertising, according to Ehrenberg and Goodhardt, is not to increase market share (there is no evidence of the sales effectiveness of advertising for established brands) but to prevent the erosion of sales levels. In other words, advertising such brands is indicative of a defensive strategy, "advertising helps to keep one's satisfied customers by reinforcing their existing habits and attitudes. It is the price to pay for staying in the market" (Ehrenberg & Goodhardt, 1979–1981, p. 6).

The ATR model applies to frequently and infrequently purchased products, new and established brands, and brands with stable sales levels as well as those with dynamic sales trends. Its importance in the present argument, however, stems from its emphasis on behavior (and behavioral change) preceding attitude formation (and attitudinal change). Only after a brand has been purchased and used can conviction and strong desire (to retain the cognitive terminology a little longer) be built and these are the result first and foremost of direct favorable experience with the item, in the absence of which, no amount of persuasive advertising will induce the repeat purchasing upon which brand marketing strategies are heavily dependent. In place of the depiction of behavioral change as a function of prior attitudinal change which in turn derives from internal information processing prior to purchase, the proposed sequence is now (i) brand trial, stimulated by the reception and acceptance of some modicum of information but, of necessity an experiment which occurs in a state of great uncertainty, followed by (ii) the reinforcement of the purchase, partly through advertising and social communication but primarily as a consequence of the user's evaluation of the merits of purchase and consumption outcomes.

The conclusions of this train of argument, though they are not necessarily all of the processes postulated by the ATR model, are consistent with a paradigm which provides an alternative framework of analysis to that of cognitive information processing and different managerial prescriptions from those hitherto discussed. This is the behavior modification perspective. Behavioral learning theory is by no means unknown in marketing and has had a distinct influence on several cognate fields of research. Members of the Yale communications research team, to which reference has been made, derived assumptions and hypotheses from such learning theorists as Hull (1935) and Doob (1947). Fishbein and Ajzen (1975, pp. 22–33) acknowledge similar influences on their own work, which has had some impact upon consumer research (cf. Eagly & Chaiken, 1993). Nevertheless, the advocacy of a behaviorist paradigm as a means of guiding general marketing and consumer research is innovatory. Although the perspective proposed by Nord and Peter, and Rothschild and Gaidis owes more to the social learning approaches of Staats (1975) and Bandura (1986), the most influential recent behaviorist is Skinner (e.g., 1938, 1953). While Skinner's proposals are undoubtedly more radical than those thus far advanced by marketing specialists, consideration of his work provides the most appropriate introduction to behaviorist principles for consumer researchers whose work is still dominated by cognitive concepts. It is interesting, in connection with this discussion of paradigms of choice, that Skinner (1974, p. 3) describes behaviorism not as the science of human behavior, but as "the philosophy of that science."

Ehrenberg and his colleagues have drawn attention to pattern of the multi-brand buying in which comparatively few consumers of a product are loyal to any one brand in the sense of always choosing it. Multi-brand purchasing is the norm to the extent that even the heaviest purchasers of a given brand buy other brands within the category much more than they buy their favorite brand over the course of say a year (Ehrenberg, 1988/1972). Certainly for consumer non-durables, which belong to established and stable markets, most consumers show low levels of brand loyalty (e.g., 10%) during, say, one year, and that they usually choose apparently randomly from a subset of three or four brands: for instance, for two brands A and B of a product bought once a week, an individual might buy in the sequence AAABBAAAABABBBAAAA over 19 weeks.

Ehrenberg has stressed that brand loyalty be measured at this behavioral level of what consumers actually do, though other researchers are adamant that such observed patterns must be the reflection of some underlying mental loyalty which determines or at least explains behavior. Here is a classic distinction between the probability and latent process conceptions of attitude. The former is shown by Ehrenberg's counting responses, be they purchase responses or verbal evaluations of brands, which we might refer to as the "attitudes" of the consumers concerned (and which, incidentally, are as volatile for most consumers as are their brand selections over a series of shopping trips: Dall'Olmo Riley et al., 1997). The latter is apparent in other investigators who assume a psychological reality over and above the observed pattern of behavior which can be influenced not only by experience of the product but by persuasive communications such as brand advertising which changes brand beliefs.

Although the probability conception of attitude is behavioristic in a sense that would be readily understood in everyday conversation – it sticks to the observed behavior of the individual making repeated decisions – it is not behavioristic in the psychological sense of offering some explanation to account for the patterns of behavior. A behaviorist methodology would attempt to provide a more generalizable story of how the environment influences behavior over time. The following section discusses how behavior analysis attempts this.

Behavior and its control

The focus of behavior analysis is behavior itself rather than any mental antecedents or causes, which cognitive psychologists may attribute to it (Moore, 1999).[6] Interest in the prediction of responses from knowledge of stimulation (or the definition of stimuli exclusively, from descriptions of responses) without recourse to the subjective introspection which was then the hallmark of American psychology, developed during the early years of this century. Watson made *S-R* relationships the fundamental unit of psychological analysis, abandoning so called mental phenomena such as attention, will and thought. In the consequent absence of introspective, subjective evidence and cognitively founded "explanations" of action behavior was directly observed and described by a vocabulary shorn of references to inferred mental states. Miller (1962, p. 83) points out that what the prevailing mentalistic psychologists called sensation and perception, Watson classed as no more than discriminatory responses: similarly, learning and memory were described in terms of the conditioning and maintenance of *S-R* links, thinking became talking and problem solving, motivation and valuing became choice behavior, while emotion was understood in terms of the functioning of the autonomous nervous system, the glands and the muscles, "[e]verything intangible was simply reduced to its most tangible manifestation." Indeed, for Watson, though not for all subsequent behaviorists, thought itself became no more than sub-vocal verbalization.

Two distinct emphases are apparent in the history of behavior analysis. Concentration upon *S-R* associations lies at the heart of classical or respondent conditioning. "Respondents" are involuntary response behaviors controlled by preceding stimuli. The well known experiments of Pavlov (1927) were concerned with the learning of conditioned responses, those which come to follow a stimulus which originally had no capacity to elicit them but which, after being continually linked with an unconditioned or "natural" stimulus are subsequently able to bring forth the conditioned response in the absence of other stimuli. Typically, a dog would be fed meat powder (unconditioned stimulus) shortly after a bell (the conditioned stimulus) had been rung; the response was salivation. Repetition of this procedure in which the conditioned and unconditioned stimuli were paired resulted in a situation in which the presentation of the auditory stimulus alone would produce salivation.

A little more formally, classical conditioning is the process in which a neutral stimulus (such as a metronome) is repeatedly paired with a stimulus (say, food) that naturally elicits an unconditioned response (UR, salivation). Over time the metronome acquires similar eliciting properties to those of the unconditioned stimulus (US, food in this case). The neutral stimulus becomes a conditioned stimulus (CS) capable of eliciting a conditioned response (CR) which is similar in form to the original UR (Eagly & Chaiken, 1993). Hence

CS (metronome)   →   CR (salivation)
UC (food)   →   UR (salivation)

The phenomena of classical conditioning apply also in the human sphere: the first time an individual listens to a new comedian, his laughter is a response to the performer's material, but on subsequent occasions similar behavior, smiling or laughter, is likely to accompany the mere sight of the comedian (Staats & Staats, 1963).

Classical conditioning is of interest in the context of consumption and marketing because it accounts for the basic learning of associations. Much marketing effort is designed to build associations between brands or retail outlets and enjoyable events that the consumer has previously encountered. A summer's day's hike in a rural setting may constitute a US that elicits pleasant feelings of self-assurance (UR) in the consumer which a marketer wishes to transfer to a brand of perfume or clothing. By using advertising showing an attractive model self-confidently walking in the rustic sunshine and using a mellifluous voice-over to announce that the brand in question can engender a feeling of self-esteem, the advertisement links the natural stimuli that produce feelings of well-being with the brand of perfume or clothing that the model is wearing (CS). Should the consumer subsequently see the brand in a store, he or she may "automatically" feel good about him or herself as a result (CR) and purchase it, not just once but repeatedly whenever the CS is encountered. Even a brief perusal of Cialdini's *Influence: The Psychology of Persuasion* (1984) confirms that this is not the oversimplification it initially appears.

Behavior analysis is not, however, confined to the study of classical conditioning. In fact, more prevalent is operant or instrumental conditioning, which is based upon the observation that "behavior is shaped and maintained by its consequences" (Skinner, 1971, p. 23). Behavioral psychology relates the rate at which a behavior is performed to the consequences it has attracted in the past: some consequences result in the behavior or response becoming more frequent and are known as positive rewards or reinforcement; others decrease the probability of the response and are known as punishers. Because such behavior is conceptualized as operating upon the environment to produce consequences, it is known as operant behavior, the process in which the consequences come to influence the behavior as *operant* conditioning, and the behavioral psychology which studies this process as *operant* psychology. Formally, the rate of response (R) is seen as contingent on the nature of the consequences it generates, positive reinforcers (S^r) or aversive stimuli (S^a):

$$R \rightarrow S^{r/a}.$$

In addition, some prebehavioral stimuli signal the likelihood of positive or aversive consequences arising as a result of performing a particular behavioral act. These "discriminative" stimuli (S^d) can be regarded as signals or cues. They are stimuli in the presence of which the individual "discriminates" his or her behavior, performing only that response which has previously been reinforced. The central explanatory device in operant psychology, the so-called "three-term contingency," is then

$$S^d \rightarrow R \rightarrow S^{r/a}.$$

The capacity of so simple a formulation to account for complex human behavior such as consumer brand choice and marketer behavior is surprising perhaps but real for all that as a range of theoretical and empirical work attests (Foxall, 2002b; Hantula et al., 2001; Rajala & Hantula, 2000).

"Operants" are behaviors which are conditioned by their consequences; since these consequences increase the likelihood of the operant's recurrence, strengthening the behavior, they are known as reinforcers. Operant behaviors, as opposed to the reflexes elicited by stimuli in classical conditioning, are frequently described as voluntary: they are emitted by the individual who acts upon his environment and who receives the resulting, instrumental consequences (Skinner, 1974, pp. 39–40).

Whereas classical conditioning is concerned overwhelmingly with the antecedent environmental stimuli which cause behavior, operant conditioning considers post behavioral effects of behavior. The idea of reinforcement is central to behaviorist philosophy and its ramifications require further exposition if the role of this paradigm in marketing and consumer research is to be clarified. A consequence which strengthens the behavior which produced it is known as a *positive* reinforcer; *negative* reinforcement refers to the strengthening of behavior which reduces or terminates the reinforcer. This distinction is sometimes critically confusing and an example may assist. A meal is positively reinforcing to a person who is hungry; if he then cooks and eats that meal, the probability of his repeating these behaviors in subsequently occurring similar circumstances increases. A gardener's removal of a painful thorn from his thumb is negatively reinforcing and his removal of thorns which cause him pain on other occasions becomes more predictable (Skinner, 1974, p. 46). Positively reinforcing behavior involves consequences such that the individual is likely to act in ways which elicit further, similar consequences; negatively reinforcing behavior involves consequences which the individual will probably continue to avoid by operating upon his environment in ways which do not produce them.

The accumulation of behavioral consequences experienced by the individual thus constitute his or her reinforcement history which renders his or her subsequent behavior in similar circumstances predictable. Within the behaviorist paradigm, the guiding principle is to the effect that the nature of past reinforcement determines the probability that a given operant behavior will be repeated. The possibility of modifying the probabilities of occurrence of specific behavior through the creation of an environment which 'rewards' operants with appropriate consequences thus arises. It is upon this possibility that the behavioral technology promoted by Skinner rests and from which any use of behavior analysis in marketing stems.

Reinforcement and behavioral technology

This introduces another central term in behaviorist analysis: "contingencies of reinforcement." Skinner (1971, p. 24) writes that, "behavior which operates upon the environment to produce consequences ('operant' behavior) can be studied by arranging environments in which specific consequences are contingent upon it." The significance of this in paradigmatic terms is evident from his assertion that "The contingencies under investigation have become steadily more complex, and one by one they are taking over the explanatory functions previously assigned to personalities, states of mind, feelings, traits of character, purposes, and intentions." (Skinner, 1974, p. 24). Indeed, the import of the behaviorist approach in the present context derives from its utterly distinct perspective of the causation and explanation of human behavior and behavior modification. Rather than attempt to modify or maintain behavior by acting upon its alleged cognitive precursors and determinants, behaviorists advocate the manipulation of the environments within which response and reward occur – the conditions or contingencies or reinforcements. The result is an explanation of behavior which attributes action, "to the subtle and complex relations among ... the situation in which behavior occurs, the behavior itself, and its consequences" (Skinner, 1974, p. 148). These three elements and their inter-relationships constitute the "contingencies of reinforcement" which is the basic explanatory device of this paradigm.

Schedules of reinforcement

An important component of reinforcement contingencies which acts directly upon the repetition of operant behavior is the relative frequency with which reinforcers are produced in response to such behavior (Ferster & Skinner, 1957). There exist various "schedules of reinforcement." On continuous reinforcement (CR) schedules, every requisite operant behavior is subsequently and appropriately rewarded: for example the warmth made available to the individual each time he stands before a fire. There is a one to one relation between the response and the reinforcement. Sometimes, however, reinforcement is intermittent, (i.e., it does not follow every response but, in the case of an interval schedule), occurs after a particular period of time has elapsed provided at least one response has been made during the interval, or in the case of a ratio schedule, when a number of responses has been performed. Each of these types of schedule may be fixed or variable. Fixed interval schedules (FI) require that the interval remain constant from trial to trial, while in variable interval (VI) conditioning the interval changes after each reinforcer has been delivered. Fixed ration (FR) schedules require that the number of responses that must be made before reinforcement is constant from trial to trial, while in variable ratio (VR) conditioning the number of responses required changes after each reinforcement. Many consumer non-durables are purchased on FR ratios (each box of ready-to-eat cereal requires the consumer to produce a standard number of cents or pence, considered the response in this instance). From week to week, the price of a commodity may change, however, and if we were interested in the pattern of behavior over a period of say several months we might consider the consumer behavior in question to be governed by a VR schedule. Though this may seem abstract at present, all of these concepts will come into their own in the assessment of recent operant consumer research in Chapter 7.

Complex behavior

Quite complex behavior can be accounted for in terms of the three-term contingency. In a process known as *chaining*, discriminative stimuli that are frequently paired with a reinforcer may become conditioned to act as reinforcers in their own right. Complex behaviors can be understood as resulting from sequences or chains of three-term contingencies in which each discriminative stimulus not only signals the availability of a further reinforcement contingent upon the performance of a specific behavior but also in itself reinforces the preceding response. Shopping in a supermarket, for instance, is a complex series of behaviors including writing out a shopping list, leaving the house, driving to the store, leaving the car in the parking lot, entering the store, finding the products one wants and brining them to the check-out, and so on. Only paying for the goods is overtly reinforced since this is how one gets to own and keep the products. The consumer goes through the entire sequence, however, because each separate response is reinforced by its completion which acts as a discriminative stimulus for the next response. So, while only the final response in the sequence appears to be reinforced, the preceding action (taking the goods to the checkout) becomes the final discriminative stimulus for the reinforcement of that terminal response. Taking the goods to the checkout, by being paired with the actions that immediately precede it, such as brand selection, becomes a reinforcer, too. The chain of events needs to be analyzed in reverse order in order to appreciate the three-term contingencies of which it is composed. Chaining suggests that behavior that seems to be rewarded only after a considerable delay, is in fact a series of separate responses each of which has its own rewarding consequences ensuring the persistence of the individual over time.

While chaining provides a plausible explanation of behavior that is already acquired, behavior analysis requires also an account of the process of acquiring novel patterns of response. Complex behaviors do not appear either suddenly or in their entirety. A final response may become apparent only after a sequence of preceding acts which are a series of increasing approximations to the final behavior. As long as each of these is reinforced in its own right, the target behavior may be "shaped" over time. Before doing all of one's shopping at a one-stop hypermarket, for instance, one might go through a process of visiting the store, browsing, doing a proportion of one's shopping there, each of which is reinforced in its own right and which as a whole have the effect of making the terminal response more probable.

A hungry student heads for the cafeteria because on previous occasions when he has gone without food for a long period appropriate reinforcement has been forthcoming there rather than in the library. Going to the café on such occasions has been "differentially reinforced." It is a response that is reinforced in the presence of one stimulus but not another. A person who behaves differently in the presence of the particular antecedent stimulus has made a discrimination, meaning simply that he or she has made one response in those circumstances rather than another. Store choice, for example, may be explained in terms of the discriminations which the consumer has learned in the course of a history of differential reinforcement in a variety of stores over a period of time. Reinforcement is not simply a matter of rewarding a single response and thereby making its repetition more probable: reinforcement of one response may strengthen other, similar responses, and all of the responses that are rewarded by a particular reinforcer belong to the same operant class. In other words, the responses that make up an operant class all have the same consequences, i.e., produce the same reinforcement. So ordering a book by mail, asking for that book in a bookshop, or stealing it from a library all have the same consequence – getting the book – and belong to the same operant response class. (Stealing the book, of course, may have other consequences such as a job in the prison library and so its belongs also to the class of responses that lead to incarceration!)

The circumstances in which one member of an operant class is enacted may resemble (i.e., contain some of the same discriminative stimuli as) those in which other responses belonging to that class have been reinforced. Buying a food product in a particular store may, if it is reinforced, lead to one's buying a number of other similar products there. This process is *response generalization*. Another example is the trial purchase of a product marketed under the same brand name (the controlling stimulus) as previously purchased items whose purchase was positively reinforced. The consumer's behavior in each case amounts to performing a similar operant in a given setting which marks the availability of contingent reinforcement and can be explained in terms of the controlling discriminative stimulus. Also, a response that has been reinforced in one situation may generalize to other, similar (but not identical) situations – a procedure known as *stimulus generalization* – as when a consumer buys a brand in a given store and subsequently obtains it from other outlets.

Finally, when reinforcement no longer follows, the performance of a particular operant leads (usually quickly) to the withdrawal of that behavior by the individual, a phenomenon known as "extinction." Consumers may attend the cinema in large numbers to see a new movie that is scary and exciting. This behavior may be reinforcing in that they also attend the sequel. But if this movie is disappointing and if subsequent spin-off films fail to live up to expectations then cinema going, at least for this kind of movie, may decline and eventually disappear from the cineastes' behavioral repertoires.

Social technology or scientific explanation?

Behavioral science is presented by Skinner not simply as a means of describing and explaining the world as though these were self-sufficient acts but as the basis of a social technology, a means of shaping or controlling behavior. For many who have written generalized articles or textbook references to behavior analysis in marketing, it is in this respect alone that behavior analysis is likely to be ultimately judged with respect to marketing management and consumer research and it is necessary now to indicate some of the procedures involved in behavioral technology.

While classical conditioning may proceed as a result of the production of stimuli which elicit particular responses, operant conditioning clearly cannot involve the reinforcement of behavior until that behavior appears. The problem, therefore, is to obtain the behavior which is to be reinforced and this may be achieved by the shaping of behavior through successive approximations. In animal experiments, the reinforcement of the extremely forceful pressing of a lever could be achieved by waiting for an extremely forceful push to occur and rewarding it appropriately; a quicker means is the extra reinforcement of the animal's more forceful actions with the result that the average amount of force employed in the depression of the lever is increased. Similar methods have been successfully employed in the treatment of patients in mental hospitals as well as in the shaping of human behavior more generally. (Skinner, 1977, p. 381; cf. Staats & Staats, 1963, pp. 77–86). Shaping demands the careful arrangement of reinforcement contingencies and schedules so that behavior which increasingly approximates the required terminal behavior is increasingly rewarded while behavior which deviates from this pattern is not reinforced. This requires the identification and isolation of those differential aspects of the performance of a behavioral response which are to be reinforced and, if possible, their detailed specification. The result of shaping may be minor behavioral modification or novel and original behavior.

Another means by which individuals acquire new patterns of behavior is modeling in which they imitate the observed actions of others. Vicarious experience and learning may arise from the direct observation or description of the behavior of others or from the mass media. The observation of the reinforcement of others' behavior acts as a learning trial for the observer (Bandura, 1986). This phenomenon is clearly associated with the generalization of reinforced behavior: once a behavior has been reinforced in one set of circumstances, it is likely to appear in similar situations or even in situations which have only some features in common with those in which reinforcement occurred. If, however, behavior is reinforced only when a particular environmental or situational feature, the individual learns to *discriminate*: the behavior appears only when that factor is present in the situation and is said to be controlled by it. The arrangement of environments to modify behavior, that is, the placing of stimuli and rewards in such a way as to elicit and reinforce behavior of a given variety, is nowadays widely practiced. Environmental or "ecological" design involves the use of the phenomena of discrimination and generalization in order to produce required patterns of behavior.

A more crucial question than the pragmatic benefits of behavioral technology to managers is that of how far behavior analysis can provide an explanatory mechanism for consumer research and marketing management. Consumer research has made less use of behaviorist approaches than of cognitive information processing. The early work of Howard (e.g., 1965) drew upon learning theory but there has otherwise been little systematic application and certainly no transfer of the psychological paradigm of behaviorism to marketing. However, in so far as marketing behavior represents a microcosm of human social and economic behavior in general it is possible to describe much buyer and managerial behavior in terms of this paradigm and to cast prescriptions for consumer research accordingly. Nord and Peter (1980) and Rothschild and Gaidis (1981) have attempted to show the relevance of behavior analysis to these areas by indicating how accounts of current marketing practice may be recast in behaviorist terminology, by suggesting extensions of the use of behaviorist analysis in marketing management and research, and by identifying future academic and commercial research imperatives. Many of the actual and potential applications of the behaviorist framework of analysis and research to marketing may well have suggested themselves already to the reader. The following account illustrates these applications but is by no means exhaustive. Classical conditioning, which involves the pairing of environmental stimuli may be used in such a way as to associate stimuli like sporting events, to which the audience has learned a positive or favorable response with the attributes of a particular product or brand or with store characteristics. The incorporation of opinion leaders and other positive reference groups in advertising, sports event sponsorship, point of sale advertising and the use of in-store music and in television and radio commercials further exemplify the application of respondent conditioning techniques in which prior stimuli are expected to produce certain responses. There remains a deal of research to be conducted in this area, particularly, experimentation with the deliberate pairing of stimuli to ascertain the actual effects of human respondent conditioning in the marketing context and, where valid and appropriate, to facilitate the more effective arrangement of stimuli.

Operant or instrumental conditioning, in which environments are so arranged that the consequences of particular behaviors reinforce those behaviors, probably offers a greater challenge to marketing managers and researchers. The use of rewards is already pervasive in marketing which, after all, depends vitally upon the provision of economic material reinforcers. Apart from the clear necessity to arrange product attributes so as to produce appropriate reinforcement of purchase and consumption patterns, marketers might do far more to operationalize facets of the Skinnerian paradigm by the more skilful arrangement of contingencies of reinforcement, that is, the circumstances and conditions in which behavior occurs which determine its consequences and thus whether it will be repeated. Most economic reinforcers employed in marketing – notably in the form of product attributes – are arranged in schedules of continuous reinforcement. Every purchase or use of the item is intended to produce the same consequences and elaborate systems of quality control, efficient distribution and brand identification are employed in order to ensure that positive reinforcement of consumer behavior occurs on every occasion. Continuous reinforcement is invaluable in increasing the rate at which the learning of a new task occurs but subsequent consolidation of what is learned is usually better accomplished through the use of intermittent reinforcers. As far as product attributes are concerned, it would be an extremely dangerous strategy to make positive reinforcement contingent upon several brand trials; indeed the result would be that many purchases and consumptions would be negatively reinforced, customers turning to alternative brands which had previously been positively reinforcing. Rather than encouraging non-continuous reinforcement behaviorist analysis in marketing encourages the use of quality control and consistent branding strategies. Individuals who are habitually reinforced on continuous schedules become extremely frustrated and depressed when the 'expected' reinforcement is not forthcoming (Skinner, 1974, p. 58, 1978, pp. 163–70.) The implication for marketing is that product quality and continuity are essential components of effective strategy.[7]

The most important implication of behavior analysis to the present context, however, is the treatment of the concepts of attitude, attitude change and persuasion. The formation and changing of attitudes, which loom so large in cognitive information processes, are accorded little if any explicative power in behavior analysis; mentalistic views of the effects of attitudes on overt behavior are certainly absent from behaviorists' accounts of the antecedents and causes of behavior. Behaviorists are concerned rather with the conditioning of behaviors by the consequences: the verbal responses which provide the raw material of 'attitude data' in consumer research and much cognitive psychology are simply one sort of behavior. Verbal and "overt" behaviors are, according to this perspective, likely to be consistent with and predictable from each other only when their consequences coincide, when the individual makes no discrimination between the two classes of behavior or their consequences. If the word "attitude" is employed at all in this framework, it refers either to verbal behavior or to the consistency of behavioral responses toward an entity, recorded simply on the basis of observation of a series of behaviors.[8]

This difference in perspective has immense implications for behavioral technology in general and for attempts to modify consumer behavior in particular. While cognitive learning approaches are founded upon the assumption that the "internalization" of a persuasive message which modifies attitudes and other internal states or process is a necessary prerequisite of behavioral change, behaviorist approaches point simply to the necessity of providing the reinforcement required if the behavior is to be repeated or altered.[9]

3
The Behavior of Consumers' Attitudes

Attitude research forms a formidable body of social scientific knowledge. Eagly and Chaiken's (1993) *The Psychology of Attitudes*, which swiftly established itself as the "bible" of attitude theory and practice, attests vitally to this, as does the literature to be found in the relevant pure and applied journals. Yet the very conceptualization on which this intellectual corpus is built is not without difficulties. To refer to the tendency or inclination to behave consistently in some particular way as an "attitude" or as corresponding to an "attitude" is to use the term metaphorically. "Attitude" implied originally the literal leaning of a building or a bodily posture and has only comparatively recently been used to describe behavioral dispositions, opinions or their underlying patterns of thought. Figurative uses of words are seldom as rigorously circumscribed as their literal applications and there is a range of definitions of attitude in psychology and marketing. There is some agreement that the term refers to *"a learned predisposition to respond in a consistently favorable or unfavorable manner with respect to a given object"* (Fishbein & Ajzen, 1975, p. 6, italics in original) but, as they authors demonstrate, even this is a highly ambiguous statement and permits a variety of methodologies and explanations of behavior.[1]

Some meanings of attitude

The general understanding in social psychology – in line with the latent process conception – is that *attitude* is a mediating variable corresponding to mental processes or states which account for the consistency of an individual's favorable-unfavorable and cross-situational responses toward an object. Petty et al. (1994, p. 70) state that "attitude is a general and relatively enduring evaluation of some person (including oneself), group, object, or issue." A degree of endurance implies that long term memory acts as a repository for the evaluation that the individual has attached to the attitude object; and generally indicates that it is an overall or global appraisal. Their basic definition is borne out by Eagly and Chaiken (1993,

p. 1) who refer to an attitude as "a psychological tendency that is expressed by evaluating a particular entity with some degree of favor or disfavor" (cf. Olson & Zanna, 1993; Tesser & Shaffer, 1990). "Psychological tendency" denotes an intrapersonal state, and "evaluative" encompasses all varieties of evaluation responding: overt or covert, and – an espousal of the traditional tricomponential view of attitude structure and function – cognitive, affective or behavioral. Attitudes develop out of evaluative responding of one of these three kinds, are mentally represented in memory, and are activated in the presence of the object to which they refer with the effect of shaping further behavior toward it (Eagly & Chaiken, 1993).

Indeed, it is not the behavior involved in the formation of attitudes which has received the lion's share of attention from attitude researchers and theorists, but that to which attitudes are understood to lead. Since the pioneering conceptualization and measurement in the third and fourth decades of this century (Bogardus, 1925; Likert, 1932), attitude has been portrayed as an organocentric predisposition to *behave* consistently toward the object to which it refers wherever it is encountered. The verbal statements by which attitudes are recorded in response to questionnaires have been assumed to express accurately the underlying 'real' or 'true' attitude held in mind and thus predict and explain its nonverbal manifestations.

Foundational definitions of attitude therefore emphasized its motivating capacity: in Allport's oft-quoted words, an attitude is "a mental and neural state of readiness, organized through experience, exerting a directive or dynamic influence upon the individual's response to all objects and situations with which it is related." The tacit assumption was then, as it generally is now, that to know an individual's attitude was equivalent to being able to predict his or her actions (Fazio & Zanna, 1981, p. 162). The attitude-behavior relationship came to be most contingent in those definitions which claimed that only if consistent behavior followed from measures of cognition, affect or conation, could an attitude be held to exist (Doob, 1947; Fazio, 1986 p. 205).

However, while the conceptual development of the construct is interesting in its own right, more germane to the present argument is that the most important lesson of the empirical work on attitudinal – behavioral consistency over recent decades is the necessity of not only refining but by supplementing the construct of *attitude* in order to achieve anywhere near acceptable levels of predictive capacity.

A brief history of attitude research

Attitude psychology has a familiar history: while its most optimistic phase culminated in the mid-1960s, its most successful era extends from the mid-1970s to the present. The objectives of attitude study naturally embrace far more than the prediction of behavior but, within social psychology and consumer research, and especially in the analysis of social cognition in which both fields have a current interest (Wyer & Srull, 1994a, 1994b), the external validity of attitude constructs and measures continues to maintain a central position. Only by delving briefly into that not-so-far-off history of attitude theory and research can we appreciate the present theoretical position. Current emphases in attitude theory and research stem from the dire assessments of the evidence for attitude-behavior consistency published in the late 1960s and early 1970s. Wicker (1969), whom we met briefly in Chapter 1, showed that early attitude research (from the 1930s to the 1960s) generally revealed positive but insipid relationships between attitudes and behaviors. The extent to which attitudinal variance accounted for behavioral variance was small indeed. Rather, as Fishbein (1972) noted, the evidence favored the prediction of attitudes from behavior rather than the expected position.[2]

The evidence for attitudinal-behavioral consistency that has accrued during the last twenty years or so can be fully comprehended and interpreted only through a short detour into the period of pessimism that intervened between those of optimism and success. The original objective of attitude psychology to predict behavior toward an object from measures of a person's attitude toward that object, became problematical as a result of Wicker's (1969) review of 46 mainly experimental studies of behavior with respect to various attitude objects. Wicker examined forty six empirical studies of attitudes and behavior in which: (i) individuals rather than groups had been the unit of observation; (ii) at least one attitudinal measure and one measure of behavior toward a common object had been taken of each subject; (iii) attitudes and behavior had been measured on separate occasions; and (iv) overt behavior had not been measured simply by subjects' post behavioral self-report.

These are stringent requirements; few marketing studies of attitudes and behavior certainly conform to them even now. Moreover, studies of attitudinal and behavioral change were excluded, and the chosen investigations covered a diversity of verbal measures of attitude: Thurstone's (1931) method of equal-appearing intervals, the summated ratings technique, devised by Likert (1932), Osgood et al.'s (1957) semantic differential, and interviews. A range of measures of behavioral response (for example willingness to be photographed with a member of a racial minority, attendance at meetings, cheating in examinations) is also apparent from the studies reviewed. In addition, there was a wide selection of sampling frames (including maternity patients, union members, students and oilfield workers). But Wicker's conclusions could not be more damaging for psychologists who adopt the latent process conception. He lambasted the notion that attitudes and behavior were empirically consistent on the grounds that correlations were typically small, even if statistically significant. Even the direction of causality between the variables was in doubt. "Taken as a whole", he wrote:

> these studies suggest that it is considerably more likely that attitudes will be unrelated or only slightly related to actions. Product-moment correlation coefficients relating the two kinds of responses are rarely above 0.30, and are often nearer zero. Only rarely can as much as 10 per cent of the variance in overt behavior measures be accounted for by attitudinal data. In studies in which data are dichotomized, substantial proportions of subjects show attitude-behavior discrepancies. This is true even when subjects scoring at the extremes of attitudinal measures are compared on behavioral indices. (Wicker, 1969, p. 65).

Wicker's review also failed to reveal a predictable pattern of causation between the attitudinal and behavioral variables. Six studies indicated that, when measures of overt behavior or behavioral commitment preceded the measurement of attitudes, attitudinal-behavioral consistency was greater than when this procedure was reversed; but four others demonstrated inconsistencies. A few years later, Fishbein summed up the position by saying that: "...what little evidence there is to support any relationship between attitudes and behavior comes from studies showing that a person tends to bring his attitude into line with his behavior rather than from studies demonstrating that behavior is a function of attitude" (Fishbein, 1972).

The evaluation of the empirically-based evidence for attitudinal-behavioral consistency led, then, to pessimistic conclusions: published studies indicated at best only very weak relationships between attitude toward an object and behaviors performed with respect to it; attitude change was not an inevitable precursor of behavioral change; and attitudes might be nothing more than post-behavioral epiphenomena. Such conclusions as these cast considerable gloom on both social psychological and marketing research since both had been firmly predicated upon the expectation that a demonstrable relationship existed. While some psychologists and market researchers argued that the conclusion that attitudes never predicted behavior was too dire, others appeared prepared to dispense altogether with the concept of attitude (cf. Fishbein, 1973; Lunn, 1971; Foxall, 1980; Abelson, 1972). It is, then, superficially surprising to find reviews of the attitude-behavior literature a few years later reporting a rather different state of affairs. Indeed, disappointment was quickly to lead to innovations in methodology and conceptualization that have since then revolutionized the field (Upmeyer, 1989). A much greater spirit of optimism is apparent in these accounts (see, for example, Ajzen & Fishbein, 1977; Schuman & Johnson, 1976). Schuman and Johnson (1976, p. 199) conclude, for example, that, "Our review has shown that most A-B [attitude-behavior] studies yield positive results. The correlations that do occur are large enough to indicate that important causal forces are involved." And Seibold (1980) notes the moderate to strong correlational consistency indicated by numerous empirical studies concluded since the publication of Wicker's analysis.

Transformation

More recent work has generated still higher correlations and, perhaps more important, has pointed the way to the full gamut of cognitive *and environmental* influences that shape behavior. The accurate prediction of behavior requires an understanding of why this change has come about. Some of the reasons for this transformation are relatively easy to find. DeFleur and Westie (1963, p. 30) argued convincingly that definitions of attitude should be more closely linked with the methods employed in attitude measurement:

> Exact specification of the class of response (verbal, overt, motional–autonomic) would aid considerably in the clarification of thinking concerning the degree to which predictions can be made from one class of response to another. The fallacy of expected correspondence resulted historically from the conception of attitudes as *general* response tendencies which implied that consistency should appear from one class of behavior to another, that verbal attitudes 'should' predict overt behavior. It has taken a quarter century of research ... to refute this conception. Attitudes appear to be most usefully conceptualized as *specific*, in the sense that they may be viewed as probabilities of specific forms of response to specific social objects, or specific classes of social objects.

This would, of course, detract from the use of intervening constructs to predict behavior. Wicker (1969) points out, moreover, that most investigators of attitudinal-behavioral relationships argue that factors other than attitudes impinge upon the measured behavior and that these "other factors" must, therefore, be considered when behavior is predicted. Personal factors, which include other attitudes, compelling motives, and verbal, intellectual and social abilities, and situational factors such as the actual or assumed presence of other people, normative prescriptions of proper behavior, alternative available behaviors, lack of specificity of the attitude objects, unforeseen extraneous events and the actual or expected consequences of various acts have all been suggested as causes of the inconsistency countered between measures of attitudes and behavior. Methodological problems have also been noted as contributing to the disappointing results of the search for attitudinal-behavioral consistency, though these often reflect lack of attention to variation in situational variables. Thus the selected attitude measure, behavioral criterion, and the circumstances in which both are measured may lead to the collection of incomparable data.

The "other variables"

The optimism of those psychologists who have reported relatively high levels of attitudinal-behavioral consistency derives from research in which the relationships between circumstantial factors and measured levels of attitudinal-behavioral consistency have been carefully identified and specified. Seibold (1980) arranges the "other variables" issues that arise in this research into three groupings. The first two are concerned with the measurement of attitudes and behavior in ways which render the correspondence and congruity of the measured variables probable on more than simplistic, intuitive grounds.

With respect to the measurement of attitudes, Seibold emphasized, first, that the attitude measure should be constructed with the same level of specificity as the behavioral criterion; this replaces the practice of employing general measures of attitude toward the object to predict particular behaviors; second, that attitude toward the act should be measured rather than attitude toward the object; act or situation-specific measures with the latter may, however, increase predictive value; and, third, that multiple-item attitude scales should be used.(cf. Schuman & Johnson 1976). Finally, he argued that measurement error or inter-measurement change should be considered.

With regard to the conceptualization of behavior, he argued, first, that attitude–behavior correlations are higher when general attitude measures are used to predict multi-act behavioral criteria *and* when specific measures of attitude are employed in the prediction of single act behavioral criteria. The latter produce higher correlations than the former and measures of attitude toward the act increase correlation coefficients. Second, close correspondence between attitudes and behaviors increases correlated consistency. Third, attitude measures provide better predictions of symbolic behaviors such as making a commitment than of actual experience with the attitude object. Fourth, consistency is higher when the behavior measured is highly institutionalized, routine or familiar, when individuals can foresee their behavior and are willing to reveal their behavioral intentions. And, last, measured consistency is higher, the shorter the time interval between the measurement of the variables.

Seibold's third set of issues relates to contextual and moderating variables which he illustrates by summarizing Schuman and Johnson's (1976, pp. 185–99) observations that, first, the degree of consistency varies according to the attitude object and situation; second, normative beliefs may influence behavior both separately from and conjointly with attitudes; third, immediate social pressures impinge on attitude-behavior correspondence in a manner consistent or inconsistent with previously measured attitudes; fourth, privately expressed attitudes may not be consistent with public behavior; fifth, attitudinal-behavioral consistency varies directly with attitudinal certainty, confidence, salience, intensity, internal consistency, and stability; sixth, inconsistency between one's own attitudes and those perceived as belonging to reference groups decreases personal *A-B* consistency; and, last, attitudes whose formation results from direct, personal experience show greater consistency with relevant behaviors than those formed through indirect experience.

Seibold's conclusion is that literal consistency is no longer expected. Previous failures to establish consistency were often based upon the expectation of an isomorphic relationship between verbal and overt behaviors. Correlational consistency, which indicates the extent to which individuals are ordered on both measures, is now generally sought and acknowledges that consistency may be moderated by factors extrinsic to attitude-behavior relationships. Schuman and Johnson (1976, p. 164, p. 200) set particularly high standards for the contextual framework within which attitudinal-behavioral consistency may be genuinely inferred, independently of researcher or experimenter effects:

> Methodologically, a fully adequate investigation of an A-B [attitudinal-behavioral] relationship should involve measuring actual behavior objectively and unobtrusively, without signaling in any way its connection to the prior or subsequent attitude assessment phase... Ideally, attitude and behavior need to be measured in ways that dissociate the two completely in the subject's mind, or else the need to present a temporarily consistent picture may result in spuriously high A-B relationships.

Their review, not surprisingly, contains reference to few studies which attain this ideal but it remains a useful benchmark by which to assess deviations in evaluating the results of empirical studies.

With or without this ideal level of dissociation, however, studies of attitudinal-behavioral relationships report greater consistency the greater the correspondence between the measures of attitude employed and the measures of behavior. Ajzen and Fishbein (1977) argue that attitudinal and behavioral phenomena each comprise four elements: the *action*, the *target* of that action, the *context* within which the action occurs, and the *time* at which it takes place. (Fishbein had, moreover, long argued that attitudes toward performing a specific behavior with respect to an object should be measured rather than the much more general attitude toward the object.) Correspondence between the attitudinal predictor and the behavioral criterion depends upon the degree to which the attitude measure matches the behavioral measure on these four elements. Consistent strength in the relationship between an individual's attitude and his behavior is found when both are directed toward an identical target and both refer to the same action. (Ajzen and Fishbein's review concentrates upon studies fulfilling these two criteria of correspondence because so few investigators provide data about the others). Their results for the 142 studies of attitudes and behavior they review are summarized in Table 3.1. It may be argued that the criterion upon which the level of attitudinal-behavioral consistency is judged to be high or low is not especially rigorous. If $r = 0.40$, only 16 per cent of behavioral variance has been explained in terms of attitude. There are, furthermore, dangers in aggregating the correlation coefficients obtained in diverse investigations. But it is clear from this table that the authors' general point has been made: to put it in its least persuasive form, when correspondence is low, so is the correlational consistency between attitudes and behavior.

Furthermore, the twenty six studies in the high correspondence condition which employed "appropriate measures" all showed high levels of attitudinal-behavioral relationship.

The "other variables" have been increasingly studied in the wake of disappointment over the inability of empirical research to demonstrate sufficiently convincing levels of attitudinal-behavioral consistency to substantiate the latent process idea. Any serious attempt at arguing in favor of attitudes as latent processes on the basis of the evidence of hundreds of field studies is severely qualified by the inclusion of a broad range of constraints which re-enact the need for attitude and behavior measures to correspond very specifically, to treat behavior in a given situation, and to take into account the direct effects of situational variables upon behavior. Seibold (1980, p. 221) who is an able exponent of the latent process conception concedes that, "Behaviors are a consequence of personal social and environmental influences, and attitudes are but one of the factors affecting action." He proposes that theory must treat "situated actions in terms of specific configurations of those influences."

In the review which cast grave doubts upon the expectation of attitudinal-behavioral consistency, Wicker (1969, p. 76) noted that the possibility that non-attitudinal factors entered significantly into the determination of overt behavior was commonly assumed, especially by researchers who had attempted and failed to establish that consistency empirically. The

Table 3.1 Correspondence and Attitudinal-Behavioral Consistency

Attitudinal-behavioral relationship	Level of correspondence		
	Low	Partial	High
Not significant	26	20	0
Low or inconsistent ($r < 0.40$)	1	47	9
High ($r \geq 0.40$)	0	4	35

Source: Derived from Ajzen and Fishbein (1977, p. 913).

actual effects of these "other variables" were, at that time, largely unsubstantiated by research findings, however, though Wicker concluded that, "once these variables are operationalized, their contribution and the contribution of attitude to the variance of overt behavior can be determined" (p. 75). The extent to which this has been the case in the interim can be judged by consideration of an approach to the attitude-behavior problem which has been variously described as "fashionable," "a fad," and "the most influential model" in applied psychology: Fishbein's behavioral intentions model which Fishbein and Ajzen (1975) elaborate in the context of their Theory of Reasoned Action. The theory predicts *behavioral intentions*, which are assumed under specific circumstances, to approximate *behavior*; the subset of behavioral intentions it predicts are those for which reasons can be adduced; moreover, the behavior in question must be under the volitional control of the individual.

Among several approaches to the attitude–behavior problem, Fishbein's work has proved especially productive of solutions and is probably the current basis of most attitude research in marketing and related areas (Fishbein & Ajzen, 1975; Ajzen & Fishbein, 1980). In a judgment that was to foreshadow the role of specificity in future research, Fishbein registered that the relationships probed by earlier research were generally between global measures of attitude toward an object and very particular indices of behavior toward the object. Fishbein's approach had other simplifying features. Wicker had argued that the prediction of behavior required that consideration be given to numerous additional variables including *personal factors* (other attitudes, competing motives, activity levels) and *situational factors* (presence of others, normative prescriptions, specificity of attitude objects, the expected and/or actual consequences of various acts). Incorporating such a wide diversity of "other variables" would require a model of immense complexity. Fishbein's emerging approach concentrated on finding the summary variables that would prove most predictive of behavior:

> Rather than viewing attitude toward a stimulus object as a major determinant of behavior with respect to that object, the theory identifies three kinds of variables that function as the basic determinants of behavior: (1) attitude toward behavior, (2) normative beliefs (both personal and social), and (3) motivation to comply with the norms. (Fishbein, 1967a, p. 490; see also Fishbein, 1967b)

The multiattribute theories

This formulation became the mainstay of the well-known "multi-attribute" theories of attitudes and behavior.: the Theory of Reasoned Action (Fishbein & Ajzen, 1975), which is relevant to behavior that is under the volitional control of the actor (Figure 3.1), and Ajzen's (1985, 1988) Theory of Planned Behavior (Figure 3.2) which is specifically adapted to situations in which behavior is not entirely under voluntary control. The former sought to predict behavioral intention, the immediate precursor of behavior itself, from measures of the individual's *attitude toward that behavior* and his or her *subjective norm,* an index of social pressure to engage in the behavior in question. The latter added a further cognitive variable, *perceived behavioral control*, to account for the extent to which the respondent felt able to undertake the behavior under investigation in order to achieve a

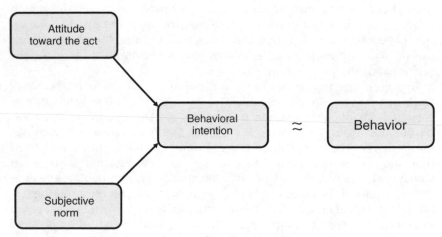

Figure 3.1   The Theory of Reasoned Action: Key Variables and Relationships

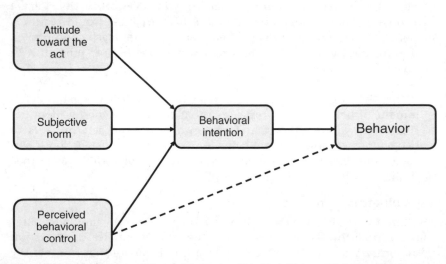

Figure 3.2   The Theory of Planned Behavior: Key Variables and Relationships

goal (losing weight or taking exercise, for instance). As Figure 3.2 shows, perceived behavioral control may act both directly on behavior or indirectly via behavioral intention.

Models that predict an individual's behavior on the basis of his or her immediately preceding intentions have become widely influential during the last 20 years (Eagly & Chaiken, 1993; Olson & Zanna, 1993; Sheppard et al., 1988). An index of their popularity is provided by the reviews and meta-analyses of their predictive efficacy and the widespread discussion of the measurement and conceptual issues they raise. These theories have generated predictions of behavior, including consumer behavior, which are considerably more accurate than those reported in the studies reviewed by Wicker. A meta-analysis of studies employing the Theory of Reasoned Action, reported by Sheppard et al. (1988) found an average correlation of behavioral intention with behavior of .53, while a more recent meta-analysis (Van den Putte, 1993) reports an average of .62. Ajzen (1991) reports similar success for the Theory of Planned Behavior, albeit based on a less formal analysis, partly because of the small number of studies that had been undertaken by that date. More recent meta-analyses and comparative evaluations have indicated that the Theory of Planned Behavior adds significantly to the explanation of behavior compared with the Theory of Reasoned Action (Armitage & Connor, 1999a, b; Sutton, 1998). More important with respect to the intentions–behavior relationship that is central to the present chapter is Sheeran's (2002) meta-analysis of ten meta-analyses of studies of this association. Although the correlations reported in the studies included in his review ranged from .40 to .82 (sd = 0.12), Sheeran found a sample-weighted average correlation of .53 (N = 82, 107). The pervasive problem raised by the psychology of attitude–intention–behavior prediction is that of interpreting results such as these. At first glance, this finding that 28% of behavioral variance is explicable in terms of variance in intentions appears disappointing, but Sheeran (2002, p. 15) argues that this "should probably be considered 'good'" on the basis of Cohen's (1992) assessment that $r_+ = 0.5$ is "large."

Whatever one's judgment on this matter, there is clearly an improvement in results here which can be traced to attitude researchers' having incorporated into their models the awareness of situational variables which Wicker argued was essential. Specifically, two situational factors have been taken into account by the theories of Fishbein and Ajzen – known as "deliberative theories" – since they assume that prior to behaving in a particular way, the individual reasons or deliberates in his or her actions and their consequences – which provide important clues to the development and testing of a comprehensive model of consumers' attitudes and behavior. These two factors are *situational correspondence* among the cognitive and behavioral measures included in the model, and the *learning history of the respondent*, his or her previous behavior with respect to the attitude object and its positive and negative, rewarding and punishing, consequences.

Before we explore these multi-attribute theories in more detail, it is useful to place them within the context of the two broad courses of research that have been pursued since the beginning of the 1970s were intended to come to terms with the critical conclusions of Wicker and others.

Spontaneous and deliberative processing

The approach associated predominantly with Fazio and Zanna (e.g., 1978a, 1978b, 1981) retains the original problem of demonstrating a relationship of consistency between global attitude toward an object and behavior enacted toward that object. That associated predominantly with Fishbein and Ajzen (e.g., 1975; Ajzen, 1988; Ajzen & Fishbein, 1980) and, by extension, with Bagozzi and Warshaw (1990), has adopted a narrower route to the conceptualization and measurement of attitudes and behaviors, and has concentrated on identifying and implementing the methodological developments necessary if the latter are to be accurately predicted from the former. Fazio's (1990) ex post categorization of these approaches suggests that they are complementary (cf. Olson & Zanna, 1993). The "global" approach has dealt with attitude elicitation that is apparently spontaneous, reliant on little if any mental processing and leading directly to action. The information processing associated with it is reminiscent of, though not identical with the peripheral route to persuasion of the elaboration likelihood model which we encountered in Chapter 2 and which continues to inspire work in consumer research, persuasive communications, and marketing (e.g., Knowles & Linn, 2004), and of the heuristic processing proposed by Chaiken (1980). The "reasoned" approach has concentrated on the mental processing involved in deliberating on the consequences of undertaking an action before forming an intention to do so. It assumes a level of information processing more reminiscent of the central route to persuasion (Petty & Cacioppo, 1986a, 1986b) and of systematic processing (Bohner et al., 1995).

Spontaneous processing

This avenue of investigation retains the objective of predicting specific behaviors from general measures of attitude toward an object. While, as we shall see, many researchers have adapted the underlying problem by seeking whatever measures correlate with behavior, Fazio (1986; Fazio & Zanna, 1981) focuses on the original general-to-specific problem of correlating global attitude measures with specific behavior criteria.

While some attitude-behavior correlations are low using this approach, some are high and an important goal of this research program has been to understand *when* attitudes correlate with behavior. It is the nonattitudinal variables, which people fail to take into account when they form and report attitudes toward targets, that confound attitude-behavior consistency. Therefore, these investigators have argued that nonattitudinal factors be taken into consideration in the prediction of behavior from attitudes to objects. The variations in correlations between attitudes and behaviors depends on the variability in nonattitudinal factors from situation to situation, which is considerable. i.e. nonattitudinal factors *moderate* the relationship of attitude toward an object and behavior toward that object (Eagly & Chaiken, 1993).

Attitudes as object-evaluation associations. Fazio (1986, p. 214) defines an attitude as involving "categorization of an object along an evaluative dimension": specifically, an attitude is an association between a given object and a given evaluation (Fazio, 1989, p. 155; Fazio et al., 1982). This definition of 'attitude' corresponds to the affective component of the tricomponential portrayal of this construct preferred by other researchers and consisting of cognition and conation as well as affect.

The simple idea that an attitude is an association suggests that the strength of attitudes, and hence their capacity to influence behavior, will vary, just as the strength of any relationship which is the result of associative learning will vary (Fazio, 1989, p. 155). Fazio's model of the attitude-behavior process thus attempts to answer the question '*When* is attitude related to behavior?' rather than the more pervasive *why?* question. It assumes that social behavior is substantially determined by the way in which the individual perceives the immediate situation in which the attitude object is presented as well as the way in which he or she perceives the object itself.

Situations are generally ambiguous and the individual's definition of any particular situation depends on how he or she interprets it. Behavior is guided by perceptions of the attitude object but also by perceptions of the situation in which it occurs: that setting is said to determine the event. For instance, behavior toward a particular person (attitude object) naturally depends on the individual's perception of him or her: but the style of that behavior will differ depending on whether the attitude object is encountered in his or her home, or a store, or at a party, or in church. "It is this definition of the event – perceptions that involve both the attitude object and the situation in which the object is encountered – that the model postulates to act as the primary determinant of an individual's behavior" (Fazio, 1986, p. 208).

When attitudes guide behavior. The extent to which an attitude guides behavior depends on the manner of its formation. Attitudes formed from direct experience with the attitude object are expected to differ from those stemming from indirect experience (e.g., word of mouth, advertising) in terms of their capacity to predict behavior. Especially when they have to articulate an attitude (e.g., to a researcher or to fill out a questionnaire, people draw on past experiences which "are organized and transformed in light of current contingencies;" Rajecki, 1982, p. 78; Schwartz, 1978); moreover, even enquiries about intentions can influence behavior (Morwitz et al., 1993). There is corroborative empirical evidence that the attitudes of people who have had direct experience with an attitude object (target) correlate moderately with subsequent attitude-relevant behaviors; attitudes where such experience is lacking correlate only weakly. Attitude-behavior consistency is higher when the preceding sequence has been behavior-to-attitude-to-behavior, rather than when it has been simply attitude-to-behavior.

Whether an attitude guides behavior depends also on the accessibility of the attitude from memory (Berger, 1992; Kardes, 1988; cf. Bargh, 1994). Attitudes formed behaviorally lead to a stronger object-evaluation bond than those formed indirectly and are as a result more easily accessed from memory. This is consistent with Bem's (1972) view that the difficulty people encounter in assessing their attitudes (their evaluations of an object) is overcome by engaging in behavior with the object or by observing their own behavior with it. Information gained through behavior or behavioral observation is more trustworthy than that presented by another person or medium (Stayman & Kardes, 1992).

Dealing with direct experience.   A feasible deduction from Fazio's demonstration of the significance of direct experience with the attitude object is that the consequences of relevant past behavior are responsible wholly or in part for the probability of current responding in the presence of the attitude object. Current behavior could then be explained as having come under the stimulus control of the attitude object, such control having been established through the reinforcement resulting from previous experience with the stimulus. In other words, the entire episode might be depicted as operant conditioning and investigation might be directed toward identifying the consequences of behavior that accounted for its future probability. However, the explanation that has predominated is cognitive: attitudes formed through direct experience are held to be more accessible from memory than those formed indirectly. And accessibility, measured as verbal response latency (i.e. the speed with which the attitude is activated or recalled in the presence of the attitude object) is hypothesized to be directly proportional to behavior change (Fazio & Zanna, 1981; Fazio et al., 1982, 1989). The strength of an attitude, its capacity to influence behavior in the presence of the attitude object, increases with such structural attitude qualities as clarity, confidence, stability and certainty (Bargh et al., 1992; Downing et al., 1992).

An attitude's strength is also increased through its repeated verbal expression (Fazio et al., 1982), though repeated expression is also related to attitude polarization (Downing et al., 1992; Smith et al., 1994). Accessible attitudes are, moreover, activated automatically in the presence of the attitude stimulus – without conscious and volitional cognitive processing (Eagly & Chaiken, 1993, p. 197; see also Bargh et al., 1992; Blascovich et al., 1993; Fazio, 1994; Haugtvedt & Petty, 1992; Myers-Levy, 1991; Tesser et al., 1994).

Not all of the evidence supports this: there are contra-indications that *all* attitudes are automatically activated in the presence of the attitude object, regardless of their accessibility (Bargh et al., 1992). Prior knowledge about the attitude object also increases attitudinal-behavioral consistency presumably because such knowledge is attained through direct experience (Eagly & Chaiken, 1993 pp. 200–201; cf. Tripp et al., 1994). As will be documented, there is empirical evidence that such verbal repetition increases the chance that the evaluative behavior described as an attitude will become a self-instruction that guides further responding.

Deliberative processing

Many familiar conclusions of attitude researchers in the era since Wicker's (1969) review and his (1971) call for the abandonment of the attitude concept derive from the application of Fishbein's (1967b) intentions model which gave rise to the Theory of Reasoned Action (Fishbein & Ajzen, 1975) and the Theory of Planned Behavior (Ajzen, 1985). The emphasis – as in the case of work by Bagozzi and Warshaw (1990, 1992) – is largely on the methodological refinements required in order to increase the accuracy of prediction.

This group of attitude theories revolves around the belief that the degrees of specificity with which attitudinal and behavioral measures are each defined must be identical if high correlations are to be found between them. Global attitude measures are therefore consistent with multiple-act measures of behavior toward the attitude object. It follows that the prediction of single acts is only likely to result from equally narrow measures of attitude, those that correspond exactly in level of specificity to the act to be predicted; those, moreover, that are framed as measures of the respondent's attitude toward performing that act in closely designated circumstances (Fishbein & Ajzen, 1975).

This is not the initial intellectual problem posed by attitude research (Cohen, 1964), but its pragmatic departure from the constrictions inherent in that problem has produced a reformation in the technology of behavioral prediction (Ajzen & Fishbein, 1980). Nor is the requirement of situational compatibility confined to measuring attitude toward a specific target behavior rather than attitude toward an object: Ajzen and Fishbein's (1977) analysis of numerous studies of attitudinal-behavioral consistency revealed that high correlations are probable only when the measures of attitude and behavior coincide with reference to the precise *action* to be performed, the *target* toward which the action is to be directed, the *context* in which the action would occur, and its *timing* (see Table 2.2).

A further important recognition was that measures of the cognitive pre-cursors of attitude will be highly predictive only when there is maximal temporal contiguity of the behavioral and antecedent measures (Ajzen & Fishbein, 1980). The greater the temporal gap between attitude or intention and the behavior to which they refer, and hence the extent of situational intervention that potentially separates them, the lower will be their correl-ative consistency. Though this remains a significant problem in all of the theories reviewed below, it is not necessarily a handicap to prediction. Even a temporal gap of some fifteen years does not impede prediction in some cases, though the correlation may be positively influenced by the use of self-report measures of behavior (Randall & Wolff, 1994). Certainly, there appears abundant empirical evidence that the intention which *immediately* precedes behavior is highly predictive (Ericsson & Simon, 1993), and that is all that the models now considered explicitly claim.

The Theory of Reasoned Action.   The Theory of Reasoned Action (TRA), which represents a culmination of Fishbein's and Ajzen's work on the pre-diction of attitude-consistent volitional behaviors, incorporates both these observations and several other innovations (Fishbein & Ajzen, 1975). While it was originally derived from the theory of propositional control put forward by Dulany (1968) and has much in common with the version of expectancy-value theory advanced by Rosenberg, the Fishbein model, from its inception to its most recent theoretical and methodological elabora-tions, has played a distinct role in the study of attitudes and behavior in both social psychology and marketing (Fishbein, 1967b). Fishbein defines attitude solely in terms of affect (overall evaluation) while defining cogni-tions in terms of the beliefs of which attitudes are a function, and conation as the behavioral intentions which mediate overt behavior. He avoids the classic problem of attitudinal-behavioral consistency in social psychology which is framed in terms of the relationship between attitudes toward an object and subsequent behavior toward that object. He argues that indi-viduals hold a multiplicity of attitudes toward an object and there is no reason why any one of them should predict all of the possible behavior pat-terns of that individual with respect to the object. Rather he concentrates upon the individual's attitude toward performing a given behavior or act with respect to the object in closely defined circumstances. Thus, rather than enquire simply of attitudes toward, say, frozen peas, the consumer researcher might pose questions or attitude statements which enquire specifically of the use of frozen peas as part of a family meal or a dinner party or in salads, or of their purchase in defined quantities, at given prices, from particular retail outlets.

The theory predicts not behaviors themselves but intentions to engage in them provided, first, that reasons can be adduced for doing so, and, second, that there is no let or hindrance to the respondent's doing so. It thus refers to reasoned behavior that is under the individual's volitional control. Such behavior, despite the authors' caution in delineating the predictive scope of their model, is assumed to approximate intentions toward its performance.

Intentions are, in their turn, determined by two belief-based cognitions. The first, attitude toward performing the target behavior, is measured as the respondent's belief that a particular action will have a given outcome or consequence, weighted by his or her evaluation of that outcome. Only *salient* behavioral beliefs enter into the calculation of behavioral attitude, which is presented as a multi-attribute model:

$$A_B \propto \sum_n b_i e_i \tag{2.1}$$

where A_B is the respondent's attitude toward performing behavior, B; b_i is the belief (subjective probability) that performing B will lead to outcome $_i$; e_i is the evaluation of outcome $_i$; and n is the number of salient behavioral beliefs over which these measures are summed (Ajzen, 1985, p. 13).

The second cognitive variable that determines intention is the respondent's subjective norm, his or her perceptions of the evaluations that important social referents ("significant others") would hold toward the respondent's performing the target action, weighted by his or her motivation to comply with them. Hence

$$SN \propto \sum_n b_j m_j \tag{2.2}$$

where SN is the subjective norm; b_j is the normative belief concerning referent $_j$; m_j is the respondent's motivation to comply with referent $_j$; and n is the number of salient beliefs.

Subjective norm is an attempt to capture the nonattitudinal influences on intention and, by implication, behavior. By permitting this consideration of perceived social pressure to enter the calculation of behavioral intentions, the theory takes account of some at least of the situational interventions that may reduce the consistency of the attitude-behavior sequence. There is empirical evidence that people actually distinguish behavioral and normative beliefs (Trafimow & Fishbein, 1995).

These belief-based measures predict not behavior itself but the *behavioral intentions* which are its immediate precursor and which it is assumed to approximate. Hence

$$B\_I \propto [w_1 + A_B + w_2 SN] \tag{2.3}$$

where B is the behavior of interest, I is the respondent's intention to perform B, A_B is his or her attitude toward performing B, SN is his or her subjective norm with respect to the performance of B, and w_1 and w_2

are empirically determined regression weights indicating the relative importance of A_B and SN (Ajzen, 1985, pp. 13–14).

The initial problem of attitude research has thus been modified further by the assumptions that the relationship between attitude and behavior is mediated by the behavioral intention which is the immediate precursor of the targeted action, and that behavioral intention is determined by both attitudinal and nonattitudinal factors (Sparks et al., 1991). But this approach has proved successful in as much as the prediction of behavior, albeit under the specialised circumstances to which the theory applies, has been achieved. Hence, the technological achievement of the TRA is that as long as its variables are measured under conditions maximally conducive to high correlations, which, as noted, refer to conditions of close situational correspondence, rather higher correlations than those reported pre-Wicker are usually obtained by the TRA.

The theory quickly found a pivotal place in consumer research: at the academic level – for instance, the *Journal of Consumer Research* was dominated by articles on multiattribute modeling from the mid- to late-1970s – and commercial market research conferences and journals were similarly concerned throughout that decade. The fascination continues, as perusal of current journals and textbooks alike attests. In summary, Petty et al. (1994) furnish us with a general evaluation of the TRA that reflects its popularity: while doubts occasionally arise with respect to some aspect or other of the model, they write, "a monumental body of research supports the idea that attitudes toward objects, issues, and people become more favorable as the number of likely desirable consequences (or attributes) and unlikely undesirable consequences associated with them increase" (p. 77).

Summing up the TRA.   In the extended model, known also as the Fishbein behavioral intentions model, behavioral intentions are posited as a function of attitudes toward performing an act in a specific situation (as defined above) plus the subject's normative beliefs about the social expediency of performing this act as they are aroused by her motivation to comply with the social norms as he perceives them. Thus, neither behavioral intentions nor the behavior they are assumed to approximate is depicted simply and exclusively as a function of attitude. This alone places the Fishbein model beyond the scope of simple attitudinal-behavioral relationships.

The effects of social environment on behavior are accounted for in the behavioral intentions model by a term which subsumes the individual's expectations that a specific reference group's members expect her to behave in the particular manner under investigation. Since different reference groups make various demands on the individual, some of which he ignores in order to reduce role conflict, her motivation to comply with the expectations of specified reference groups is used to weight the normative beliefs component. The intentions theory thus takes the following form when a single or generalized significant other is assumed:

$$B \approx B1 = [Aact]w_o + [NB(M_c)]w_1$$

where b = overt behavior
        $B1$ = behavioral intention
        $Aact$ = attitude toward the act
        NB = normative belief
        M_c = motivation to comply

and w_o, w_1 = empirically determined regression weights, and the following form when multiple reference groups are considered:

$$\overset{n}{\underset{i=1}{B}} \approx BI = [Aact]w_o + [\Sigma NB_i(M_{c1})]w_1$$

A great deal of work has been concerned with respective correlations of the attitudinal and normative components of the model with behavioral intentions and of the way in which these components combine to produce measures of behavioral intentions. While this underlies the internal validation of the model and is thus of concern to all researchers, for applied social psychologists and those involved in investigations of consumer choice the crucial criterion of the model's usefulness is the ability of behavioral intentions to predict actual behavior. The evidence to satisfy them is available from studies in which behavior was predicted from behavioral intentions over a variety of different contexts. These include alcohol use, voting on the building of nuclear power plants, consumer behavior, family planning, and forces re-enlistment. Although BI:B correlations range widely in these studies, it is no longer difficult to obtain evidence of strong relationships *so long as the variables are measured appropriately.*

But the question of appropriate measurement is crucial. The view was expressed earlier in this chapter that the improvement in correlations between pre-behavioral factors (attitudes or intentions) and behavior obtained subsequent to the revolution in attitude psychology which followed the inauguration of expectancy-value models and, in particular multi-attribute models such as that of Fishbein, result from the incorporation of "other variables" into the prediction of behavior.

The behavioral intentions model deliberately includes such "other factors." Fishbein does not deny their indispensability in the prediction of behavioral intentions or behavior but asserts that their full effect is subsumed in the measured components of behavioral intentions namely attitude toward the specified act and compliance with subjective norms. It is appropriate now to attempt to ascertain the extent to which the improvements in measured consistency are derived from the incorporation

of non-attitudinal factors. The following discussion of this issue is conducted in the context of the studies of consumer choice to which reference
has been made.

Critique of the TRA.   Any model of behavior contains inherent limitations.
The Fishbein intentions model is presented by Ajzen and Fishbein as a
device by which behavior may be predicted from measures of behavioral
intention *only under certain closely specified conditions* (Ajzen & Fishbein,
1972; cf. Fishbein, 1973). In short, the conditions in which measures of
behavioral intention are obtained must be, "maximally conducive to a high
correlation between BI and B" (Wilson et al., 1975, p. 40). High correlations
are obtainable *only when* the cognitive measures (of attitude toward the act,
subjective norm and behavioral intention) and of behavior are equally
specific; *and when* the period of time which intervenes between the
measurement of the behavioral intention and that of the behavioral criterion is very short; *and when* novel consequences of behavior or reference
group evaluations of the action under investigation do not intervene; *and
when* the behavior is voluntary and amenable to reason; *and when* the
intention which accurately predicts behavior is that which immediately
precedes the act.

The exogenous influences which invalidate more remote expressions of
intention no doubt account for the equivocal capability of the Fishbein
model to predict brand choice usefully in consumer research, that is in a
manner which permits the rather long term forecasts required by marketing managers. The typical results certainly give little encouragement to
anyone involved in the attempt to reduce the extremely high failure rates
of new consumer products.

But there are other criticisms to be noted here. Sheppard et al. (1988)
point out that the TRA deals with the prediction of behaviors rather than
the outcomes of behaviors: it is concerned for instance to predict the likelihood of one's studying for an examination, not that of one's passing it.
The amount of studying one does is largely under personal volitional
control but whether one's hard studying is accompanied by success in
the examination depends on factors that lie beyond that control: the cooperation of others in the household or library might not be forthcoming,
the books one most needs may not be available, one may not have invested
sufficient time and effort in attaining study skills, and so on (Liska, 1984).
Even if one is fully motivated and puts total effort into the task, circumstances may impede one's performance and achievement of the goal
(Ramsey et al., 1994; Sheppard et al., 1988).

The TRA cannot predict goal achievement because that outcome relies
upon situational factors which make the attainment of a goal uncertain.
The TRA also concentrates on the prediction of single, specified behaviors
which are not in competition with other behaviors. It thus avoids situ-

ations of choice within the class of intended behaviors or consequences (Dabholkar, 1994). The attributes taken into consideration in expectancy-value models such as the TRA correspond to attributes of the product class: to the extent that brands within that class are perceptively identical, brand choice may be unpredictable (Ehrenberg, 1988/1972). The vast majority of consumers are neither entirely brand nor store loyal and appear always to have more than one brand/outlet in mind when shopping for a particular product. The availability of choice, leading to the possible selection of one item or behavior from alternatives, is a situational constraint. Given the multi-brand purchasing behaviors of consumers, (Ehrenberg & Uncles, 1995), and their multi-store purchasing patterns (Uncles & Ehrenberg, 1990), it is doubtful whether such specific behaviors can be predicted by models of this sort.

Most significantly, the TRA has been criticized for not taking into consideration the full gamut of nonattitudinal personal and situational factors likely to influence the strength of the attitude-behavior relationship or to enhance the prediction of behavior (Brown & Stayman, 1992; Olson & Zanna, 1993). The authors of the TRA are adamant that behavior is determined by behavioral intention and that all contributing influences are subsumed by the two elements that determine it: attitude toward performing the target act and subjective norm with reference to performing that act (Ajzen & Fishbein, 1980; Fishbein & Ajzen, 1975). Yet this principle of sufficiency has been proved inaccurate by empirical work that has incorporated additional factors to increase the predictability of intentions and/or behavior (Bagozzi & Van Loo, 1991; Davies et al., 2002).[3]

Behavior that requires resources, skills and cooperation in order to be enacted is especially problematical. Consumer behavior usually requires all three, yet restricting the TRA to behavior that is volitional means it requires only motivation on the part of the individual. Studies that have supported the model have dealt with only simple behaviors that require little if anything by way of resources and skills. Fishbein and Ajzen argue that such considerations have an effect on intention and thus were taken care of in their model.

Also, Fishbein and Ajzen stressed that the intention that mattered for purposes of prediction was that obtaining immediately before the opportunity to engage in the behavior arose. Understanding what occurs between intention and behavior has become a big part of predicting actions (Eagly & Chaiken, 1993). Understanding what has gone before seems also to be of crucial importance. Fredericks and Dossett (1983), among others, have reported that once a measure of prior behavior is introduced into the Theory of Reasoned Action, it becomes the sole predictor of current behavior as the explanatory significance of the cognitive variables reduces to zero.

The theory of planned behavior

The Theory of Planned Behavior (Ajzen, 1985) adds a further cognitive variable to those contained in the TRA. *Perceived behavioral control* is posited – along with attitude toward the act and subjective norm – to determine behavioral intention. Further, on those occasions when perceived and actual behavioral control coincide or are closely approximate, perceived behavioral control is expected to exert a direct determinative influence on behavior. The theory thus applies to behaviors over which volitional control is limited. This is in contrast to the TRA which is adamantly a theory for volitional behavior.

Moreover, the extent to which perceived behavioral control adds significantly to the prediction of intentions is apparent from Ajzen's (1991) analysis of the results of several studies employing his theory which shows that the average multiple correlation was .71. Moreover, a comparison of the theories of reasoned action and planned behavior (Madden et al., 1992) involved a spectrum of ten behaviors from those rated comparatively difficult to control (e.g., shopping) to those rated comparatively easy (e.g. renting a video). The inclusion of perceived behavioral control in addition to the reasoned action variables resulted in a significant increase in explained behavioral variance.

As predicted by the Theory of Planned Behavior (TPB), perceived behavioral control was more important in the case of the behaviors rated as low in controllability. Manstead and Parker (1995, p. 72) conclude that the TPB has improved on the predictive performance of the TRA and extended the range of behaviors to which it can be applied.

Critique of the TPB.   The TPB is, nevertheless, problematical on several grounds of conceptualization and method. Like its immediate predecessor, the TPB assumes temporal contiguity between intention and behavior so that precise situational correspondence is still essential to accurate prediction (Netemeyer et al., 1991). The operationalisation of the theory remains beset by the problem of whether perceived behavioral control should be measured directly or by the recording of control beliefs (Manstead & Parker, 1995). Moreover, as Eagly and Chaiken (1993, p. 189) point out, the assumption of a causal link between perceived control and intention presumes people decide to engage in a behavior because they feel they can achieve it. This raises problems in the case of antisocial or negatively self-evaluated behaviors such as risky driving (Manstead & Parker, 1995).

Another, potentially more important technical problem is that the theory introduces only one new variable when we have seen that other factors – habit, perceived moral obligation, self-identity – may also predict behavior over and above the terms of the TRA. The theory is based on the principle of sufficiency, though the number of variables involved has been increased by just one from the TRA: there is continuing evidence that factors such as self-identity and moral judgment add predictive power over and above the measures formally incorporated into the TPB (see, for instance, Raats et al., 1995; Sparks & Shepherd, 1995; Sparks et al., 1995). Manstead and Parker (1995) argue strongly that personal norms and the affective evaluation of behavior may account for variance in behavioral intentions beyond that accounted for by the TPB (cf. Allen et al., 1992).

Taking stock

The concept of "attitude," understood within a cognitive framework, is perhaps the most widely used source of explanation for human behavior. The assumptions on which its use is based may be stated as follows: *Behavior is prefigured and largely determined by factors which exist (or can be hypothesized as existing) within the individual. Of all these intrapersonal elements, attitudes which consist of cognitions (beliefs), affect (emotion or feeling) and conation (action tendencies) are of pre-eminent importance in shaping behavior to particular objects. The prediction of behavior therefore depends upon obtaining accurate measurements of attitudes since behavior will be consistent with the individual's underlying mental dispositions. Although attitudes are dynamic and may be modified as a result of behavior, the key to changing behavior consists in the modification of one or more components of attitudes, predominantly through the presentation of informative (or persuasive) messages.* Any description of a complex perspective which is only four sentences long is naturally a simplification, but most consumer behavior specialists would agree that the above description contains the major assumptions which underlie the predominant uses of the concept of attitude in marketing.

The problem with this approach is that empirical research on attitude-behavior (A-B) relationships shows them to be unacceptably weak unless the situational correspondence between them is exceptionally high. Moreover, behavior is often predicted more accurately by measures of prior behavior than of attitudes. Yet the response of attitude researchers in consumer research is not to seek understanding of situational influences on consumer choice: it is to refine further the modeling of attitude-behavior relationships. There is a longstanding need to transcend this technical emphasis. Mostyn (1978, p. 83) wrote, based on her wide ranging review, "Instead of trying to improve the *A-B* relationship with existing techniques or even trying to improve upon the techniques, it would be more meaningful if researchers could rethink the entire assumptive philosophy underlying the *A-B* relationship." The following chapters begin to examine the proposition that an appropriate alternative might be akin to the following: *Behavior is the result, not of intrapersonal events, but of the consequences of previous behavior in similar situations. The reward or reinforcement of that behavior shapes and sustains present and future behavior of the same or similar kind. Behavior can thus be most effectively predicted from the pattern of reinforcements previously received by the individual and changing behavior depends upon modifying the situation in which it occurs in such a way as to make the reward or reinforcement dependent on new responses.* They will conclude that there is strong evidence for this proposition. But, far from advancing the crude notion that one of these paradigms is superior to the other, they will also seek a novel synthesis of the cognitive and the behavioral.

4
Prior Behavior

The search for "other variables" is far from over. Prior behavior, in particular, is an independent determinant of intention and behavior and several of the extra-TRA variables, including perceived behavioral control, are presumably related to prior behavior (e.g., Morojele & Stephenson, 1992; cf. East, 1997; Foxall, 1996, 1997a; cf. Thompson et al., 1994, 1995). East (1997) argues that "experience elaborates the belief basis of planned behavior constructs." As the consumer progresses from novice to experienced buyer, his or her behavior is influenced more by attitudes toward the behavior and perceived behavioral control and less by subjective norm, more by personal knowledge based on experience and less on the communicated preferences of other people.

The consumer who lacks specific and detailed knowledge of say a product falls back on simple notions or heuristics: social pressures to act in a particular manner will be more easily known or guessed than the benefits and costs of executing a novel behavior (East, 1997). This is supported by the finding that extrinsic cues such as product price and appearance are used in decision making by consumers with little or no direct experience of consuming the item (Rao & Monroe, 1988); moreover, the less consumers are familiar with a product the more they tend to infer its quality from its price and to have lower price limits suggesting that they have little idea of the product qualities worth paying for (Rao & Sieben, 1992). East (1997) interprets this to mean that "experience seems to result in detailed product knowledge that is used to change the way in which consumer judgments are made."

Moreover, novice computer buyers rely disproportionately on subjective norms and East contends, without direct evidence, that experienced computer users would scarcely be expected to base their decisions on social pressures rather than behavioral attitudes and perceived control. There is also empirical confirmation in the case of television viewing intentions that subjective norm is the stronger influence among novices (who lack experience and knowledge of the service, breakfast-time broadcasting) as compared with experienced viewers whose intentions were more pre-dictable from behavioral attitudes (East, 1992). Further evidence comes from a study showing that non-users of mineral water, as compared with users, tend to be far more strongly influenced by subjective norm (Knox & de Chernatony, 1994). Past behavior correlates more highly with beha-vioral attitude and perceived behavioral control than with subjective norm for a variety of consumer behaviors including applying for shares in a pri-vatized utility, four redress seeking behaviors, theatre-going, complaining in a restaurant, taking out a pension scheme, and playing Britain's National Lottery (East, 1997); the data also indicate that the inclusion of a measure of past behavior in a regression equation predicting intention from the TPB variables reduces the beta weights to a greater degree for behavioral attitude and perceived behavioral control than for subjective norm. Subjective norm, after all, is unlikely to be affected by or to increase in salience as a result of experience. One approach to the problems remaining in the TPB has been to investigate how people formulate plans and translate intentions into behavior, something the theory fails to address (Eagly & Chaiken, 1993). It is, however, a theme confronted by the theories of self-regulation and, especially, the theory of trying.

The theory of trying

An attempt to uncover the factors responsible for the translation of inten-tions into behavior was made by Bagozzi (1986, 1992, 1993; Bagozzi et al., 1992a, 1992b) in the theory of self-regulation. The novel thinking behind this approach is that attitude provides only a measure of the extent to which an individual is affectively involved with a behavior: his or her motivation to act in the specified way depends on their desire to engage in the behavior. It can be hypothesized, therefore, that desires would show a stronger effect on intentions than would attitudes, that attitude affects would ideally disappear, and that if desires contain explanatory content over and above that provided by subjective norm and past behavior, they will predict intentions even though these addi-tional variables are included in the measure of antecedents to intention (Bagozzi & Kimmel, 1995).

Bagozzi and Warshaw (1990) argue that goal attainment is determined by trying, i.e., cognitive and behavioral activities that mediate the expression of an intention to achieve a goal and its actual achievement (Figure 4.1). Trying thus incorporates the effectual tasks on which the attainment of a goal depends (Eagly & Chaiken, 1993, p. 190). This is, therefore, a based-based approach which takes into consideration the planning people engage in in order to achieve remote goals. Moreover, as a later section elaborates, it is precisely what the behavior analysis of rule-governance concentrates on.

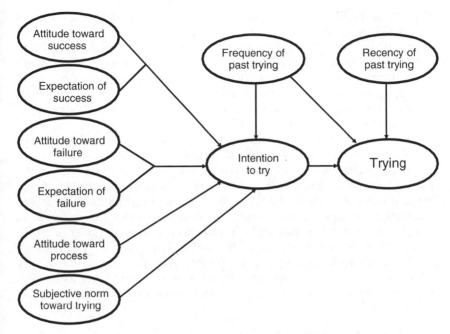

Figure 4.1 The Theory of Trying: Key Variables and Relationships

The theory of trying is intended to explain the link between intention and behavior by investigating the striving people undertake in order to perform a behavior or attain a goal, especially one which is difficult (Bagozzi & Kimmel, 1995). It assumes that when individuals *try* to achieve such a goal they discern it as potentially burdensome to the extent that it has only a probability of success; i.e. they are concerned about the likely outcome in view of the expenditure of effort that performing the behavior will entail. They will specifically be concerned with the possibilities of two final consequences – succeeding, having tried, and failing despite trying – and they will certainly incur the intermediate consequences inherent in the process of striving itself.

This approach differs from the theories of reasoned action and planned behavior in three respects. First, those theories measure attitude as an overall and unidimensional construct, averaging the effects of separate component attitudes and thereby masking their individual effect on intention which may differ from situation to situation. The three component attitudes, confirmed in a study of respondents' trying to lose weight (Bagozzi & Warshaw, 1990) are toward (i) success, (ii) failure, and (iii) the process of striving. Second, the theory of trying posits a novel idea of the manner in which attitudes operate in influencing intentions: attitudes toward success and failure will result in intentions to engage in a particular behavior to the degree that expectations of success are high and expectations of failure are low.

Bagozzi and Warshaw (1990) found evidence for the interaction of attitude toward success and expectations of success, and of a significant main effect of attitude toward the process; they found mixed support for the interaction of attitudes toward failure and expectations of failure. Third, the theory of trying explicitly includes the effect of past behavior on current trying. Despite Ajzen's (1987, p. 41) denial of the usefulness of including past behavior in causal theories of human action, numerous studies indicate the importance of this variable. Bentler and Speckart (1979) compare the TRA with (a) an alternative model that incorporated, in addition to the usual TRA variables, a direct causal path from attitude to behavior that was not mediated by intention) and (b) a further model that also added a new independent variable, *past behavior*, which was assumed to affect behavior both directly and via intention. This final model provided the best fit with the data: direct paths from attitude to behavior and from past behavior to behavior were supported. Attitude and past behavior explained variability not explained by intentions, though drug consumption, the focal behavior investigated, is not necessarily volitional (Eagly & Chaiken, 1993).

Evidence on past behavior

Other studies have shown that measures of past behavior improve predictions of behavior over those provided by attitudes/subjective norm/intention alone: e.g., giving up smoking (Marsh & Matheson, 1983; Sutton et al. 1987); studying and exercise (Bentler & Speckart, 1981); students' class attendance (Ajzen & Madden, 1986; Fredericks & Dossett, 1983); voting (Echabe et al., 1988); seat belt use (Budd et al., 1984; Mittal, 1988; Sutton & Hallett, 1989; Wittenbraker et al., 1983); blood donation (Bagozzi, 1981; Charng et al., 1988); and in consumer behavior (East, 1992, 1993).[1]

It is apparent from these studies that past behavior influences current behavior without being mediated by intentions, and that past behavior may influence intentions without being mediated by attitude or subjective norm. Bagozzi and Warshaw (1990) measured past behavior in two ways: frequency and recency, both of which were expected to impact the target act under investigation; of the two, only the frequency of past behavior was expected to impact intention to perform the act. They reported that both the frequency and recency of past trying had a direct influence on subsequent trying; moreover, frequency also influenced intentions to try to lose weight.

Bagozzi and Kimmel (1995) compared all four of the theories considered thus far in a study of two activities thought to have low perceived behavioral control: exercising and dieting. In the case of the TRA, intentions entirely predicted exercising and dieting responses but, while intentions for both were predicted by attitudes, subjective norms predicted intentions for neither. Their test of the TPB revealed that exercising was predicted by perceived behavioral control but not by intentions; however, intentions but not perceived behavioral control predicted dieting. Results for the prediction of intentions were also mixed: perceived behavioral control predicted this variable in the case of exercising but did not achieve this in the case of dieting.

The direct influence of perceived behavioral control is thus substantiated for exercising; but neither the hypothesized direct and indirect effect of perceived control on dieting was confirmed. Attitudes again predicted intentions for both actions but subjective norms failed to do so in either instance. As predicted by the theory of self-regulation, desires strongly influenced intentions for both behaviors; intention to exercise was impacted by attitude but not intention to diet; moreover, subjective norm again failed to predict intention in either case. However, behavior was significantly related to intention for both exercising and dieting. When past behavior measures were used to augment the theory of self-regulation, both frequency and recency significantly impacted behavior but the effect of intention on behavior became nonsignificant.

The findings provide mixed evidence for the theory of trying. While intention predicted dieting but not exercising, the measures of past behavior, frequency and recency, each had a significant impact on both behaviors. A significant interaction between attitude toward success and expectation of success was found only in the case of exercising; frequency and subjective norms also had a significant effect for this behavior but neither attitudes toward the process nor the interaction of attitude toward failure and expectations thereof fulfilled the hypothesized relationships. Intentions for dieting were functions of frequency, subjective norms, and attitudes toward the process of striving, but neither of the hypothesized interactions was confirmed.

Madden and Sprott (1995) report a partial confirmation of Bagozzi and Kimmel's results. They compared the TRA, TPB and the theory of trying in two contexts: renting a video cassette, which represented high volitional control, and obtaining a good night's sleep, which represented low volitional control. The TPB's predictions of intention exceeded those of the TRA, but were no more predictive of behavior once intentions had been taken into account. In the case of the theory of trying, Madden and Sprott failed to confirm Bagozzi and Warshaw's (1990) finding that frequency and recency of past behavior significantly affected trying. Intentions to try appear to subsume these effects for these admittedly familiar behaviors: indeed, past behavior in the form of recency of trying impacted significantly on intention in both cases.

The inclusion of a measure of past behavior improved on the predictions of behavior generated by the TRA and TPB in the case of sleeping but not video rental. Past trying frequency improved predictions of intention for both behaviors over those produced by the TRA and TPB, a confirmation of the results reported by Bagozzi and Kimmel (1995). A test of the TRA and an augmented version of that model containing measures of the frequency and recency of past behavior as covariates (Bagozzi & Warshaw, 1992) also indicates the importance of past behavior as an explanatory variable. The investigation demonstrates the capacity of the TRA to predict some behaviors under some circumstances when it is not augmented by measures of past behavior. In the case of losing weight, the theory performed as expected: behavior was predicted by intentions, and intentions were predicted by attitude and subjective norm. Neither attitudes nor subjective norm predicted behavior, i.e. the effect of each on behavior was fully mediated by intention. However, the other behavior examined, initiating a conversation with an attractive stranger, was not predicted by intentions; attitude predicted intention but subjective norm had no impact upon it. Moreover, behavior was directly influenced by attitude.

These results on the whole are not consistent with the relations hypothesized by the TRA. When the measures of past behavior were added to the analysis, neither of the behaviors investigated could be attributed to processes of reasoning or volition (Bagozzi & Warshaw, 1992). For neither behavior was there an influence from intentions to behavior; nor did attitude have a direct effect on either behavior. "The Theory of Reasoned Action therefore fails to explain behavior, once we control for the effects of frequency and recency of past behavior" (ib.) Intentions to lose weight or initiate a conversation were unstable after the partialling-out of frequency and recency effects, indicating that neither behavior can be attributed to volitional control. "Significantly, strong recency effects are found for trying to lose weight... and initiating a conversation... No other determinants of behavior are found..." (ib.) Bagozzi and Warshaw (1992, p. 631) conclude that because of the failure of attitude, subjective norm and intention to act as antecedents of behavior doubt is cast on their role in the explanation of human action. In a reversal of the explanatory sequence presumed by the TRA, their results indicate that intentions and attitudes arise out of behavior.

Dealing with prior behavior

Authors of deliberative processing models have generally sought the rationale for the relation between past and current behaviors by invoking a cognitive framework. Hence, it is proposed that frequency effects on intentions operate when attitudes fail: either because the information needed to form a belief and/or evaluation is absent or because it is unclear (Bagozzi & Warshaw, 1992, p. 605). Inability to access or comprehend one's attitude will similarly increase the salience of frequency effects for intention formation. Frequency might exert a direct effect on behavior when the individual has formed no plan of action, even though his or her attitude and intention are in place, or when choice involves a multitude of similar options, or when there is no time pressure to act. But, in addition, "frequency effects might reflect desires or cognitive urges" (ibid.; Bagozzi, 1991). Frequency effects on behavior are also likely when "cognitions and evaluations are primitive or undergoing change," or because the behavior in question is "mindless or scripted, such as biting one's fingernails" (ibid.; Abelson, 1981; Langer, 1989b).[2]

Further, an inability to activate intentions, caused by absence of control, situational interventions, or "internal impediments" may stand in the way of a conscious intention's activating behavior (Bagozzi & Yi, 1989; Bagozzi et al., 1990). Frequency of past behavior can also substitute for actual control (Ajzen & Madden, 1986; Beale & Manstead, 1991). Recency acts upon intentions by increasing availability and anchoring/adjustment biases into reports thereof (Tversky & Kahneman, 1974). Recent behavior exerts a disproportionate influence on the perceived likelihood of an event; and on the anchor value used to estimate subjective probability of an event; both influence one's intention to perform it. When intentions do not automatically lead to behavior, recency of behaving may act to "capture any residual automatic reactions that are triggered by conditioned releasers or stimulated directly by learned dispositions to respond" (Bagozzi & Warshaw, 1992, p. 606). Finally, situational factors may just block an intended behavior and recency effects may operate by suggesting alternative paths to the goal.

In summary, past behavior will predict current when cognitive determinants are absent or ineffective or goal attainment is blocked; and when behavior is either mindless or scripted or incapable of fulfillment even though it is attitude-driven or intentional. The analysis also carries the implication that routine (mindless/scripted/low involvement) behavior is to be accounted for by behavioral variables whilst novel (high involvement) behavior is to be accounted for by cognitive variables. As the following section on the behavior analysis of choice and decision making indicates, however, there is no reason to accept this. Either behavioral explanation can cover both or the behavioral and cognitive approaches to explanation should be seen as complementary rather than supplementary: cognitive accounts for proximal causation, behavioral for distal.

Current research

The social cognitive research tradition continues apace, continually getting closer to behavior as a predictor of subsequent behavior, while insisting on the cognitive mediation of action. The theory of trying "conceived of trying as a singular subjective state summarizing the extent to which a person *believes* that they have tried or will try to act. Trying was presumed to mediate the influence of intentions to act on actual actions..." (Bagozzi,

2004, p. 2; emphasis added). Yet the mental precursors of behavior tend to reach out toward and even blend with effortful behavior itself: "Bagozzi (1992) proposed that, following a decision to act, some subset of the following might constitute trying: planning, monitoring of progress toward a goal, self-guidance and self-control activities, commitment to a goal or intention or action, and effort put forth" (ibid). The empirical arm of this program increasingly equates trying with both mental and physical activities (e.g., Bagozzi & Edwards, 1998, 2000; Bagozzi et al., 1998, 1990; Taylor et al. 2001), Bagozzi (2004, p. 4) admitting that "The line, then, between trying and intentions, volition, and goal-directed behavior may be difficult to draw, and an argument could be made that 'trying' is an omnibus term... ."[3]

Syntheses of attitude-behavior relationships

In addition to ongoing analysis of this kind, several attempts have been made to produce syntheses of the evidence on spontaneous and deliberative attitude–behavior relationships,[4] the cognitive processes inferred to underlie them, and the extent to which behavior enters into the definition and evaluation of cognitive events. Several of these attempts have highlighted the questions of *when* each method of processing is relevant to the determination of behavior, and the possibility that they may work in tandem. What is particularly interesting about them, however, is the variety of ways in which they take prior behavior into consideration.

MODE: motivation and opportunity as determinants

Fazio (1990) points to the two ways in which attitudes guide behavior – spontaneously and through deliberation – and argues that one or other of these processing modes will be activated according to the circumstances of motivation and opportunity present. Deliberative processing is probable when the expected costliness of the prospective behavior induces rational evaluation of the merits and demerits of assuming a given course of action. At this time, motivation to avoid the expense of making and acting upon a poor judgment overrides the spontaneous mechanism whereby attitudes might be activated from memory without cognitive effort. Assuming that an opportunity to deliberate is available, the individual can be expected to engage in extensive prebehavioral mental deliberation.

Where the motivation to avoid heavy costs misjudgment is low and/or an opportunity to deliberate is not forthcoming, attitudinal influences on behavior will occur via spontaneous processing. The extent to which attitude influences behavior in these circumstances reflects the strength of evaluative association that has been built with respect to the attitude object through direct experience or by means of verbal rehearsal of the attitude. Provided that this association is sufficiently strong, the individual's definition of the event will be wholly or predominantly attitude-determined. When the attitude association is weak, however, this defini-tion of the event will be based mainly on non-attitudinal factors: behavior toward the attitude object will then depend predominantly on the salient features of the attitude object itself and the situation (Fazio, 1990, pp. 93–94).

HSM: the heuristic-systematic model

A broadly similar spectrum underlies Chaiken's (1980) heuristic-systematic model (HSM) which arrays processing strategies on the basis of the amount of cognitive effort they involve. The extremes of the processing continuum she proposes are *systematic* processing which is potentially effortful, requir-ing the evaluation of multiple interpretations of the situation before a definitive impression is formulated, and *heuristic* processing which requires minimal information handling, relying on established rules to make sense of the current situation. On the understanding that individuals minimize effortful activity, systematic processing is likely only when the person is highly motivated and has the cognitive capacity and resources to engage in it. Nevertheless, individuals are also assumed to balance effort mini-mization with the confidence they feel in their social perceptions. When heuristics based on experience can be substituted for systematic processing, they will be activated by elements of the current situation that signify their relevance (Bohner et al., 1995). Decision making may, however, result from the simultaneous activation of both processes, reflecting both "content-related thinking" (systematic) and "cue-related evaluations" (heuristic) (van Knippenberg et al., 1994). Recent reviews of the empirical work prompted by the HSM can be found in Eagly and Chaiken (1993); in addition, Bohner et al. (1995) present the most recent version of the model and review research which has applied the model in the spheres of mood, persuasion and minority influence.

The Eagly-Chaiken composite model

Eagly and Chaiken (1993) present an integrative model of the attitude-behavior relationship which incorporates both the attitudes toward objects ("targets") implicated in spontaneous processing and the attitudes toward behaviors implicated in deliberative processing. Each kind of atti-tude is operational at a different stage in a dynamic sequence leading to behavior. Attitude toward a behavior is determined by *habit* (successive instances of an action that occur automatically or at least in the absence of self-instruction); *attitude toward the target*; and three sets of outcomes: *utilitarian*, rewards and penalties expected to follow from the performance of the behavior, *normative*, the endorsement or denunciation expected of significant others toward the action, plus the self-administered rewards like pride, and punishments like guilt, resulting from internal moral rules;

and, when these self-administered consequences relate to the self-concept, *self-identity*.

Attitude toward behavior impacts in turn upon intention which in turn impacts upon behavior. Intention is also partly determined by normative and self-identity outcomes; and behavior, by habit and attitude toward behavior (Eagly & Chaiken, 1993, pp. 209–11). This is corroborated by the functional approach to attitude theory and research taken by Shavitt (1989) who proposes that an object may evoke one or more of three functions: *utilitarian* (coffee, for instance) which arises from the reinforcing and punishing outcomes of using the item; *social identity* (e.g., a wedding ring) that communicates social status, identity and prestige; and *ego-defensive/self-esteem* (e.g., one's appearance). Shavitt has shown that many objects evoke a single attitude function and that promotional appeals based on the appropriate function for each product are more persuasive than appeals based on different criteria.

Prior behavior and cognitive explanation

So much in the preceding account points to the determinative role of prior behavior (at least in predicting, and possibly in causing, current behavior) that this variable apparently has the potential to modify the paradigm for attitude research, shifting the emphasis from intrapersonal sources of explanation toward a based-based perspective. More than being just an additional influence that increases attitudinal/intentional-behavioral consistency or accounts for inconsistency, prior behavior has a deter-minative influence on behavior inasmuch as its inclusion in models has direct implications for the predictive and explicative power of cognitive variables and may even render them redundant. As will be shown, its influence on "intentions" can be interpreted in a behavior analytic account as an influence on verbal behavior which acts as an instruction to further responding.

The pressure of the evidence is for the incorporation of prior behavior more fully into explanations of behavior. However, although prior beha-vior is finding a place at the level of measurement, the implications of the empirical findings for this factor impinge little on the epistemology of atti-tude researchers and theorists. By and large, they have opted for a cognitive framework to embrace the influence of prior behavior on current respond-ing. The nonattitudinal variables considered by Eagly and Chaiken to mod-erate attitude toward an object and behavior toward that object include 'vested interest' (which is surely an aspect of learning history), personality, including moral reasoning level, and having a doer self-image (both of which can be conceptualized as arising in the individual's learning history). But these authors do not consider these further, let alone as denotive of a history of reinforcement and punishment, because they do not fit into a unified theoretical framework. Rather they press on with their assumption that "attitude-behavior correspondence is affected by the nature of the attitude and by the implications that that attitude is perceived to have for the behavior that is assessed" (Eagly & Chaiken, 1993, p. 194). Even authors who speak of learning history as determinative (Eiser 1987), refuse the full operant alternative to cognitivism. There might be good reason for this (see Chapter 8), but there is an alternative strategy.

The continuity of behavioral effects on behavior is presumably traceable to situational influences, i.e., to stimuli that are either identical or "functionally equivalent," as the behaviorists would say, on each occasion that the behavior is enacted. The alternative strategy is based on the thinking that since the degree to which situational effects on attitudes should be weighted as compared with intrapersonal factors is unknown, a model of environment–behavioral influence that puts the entire onus on situational factors is a good starting point. If, and as and when, this becomes inadequate as either a predictive or explanatory device, additional variables can then be incorporated as required. This is the approach on which the research program from which this book derives has been based and the following chapters will expand upon its implications for attitudinal–behavioral research. While it may not be the sole strategy for research in this area, it seems to reflect an undue conformity to the cognitive paradigm to respond to a crisis of prediction and explanation by incorporating ever greater numbers of cognitive variables into one's models, even if these are attempting to capture situational influences indirectly, rather than to rethink one's approach.

Some reviewers have, admittedly, been willing to accommodate behavioral as well as cognitive precursors of attitude as factors that increase attitudinal-behavioral consistency. Eagly and Chaiken (1993, p. 202) sum up their extensive review of the factors involved in generating such consistency: "Attitudes that are based on more input are likely to relate more strongly to attitude-relevant behaviors, whether this input is behavioral or cognitive. Thus, research on behavioral experience has shown that increased behavioral input increases attitude-behavior correspondence, and research on prior knowledge has suggested that increased cognitive input has the same impact. Unfortunately, research on affective experience is lacking, but increased input from this source may similarly increase attitude-behavior correspondence." Yet this approach, though it tries to incorporate both behavioral and cognitive influences evenhandedly, is limited in two ways by its implicit acceptance of a cognitive reference structure.

First, there remains an overwhelming inclination toward explaining attitudinal-behavioral consistency in cognitive terms. The general thrust of the evidence gained subsequently to Wicker's (1969) review, and the disappointment and consternation it generated, has tended toward the importance of including noncognitive factors in the prediction of behavior.

But current attitude theory does not reflect this sufficiently. Extra-attitudinal cognitive factors were, of course, always implicated in the quest for greater consistency, but seminal contributions have emphasized situational and behavioral influences (Seibold, 1980).

The implication of the tight situational compatibility required of measures of target behavior and measures of its antecedent cognitive predictors (Ajzen and Fishbein, 1977) is that situational factors are highly significant for the correlational consistency of attitudes/intentions and behavior. Only when the situational influences governing both the prebehavioral and the behavioral variables are "functionally equivalent" are high correlations found. That the intertemporal period between prebehavioral and behavioral measures must be minimal if high correlations are to be found corroborates this view by pointing to the undesirability of unexpected situational demands reducing the predictive value of measured intentions (Foxall, 1983, 1984, 1996).

Ajzen's and Fishbein (1980) claim that situational factors that intervene between intention and behavior can be ignored for purposes of prediction since the changes will likely cancel one another out and thus not influence the predictive accuracy of the intention also requires comment. While the problem of prediction has been overcome – albeit only to the extent that, for the individual, the predictive intention is that which immediately precedes the opportunity to behave in accordance with it – that of explanation remains. For there can be no claim to have explained behavior in terms of its antecedent reasons if situational interventions can play so large a part in the determination of behavior (Sarver, 1983).

This is no deterrent to Fishbein and Ajzen whose insistence on attributing behavior to intentions – and in turn to attitudes and subjective norms – reveals a deliberate predilection to interpret behavior by reference to underlying causative mental dispositions. The practical importance of predictive methods closely following theoretical expectations is clear from the marketing of new consumer products in which process about eighty percent of innovations fail at the point of market acceptance even when their launch has been preceded by sophisticated market research based on the measurement of prospective consumers' attitudes and intentions. Only behavior with the product, including product tests and test marketing, predicts trial and repeat purchase with any acceptable degree of accuracy (Foxall, 1984).

But the point here is that context and situation deserve a more central place in the explanation of behavior which is denied them by the partiality inherent in acceptance of the preeminence of the cognitive paradigm. Yet the reasons why past and current behavior are consistent are discussed by attitude theorists in predominantly cognitive terms: the possibility that the consistency is due to environmental influences does not appear to enter their research agenda. Moreover, the tripartite comprehension of attitude prevails as the paradigm for further investigation and explication.

Second, although Eagly and Chaiken mention in passing a behavioristic approach, their apparent understanding of the possibilities thereof seem severely limited. They accept, for instance, that including measures of past behavior is reasonable from a behaviorist standpoint which holds that "behavior is influenced by habit, or more generally, by various types of conditioned releasers or learned predispositions to respond that are not readily encompassed by the concepts of attitude and intention" (Eagly & Chaiken, 1993, p. 179).

But this avoids the fact that the explanatory power of past behavior is frequently sufficient to make cognitive variables superfluous; that a behavior analytic theory may be capable of explaining or interpreting the evidence on attitudinal-behavioral consistency in full; and that in any case the reason for including a behaviorist perspective is to identify the consequences that past behavior has produced to account for the consistency of that prior responding and thus to use those consequences to predict future behavior.

A further tendency is to refer to repetitious behavior as habit. Triandis (1977, 1980) defined habit as "situation-specific sequences that are or have become automatic, so that they occur without self-instruction" (Triandis, 1980, p. 204). In similar vein, Eagly and Chaiken (1993, p. 180) comment that "the concept of habit implies that a behavior has become so routinised through repetition that a person has ceased to make any conscious decision to act yet still behaves in the accustomed way." Another way of putting this is that habitual behavior is that maintained by direct contact with the contingencies of reinforcement rather than instructed through verbal behavior. The alternative paradigm to which this description belongs suggests a means by which the import of prior behavior may be more fully understood. However, this is not the usual emphasis in attitude theory and research. Ronis et al., (1989, p. 218) refer to a habit as an action that has been carried out with such frequency that it has become automatic; its performance is devoid of conscious thinking.

A great deal of consumer behavior is apparently of this kind. How is it to be explained? Unfortunately, it is often "explained" in terms that are frankly tautological. Hence Ronis et al. (1989, p. 217) argue that "the continued repetition of behaviors is often determined by habits rather than by attitudes or beliefs." But this is meaningless given their definition of habit: a habit, as they understand it and as the word is used in everyday discourse, *is* the repeated behavior. Such behavior must be accounted for – unless we think it is uncaused – by reference to other factors; in an operant account, for instance, it would be ascribed to the contingencies of reinforcement. These authors attribute the causative habits to repeated behavior (p. 219), an assignation that completes the tautology of their argument. Eagly and Chaiken similarly refer to habits as "nonattitudinal determinants of behavior" and as one of several "psychological tendencies that regulate behavior" (Eagly & Chaiken, 1993, p. 216, p. 671).

Ronis et al. (1989, pp. 216–18) uncontroversially point out that the explanation of habit requires that attention be given to two component processes: *initiation*, that in which the behavior comes about, requiring decision-making; and *persistence* which implies automaticity, lack of conscious direction. They associate attitudes with initiation, but not persistence. A decision, almost by definition, involves conscious thought and reflection on one or more alternatives to the chosen behavior. They also point out that initiation (novel behavior) is predictable from attitudes, while persistence is not; that prior behavior is also a strong predictor of novelty; and that habit predicts future behavior more effectively than intentions (Ronis et al., 1989, p. 221).

In other words, attitudes correlate with habitual behavior under some circumstances, not others. In a behavior analysis, there is evidence that nonverbal behavior is consistent with rules in the long term only if the contingencies bear out the rules. Moreover, note that the behavior analytic demonstration is that behaviorist explanation can account for both decision and habit: it is not the case that behavior analysis is confined to habit while decision is accounted for as social cognitivism.

Behavior and attitudes

According to the social cognition interpretation, consumer behavior is the result of information processing in a social context. It is attitude-consistent either because prior experience of the object is sufficient to allow evaluations to control behavior spontaneously or because, in the absence of such experience, the individual must deliberate, examining the likely consequences of each course of action apparently available and consciously selecting one which he or she intends to perform if circumstances permit. Most consumer behavior contains elements of both spontaneous and deliberative processing. The tendency of adherents to this paradigm is to interpret evidence for the environmental control of behavior in terms of additional cognitive processing.

But the factor that emerges again and again as predictive of current behavior is neither attitude nor intention but *preceding* behavior. Moreover, this neglected but clearly central explicator has two components. The first is the set of similar overt motor responses performed by the individual in the past, what attitude theorists and researchers including Fishbein, Ajzen, Bagozzi and Warshaw have referred to as past behavior or prior behavior. This stream of similar responses cannot be considered in the absence of the consequences it has produced and their implications for the probability that similar behavior of the same kind will be emitted again. In the terminology of behavior analysis, and on the assumption that they are similarly reinforced, these responses belong to the same operant class and their future rate of emission depends upon the learning history of the individual.

The second sense in which preceding behavior may be understood is that of the verbal behavior which instructs the current responding of an individual. This verbal behavior might consist of instructions or rules articulated by someone else or of the self-instructions generated by the individual for him/herself. These verbal discriminative stimuli are the antecedent source of the rule-governed behavior of humans: such behavior is distinguished from the contingency-shaped behavior of nonhumans and, on occasion, humans. The broader category of verbal behavior, which includes both the rule-provision of the speaker and the rule-compliance of the listener, allows radical behaviorism to investigate and interpret the phenomena of thinking, reasoning, problem-solving and deciding that have traditionally fallen within the purview of cognitive psychology (Skinner 1974; Ribes 1991, 1992). The paradigm which offers understanding of the role of instructed behavior and to underpin the argument made here is behavior analysis.

Our need is for a paradigm that takes account of the import of behavior itself. The account of consumer behavior we have just left draws our attention to the significance of prior behavior in the analysis of current consumer choice, to the need to consider the context in which behavior has been learned in order to interpret properly its present meaning, and to the necessity of understanding the ways in which environmental influences shape and maintain patterns of consumer behavior over time. All of these criticisms of social cognition derive from work within that paradigm, though there does not appear to be recognition among its practitioners that, cumulatively, these findings might render their perspective untenable for the comprehensive modeling of consumer behavior.

If we are dissatisfied with social cognitive accounts of consumer choice, we may react constructively in two ways. One is to improve the techniques we are using; for instance, increasing the number of variables we employ to predict a response, or expanding the accuracy of our measures by relying more on observation of the behavioral target rather than on respondents' self reports of what they have done. As long as we wish to continue to work within the social cognition paradigm, this process of amelioration is inevitable. The thrust of attitude and consumer researcher's effort has been so directed: from early attempts to establish statistical consistency between measures of attitude-toward-the-object and object-toward-the-object, through the Theory of Reasoned Action, the Theory of Planned Behavior, the theories of self-regulation and trying, as well as by the more radical reformulation in terms of spontaneous processing. Moreover, while these attempts might not be definitive in resolving the problems of attitudinal-behavioral consistency, they are forceful in identifying the situational coherence required for the comprehension of verbal and nonverbal behaviors.

The other approach to any professional disappointment we may feel with current attempts to understand and predict consumer behavior is to take an altogether different approach. But this does not make radical behaviorism, a paradigm founded upon antithetical assumptions about the causation of human behavior, the obvious choice as the alternative framework of conceptualization and analysis. Why, then, are the following chapters devoted to it?

Radical behaviorism is an approach to the analysis of behavior which emphasizes behavior itself, rather than its alleged intrapersonal determinants, be they mental (information processing, attitudes, intentions), neural (physiological processes), or conceptual (hypothetical constructs purportedly existing only in the mind of the observer). Moreover, radical behaviorism seeks to explain the occurrence of behavior in relation to the outcomes produced by similar behavior in the past – notably, the rewards and sanctions which affect the probability of such behavior's being repeated in similar circumstances. That is, its explication of behavior relies on events that happen *in the environment* rather than within the individual (Moore, 1999; Smith, 1986; Zuriff, 1985).

An obvious stratagem, therefore, is to turn to the consideration of a paradigm which claims to understand behavior in context and which has been dedicated for well over half a century to the practical demonstration that "the variables of which behavior is a function lie in the environment" (Skinner, 1977, p. 5) and to the philosophical grasp of its findings to that apparent effect. Not because this way lies Truth but because our intellectual quest requires it. Radical behaviorism is not even the sole perspective on behavior which seeks to relate it to its consequences. Social learning theory (Bandura, 1986) and social exchange theory (Homans, 1974) are but two of the alternatives, each of which owes its emphasis on the environment to radical behaviorism and yet takes account of cognitive processes in its own way. Perhaps our search for a novel approach will lead to one of these or to a close relative. But there are certain advantages in beginning with the more extreme position presented by radical behaviorism.

By examining the claims of this approach to have dealt successfully with the extra-personal explanation of behavior, and by working with it in the specific context of consumer behavior rather than as an abstract philosophy, we shall be able to evaluate those claims in terms of their capacity to elucidate consumer choice beyond the point to which social cognitivism has brought our understanding.

Although we shall approach it positively, it would be naive to think that radical behaviorism will not ultimately prove to have shortcomings of its own. Every system does. But we are not seeking religious certainty: rather we want as full a view of human behavior as possible and the more explanatory systems we take into consideration, critically evaluating one from the standpoint provided by another, the more comprehensive will that view become. It may emerge that the very problems we encountered in social cognition are common to radical behaviorism, or that it has shortcomings of its own with which to impede consumer research. The kind of consumer research, academic as well as commercial, which is concerned with selling soap (or brotherhood) will probably not benefit from our peregrinations. But, if consumer psychology and marketing research are to hold their own in the academy, we must undertake them. Moreover, our excursions abroad are a vital source of inspiration if we are to maintain our own sense of intellectual excitement, as students of human economic behavior, in the face of the dull strictures our disciplines would impose upon us and the shaping of the academy by those who do not do such work.

Such consideration must, nevertheless, be upon the pragmatic level of judgment rather than that of philosophical comparison. Every system of thought is both supported and destroyed by philosophical criticism, which seems to provide no enduring answers nor to convince anybody of anything for long, let alone change the views of whole scientific communities which remain as fragmented as ever. (No need to consult the history of philosophy for proof of this: the numerous philosophical arguments which have littered the pages of marketing and consumer behavior journals, conference proceedings and books since the early-1980s are ample demonstration: none has apparently informed subsequent empirical or theoretical research to any appreciable degree.) There are always grounds, at this level, to reject what is yet useful. Thank goodness: for it is the variety of our ontologies, methodologies and epistemologies, and their critical interaction, that ensures scientific progress, or at least the growth of knowledge.

Decisive shifts of perspective do not occur in the social sciences, even in psychology which so wants to be a paradigm science. Tides come and go, but each continues to say something relevant to our scientific endeavors. We may come to reject radical behaviorism in its present form or to reformulate it more usefully. But at least we shall have done so not because its death was announced in a psychology or philosophy text written by someone else but because we appreciate its value as well as its drawbacks and, therefore, what we can do with it as consumer researchers.

The possibility that behaviorism can provide an appropriate general methodological framework for consumer research fills many people with dread. For behaviorism seems to deny the very humanness of our subject matter (Webster, 1996). This would be true of radical behaviorism were it the stimulus-response psychology for which it is usually mistaken (Lee, 1988). An ontologically credible behaviorism must be capable of dealing with the private events such as thoughts and feelings which this paradigm is most frequently represented as ignoring. Indeed, it must take them as central to its subject matter and, on this point, radical behaviorism is ontologically distinct from the stimulus-response formulations of classical conditioning.

Conclusions

The lesson of this and the preceding chapters is that the relationship between consumers' attitudes and their behavior cannot be properly appreciated unless situational influences on both are taken properly into consideration. The success of the Theories of Reasoned Action and Planned Behavior appear to stem from their incorporation of concepts that belong to behavior analysis: the individual's learning history, the setting in which he or she behaves, and the consequences of behaving that are foreshadowed by that setting. Prior behavior has emerged as a central "other variable" that is, at least, correlated with current activity and therefore capable of predicting it, and, at most, causally linked with the present. The following chapter is concerned with the way in which those factors combine into a model of consumer choice that relates it systematically to its situational determinants, and thereby shows how attitudes, behavior, and situations interact. The Behavioral Perspective Model which is the culmination of the theoretical and practical developments pursued in this chapter was developed independently of the progress of the attitude research discussed above; it provides, nevertheless, an appropriate framework for the empirical investigation of situational influences on attitudes and behavior in light of attitude researchers' reaching out for analogues of the settings in which behavior occurs and the consequences of behaving in specified ways.

It is not enough to have identified the factors that have made the prediction of behaviour more accurate, notably *situational correspondence* and *behavioral history*. The evidence that these methodological refinements increase the precision of our explanations of behaviour lies scattered in the reports of dozens if not hundreds of empirical investigations which have taken them deliberately but unsystematically intro consideration. There is no guarantee that further attempts to do so will automatically succeed; nor – and this is vitally important in an applied field such as marketing – that the results of research based hopefully but haphazardly on the inclusion of these factors will yield productive applications. "Situational correspondence" and "behavioral history" are useful terms in so far as they summarise the methodological improvements introduced by deliberative attitude theory and research. But they are scarcely a guide to action for either marketing research or marketing management.

The question is how they relate to the realities of consumer situations in marketing-orientated economies and it must be answered in a way that makes these factors concrete bases for research and action. For this we require a more formal representation that relates situations, attitudes and behavior reliably. The Behavioral Perspective Model (BPM) is an attempt to incorporate the situational variables that recent attitude theory has only implicitly recognized and to do so in such a way that consumers' attitudes and behaviors can be predicted and understood.

5
The Situated Consumer

Recognition that attitude research had failed to produce convincing predictions of behavior came relatively early in the history of social psychology. We have seen that Wicker and Fishbein, in particular, though among others, realized that attitudes would be implicated in the prediction and explanation of behavior only if drastic but appropriate measures were taken to incorporate situational variables. This chapter argues first that the relative success of attitude research since the early 1970s has been achieved by precisely the kind of situational reasoning required to take environmental variables into consideration. Second, it argues that these situational variables are precisely those arrived at independently in the development of the Behavioral Perspective Model of consumer choice (BPM), namely the consumer's learning history and the setting in which consumption occurs. Third, the chapter presents evidence that the formalization of these situational influences on consumer choice has enabled the prediction of consumer behavior to take place in ways that identify the specific setting variables that influence choice in a marketing context.

The model is a fairly simple representation of consumption history and behavior setting and reflects the influences of functional and symbolic influences on consumer choice. That consumer behavior is shaped by more than technical and economic considerations, that it is determined also by social and psychological influences, is hardly novel, at least for marketing scientists (though, as Mason, 1998, argues, it has apparently long eluded economic theorists). Although these factors are basic to understanding consumer choice, the lack of a conceptual framework by which they might be comprehended has inhibited the development of marketing theory, a process which requires that explanations be sought and empirically tested in a systematic manner. The framework within which the BPM developed for this purpose is behavior analysis, an approach which makes particular assumptions about the nature of human behavior and choice and within which the findings of empirical research can be evaluated in order to critique the framework itself and to develop consumer and marketing theory further. Because the derivation of the model has been described elsewhere, the following exposition briefly introduces it and its relevance to the pursuit of attitudinal – behavioral consistency.

Situational correspondence

The deliberative theory approach indicates that in order to obtain high correlational consistency among attitude, intention and behavior these variables must be measured at identical levels of situational specificity. The first source of evidence concerns measurement specificity. The systematic processing group of attitude theories revolves around the belief that the degrees of specificity with which attitudinal and behavioral measures are each defined must be identical if high correlations are to be found between them. Generic attitude measures are therefore consistent with multiple-act measures of behavior toward the attitude object. It follows that the prediction of single acts is only likely to result from equally narrow measures of attitude, those that correspond exactly in level of specificity to the act to be predicted; those, moreover, that are framed as measures of the respondent's attitude toward performing that act in closely designated circumstances.

A second source of evidence is the quest for setting correspondence. We have seen that Ajzen and Fishbein's (1977) analysis of numerous studies of attitudinal-behavioral consistency revealed that high correlations are probable only when the measures of attitude and behavior coincide with reference to the precise *action* to be performed, the *target* toward which the action is to be directed, the *context* in which the action would occur, and its *timing* (usually summarized in the acronym TACT). Evidence is finally available from the insistence on temporal contiguity. An important recognition was that measures of the cognitive precursors of attitude will be highly predictive only when there is maximal temporal contiguity of the behavioral and antecedent measures (Ajzen & Fishbein, 1980). The greater the temporal gap between attitude or intention and the behavior to which they refer, and hence the extent of situational intervention that potentially separates them, the lower will be their correlative consistency. It is the intention which *immediately* precedes behavior that is predictive (Ericsson & Simon, 1993).

The implication of the tight situational compatibility required of measures of target behavior and measures of its antecedent cognitive predictors (Ajzen & Fishbein, 1977) is that situational factors are highly significant for the correlational consistency of attitudes/intentions and behavior. Only when the situational influences governing both the prebehavioral and the behavioral variables are functionally equivalent are high correlations found. That the intertemporal period between prebehavioral and behavioral measures must be minimal if high correlations are to be found corroborates this view by pointing to the undesirability of unexpected situational demands reducing the predictive value of measured intentions.

Context and situation deserve a more central place in the explanation of behavior which is denied them by the partiality inherent in acceptance of the preeminence of the cognitive paradigm. The explanatory power of past behavior is frequently sufficient to make cognitive variables superfluous; that a behavior analytic theory may be capable of explaining or interpreting the evidence on attitudinal-behavioral consistency in full; and that in any case the reason for including a behaviorist perspective is to identify the consequences that past behavior has produced to account for the consistency of that prior responding and thus to use those consequences to predict future behavior.

Moreover, consideration of the ways in which the components of the Theory of Reasoned Action are disaggregated and measured by users of this method indicates that these components refer in practice to elements of behavior setting and learning history. *Subjective norm* is a reflection of the demands of the situation conceptualized and measured as a set of beliefs about what the respondent believes a significant other thinks about the respondent's performing the behavior in question

My partner thinks that
I should – —: – —: – —: – —: – —: – —I should not
buy organic vegetables.

weighted by the respondent's motivation to comply with the referent

In general, how much do you want to do what your partner thinks you should do?

_____ Not at all
_____ Slightly
_____ Moderately
_____ Strongly.

This also represents a learning history which reflects the extent of social pressures to conform with the demands of the situation and a history of compliance or non-compliance with the perceived wishes of a significant other.

Behavioral history

The individual's behavioral history – what he or she has done in the past with respect to the attitude object and the consequences of such behavior – is captured in the attitudinal variable (A_{act}) which measures what the respondent thinks the consequences of behaving in a particular way vis-à-vis the attitude object will be and his or her evaluation of those consequences. It is clear that the formulation of an attitude toward an act depends on having had prior experience with the attitude object and having prior experience of the consequences of such behavior: it is a behavioral outcome. *Attitude toward the act* is operationalized as "The person's beliefs that the behavior leads to certain outcomes and his evaluations of those outcomes. [Hence] [a]ccording to our theory, a person's attitude toward a behavior can be predicted by multiplying her evaluation of each of the behavior's consequences by the strength of her belief that performing the behavior will lead to that consequence and then summing the products for the total set of beliefs" (Ajzen & Fishbein, 1980, p. 8, p. 67). The particular measurement technique involves respondents' engaging in verbal behavior that rates the attitudinal behavior in question according to a small number of its consequences (those representing *salient* behavioral beliefs that have been ascertained in previous qualitative research. In the case of the behavior: buy*ing organically-grown vegetables,* and its context: *at your usual supermarket next time you shop for groceries*, the required behavior might be elicited thus (the example uses only two belief dimensions for ease of exposition – there would normally be three or four – and shows the reversal of the rating dimension):

Buying organic vegetables when I shop for groceries is
expensive – —: – —: – —: – —: – —: – —: – —inexpensive
environmentally harmful – —: – —: – —: – —: – —: – —: – —environmentally
friendly

In order that the belief statements elicited in this way can be weighted by the individual's strength of expectation that the behavior will actually lead to the stated positive or negative consequence, the respondent will be asked a question such as, *How certain are you that buying organic vegetables will prove environmentally friendly?* and will be asked to answer "Not at all certain" (scores 0), "Slightly certain" (+1), "Quite certain" (+2) or "Extremely certain" (+3). Verbal behavior of this kind requires experience, and, if it is to have a strong effect on behavior, a learning history. We have seen from the research on spontaneous processing that an attitude learned indirectly (e.g., through the persuasive arguments of another person or an advertisement) is weaker than one that is learned via personal experience. That is, in fact what is being measured by means of this technique of attitude assessment.

Perceived behavioral control (PBC) is a similar variable that gains potency by experience of self-efficacy (Bandura, 1997). It is measured, for example, as

How much control do you have over the kinds of vegetables you buy?
complete control – —: – —: – —: – —: – —: – —: – —very little control

For me, to buy organic vegetables is
very difficult – —: – —: – —: – —: – —: – —: – —very easy
If I wanted to, I could buy organic vegetables every time I shop
extremely likely – —: – —: – —: – —: – —:'– —: – —extremely unlikely.

The importance of prior behavior is also shown by the fact that this variable often exerts a main effect on behavior in its own right, something explored at some length in Chapter 4. The cognitive bias of most attitude research does not encourage researchers to investigate *why* past behavior is a primary predictor of current and future action – a more behavioral approach would attribute its effects to the rewarding and punishing consequences of that prior behavior (Foxall, 1997a, b). Fishbein and Ajzen's approaches are more ready to find expression of such consequences through respondents' attitude statements.

Behavioral intention also reflects past behavior. Intentions are measured in a way that will by now be familiar:

I will buy organic vegetables on my next shopping trip
Probable   – —: – —: – —: – —: – —: – —: – —Improbable
extremely quite slightly neither slightly quite extremely

BPM: A model of the consumer situation

It is not enough to have identified the factors that have made the prediction of behavior more accurate, notably *situational correspondence* and *behavioral history*. The evidence that these methodological refinements increase the precision of our explanations of behavior lies scattered in the reports of dozens if not hundreds of empirical investigations which have taken them deliberately but unsystematically into consideration. There is no guarantee that further attempts to do so will automatically succeed; nor – and this is vitally important in an applied field such as marketing – that the results of research based hopefully but haphazardly on the inclusion of these factors will yield productive applications. "Situational correspondence" and "behavioral history" are useful terms in so far as they summarize the methodological improvements introduced by deliberative attitude theory and research. But they are scarcely a guide to action for either marketing research or marketing management.

The question is how they relate to the realities of consumer situations in marketing-orientated economies and it must be answered in a way that makes these factors concrete bases for research and action. For this we require a more formal representation that relates situations, attitudes and behavior reliably. The Behavioral Perspective Model (BPM) is an attempt to incorporate the situational variables that recent attitude theory has only implicitly recognized and to do so in such a way that consumers' attitudes and behaviors can be predicted and understood. Since the derivation and refinement of the model has been described in detail elsewhere, the following account is designed to be succinct.

The numerous ways of deriving theories of consumer behavior differ according to the extent to which they rely on description of marketing phenomena in themselves and the extent to which they include concepts and measures borrowed from the social sciences. This is no place to debate the pros and cons of these avenues to our greater understanding of consumer behavior and marketer response, but it is likely that none has an absolute advantage over the others. The selection of one or other depends largely upon the purposes of the investigator.

However, a relative advantage of models built on some systematic knowledge base such as is provided by psychology is that the reasoning on which the model rests and the findings it generates can be evaluated according to pre-existing, tried and tested canons of judgment. There is no doubt that the essential features of the BPM can be found in simple description of consumer behavior and the marketing system: the capacity to specify the model in such terms is vital to its relevance to marketing (Foxall, 1997a). That it is developed in the context of behavioral psychology has the additional benefit, however, that the nature and scope of the resulting theory can be gauged and the findings can be related to those produced in differing contexts by other researchers.

The consumer situation

The central explanatory component of the BPM is the *consumer situation* which exerts a direct influence on the shaping and maintenance of consumer behavior in specified surroundings (Figure 5.1). The consumer situation is defined as the intersection of the *consumer behavior setting* and the consumer's *learning history*. A consumer behavior setting comprises the stimuli that form the social (including regulatory) and physical (including temporal) environment. These initially neutral stimuli are transformed into the discriminative stimuli that signal the probable outcomes of approach and avoidance responses in the setting by their intersection with the consumer's pertinent history of reinforcement and punishment. It is this learning history that adds meaning to the otherwise neutral setting stimuli by investing them with the consequences of previous approach-avoidance behaviors in similar circumstances.

The consumer behavior setting

The concept of a behavior setting owes much to the pioneering work of the ecological psychologist, Roger Barker and his colleagues (see, especially, Barker, 1968; Schoggen, 1989; Wicker, 1979). Although Barker's conception will not prove the final resting place for the model we seek to establish

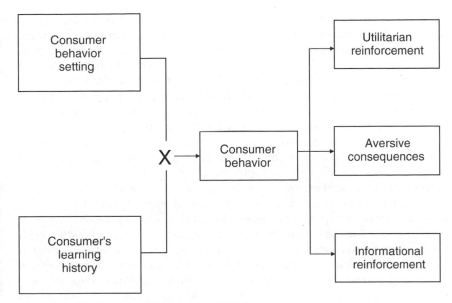

Figure 5.1   The Behavioral Perspective Model

here, it is soundly based on empirical observation and rightly emphasizes the environmental determinants of behavior. It is therefore a valuable starting point.

On the basis of over 25 years' observation of behavior in a southern United States town, Oskaloosa, Barker severely criticized what he saw as the prevailing basis of psychological research: that human behavior can best be understood as a property of the person who enacts it; that the best way to study such behavior is to interrupt it, probe it and rearrange it in line with the concerns of the investigator through experiments, questionnaires, interviews and intrusive measurements; that behavior can be most effectively observed by homing in on "delimited segments or aspects of it" and restricting observation to the dimensions that the observer has predefined; that the physical and social environments in which behavior occurs are unstructured, random and passive: the individual's mental apparatus makes sense of this chaos and imposes some degree of order on it; theory must precede data gathering. By contrast, Barker argued that the Oskaloosa program indicated that: human behavior has both an individual form but also an extra-individual form: a characteristic pattern of behavior is engendered by environmental units like churches, stores, and schools: this pattern of behavior in each case is independent of the people involved and their ideographic features such as personality traits, attitudes, intentions and motivations; the order and stability that is apparent in human behavior stems from the "ecological environment" that is from the "structured, homeostatic, coercive behavior settings that people inhabit;" since every way of seeing is a way of not seeing, theories can get in the way of scientific progress; methodological imperatives such as an insistence of experimental techniques can arbitrarily break up naturally-occurring behaviors that deserve to be studied in their own right. Barker and his colleagues came to realize that the physical and social environment in which behavior takes place and the behavior pattern that is characteristic of that environment form a unit, what they called the *behavior setting*.

The consumer behavior setting consists of the current discriminative stimuli that signal reinforcement and punishment contingent upon the emission of a purchase or consumption response. The discriminative stimuli that compose the setting may be physical (e.g., point-of-sale advertising, the product array, a store logo), social (principally the physical presence of co-shoppers, other diners in a restaurant, the waiter, the salesperson), temporal (the hours of opening of a store, the duration of a special offer, Christmas) or regulatory (self- and other-rules that specify contingencies). Rule-governed behavior is actually a social phenomenon but deserves separate treatment (Guerin, 1994a; Hyten & Burns, 1986).

Rule-governed behavior

When a listener's behavior results from the verbal activity of a speaker, it is said to be instructed or rule-governed. The rule in question acts as a verbal discriminative stimulus which takes the place of the contingencies themselves. The provision of rules is especially pertinent in changing behavior the consequences of which are delayed, improbable or small (Malott, 1989). If it is effective over time, such control requires a degree of consistency between the instructions and the contingencies they describe. But instructed behavior has noteworthy properties of its own arising from its insensitivity to changes in the consequences of responding (Catania et al., 1989, 1990).

Instructed behavior is always subject to two sets of contingencies: the social consequences that maintain the rule-following, and the natural contingencies that eventually take over if the instruction is effective (e.g., Baum, 1994). Moreover, if the instructed behavior is to be effectively learned, the consequences of rule-compliance must be more powerful than the natural consequences that would follow trial-and-success behavior in the absence of the instruction. Since these natural contingencies are often remote, delayed and weak, learning from them alone (i.e., in the absence of instructions) would be slow or dangerous – as in the case of learning to drive a car – or possibly never-acting. This may supply part of the reason why instructed behavior is often insensitive to changes in the natural contingencies. Shaped behavior does not show this insensitivity: the acquisition of a practical skill such as glassblowing must, in many of its aspects, be directly shaped by hands-on experience that confers positive environmental consequences.

The functional categorization of rule-following presents difficulties, though that suggested by Zettle and Hayes (1982), paralleling somewhat Skinner's (1957) definitions of the functional units of the behavior of the speaker, has found support and prompted both empirical and theoretical investigations (Hayes, 1989; Hayes & Hayes, 1989; Chase & Danforth, 1991; Malott, 1989). Skinner posited two such units in particular, manding and tacting. The *mand* denotes the consequences contingent upon following the instructions of the speaker or of imitating his or her example. Much advertising consists of mands – "Buy three and get one free!" "Don't forget the fruit gums, mum" – which indicate contingencies that are under the control of the speaker. *Tacts* present a con*tact* with part of the environment and, depending on learning history, a potential for behavior on the part of the recipient. A trade mark or logo may be followed by making a purchase or entering a store. Zettle and Hayes suggest the following units of analysis for the recipient's responding that match these phases of the prompter's behavior or presence. Corresponding to manding is *pliance* which is rule-governed behavior controlled by consequences that the speaker (or his/her agent) regulates (or claims to regulate). The rule, known as a *ply*, refers, therefore, to the social consequences of compliance or noncompliance: "Keeping my breath fresh will get me more dates." Corresponding to *tacting* is *tracking* which is instructed behavior which, according to the rule, is under the control of the nonsocial environment. A *track* specifies the arrangement of contingencies within that physical or temporal context: "If I turn left at the next intersection, I'll come to Sainsbury's." 'If I arrive by seven, the shop will still be open."

A third functional unit of listener behavior has no corresponding unit for the speaker: the *augmental* (Zettle & Hayes, 1982) is a highly motivating rule that states emphatically how a particular behavior will be reinforced or avoid punishment. "Just one more packet top and I can claim my watch!"

The scope of the setting

The extent to which consumer behavior can be attributed unambiguously to control by environmental contingencies varies with the *scope* of the setting in which it takes place. The animal laboratory, from which principles of operant behaviorism were derived, presents a particularly closed setting, one in which the elements of the three-term contingency can be objectively identified and behavior therefore traced unambiguously to its environmental effects. The further behavior settings stray from this degree of closedness, the harder it is for the operant psychologist to ascribe activities within them unreservedly to operant conditioning. Even in the animal laboratory, there exists scope for alternative interpretations: in terms, for instance, of classical conditioning or cognitive decision making. The human operant laboratory, for example, presents a less closed context, one from which escape is relatively easy; while nonhumans face no option but being in the setting, human participants on occasion remove themselves from the experimental situation.

The settings in which human consumer behavior takes place are more open still: though a continuum of such settings is evident, from the relatively closed confines of a large group awareness training session to the relatively open variety store. Closed and open settings may also be distinguished in terms of the verbal behavior that characterizes each. In closed settings, the other-instructions and contingencies are precise: in order to get a passport, a consumer must obey the rules to the letter. In open settings, the consumer has more control over his or her behavior through self-instructions, and specific other rules are less likely to be determinative.

There may be several other-rule configurations to choose among; further, there is the possibility of behavior being directly controlled by the contingencies: as one spots new products, devises new ways of finding presents, and so on. Even if the view is taken that most consumer behavior is rule-governed, open settings allow self-rules to a far greater extent than closed. Moreover, human behavior that is entirely contingency-shaped is rare. Self-rules, devised and followed by the same individual, are particularly effective instructions, which may be more isolated from the contingencies than other-rules (Catania et al., 1990, p. 227).

Thus *behavior setting scope* is the extent to which the current consumer behavior setting compels a particular pattern of behavior (as a national opera house induces people to wear evening dress, remain seated and silent during arias, and applaud wildly at the end; compare a rock concert where one is free to walk about, shout, sing, smoke, eat and drink and do many other things during the performance). The scope of the former is said to be (relatively) closed; that of the latter, (relatively) open. Hence, the spectrum of behavior settings encompasses the different ranges of applicability of the Theories of Reasoned Action and Planned Behavior, the former to behavior in situations over which the individual is assumed to have volitional control, the latter to those in which such control is circumscribed.[1]

Learning history

The importance of learning history is amply demonstrated by the repeated finding that prior behavior is an important determinant of current responding. We have seen that it is not sufficient to attribute the influence of prior behavior simply to 'habit', which is to redescribe it rather than explain it. The continuance of behavior is to be accounted for by the consequences it produces and whether or not a stream of behavior is continued into the near future depends on the stimulus control which influences it and the maintenance of the pattern of reinforcement that is its distal cause.

The deliberative processing models such as the TRA are centrally concerned with the self-reported consequences of behaving in a given way, which constitutes a personal summary of the respondent's learning history.

The elicitation of subjective norm beliefs and evaluations is also indicative of a history of rule-compliance. The spontaneous processing models emphasize direct experience with the attitude object, which both constitutes a learning history in itself and serves to establish the attitude object as a discriminative stimulus for further responding. The rehearsal of attitude statements, especially if they have their origin in other-instructions, constitutes prior verbal behavior which also exerts an environmental influence on the probability of current responding.

The potency of a learning history is manifested within a particular behavior setting: prior learning establishes what will act as a discriminative stimulus in that setting by embodying the consequences, reinforcing and punishing, of earlier behavior in the presence of the relevant setting elements. The functional approach to attitude theory and research taken by Shavitt (1989) corroborates the BPM by indicating several functions of behavioral consequence in controlling verbal and nonverbal current responding (usually via preceding verbal behavior/instructional control). The bases of the attitude functions she proposes appear closely related to the nature of the reinforcement associated with these products – utilitarian (her "utilitarian" function) and informational (her "social identity" function). The distinction between utilitarian and informational reinforcement is consonant with that between the utilitarian and social identity functions of attitudes (Shavitt, 1989). Shavitt argues that the function of a person's attitude towards an air conditioner is principally utilitarian "because one's attitude toward it should be based largely on rewards (e.g., comfort) and punishments (e.g., high energy bills) intrinsically associated with it. One's attitude toward an air conditioner should guide behaviors that maintain the rewards and avoid the punishments associated with this object (e.g., using the air conditioner on a hot day, turning it off at times to conserve energy" (p. 324). However, an individual's attitude towards a wedding ring performs contrasting functions: "one's attitude toward it should be based largely on what it symbolizes. Furthermore, wedding rings are worn (in public) primarily to communicate information to others about the wearer, and one's attitude toward wedding rings and what they symbolize should guide this behavior" (ib.)

The components of Eagly and Chaiken's (1993) composite model of attitude-behavior relationships are also supportive of the BPM: all of the determinants of attitude towards behavior – habit, attitudes towards the target, utilitarian, normative and self-identity outcomes – are indicative of learning history. Habits form only if the behavior of which they are composed is sequentially reinforced; attitudes towards target develops only through experience; and, although conceptualized as expectations of what will result from behaving in a specified way, the outcomes can result only from environmental history, either in the form of contingency-shaping or through instruction. Moreover, utilitarian outcomes closely resemble the utilitarian reinforcement of the BPM, while normative (including self-identity) outcomes are akin to informational reinforcement.

Intersection

The BPM links past behavior, behavior setting elements, and outcomes by arguing that learning history primes elements of the setting to act as discriminative stimuli for utilitarian and informational reinforcement/punishment contingent upon the performance of specific responses. It thereby provides an alternative, noncognitive synthesis of empirical results gained in both attitude research and operant investigations of instructed behavior.

The resulting discriminative stimuli define the *scope* of the consumer behavior setting, its capacity to facilitate or inhibit consumer responses such as browsing, choosing, and purchasing (approach) or delaying, deferring, and leaving the setting without purchasing (avoidance). A relatively *open* consumer behavior setting is one in which several responses are available to the consumer who has discretion over which is chosen; behavior under these circumstances may take several forms and its topography is difficult to predict. A relatively *closed* setting is one in which the consumer is denied such wider discretion; the consumer's behavior is determined by agents (e.g., retail designers) who control the setting but are not themselves subject to its contingencies. Such behavior is relatively prescribed and is easier to predict.

One of the most restrictive closed settings encountered in human societies is the "total organization" or "asylum" described so effectively by Goffman (1968). Such settings are "encompassing to a degree discontinuously greater than the ones next in line. Their encompassing or total character is symbolized by the barrier to social intercourse with the outside and to departure that is often built in right into the physical plant, such as locked doors, high walls, barbed wire, cliffs, water, forests, or moors." (pp. 16–17) Goffman has in mind a range of such closed societies from homes for the blind, and the homeless, through mental hospitals, prisons, boarding schools and the servants' quarters of large mansions, to monasteries and abbeys. Some of these are susceptible to an analysis in terms of consumer choice, but by and large they are more closed and more restrictive than the consumer behavior settings with which we are concerned here.

Classes of consumer behavior

The consequences signaled by the discriminative stimuli that compose the consumer situation are of three kinds: utilitarian reinforcement, informational reinforcement, and punishment.

Utilitarian reinforcement consists in the tangible functional and economic benefits which stem from purchase, ownership and consumption. The driver of a Lada, for instance, is principally concerned with the utilitarian benefits that all cars provide: the most obvious is getting from A to B, door-to-door transportation. Utilitarian reinforcement consists in the practical outcomes of purchase and consumption – the functional benefit, value-in-use, economic/pragmatic/material satisfactions received by consumers as a result of acquiring, owning and/or using an economic product or service. It is purely instrumental, consisting in itself and for itself; it is concrete and likely to be constant across social systems. Incentives are usually of this kind.

Hence, utilitarian reinforcement arises from the characteristics of the product or service obtained in purchase or used in consumption; this corresponds to the use of utility in economics to refer to "the direct satisfaction that goods and services yield to their possessors" (Gould & Kolb, 1964, p. 303, p. 740). Utility theory in economics derives essentially from the psychology of hedonism (Viner, 1925; Black, 1987; Griffin & Parfitt, 1987; Menger, 1956). Hence, while utilitarian reinforcement is akin to value-in-use, it derives not only from the functional performance of a product or service but from the feelings associated with owning and consuming it. In addition to the functions performed by a product or service, utilitarian consequences of consumption include the positive affect generated in the process. Utilitarian reinforcement refers, therefore, to all of the benefits derived directly from possession and application of a product or service, it is reinforcement mediated by the product or service; it inheres in the use-value of the commodity.

Informational or symbolic reinforcement, on the other hand, is more likely to involve a lifestyle statement by which the consumer seeks to convey his or her social status or to bolster esteem and/or reported feelings of self-esteem. The driver of a Mercedes or a Bentley or a Porsche, clearly gets from A to B in it but, in addition, gains the social esteem and status provided by friends and acquaintances who admire these prestige products and from members of the general public who see him driving around in a socially-desirable vehicle. The social status and esteem that driver is accorded are the symbolic rewards of consumption. Informational reinforcement, by contrast, is symbolic, usually mediated by the responsive actions of others, and closely akin to exchange value. It consists not in information per se but in feedback on an individual's performance. Informational reinforcement attests to the level of correctness or appropriateness of a person's performance as a consumer; whereas utilitarian reinforcement stems from economic and functional payoffs of buying and using goods, informational reinforcement results from the level of social status, prestige and acceptance achieved by a consumer by his or her efforts. It is usually publicly determined, judged by others according to the rules, and thus of primarily social significance. In as much as it is mediated by other people, it is verbal (Skinner, 1957), consisting in speech, gestures and – where the individual provides his or her own informational reinforcement and thus becomes the "other" person – in private thoughts (Skinner, 1974).

From the viewpoint of the consumer, informational reinforcement rests on a comparative judgment of how well he or she is using time and energy relative to other uses to which they would be put: "How well am I exchanging my time and effort for the acquisition of groceries?" If the consumer is being relatively inefficient, he or she may either speed up the shopping trip or postpone purchasing further items. If efficient, they can use the time and energy left over to accomplish something else. From the social viewpoint, the public consumption of a prestigious product or service is exchanged for the goodwill, praise, positive responses and so on of others, i.e., for esteem and social status. Informational reinforcement is thus fundamentally social and verbal.[2]

The feedback on the level of performance or achievement of the consumer in which informational reinforcement consists takes one or both of two forms, public and private. Public informational reinforcement is the social honor, esteem or status accorded by others for the position achieved or level of accomplishment conferred on the consumer for his conspicuous acquisition, ownership, or use of products and services. It may be positive, when the product or service is valued by the social group; or negative, when it is despised. Private informational reinforcement consists in the individual's own evaluative reaction to his performance: it may take the form of a verbal "slap on the back," a silent or at least solitary "Well done!" given to oneself by oneself. It may also be accompanied by such collateral (though not epiphenomenal) responses as feelings described as pride and self-esteem. These responses may act as reinforcers in the BPM framework, though strictly speaking in a radical behaviorist interpretation they are ascribed only the status of responses). Public or private, informational reinforcement is symbolic, representative, referential, cultural; the behaviors it reinforces are likely to differ sharply from social system to social system.

Informational reinforcement is most clearly exhibited in affluent economies in the form of conspicuous consumption which has been described by a host of social scientists and commentators from Veblen (1899) to Galbraith (1967), and which has been analyzed in the context of economic theory and social science generally by Mason (1998). Mason (1998, p. 130) notes recent renewed acknowledgment of

> the use of products to mark social differences and to act as status communicators [which] represented a major shift from cultural and social identity linked to production and toward new interpretations centered on consumptions and the "commodity sign" (Baudrillard, 1970; Bourdieu, 1984). Evident, too, was a far greater preoccupation with "style" (Featherstone, 1991, Ewen, 1990) as a device of conformity or of opposition, where projection depended crucially, again, on the use and display of products. Considerations of style began to overlay the world of goods, and certainly influenced consumer choice to a far greater extent than previously.

Mason traces the incorporation of social consumption by economists such as Hirsch (1976) who distinguished "positional" from "nonpositional" goods, the latter whose "value to the individual depended strongly on how they compared with things owned by others, and hence to the degree of scarcity attached to the products in question." (p 135; see also Mason, 1984). Just as Mason is keen to emphasize that conspicuous consumption is to be encountered in all social classes, so it must be stressed that all products (and services, and consumption settings) promise and provide both utilitarian and informational reinforcement, albeit in vastly differing degrees.

In short, *utilitarian* reinforcement refers to the acceptance of positive benefits of purchasing, owning or consuming economic products and services (goods); these benefits are functional, conferring material satisfactions, the utility of orthodox microeconomic theory. Utilitarian reinforcers are frequently referred to as incentives both in general discourse and in applied behavior analysis. *Informational* reinforcement is performance feedback, an indication of how well the consumer is doing, how well he or she is following rules, whether these are derived from others or, after rumination, from one's own analysis of the contingencies of reinforcement. Such rule-governed behavior may confer social status and/or self-satisfaction, or it may simply constitute a reference point denoting progress to date.[3]

Informational reinforcement is associated with verbal behavior because the meaning of the behavior is always mediated by a person, usually someone other than the actor but perhaps by him/herself. There is empirical evidence that utilitarian and informational reinforcement have separate influences on behavior in both human operant experiments conducted under laboratory conditions (Wearden, 1988), in token economy studies, and in the field experiments of applied behavior analysis directed toward the reduction of environmentally-deleterious consumption (Foxall, 1995, 1996, 1998a).

Finally, there are aversive consequences which, if suffered, reduce the chance of this behavior being repeated. A defining characteristic of economic behavior, since it includes a reciprocal transfer of rights, lies in its being simultaneously reinforced and punished (Alhadeff, 1982). It incurs reinforcement and punishment as direct and specific consequences of its being performed. Economic behavior is determined by the interaction of two response strengths: approach and avoidance, each of which is dependent upon the consumer's learning history, the quality and quantity of reinforcement, reinforcement schedules, and so on (Alhadeff, 1982). These *punishing or aversive consequences* – in everyday language, costs – are an inevitable outcome of consumer behavior which always meets with results that tend to diminish its rate of future enactment as well as reinforcers which tend toward increasing this rate.

Most products and services, most situations of purchase and consumption present elements of both the instrumental and the symbolic. A mobile phone not only provides communications services when and where the consumer wants them; because it is a Nokia and therefore has interchangeable colored cases, it may also signal to that consumer's social group that he or she is cool. Similarly, a Harley-Davidson motor cycle not only provides fast transportation: it is also the basic means of belonging to a group of bikers.[4]

Four operant classes of consumer behavior can be distinguished depending on the pattern of relatively high/relatively low utilitarian reinforcement and relatively high/relatively low informational reinforcement which maintains the responses of which these classes are composed (Figure 5.2). *Accomplishment* is consumer behavior maintained by relatively high levels of both utilitarian and informational reinforcement; *hedonism*, by relatively high utilitarian and relatively low informational reinforcement; *accumulation*, by relatively low utilitarian and relatively high informational reinforcement; and *maintenance*, by relatively low levels of both.[5]

The eightfold way

Adding the dimension of consumer behavior setting scope to this operant classification of consumer behavior gives the eightfold categorization of the contingencies that may control consumer behavior shown in Figure 5.3. Each of these eight "contingency categories" (CCs) may accommodate numerous functionally-defined consumer situations in which behavior is maintained by a specified matrix of structural factors.[6] In so far as consumer choice is understood as functionally determined by the environment, Figure 5.3 proposes an exhaustive categorization of such contingencies. Consumer behavior is expected to vary depending on these structural components of the consumer situation. The derivation of the labels which Figure 5 gives these eight contingency categories is discussed further in Foxall (2004b, 1990).

An interpretive device

The BPM was initially conceived primarily as an interpretive device.[7] In this section we explore how it might be applied to the description of consumer behavior as it relates to the environmentally-located contingencies which

	High utilitarian reinforcement	Low utilitarian reinforcement
High informational reinforcement	ACCOMPLISHMENT	ACCUMULATION
Low informational reinforcement	HEDONISM	MAINTENANCE

Figure 5.2 Operant Classes of Consumer Behavior defined by Pattern of Reinforcement

Behavior setting scope

	Closed	Open
ACCOMPLISHMENT	CC2 "Fulfillment"	CC1 "Status consumption"
HEDONISM	CC4 "Inescapable entertainment"	CC3 "Popular entertainment"
ACCUMULATION	CC6 "Token-based consumption"	CC5 "Saving and collecting"
MAINTENANCE	CC8 "Mandatory consumption"	CC7 "Routine purchasing"

Figure 5.3   The BPM Contingency Matrix

apparently maintain it. (The following section describes its use in empirical studies of attitudes, situations and behavior). In other words, despite the qualification made above that the BPM operant classification and the contingency matrix are based upon functional possibilities rather than final taxonomies of consumer behaviors, is it possible to allocate broad examples of consumer choice to each of the contingency categories at least on a provisional basis? Single responses such as browsing, inspecting, signing, paying, transporting, preparation and using are to be found within any of the categories, but do more molar patterns of consumer behavior *reasonably* belong to specific classes and categories given the logic on which the classification and the matrix were constructed? There is no harm in making the attempt so long as our surmising is at some stage open to empirical examination.

Therefore, arbitrary or useful as they must ultimately be, the following generalized descriptions of consumer behaviors and situations which appear to belong to each of the contingency categories provide a summary of consumer choice in relation to the contingencies that maintain it.

Accomplishment

Accomplishment in an open setting consists in general in the *purchase and consumption of status goods*. A familiar instance is pre-purchase consumer behavior for luxuries and radical innovations such as TV satellite dishes, video recorders, exotic vacations, and home computers. These behaviors, including window-shopping and browsing, involve search for and comparative evaluation of information about many products and services. Most of the items in question are possessed and used for the pleasure or ease of living they confer, the wellbeing they make possible for the individual: they thereby provide extensive hedonic rewards. But they are often status symbols and their conspicuous consumption also strengthens the behavior in question. They attest directly, and often publicly and unambiguously, to the consumer's attainments, especially economic. Goods in this category are usually highly differentiated – by novel function in the case of innovations, by branding in the case of luxuries.

In a closed setting, accomplishment can be generally described as *fulfillment*. In such a context, it comprises personal attainments gained through leisure, often with a strong element of recreation or excitement as well as achievement. This category refers to the material contribution to *fulfillment* and could include both the completion of a personal development seminar or a casino. Gambling in so closed a setting is an activity maintained by both hedonic and informational consequences. In addition, few consumer behaviors are maintained so thoroughly by social rules. All these elements of the setting unambiguously signal both the positive consequences of approved approach behaviors and the potentially punishing implications of escape or avoidance responses which flout established rules and gaming conventions. Although several games may be available in the casino, there is one principal reinforcer: winning. Pleasure and social approval stem mainly from success, though a certain amount of enjoyment and prestige may be derived from being part of a somewhat exclusive social group and conforming to its code of behavior. Closely defined acts must be performed in order to participate, including obtaining membership, dressing appropriately, entering the game at the right time and in an acceptable manner.

Hedonism[8]

In an open setting, this behavior generally consists of *popular entertainment*. Obvious examples are watching television game shows which provide near-constant hedonic reward, and the reading of mass fiction which contains a sensation on almost every page. Personal cassette players and DVDs have made such reinforcement more immediate to the point of its being ubiquitous. Mass culture presents frequent and predictable, relatively strong and continuous hedonic rewards which are not contingent on long periods of concentrated effort. Indeed, the arrangement of reinforcers is such that viewing, listening or reading for even a short interval is likely to be rewarded. Informational feedback is more obvious on some occasions than others, as when game shows allow the audience to pit their own performances against that of the competing participants, but it is not the main source of reward.

Hedonism in closed settings consists as a generalization of inescapable entertainment and amelioration. The behaviors in question are potentially pleasurable but – in this context – may be irksome because they are unavoidable. As a result, consumption of these products and services may be passive rather than active. An example is the situation in which long distance airline passengers must purchase meals and movies along with their travel. The meals are usually consumed, like the in-flight movies which follow them, without alternative. The setting, which cannot be other than highly restrictive if one is to arrive safely, is further closed by the pulling of blinds, the disappearance of cabin staff, the impossibility of moving around the plane, and the attention of one's fellow passengers to the movie. To try to read or engage in other activities may even invite censure.

Accumulation

In an open setting, Accumulation is generally described as *saving and collecting*. For example, purchases for which payments are made prior to consumption – installments for a holiday which can only be taken once the full amount has been paid. Another example is payments into a Christmas club. Discretionary saving with the intention of making a large purchase once a certain amount has accumulated, would fall into this category, too. Promotional deals requiring the accumulation of coupons or other tokens before a product or service can be obtained also belong here. The important reward, in every case, is informational, feedback on how much one has accumulated, how close one is to the ultimate reinforcer.

Accumulation occurring in a closed setting may be described, in general terms, as *token-based buying*. This also involves collecting – through schemes in which payment for one item provides tokens which will pay for another. Although some examples of this are quite recent, the practice is simply an extension of the familiar prize schemes open to collectors of cigarette cards or trading stamps. For example, the "air-miles" earned by frequent flyers on domestic and international airlines constitute informational reinforcers (Foxall, 1997b). Some hotels also offer gifts to customers who accumulate points by staying there frequently. The collection of these tokens is reinforced by gaining additional free air travel or hospitality, or by access to different types of reinforcer such as prizes. Purchase and consumption of the basic product, the air travel or accommodation originally demanded are maintained by both the intrinsic hedonic rewards they embody and the feedback on progress that is being made toward the ultimate incentive. The setting is relatively closed because the first item would probably be purchased anyway in some form or other and the consumer's income constraint makes it likely that the second or backup reinforcer would be obtained only in this way.

Maintenance

In an open setting, Maintenance may be generally described as *routine purchasing and consumption*. This includes the regular buying of goods necessary for survival. For example, the habitual purchasing of grocery items at a supermarket. Consumer behavior in these circumstances is indeed routine: it occurs as if reinforcement were available only at fixed intervals. Further, contrary to the usual depiction, the frequent consumer of , say, baked beans is highly rational, having tried and evaluated many brands in the relevant product class. But his or her behavior is not static: again in contrast to the received wisdom of the marketing texts, comparatively few such consumers are brand loyal in the sense of always choosing the identical brand in a long sequence of shopping trips. There is so much choice that the consumer enjoys considerable discretion among versions of the product (Ehrenberg, 1988/1972).

Maintenance is generally characterized in closed settings as *mandatory purchase and consumption*. It includes all forms of consumer behavior necessary to remain a citizen: the payment of taxes for public and collective goods, for instance; less extremely, it includes payments into pension schemes linked to employment, payments of endowment insurance premiums linked to mortgages. To this extent, Maintenance is the consumer behavior inherent in pursuing the normal business of citizenship. In the workplace, it may include the enforced use of areas under smoking bans which, for smokers, represent a severe limitation on behavior (though for nonsmokers, particularly the allergic, they constitute an opening of the setting, a measure that permits a wider range of behaviors).

An interpretation of consumer decision making

An integral part of the consumer situation is the extent and nature of consumer decision making required before an operant response is emitted. The preceding analysis of verbal behavior and the BPM interpretation permit this aspect of consumer choice to be covered now in detail.

Table 5.1 shows how the mechanisms for decision making and persuasion proposed by Fazio's MODE model (1990), the Elaboration Likelihood Model (Petty & Cacioppo, 1986a) and the Heuristic-Systematic Model (Chaiken 1980) relate to consumer decision making in behavioral perspective. In the BPM interpretation, "motivation" is supplied by the individual's learning history (or lack thereof) in combination with the stimuli that compose the current behavior setting; where a learning history is absent or weak, other-rules become all-important in motivating behavior. It is this which determines the likelihood that the outcome of a particular action will be relatively costly or rewarding and which leads to more or less prebehavioral reviewing of the contingencies, i.e. the probability of particular positive and aversive outcomes emerging from each of the behaviors available.

Table 5.1 Behavioral and Cognitive Approaches to Decision Making

	Low experience/high cost	High experience/low cost
BPM	Other-rules. Consumer's lack of a relevant learning history prompts search for other-rules.	Self-rules. Acquisition of a learning history from which self-rules can be extracted.
Elaboration likelihood	Central route	Peripheral route
MODE	Deliberation	Spontaneity
Heuristic-systematic processing	Systematic processing	Heuristic processing

Such review is not, according to a radical behaviorist interpretation, mental processing: it is, rather, behavior, verbal behavior which is often private. Where deliberation takes place it consists of a review of rules, self-rules generated on the basis of direct learning experience of the contingencies, and other-rules provided by those whose instructions have proved accurate and reinforcing if followed in the past and/or who themselves have relevant experience of the consequences which can be publicly ascertained. Self-rules correspond to the attitude toward the act of the Fishbein/Ajzen formula: how would one identify learning history through self report other than by asking what an individual believed would be the outcome of acting in a given way in specific circumstances and weighting this by that same individual's appraisal of those consequences? Questions that elicit attitude toward the act may be equally understood as indicating a history of reinforcement. The rules revealed in this manner ("Eating fresh greens every day will result in a clear complexion") are akin to the tracks identified by Zettle and Hayes (1982): they specify how to get to a particular goal point. By this time, behavior is "scripted" (Langer, 1989a, 1989b), following not from conscious intentions or plans but under the control of self-rules and/or immediate stimuli.

Other-rules correspond to the subjective norm of the Fishbein/Ajzen model: acting as plys, they specify the social consequences of compliance or noncompliance with a specified course of action. Evidence for the progression from other-rules, via deliberation, experience and self-observation, to action based on self-rules is provided by research on the TPB by East (1992, 1997) which was reviewed above. (A comparative review of the cognitive and behaviorist approaches to problem solving is found in Reese, 1994; cf. Chase & Bjamadottir, 1992; Fantino, 2004; Reese, 1992a, 1992b; Ito, 1994).

The probability of a particular response depends also upon the non-regulatory components of the consumer behavior setting, the physical, social and temporal discriminative stimuli given meaning in any particular setting by the individual's learning history. Where they have figured in the past as controlling antecedents, they will now act to signal the kinds of consequences that are contingent on each possible response. They will thus play an integral role in prebehavioral deliberation, each setting the occasion for behavior with predictable results in the form of positive and aversive consequences.

When the learning history of the individual is such that known consequences have followed regularly and unimpeded from specific acts, the discriminative stimuli in the current setting will provide signals that quickly result in the performance of the requisite behavior; when the individual has little appropriate learning history, or the history is ambiguous with respect to the kinds of reinforcer or punisher likely to result from behavior, the magnitude of these consequence and their probability, greater deliberation including the formulation, weighing and use of rules will be normal.

The self- and other-instructions activated to a greater or less extent in either deliberative or spontaneous processing, plus the power of current discriminative stimuli – conferred in a history of reinforcement and punishment – determine the probability of a specific response. The immediate prebehavioral verbal self-instruction or prediction the individual is capable of making (on the question of introspection entering into rule-formulation, see Moore, 1994; on that of self-editing in rule-formulation, see Hyten & Chase, 1991; cf. Vaughan, 1987) – equivalent to what deliberation theorists call behavioral intention – is another kind of rule, an augmental, the proximal motivating factor leading to the consummation of a particular act.

Behavior formed through direct experience is contingency-shaped: its persistence is due to continued reinforcement and its emission is likely to come under the stimulus control of the physical, social and temporal elements of the behavior setting. Such behavior may be described as "spontaneous" or "automatic" – finger tapping, for instance – when it is entirely under the control of these historical and current contingencies (Catania, 1992a). However, it is unlikely that a great deal of human behavior is formed and maintained entirely through the direct action of the environmental contingencies.

Humans are rule-formulating animals and routine/habitual behavior is likely to be guided by self-rules, formed through experience and observation, and taking the form largely of tracks. Private tracking probably controls a great deal of repetitive consumer behavior such as weekly or monthly supermarket shopping. Although such behavior as brand choice shows 100% loyalty in only a small minority of the users of a product class, most consumers' multi-brand purchasing is confined to a small repertoire of tried and tested brands in each class (Ehrenberg & Uncles, 1995). Brand choice within this repertoire may look haphazard but it is far from random. It differs from finger tapping in that it is highly functional and economically/consumption rational, and most consumers have no difficulty in describing the rules employed in finding and selecting brands of fast-moving consumer goods, as protocol analysis readily shows.

Self-rules in the form of tracks are undoubtedly analogous to global attitudes toward the object – in this case a known subset of substitutable brands within a product class – which are easily/automatically elicited by the discriminative stimuli in the purchase setting. Formed through repeated purchasing, observation and imitation, including a long period of consumer socialization, they are readily available to guide immediate, familiar purchasing in the presence of such antecedent controlling stimuli as the label on a can, a familiar brand name or a logo. This resembles the spontaneous processing in the presence of a known attitude object identified by Fazio as prerequisite to unpremeditated, automatic, routine processing.

Behavior instructed by the rules provided by others is formed through indirect experience: TV advertisements, neighbors' recommendations, parents' approbation, and so on. Such rules are most likely to be effective when the listener's relevant learning history is minimal or non-existent and/or when the behavior setting in which he or she is acting is closed (the latter a function of how much control the speaker has over the setting). Other-instructions are far more likely to be productive in situations unfamiliar to the listener, when a novel course of action is commended – perhaps buying a radically innovative product or moving house or just trying a new make of computer disc. Such behaviors usually require some degree of deliberation since no self-rules exist to "spontaneously" guide action. Depending on previous rule-compliance and its outcomes, the consumer will be more or less disposed to follow the other-instructions without demur: a friend whose advice has proved worthwhile may be able to offer recommendations that are immediately taken up and acted upon, providing the new sphere of consumption is not too far removed from that previously instructed. But a stranger appearing in a TV commercial may not be able to rely on audience members' having so motivating a reinforcement history with respect to following other-rules. Other-rules of these kinds take the form of plys: in the absence of direct experience on the part of the listener, and especially if the rules come from a remote/unfamiliar/impersonal source, they are more likely to lead to deliberation than immediate action.

The consequent review of the contingencies is interpreted by Skinner (1974) as behavioral, a series of private events in which the ultimate causes of behavior are scrutinized. Verbal rules toward specific courses of action (like attitudes toward target behaviors in the cognitive theories) may result from this process. The consumer who initially had no self-rules for the proposed course of action (as a result of having little or no direct experience thereof, little or no relevant learning history) eventually may form such rules, translating the plys provided by others into the private tracks necessary to guide particular behavior in a clearly defined situation (corresponding to that defined in terms of target, action, timing and context by the multi-attribute modelers).

To reach a decision, choosing one action from among several, is to form a behavioral intention in the deliberative models; in the BPM, it appears to involve a third kind of rule, an augmental, which motivates the individual to behave in a specific manner. Augmentals of this kind result from deliberation and are succeeded by positive motivation, perhaps the outcome of a cost-benefit analysis that indicates that the reinforcing consequences of the proposed act are likely to exceed the aversive, a review of the contingencies that suggests one action will generate greater net benefits than any other.

If the action is performed and reinforced, the plys provided as other-rules gradually become track-based self-rules and, ultimately, the contingencies themselves exert a greater share of control than instructions: the behavior becomes routinized and apparently habitual. Much behavior is of course a mixture of contingency-shaped and rule-governed, subject to adjustment as new contingencies arise and as new instructions from others and oneself emerge to be evaluated and otherwise deliberated upon. Guerin (1994a, p. 192) distinguishes two kinds of decision making, intuitive and nonintuitive, which have the capacity to bring together the findings of social cognitive research and those of behavior analysis. "Intuitive decision making," he writes, "refers to behaving in accordance with the multiple environmental contingencies acting at that time [while] nonintuitive means that decision behavior has become verbally governed in some way and verbal rules are controlling the decision behavior through pliance or tracking."

The preceding analysis goes beyond this, however, eschewing the simple dichotomy it implies. The theory expounded above assumes that, where there is little direct learning history, behavior is guided by other-rules (especially, plys); where there is a well-established learning history it is guided by prior contingency shaping and the discriminative stimuli of the current behavior setting including self-rules (especially, tracks). Between the two is a period of contingency shaping through which the self-rules that come to guide behavior apparently spontaneously are formulated. At this stage, the nonverbal contingencies that guide current behavior are notoriously difficult to distinguish from the self-rules that may do so (Hackenberg & Joker, 1994; Hayes et al., 1986). The choice of explanation is methodologically-based: some behavior analysts refuse to admit variables represented by private events that are not amenable to an experimental analysis of their subject matter (e.g., Hayes, 1986); others are willing to interpret observed behavior in terms of nonpublicly available entities of this kind (e.g., Catania, 1992a; Horne & Lowe, 1993).[9]

Hence, the debate about the direction of causation between attitudes and behavior is redundant: a consumer who has simply seen an advertisement for a brand will have an attitude in the sense of being able to express some verbal evaluations, perhaps only in the form of *echoics* (repetitions of what has been heard; Skinner, 1957), or possibly some minimal verbal evaluation of the brand. But such an attitude is less likely to act as a self-instruction to guide behavior than that which is formed through experience with the brand.

6
Attitudes, Situations, and Behavior

Empirical tests of the BPM in the context of consumers' attitudes have involved the prediction of consumers' verbal responses to descriptions of consumer situations representative of each of the eight feasible categories of environmental contingencies shown in Figure 5.3. The range of verbal responses is suggested by Mehrabian and Russell's (1974a) verbal measures of the three affective reposes to environments which they argue are exhaustive: *pleasure, arousal* and *dominance*. An array of consumer situations (Foxall, 2004b, 1990) was subjected to the judgment of panels of consumers and market research executives who successfully allocated each to the theoretical contingencies (Foxall, 1999b). Mehrabian and Russell (1974a) propose that physical and social stimuli in the environment directly influence the emotional state of an individual and as a result shape the behaviors he or she enacts within that environment. *Pleasure, Arousal*, and *Dominance* are the three emotional variables which summarise the emotion-eliciting qualities of environments and mediate a variety of approach-avoidance behaviors such as preference, exploration, affiliation and work performance. These authors hypothesize that judgmental responses of evaluation, activity and potency on the semantic differential correspond to the emotional (connotative, affective, feeling) responses of pleasure, arousal, and dominance, respectively, and that variations in these emotional reactions constitute the common core of human emotional responses to all situations (Figure 6.1).

Mehrabian's three-factor model of emotionality

Mehrabian's three-factor theory seeks to identify those reactions that are the immediate responses to environmental stimulation and which are present in all environments in some degree or other (Mehrabian, 1980; Mehrabian and Russell, 1974a, 1974b). The three variables employed, *pleasure, arousal*, and *dominance*, were chosen on the basis of their having multi-modal (synesthetic) effects, reports of physiological reactions to such

+P +A −D	+P +A +D
Amazed, infatuated, surprised, impressed, loved	Bold, creative, vigorous, powerful, admired
+P −A −D	+P −A + D
Consoled, sleepy, tranquilized, sheltered, protected	Unperturbed, untroubled, quiet, relaxed, leisurely
−P +A −D	−P +A +D
Humiliated, pain, puzzled, unsafe, embarrassed	Cruel, hate, scornful, disgusted. hostile
−P −A −D	−P −A +D
Lonely, unhappy, bored, sad, depressed	Uninterested, uncaring, unconcerned, uninterested, selfish, proud

Figure 6.1 Mehrabian's Comprehensive Framework of Affective Responses to Situations

intermodal stimulation, and the findings of work using the semantic differential method of verbal scaling (Osgood et al., 1957, 1975) which established *evaluation, activity,* and *potency* as the basic dimensions in which the meanings of concepts could be delineated. Subsequent research has provided further evidence for the conclusion drawn by Mehrabian that *pleasure, arousal* and *dominance* are the primary emotional reactions to environments:

> To summarize, studies of intermodality associations, synesthesia, physiological responses to stimuli, and the semantic differential all suggest that a limited set of basic emotional responses exists for all stimulus situations independent of the sensory modality involved. Judgmental responses of evaluation and activity on the semantic differential are hypothesized to correspond to the emotional responses of pleasure and arousal respectively. The judgmental response of potency corresponds to an emotional reaction that may be labeled dominance versus submissiveness, such that low stimulus potency elicits a feeling of dominance, and high stimulus potency elicits a submissive feeling. Pleasure, arousal and dominance constitute a parsimonious description of the common core of human responses to all situations (Mehrabian, 1980, p. 15).

Other researchers have favored a two-factor, circumplex model that omits dominance (Russell & Pratt, 1980). Although the two-factor model was preferred by Russell (1980), even he acknowledged that unexplained variance was attributable to "control" or "dominance" (Russell, 1980; cf. Russell & Mehrabian, 1977). Shaver et al. (1987), who compared the two- and three- factor models of emotional states, found predominant evidence for the 3-factor model and concluded that it "is clearly more informative as a representation of emotion knowledge than the two-dimensional solution" (p. 1071). Morgan and Heise (1988) note that, while up to 11 factors have been advanced in the literature to account for the structure of emotions, the two-factor model remains highly popular. However, their exhaustive empirical work on the semantic differential scaling of the "lexicon of pure emotion adjectives" indicates that only a three-factor model satisfies the statistical and substantive requirements of their data set. Most significantly, they adduce evidence for the necessity of including potency in any model of emotional structure. Their second study, employing multi-dimension analysis, confirmed this.

> The correspondence of dimensions obtained in the two studies de-monstrates that emotion terms array themselves naturally in the three-dimensional space involving evaluation, activation, and a sense of potency... [T]he affective dimensions correspond to basic mental processes, as Mehrabian (1980) and others have argued, and ... much of people's cognitive information concerning emotions is generated within the dimensional framework. ... We favor three dimensions of affective response not only because of the empirical evidence presented in this and other works... but also because it is demonstrable that three dimen-sions are required to produce adequate simulations of social interaction (Morgan & Heise, 1988, p. 26, p. 29, p. 30).

Reviewing the PAD scales in the context of "marketing success," Huang (2001, p. 241) summarizes: "This theory has been seen as useful for exam-ining emotions during consumption in retail environments (e.g., Donovan & Rossier, 1982; Mano & Oliver, 1993; Sherman et al., 1997), and for cap-turing the emotional component of consumption experience (Havlena & Holbrook, 1986). However, it is not clear whether it is applicable to ad-vertising emotions, with Holbrook and Batra (1987) reporting positive evidence, and Havlena et al. (1989) presenting the contrary viewpoint."

Pleasure, arousal, dominance

Mehrabian and Russell argue that pleasure-displeasure is a feeling state that can be assessed readily with self-report, such as semantic differential measures or with behavioral indicators, such as smiles, laughter, and, in general positive versus negative facial expressions. Arousal is a feeling state varying along a single dimension ranging from sleep to frantic excitement. Arousal is most directly assessed by verbal report or with behavioral indicators such as vocal activity (positive and negative), facial activity (positive and negative expressions), speech rate, and speech volume.[1] Dominance-submissiveness is a feeling state that can be assessed from verbal reports using the semantic differential method. It is assumed that there is an inverse relationship between dominance and the judged potency of the environment. Behaviorally, dominance is measured in terms of postural relaxation, i.e., body lean and asymmetrical positioning of the limbs. An individual's feeling of dominion in a situation is based on the extent to which he or she feels unrestricted or free to act in a variety of ways. This feeling can be hampered by settings that limit the forms of behavior, and enhanced by settings that facilitate a greater variety of behaviors, e.g., an individual has greater freedom (more dominance) in his own territory (e.g., reading a book at home rather than in the library). Also a person is less dominant in the presence of others of higher status (compare the perspectives of a patient and a physician in a hospital ward).

The consideration of emotions as the lowest common denominator of response to environments, provides a set of three basic variables that are related both to any aspect of environments and to most aspects of behavior. The three *environmental descriptors* are response-defined, thus, the pleasantness, arousing quality, and dominance-eliciting quality of an environment are defined as the average *pleasure, arousal* and *dominance* respectively, reported by a group of raters in that environment. These three variables can be considered as legitimate environmental descriptors because, once a particular group provides the ratings of a setting, predictions can be made about the behaviors of people in general for that same setting (Mehrabian and Russell, 1974a; Russell and Mehrabian, 1976). The range of verbal responses is suggested by Mehrabian and Russell's (1974a) verbal measures of the three affective reposes to environments which they argue are exhaustive: *pleasure, arousal* and *dominance*.

Mehrabian and Russell assess *pleasure* in terms of the environment's being: *happy* as opposed to *unhappy; pleased* as opposed to *annoyed; satisfied* as opposed to *unsatisfied; contented* as opposed to *melancholic; hopeful* as opposed to *despairing;* and *relaxed* as opposed to *bored. Arousal* is assessed by verbal reactions to an environment which show the respondent to be: *stimulated* as opposed to *relaxed; excited* as opposed to *calm; frenzied* as opposed to *sluggish; jittery* as opposed to *dull; wide-awake* as opposed to *sleepy;* and *aroused* as opposed to *unaroused.* Finally, *dominance* is reflected in verbal appraisals in which the respondent feels: *controlling* as opposed to *controlled; influential* as opposed to *influenced; in control* as opposed to *cared-for; important* as opposed to *awed; dominant* as opposed to *submissive; autonomous* as opposed to *guided.*[2] These three responses mediate more overt consumer behaviors such as a desire to affiliate with others in the setting, desire to stay in or escape from the setting, and willingness to spend money and consume (Mehrabian, 1979; Mehrabian & Riccioni, 1986; Mehrabian &

de Wetter, 1987; Mehrabian & Russell, 1975; Donovan & Rossiter, 1982; Donovan et al., 1994; Russell & Mehrabian, 1976, 1978). Russell and Mehrabian (1976) argue that desire to purchase increases with the pleasantness of the setting and, since arousal has a curvilinear relationship with approach behavior, that such desire is maximized in settings which evoke an intermediate level of arousal.

PAD variables and consumer behavior

The empirical research was based on the expectation that in general levels of consumer behavior such as time spent in the setting would increase as each of the structural variables of the BPM – utilitarian reinforcement, informational reinforcement and the scope of the setting – increased. Each of these structural variables was, further, expected to result in high levels of one or other of the attitudinal reactions to environments predicted by Mehrabian and Russell. The strength of reported *pleasure*, for instance, is an index of the utilitarian reinforcement signaled as contingent upon approach behavior by the discriminative stimuli that make up components settings of operant classes that feature high levels of this variable. The verbal behavior that is probable responses to the promise of such reinforcement would, by definition, reflect the economic, instrumental benefits which classical economists labeled hedonic. Four of the items composing the factor which Mehrabian and Russell label pleasure largely describe the satisfaction or utility which this term denotes: happy, pleased, satisfied and contented. Hence, pleasure was expected to be higher for responses associated with those consumer situations maintained by relatively high levels of utilitarian reinforcement than for those maintained by relatively low levels of utilitarian reinforcement (i.e., the pleasure means for CCs 1,2,3 and 4 (Figure 5.3) will each be significantly higher than those for CCs 5,6,7 and 8).

The strength of reported *arousal* is a measure of the information rate of an environment which increases with the novelty, complexity, intensity, unfamiliarity, improbability, change, mobility and uncertainty of the setting. Most of these are channels of feedback from the environment to the individual; while information rate is not coterminous with informational reinforcement, it includes the feedback on performance in which informational reinforcement consists, and the verbal responses nominated arousal by Mehrabian and Russell can be expected to increase in strength as this structural dimension increases in importance.[3] Given Mehrabian and Russell's (1974a) hypothesis that the *arousal level* elicited by an environment is a *direct correlate of its information rate*, there should be greater arousal in response to variability in colors or lighting, to unusual or ambiguous situations, and to more or closer people. The information rate of an environment increases with the novelty, complexity, intensity, unfamiliarity, improbability, change, mobility and uncertainty of the setting.

Most of these are channels of feedback from the environment to the individual; while information rate is not coterminous with informational reinforcement, it includes the feedback on performance in which informational reinforcement consists, and the verbal responses nominated arousal by Mehrabian and Russell can be expected to increase in strength as this structural dimension increases in importance. Hence it was expected that arousal would be higher for responses associated with those consumer situations maintained by relatively high levels of informational reinforcement than for those maintained by relatively low levels of informational reinforcement. (i.e., that the arousal means for CCs 1, 2, 5 and 6 will each significantly exceed those for CCs 3, 4, 7 and 8).

Finally, *dominance* indicates the verbal responses whose strength is predicted to increase with the degree of openness of the consumer behavior setting. The consumer who reports feeling controlling, influential, in control, important, dominant and autonomous is likely found in an open as opposed to a closed setting. Hence it was expected that dominance would be higher for responses associated with those consumer situations characterized by the relative openness of the setting scope than for those characterized by the relative closeness of the setting scope. (i.e., that the dominance means for CCs 1, 3, 5 and 7 will each significantly exceed those for CCs 2, 4, 6 and 8).

These expectations are summarized in Table 6.1. Two additional predictions were made in connection with the expected levels of approach and avoidance characteristic of each of the operant classes of consumer behavior, and of open as opposed to closed consumer behavior settings. In that behavior would be expected to increase with the total quantity and quality of reinforcement available to reinforce it, *approach* was expected to be higher for Accomplishment, which is characterized by relatively high utilitarian and relatively high informational reinforcement than for other operant consumer behavior classes. On this basis Maintenance would exhibit the lowest level of *approach*, and the remaining operant classes, Hedonism and Accumulation, intermediate levels. Hence it was expected that approach-avoidance scores for accomplishment and hedonism would significantly exceed those for accumulation and maintenance. Similarly, approach-avoidance behavior was expected to

Table 6.1 Expected Pattern of Situational and Attitudinal Correspondence

	Closed setting scope		Open setting scope	
Accomplishment	*CC2*	+P +A −D	*CC1*	+P +A +D
Hedonism	*CC4*	+P −A −D	*CC3*	+P −A +D
Accumulation	*CC6*	−P +A −D	*CC5*	−P +A +D
Maintenance	*CC8*	−P −A −D	*CC7*	−P −A + D

increase with the openness of the consumer behavior setting. The penultimate prediction was therefore that approach avoidance scores for open consumer behavior settings will significantly exceed those for closed settings. Finally, the underlying assumption that consumer situations defined in terms of the BPM framework would exhibit acceptable levels of attitudinal–behavioral consistency led to the prediction that approach-avoidance would be determined by the attitudinal variables pleasure, arousal and dominance.

Table 6.2 illustrates the kinds of consumer situation employed in the research by portraying those used in the Venezuelan study.

Because the results have already been published in detail (see Foxall, 1997c; Foxall & Greenley, 1998, 1999, 2000; Foxall & Yani-de-Soriano, 2004; Soriano et al., 2002), they will only be summarized here. All of the expectations were supported by the evidence from both the English and the Venezuelan studies. Indeed, evidence was found for main effects of pleasure, arousal and dominance on approach–avoidance; pleasure/ arousal interactions were found in half of the six studies conducted. Most important, approach–avoidance was for the first time shown to be a function of dominance, presumably because the theoretical model being tested successfully discriminated between open and closed settings, something which no previous study had attempted.

Pleasure means were found to be significantly higher for consumer situations maintained, according to the BPM, by high levels of utilitarian reinforcement than for those maintained by relatively low levels of utilitarian reinforcement: i.e., for Accomplishment and Hedonism compared with Accumulation and Maintenance. The *arousal* means proved significantly higher in those operant classes of consumer behavior theoretically characterized by relatively high levels of informational reinforcement, namely Accomplishment and Accumulation, than in Hedonism and Maintenance. Finally, the *dominance* means were significantly higher in consumer behavior settings which according to the theory are relatively open than in those which are relatively closed.

The behavioral variables also formed the expected patterns: each of the *approach* means for accomplishment and hedonism exceeds each of those for accumulation and maintenance; each of the *avoidance* means for accumulation and maintenance exceeds each of those for accomplishment and hedonism; and each of the *aminusa* means for accomplishment and hedonism exceeds each of those for accumulation and maintenance. In addition, the scope of the consumer behavior setting was found to exert an influence on reported behavior. Each of the approach means for the open settings significantly exceeds each of those for the closed settings; the avoidance means for the closed settings similarly significantly exceed those for the open settings; the aminusa means for the open setting significantly exceed those for the closed settings.

Table 6.2   Descriptions of Consumer Situations Used as Stimuli

CC	Sub-study 1	Sub-study 2
1	You are on holiday, let's say, on a Mediterranean cruise or on a tour of the Fijian Islands in the Pacific Ocean.	You are showing off your new Mercedes Benz sports car to your family and friends.
2	You are on a training course as part of your job or to learn a new technique (for your job or for a hobby). This involves attendance at class and at practical sessions.	You are playing roulette in an exclusive casino. Around you, there are a lot of people playing and enjoying themselves.
3	You are at a party. You hear your favorite music. Around you, people are talking in a lively manner.	You are watching an entertaining program on TV: a sportscast, a game show, a soap opera, or whatever programs you generally watch regularly. You use the remote control to change channels and see similar programs.
4	You are at the cinema watching documentaries and advertisements while you wait for the beginning of the film you went to see.	While you wait on the phone, you are listening to background music.
5	You are flipping though the latest issue of a magazine collection that you buy every month (the collection will turn into an encyclopedia or manual on something that interests you).	You are saving to buy something quite important. Each fortnight you deposit money in a special savings account that earns interest at 5% more than the inflation rate and is tax-free. You have just received a credit note from the bank stating the amount of interest that will be added to your savings.
6	You are using the credit cards from a particular bank because they give you points for free travel (for every 2,000 Bolívares charged to the card, you get one point; and after reaching a certain number of points you will be able to exchange them for air tickets). You check on how many points you have and how many you still need to get the trip that you would like.	You are collecting "loyalty points" when you buy at a certain supermarket (when you reach a certain number of points, you will have the right to exchange them for products, or request a discount, for the equivalent amount of Bolívares, on your next purchase).
7	You are doing your weekly shopping at a large supermarket. You go round the supermarket with your cart, placing products in it.	On the way to work, you call at the newsstand to buy a newspaper, just as you do every day.
8	You are waiting at an airport terminal for your flight to leave. You know that you are going to be at the terminal for a good while.	You are waiting in line to deposit a check at the bank.

CC = Contingency category.

The results indicate that the necessity of taking situational influences on attitude formation and attitude–behavior consistency into account (Wicker, 1969) can be accomplished by means of the Behavioral Perspective Model. The BPM's eightfold categorization of consumer situations in terms of the scope of behavior setting and the consumption history of the consumer is closely related to the three attitudinal or verbal variables – *pleasure, arousal* and *dominance* – that Mehrabian and Russell have shown to encompass individuals' characteristic emotional responses to social and physical environments. That the consumer behavior setting scope and the pattern of utilitarian and informational reinforcement are sufficient variables to define the influence of situational factors responsible for attitudinal variance is clear from the results which show the expected patterns of attitude strength across the theoretically defined range of consumer situations and do so for cross-cultural settings. The model is also capable of taking cultural differences into consideration as is shown by the capacity to accommodate differences in inflation rate etc. In addition, the use of Mehrabian and Russell's theoretical framework and measures across the range of environments functionally defined by the BPM has produced in both England and Venezuela evidence that *pleasure, arousal* and *dominance* explain a significant proportion of behavioral variance. The results of our regression analyses indicate a stronger relationship between these affective variables and approach – avoidance behavior than is apparent in Mehrabian and Russell's (1974a, b) own empirical work or in that of marketing researchers (e.g., Donovan et al., 1994) who have employed their instrument.

The evidence for attitudinal–behavioral consistency over the range of situations investigated is also encouraging. Attitudes defined as emotional responses to environmental stimuli (Staats 1996) and measured in terms of Mehrabian and Russell's (1974a) *pleasure, arousal* and *dominance* explained 26–37% of the variance in approach–avoidance in the three studies reported, well in line with the proportion of behavioral variance shown by the meta-analyses of research employing the Theory of Reasoned Action (Sheppard et al., 1988; Van den Putte, 1993), though perhaps falling short of the (possibly untypical) proportions reported by Ajzen's (1991) analyses of a small number of studies employing the Theory of Planned Behavior. The results for the BPM are, of course, founded on a much slimmer data base. At the academic level, this implies that those theories adequately take situational factors into consideration but, at the level of managerial performance, the approach developed and tested here is sufficiently sensitive to the fabric of consumer situations to enable us to make recommendations for marketing practice. It is particularly noteworthy in this context that the research reported in this chapter is the first to relate dominance to approach – avoidance behavior: Mehrabian and Russell's empirical investigations failed to find an explanatory role for this affective variable, possibly because the range of environments they considered was not theoretically generated to reflect the structural components of consumer situations identified by the BPM (Yani-de-Soriano & Foxall, 2004). Later work has either removed *dominance* from consideration (Russell & Pratt, 1980) or ignored it (Donovan et al., 1994). Our finding that the scope of the consumer behavior setting (which manifests in feelings of *dominance*) is as important in predicting *approach–avoidance* as are utilitarian and informational reinforcement (which manifest respectively in feelings of *pleasure* and *arousal* is, therefore, of considerable scientific and pragmatic interest. It is now feasible to relate consumers' attitudes and behavior in specific situations comprehensively to one another and to commend the approach adopted here for the design of retail and consumption environments.

Predicting attitudes and behavior with sensitivity to situations

The research provides hope that the problem of integrating situational and attitudinal variables in order to predict consumer behavior is being solved. The development of an integrative model of attitude–situation–behavior not only substantiates the view that all three are closely related but indicates how they are linked. This in turn gives confidence that managerial prescriptions based on the findings of research that supports the model will be more reliable than nostrums based on *ad hoc* investigations. Further research, which is inescapable in the context of the sort of research program of which the project reported here is a key component, should also benefit from being conducted within an assimilative framework of conceptualization and analysis. But before the implications for marketing theory and further research can be considered, it is important to determine whether the model itself can accommodate the findings and their theoretical and methodological significance.

By taking this novel approach to the problem of attitudinal–behavioral consistency which formally incorporates situational variables, it has been shown that consumer behavior, admittedly measured through self-reports, varies consistently with the attitudes expressed by respondents. This provides no more than an initial indication of attitudinal–behavioral consistency but the revealed relationships have the merit of being entirely those predicted by the model. Moreover, there is every indication from previous consumer research which has employed Mehrabian and Russell's approach to show that *pleasure, arousal* and *dominance* are directly related to such consumer behaviors as time spent in the consumer environment and amount of money spent there. All of this gives confidence that the measures of attitude-in-situation we have employed are predictive of consumer behavior. Research which can examine this proposition in detail is now the priority.[4]

We have explored two conceptions of attitude. We have seen that latent process conceptions of attitude are inherently poor predictors of behavior:

unless they are supplemented by other measures of supposed latent variables which, like measures of the behavior they are expected to elucidate, are estimated at very high levels of situational specificity, their capacity to predict behavior is low. Even when these additional measures and an appropriate level of situational specificity are achieved there is wide variation in the revealed accuracy of prediction. Moreover, gains in the accuracy of prediction due to this augmented latent process conception have stemmed primarily from the inclusion of situational variables into the deliberative and spontaneous processing models: the attitudinal and additional latent variables refer indirectly to the behavior setting and learning history of the consumer. This of itself does not establish a situational theory of consumer choice: the latent variables can always be interpreted as referring to the consumer's perception of the environment both as a prerequisite to and a consequence of information processing. This would result in an essentially cognitive model of behavior.

Equally, however, taking a radical behaviorist position that is concerned only with the prediction of verbal behavior, the results are evidence for an augmented probability conception of attitudes in which behavior is related directly to situational determinants defined in terms of the environmental consequences of prior behavior of a similar kind. These consequences have been divided into the utilitarian benefits consumers derive directly from the ownership and use of products and services but also but those which belong essentially to the branding activities of firms in concert with the social demands of the wider society: the symbolic consequences of ownership, consumption and deployment. These benefits in turn have been shown to be connected systematically to the attitudinal responses of consumers to social and physical situations. The PC and LPC approaches to attitude can be further elaborated by considering the radical behaviorist and psychological behaviorist positions in greater detail.

Explaining situational influences on attitudes and behavior

A radical behaviorist interpretation

The radical behaviorist interpretation of the results is relatively straightforward, confined as it is to the question of explaining the verbal behaviors of the respondents in providing answers to the questionnaire-based queries requiring them to respond to the situations described with words relating to the emotions of *pleasure, arousal,* and *dominance.* The interpretation is an exercise in verbal reconstruction. This involves establishing whether consumers' verbal expressions of pleasure, arousal, and dominance discriminate between theoretically significant dimensions of the structure of consumer behavior settings. Moreover, our initial interest is in the use of Mehrabian and Russell's scales as purely verbal responses to situations; in line with radical behaviorist thought, feelings are cast as collateral responses which as behaviors in their own right cannot cause other behaviors (Skinner, 1974).

The findings support an operant interpretation of consumer behavior, in which the model is understood to predict consumers' verbal responses to the situations with which they were presented. As we have noted, and seek here to emphasize, this interpretation is in accord with a strict radical behaviorist philosophy of science in which behavior has been explained when the environmental stimuli that control it have been identified. On this understanding, consumers' expressions of pleasure, arousal, dominance, approach and avoidance are overt verbal responses controlled by the discriminative stimuli that compose the described behaviors and settings with which respondents were presented and which they were asked to rate. The responses are assumed to have been reinforced when previously enacted during the history of the individual. No allusion is made to intervening cognitive or affective variables.

A radical behaviorist interpretation would propose first that the descriptions of situated consumer behaviors employed in this study are discriminative stimuli in whose presence certain types of reinforcement or punishment (utilitarian, informational, aversive) are likely to be forthcoming contingent on the performance of overt behaviors available in those situations. Such an approach would not postulate that these behaviors were mediated in any way by internal affective events such as pleasure, arousal, and dominance.

The original theoretical rationale for these studies thus differs from the S-R mediational model on which Mehrabian and Russell rely. Theirs is an S-r-s-R theory (the lower case letters denote internal responses and stimuli) which they derived from Osgood's theory of meaning which employs an 'E-A-P' classification rather than 'P-A-D' (so that Evaluation = Pleasure; Activity = Arousal; Potency = Dominance) (Osgood et al., 1957). Osgood and his colleagues borrowed in turn from Hull's concepts of a fractional antedating goal response (r_g) and its response-produced stimulus or stimuli (s_g). Radical behaviorist interpretation has always set itself firmly against mediational theories such as these, whose intrapersonal terms it regards as "explanatory fictions" (Skinner, 1950, 1963). It is entirely consistent therefore with the PC understanding of attitudinal–behavioral relationships where consistency is purely an empirical matter determined by the "functional equivalence" of the contingencies within which the verbal and nonverbal behaviors are emitted.

Even a radical behaviorist interpretation of the results need not be so parsimonious as to exclude entirely the affective responses characteristic of different consumer environments. Such feelings are, nevertheless, interpreted within the strictly operant behaviorist canon as collateral covert responses, produced by the same reinforcing events that determine overt verbal and nonverbal behaviors (Skinner, 1974). Furthermore, certain arguments within the learning psychology of self-management support the view that affective responses may be reinforcers which maintain those overt responses (Bandura, 1986; Mallot and Garcia, 1991).

However, a difficulty arises with a purely radical behaviorist interpretation insofar as the verbal responses to the PAD scales are understood to *mediate* nonverbal behaviors such as time spent in a retail setting or amount bought there. Traditionally, behaviorism has stressed that behavior may predict behavior but cannot be the cause thereof. Causes are to be located only in the environment of behavior. More recently another argument has arisen as a result of the recognition of rule-governed behavior: since rules are usually formulated in words and rules derived from the contingencies (including what others say and one's own formulation of self-rules) can motivate behavior. How else are augmentals supposed to motivate? The matter remains controversial among radical behaviorists, though especially among those who have studied instructed behavior, it is widely accepted that verbalizations can influence behavior even over and above the reward structure programmed to control responding.

Even if we accept the conclusion of those who are happy to assign causal status to verbal behavior by assuming that they perform the role of discriminative stimuli, something that seems likely at the descriptive level, there is still a problem at the explanatory level of accounting for the continuity of behavior. Why should words motivate? The stock radical behaviorist answer is that use of these words, acting on these words, must have been rewarded in the past, or the words themselves acted as reinforcers as when someone commented that a setting was pleasant and gave a sense of freedom: hence their present power to motivate. The problem of continuity is that of accounting for the ongoing power to motivate that these words have. Radical behaviorists argue that if anything is stored within the individual it is at the neuro physiological level rather than the cognitive, and that this along with the continuity of setting stimuli accounts for continuity. An alternative is to look to classical conditioning as the means of establishing the power of words.[5]

A psychological behaviorist interpretation

This alternative interpretation makes use of classical conditioning, not as an experimental tool that can be employed to provide direct empirical evidence for the relationships inferred but as an occurrence known to occur in the laboratory and borrowed from there to provide a plausible substructure to the findings of the operant-inspired research described above. This empirical approach derives from work on the classical conditioning of attitudes (Staats & Staats, 1958; Lott & Lott, 1968). The same conditioning principle that was described in Chapter 2 applies to the production of covert responses such as the affective reactions we call *attitudes*. A positive attitudinal reaction to a brand name might be conditioned, for instance, by pairing it in advertisements with an adjective that already elicits a favorable emotional response:

CS (brand name) $\rightarrow$ r_e (implicit positive evaluation)

US (positive adjective) $\rightarrow$ r_e (implicit positive evaluation)

Staats (1996) goes beyond the Skinnerian system to propose an approach to human environment that incorporates both classical and operant conditioning. The contribution of Staats's behaviorism is that it combines the roles of classical and operant conditioning into a single system in which a stimulus performs three functions. This essentially unifying approach accounts for the environment identified in this and other studies that use Mehrabian and Russell's technique by combining the reinforcing role of stimuli posited in the BPM and the subsumptive level of analysis in which the emotion-eliciting capacity of a stimulus determines what can be a reinforcer. Staats's theory also accounts for the predictions of verbal responses (pleasure, arousal, dominance, approach, avoidance) made in this study by showing that emotion-eliciting reinforcing stimuli also elicit approach-avoidance.

The first function of a stimulus is to elicit an emotional response (S $\rightarrow$ r). In classical conditioning, the emotion-eliciting function of an unconditioned stimulus is transferred to a neutral (subsequently conditioned) stimulus and, in higher conditioning, this function may be further passed to any number of originally neutral stimuli that become in turn conditioned elicitors. Emotion-eliciting stimuli are those that reinforce motor responses enacted prior to their presentation (R $\rightarrow$ S). This is the second function of the stimulus; it is thus the capacity of a stimulus to elicit an emotional response that determines what can be a reinforcer. These two functions of a stimulus show how classical and operant conditioning are related in the environmental production of emotional and motor responses. The third function of a stimulus inheres in its ability to elicit approach-avoidance. Associated with each emotional response is an emotional stimulus or stimulus function which elicits the motor response (S $\rightarrow$ r $\rightarrow$ s $\rightarrow$ R). Approaching something that elicits a positive emotional response is often reinforced. As a result, any positive emotion-eliciting stimulus will come to elicit approach. This mechanism, once learned, generalizes to any stimulus that elicits a positive emotional response. While a stimulus that elicits positive emotion elicits approach, avoidance is elicited by a stimulus that elicits negative emotion. In this incentive or directive function, the stimulus brings on approach-avoidance which thus follows it; contrast this with reinforcement in which the stimulus follows the environment it strengthens.

Staats's system suggests the following interpretation of the results of our study. The setting element prefiguring utilitarian reinforcement has been more than a discriminative stimulus: it has been an eliciting stimulus, causing an emotional response and associated stimulus that elicits approach-avoidance towards the setting and any stimuli associated with it. The setting stimulus is thus the reinforcement towards which approach or avoidance is directed. One of the classes of stimuli associated with the setting stimuli is verbal; other, synonymous verbal stimuli may come to be associated therewith over time. These are symbolic or informational eliciting stimuli. One of the classes of response these words elicit is verbal approach-avoidance, e.g., the pleasure, arousal, dominance, approach, avoidance descriptors used in the study. These utterances are reinforced by their approaching the unconditioned stimuli (utilitarian elicitors) and the conditioned stimuli (informational elicitors).

Further interpretation of the results in terms of Staats' psychological behaviorism is feasible. The descriptions of situated consumer environment contain directive stimuli that elicit the *pleasure/arousal/dominance/approach/ avoidance* responses. In the past, the words contained in the descriptions have become associated with the setting stimuli that elicit positive emotional responses. Approach-avoidance behaviors, including those that are verbal, towards the setting stimuli and the words that describe them have been reinforced. Any approach (avoidance) environment toward the setting, including positive (negative) verbal descriptions of it, will be elicited by the described consumer environment stimuli. Use of the *pleasure/arousal/dominance* and *approach/avoidance* adjectives/statements will have been reinforced and conditioned and they will thus have become appropriate approach-avoidance responses for the descriptions of situated consumer environment.

The descriptions of situated consumer environment are directive stimuli. They have previously been conditioned to the setting stimuli and the behavioral consequences enjoined within settings of the kind described. These descriptions now elicit the same emotional responses that were previously elicited by the setting stimuli and the behavioral consequences. These emotional responses have associated with them emotional stimuli that elicit the approach behaviors previously learned in operant conditioning. Depending on other elements of the situation in which the descriptions are encountered, the appropriate approach-avoidance environment will be forthcoming. In a travel agency, for instance, an appropriate approach environment would be booking a holiday. In the marketing research setting involved in our research, it would be the verbal use of the *pleasure/arousal/dominance/ approach /avoidance* wordings.

Staats's system of three-function stimulus provides an explanation in behavioral terms of the continuity between the learning of a rule and its being followed at a later time in another situation: words condition internal emotional responses which have stimulus functions associated with them that cause overt responses. Where an interpretation is not amenable to direct experimental examination, however, the criticism arises that this method is akin to inventing an internal s → r link wherever necessary to offer an "explanation" of what has been observed. It amounts, in other words, to an explanatory convenience because it lacks an empirical or philosophical logic by means of which the internal events may be legitimately and consistently ascribed.

Taking stock

A summary of the empirical results considered in this chapter might make two important points. First, latent process conceptions do not predict well unless the investigator takes situational factors into consideration; second, an approach based directly on situational influence on attitudes (conceived as evaluative verbal behavior) predicts about as well as one that is explicitly cognitive. Certainly, they do not predict with greater accuracy than an augmented PC approach which incorporates situational variables. Outwith the realms of either the managerial quest for prescriptive answers to practical problems or the confines of strict, descriptive behaviorism, however, prediction is not the final word. Broader issues of explanation arise. The following discussion considers the results of the research described in this chapter in terms of the two frameworks for understanding attitudinal – behavioral relationships raised earlier, the probability conception (PC) and the latent process conception (LPC). The argument is that the results are equally interpretable within either the PC or the LPC framework, and that the choice of explanatory perspective cannot be made on the basis of the results alone. However, independently of this, the PC methodology has some virtues of its own to which chapter 7 turns.

7
Patterns of Brand Choice

The emphasis in this chapter is on the probability concept of attitude and behavior, i.e., a *behavioral* understanding of choice, and seeks to integrate the contributions of behavioral economics and marketing science. The variety of behavioral economics involved is that in which behavior analysis and experimental analysis merge, and the distinct contribution of combining this approach with the analysis of consumer choice in the context of marketing-oriented economies is that the techniques of behavioral economics, largely confined to the animal laboratory, can be more fully exploited as a means of understanding human consumer choice. This is the domain of *consumer behavior analysis*.

The starting point is the patterns of aggregate consumer brand choice identified over a large number of product categories in many advanced economies of the world. These patterns show a considerable degree of consistency and predictability. There is a striking similarity in the gross patterns of consumer brand choice and the phenomena of "matching" identified in numerous animal and human studies of choice. This is pursued in order to determine whether matching is actually a feature of brand choice since this would, according to the behavioral economics literature based on animal research, indicate that consumers were economic maximizers. Further research described here has used the key variables of the BPM to elucidate consumer choice and what it is that consumers actually maximize.

Patterns of consumer choice

Ehrenberg (e.g., 1988/1972) has repeatedly shown that comparatively few purchasers of a product category are 100%-loyal to a particular brand over a period of time. Most consumers show multi-brand purchasing over a sequence of shopping opportunities, choosing within a small "repertoire" of available brands. Ehrenberg explains this in terms of the functional similarities of brands within a product category. Usually, they have near-identical physical formulations and perform identical tasks. The consumer typically exchanges one brand for another because the benefits gained from one are directly substitutable for those provided by others within the repertoire.

A small proportion of buyers are loyal to one brand over a sequence of 10/15 purchases of the product category (Table 7.1). Each brand attracts exclusive purchasers who are a relatively small proportion of buyers of the product category. Larger, more differentiated brands attract a rather higher proportion of exclusive purchasers than small brands. However, most customers of any brand buy other brands far more often than they buy that brand. Table 7.2 shows that a coffee customer typically makes 3 purchases of the brand per year but 9 purchases of the product category; each brand displays more or less the same pattern. Similar patterns are found for brands in other product categories: e.g., American consumers of breakfast cereals, which tend to be highly differentiated, make about 5 purchases of a brand per year, but 35 purchases of the product category; British consumers of gasoline, a product category which is much more difficult to differentiate, make 10 purchases of a given brand annually, but 50 of the product category (Ehrenberg & Goodhardt, 1979 – 81). From these figures can be calculated the annual "share of category requirements" (SCR), which is the average number of brand purchases divided by the average number of product category purchases over a year. Breakfast cereals show an SCR of 13%; for gasoline, the SCR is 20%.

Whatever the brand, its customers buy a similar range of other brands and do so in a replicated pattern. Thus, Table 7.3 indicates that Maxwell House was bought on average by 41% of the customers of each of the other brands, Maxim by about 12% of each other brand's customers. These phenomena are predictable from the penetration (and market share) levels of each brand: hence, Maxwell House's penetration was the highest; Maxim's, the lowest. Finally, it is notable that, apart from those, relatively few customers who are 100%-loyal to any brand, buyers tend to restrict their purchases to a small subset of brands rather than spreading them across the entire brand set. Even 100% brand loyal buyers are not particularly heavy buyers of their preferred brand.

The variability in consumers' choices is also borne out by the data on penetration rates and market shares which diverge markedly from brand to brand (Table 7.2). (Market share records the percentage of product category sales accounted for by each brand. Penetration measures the percentage of potential buyers of a brand who in fact purchased it in a given time period). For instant coffee, which is typical of consumer product categories, annual brand penetrations range from 6% to 24%, and market shares from 3% to 19%. Table 7.1 shows similar results for a wider range of products.

Repeat purchase loyalty tends to be similar for brands that have similar market shares: compare the repeat rates for highly-differentiated versus

Table 7.1 Annual Performance Measures for the Eight Leading Brands

Brands	Brand size			Loyalty			Category purchases/buyer	Partitioning % who also bought		
	Market share %	% buying	Purchases per buyer	% buying once	100% loyal: %	rate		1st	3rd	5th
1st	27	46	4.6	36	20	4	13	–	32	19
2nd	19	36	4.1	40	15	4	14	52	33	20
3rd	12	26	3.7	47	10	4	15	57	–	22
4th	9	24	3.3	50	10	4	14	56	36	24
5th	7	16	3.7	46	11	3	15	54	35	–
6th	5	15	3.0	55	9	3	15	56	36	21
7th	4	13	3.2	55	8	3	15	57	36	20
8th	3	8	3.9	55	7	3	16	52	32	20
Average	8	23	3.7	48	11	3	15	55	34	21

Source: Ehrenberg and Uncles (1999, p. 13). Reproduced by kind permission of the authors. Product categories: Catsup, cereals, cheese, chilled orange juice, gasoline, household cleaners, laundry detergents, paper towels, take-home beer, toothpaste. Based on panel data from Nielsen, IRI, AGB, GfK, TCI.

Table 7.2   Annual Penetration and Average Purchase Frequencies
(Leading Brands in Order of Market Share)

Instant Coffee USA, Annual	Market Share	Penetration	Average Purchases* of Brand:	of Any:
		%		
Any Instant	100%	67	–	7
Maxwell House	19	24	3.6	9
Sanka	15	21	3.1	9
Tasters Choice	14	22	2.8	9
High Point	13	22	2.6	8
Folgers	11	18	2.7	9
Nescafe	8	13	2.9	11
Brim	4	9	2.0	9
Maxim	3	6	2.6	11
Other	13	20	3.0	9
Average Brand	11	17	2.8	9

*per buyer of the brand.
Source: Ehrenberg and Uncles (1999), p. 6. Reproduced by kind permission of the authors.
Although this table refers to instant coffee, the data base is comprehensive: The product
categories investigated by Ehrenberg and his colleagues include 30 food and beverage items
ranging from cookies to take-home beer; 20 personal care products and cleaners from cosmetics
to washing-up liquids; industrial and durable goods including gasoline, aviation fuel and motor
cars; stores, store chains, and shopping trips; and audience viewership patterns for TV programs
and channels. The research summarized here was undertaken, between 1950 and 1995, in the
UK and Continental Europe, the USA and Japan).

Table 7.3   Duplications of Purchases Between Brands

Instant Coffee USA, annual	% Who Also Bought							
	1.	2.	3.	4.	5.	6.	7.	8.
Buyers of								
1. Maxwell House	–	32	29	32	38	26	13	13
2. Sanka	36	–	32	40	25	23	20	11
3. Tasters Choice	31	32	–	36	28	20	17	14
4. High Point	34	38	34	–	31	22	18	10
5. Folgers	51	30	35	40	–	25	15	11
6. Nescafe	48	39	34	40	34	–	15	8
7. Brim	33	45	39	44	27	20	– 1	6
8. Maxim	2	38	51	39	34	17	25	–
Average Duplication	41	36	36	39	31	22	17	12

Source: Ehrenberg and Uncles (1999). Reproduced by kind permission of the authors.

less-differentiated brands in Tables 7.1 and 7.2. Smaller brands not only attract fewer buyers but those buyers buy less of the brand (or buy it less frequently), a phenomenon known as "double-jeopardy" (Ehrenberg et al., 1990). Both SCRs and number of sole buyers are lower for smaller brands (Ehrenberg & Uncles, 1999). There is no evidence of rigid market partition-ing into clusters of brands that exclusively attract some customers rather than others. However, a buyer of one of the more-differentiated brands is more likely to buy another highly-differentiated brand on a subsequent purchase occasion than a less-differentiated brand (Tables 7.1 and 7.3).

Choice as behavior

Behavioral economics may throw some light on these patterns for it has in common with Ehrenberg's methodology an understanding of consumer choice as a series of behaviors extended through time. Moreover, the pat-terns of brand choice identified by Ehrenberg resemble the patterns of choice found in behavioral economics experiments and, in particular, that found in what Herrnstein (1997) who discovered the phenomenon refers to as "matching." Herrnstein defines choice not as an internal deliberative process but as a *rate* of intersubjectively observable events that are tem-porally distributed. In his analysis, the relative frequency of responding becomes the dependent variable. Herrnstein's (1961; cf. Herrnstein, 1970, 1979, 1997) initial discovery was that when animals are presented with two opportunities to respond (pecking key A or key B), each of which delivers reward or reinforcement (access to a food hopper) on its own variable inter-val (VI) schedule, they allocate their responses on A and B in proportion to the rates of reward available in A and B. In other words, response rate (B_1) is proportional to the relative rate of reinforcement (R) (de Villiers and Herrnstein 1976):

$$B_x / (B_x + B_y) = R_x / (R_x + R_y). \qquad (7.1)$$

These simultaneously available schedules of reinforcement, which are constantly encountered in matching research, are known as *concurrent* schedules and they may follow the ratio or interval or a mixed pattern of reward. A ratio schedule, as was noted in Chapter 2, is one in which a specified number of responses has to be performed before reinforcement becomes available. Fixed ratio (FR) schedules keep the number of required responses equal from reinforcer to reinforcer, while variable ratio (VR) schedules allow the required number of responses to change from one rein-forcer to the next. Concurrent variable ratio schedules, usually abbreviated to "conc VR VR," allow simultaneous choice to be investigated. It is this arrangement that most clearly resembles the purchases of brand within a product class. Chapter 2 also noted that an interval schedule maintains a constant minimum time interval between rewards (or reinforcements). Fixed interval (FI) schedules maintain a constant period of time between intervals, while on a variable interval (VI) schedule the time varies between one reinforcer and the next. The contingencies described in the text with respect to Herrnstein's original experiment enable behavioral allocation to be controlled and predicted by concurrent variable interval schedules, usually abbreviated to "conc VI VI." Although conc VI VI schedules have been used more frequently in behavioral experiments, conc VR VR are more common in naturalistic settings.

Matching provides a framework for the behavioral analysis of consumption. As long as there are no differences among reinforcers in terms of *bias*, i.e., preference for one reinforcer based on characteristics such as its physical position or color, and *sensitivity*, i.e., responsiveness to the alternative reinforcers, Equation 5.1 simplifies to

$$B_x / B_y = R_x / R_y. \tag{7.2}$$

Two sources of deviation from strict matching are apparent in *bias* between or among the alternatives on offer, and *sensitivity* to one or other of the schedules of reinforcement on which they are available. Bias is the result of a deficiency in experimental design rather than a shortcoming of the experimental subject; it represents a failure to take account of all of the independent variables that influence preference and declines as relevant independent variables are increasingly taken into account (Baum, 1974). Principal sources of bias are undetected response costs imposed in the case of one alternative but not the other(s), such as an additional effort required to shift one lever in an experiment, and a qualitative difference between reinforcers, such as an unanticipated additional value accorded to one reinforcer but not the rest (Baum, 1979; Davison & McCarthy, 1988; Pierce & Epling, 1983). In the context of shopping for grocery brands, bias is likely to result from the consumer's choice of a convenient store which carries only a subset of all brands within a product category from which she can now choose, or from the prominent positioning of brands within a shelf display on which the retailer earns a higher margin.

Sensitivity is often taken as indicative of the substitutability of the reinforcers. Two commodities, X and Y, are substitutes if a reduction in the price of X leads to an increase in the quantity demanded of X and a decrease in the quantity demanded of Y. The usual examples are of highly competitive brands in the same product category such as Coca Cola and Pepsi Cola, Cadbury's Dairy Milk and Galaxy Milk Chocolate (Kagel et al., 1995). (Complementarity is the converse: a reduction in the price of X leads to an increase in quantity demanded of Y; commodities are independent if a change in the price of one has no effect on the quantity demanded of the other). Of course, price is only one aspect of the marketing mix which might influence such changes in quantity demanded: few if any brands will, therefore, be *perfect* substitutes since differentiation based on non-price factors is likely to lead consumers to discriminate between them on non-functional grounds.

Taking bias and sensitivity into account, Baum (1974) proposed the generalized matching law:

$$B_x / B_y = b(R_x / R_y)^s \tag{7.3}$$

where B is the behavior allocated to alternatives x and y, R is the reinforcers contingent upon that behavior, and the constants b and s represent bias and sensitivity respectively. When the matching law is expressed logarithmically as a power function (Equation 5.3), unity of the exponent s indicates complete substitutability of the reinforcers.

Bias is absent when b, which is the intercept when Equation 5.3 is re-expressed in logarithmic form, equals unity. Deviations of b from unity indicate a consistent preference for one alternative over the other(s) regardless of the reinforcement rates in operation. As long as the reinforcements for each of the available responses are apparently equal and would predict a behavioral indifference between them, a measure of b greater or less than one indicates that "preference is biased by some unknown, but invariant, asymmetry between the alternatives" (Baum, 1974, p. 233).

The behavior of a subject who disproportionately chooses the leaner schedule of reinforcement (i.e., who chooses it more often than strict matching would predict) is said to exhibit undermatching; in such cases, the exponent s, slope, is less than one. The behavior of a subject who disproportionately chooses the richer schedule of reinforcement exhibits overmatching, and $s>1$. Low sensitivity to reinforcement schedules may arise because the subject is unable to discriminate the alternatives sufficiently well, especially if there is no delay in reinforcement when responses are allocated to a new choice (and are, therefore, controlled by a different schedule), and because rates of deprivation differ between the schedules (Baum, 1974, 1979). The generalized matching law can thus take a variety of data into consideration (Green & Freed, 1993).

In presenting choice as a behavioral rate, Herrnstein's matching equation presents a *molar*, as opposed to *molecular* approach to behavior (Baum, 2004). Whereas molecular explanations of behavior attempt to identify the precise environmental stimuli responsible for each and every response, molar conceptualizations relate *rates* of response to *rates* of reinforcement. Hence, as Vuchinich and Tucker (1996, pp. 136 – 137) point out, Hull's (1952; cf. Amsel & Rashotte, 1984) theory of behavior is molecular; it traces reaction potential ($_sE^R$) to drive (D), stimulus intensity (V), incentive (K) and habit strength ($_sH^R$) thus:

$$_sE^R = D \times V \times K \times {}_sH^R \tag{7.4}$$

Herrnstein's matching equation, by contrast, represents response frequencies as a function of reinforcement frequencies; hence choice is a matter of the temporal distribution of behavior as related to the temporal distribution of rewards. This represents the measurement of behavior in terms of probabilities and, if the rate of behavior is conceived of as an *attitude* this would be in keeping with a probability conception thereof. The patterns of consumer choice we shall explore in this chapter follow this reasoning in contradistinction to that which marks out the latent process approach.

Three types of analysis, each derived from behavioral economics, have been employed in order to show that the brands under investigation within a product category are genuinely substitutes (matching analysis), the sensitivity of quantity demanded of a brand to its own price and those of its competitors (relative demand analysis), and the extent to which consumers can be said to optimize brand purchasing (maximization analysis). In addition, a number of analyses have been undertaken to explore the sensitivity of consumer demand to price and, in particular, the relevance of the concepts of utilitarian reinforcement and informational reinforcement to the choice of brands over time.

Patterns of choice

In the research on consumer brand choice summarized here, data for 80 adult consumers were drawn from the Taylor-Nelson-Sofres "Superpanel" which consists of 15,000 households, randomly selected, to represent Great Britain. Panel members scan their purchases after each shopping occasion into a sophisticated barcode reader. The data are then downloaded on to the TNS mainframe computer where they are grossed up into reports that provide market trends. The data on which this paper is based are a subsample that tracked purchasing by households over a 16 week period. The prices recorded were actual prices paid for the items. The product categories investigated are fruit juice, packet tea/tea bags, margarine, butter, baked beans, instant coffee, cheese, breakfast cereals, and (sweet and savory) biscuits. The data, which included brand name, price-paid and quantity-bought information, were collected initially for clients in the fast-moving consumer goods industry, principally food.

Matching

The idea of matching needs to be carefully defined in the context of buyer behavior. It is important to recognize that the matching law says nothing about consumption. All reinforcers obtained are assumed to be consumed. If matching implied simply that the proportion of buying responses for Brand A equals the proportion of reinforcers obtained from that brand, it would be a truism. Assuming that the reinforcement value from consuming a commodity is constant, and that all commodities purchased are consumed (and these seem to be reasonable assumptions), then the proportion of "purchases" would always match the proportion of "reinforcers."

The application of matching to marketing must avoid this tautology. The problem derives in part from the fact that matching was developed on interval schedules (where reinforcement rate can be used as an independent variable) and purchasing behavior is based on a ratio-like schedule. The true independent variable on a ratio-like schedule (price) does not translate nicely into the independent variable of the matching law (reinforcement rate) because reinforcement rate is dependent on response rate on ratio schedules. As a result, translations between the matching law and consumer behavior are not straightforward. More suitable variables for consumer behavior have the advantage that they are readily measurable, however. In the analysis of consumer behavior, an appropriate unit of choice (i.e., the dependent variable) is *spending*, not purchasing. Spending would be measured in monetary units such as dollars or pounds. An appropriate unit of reinforcement is the number of actual purchases made, given a particular ratio of spending (i.e., price per unit by volume, weight or size). This is not a true independent variable because it is determined by spending patterns. Unfortunately, this is a byproduct of using the matching law with ratio-like schedules.

With these adjustments, the matching law comes to state that "The proportion of dollars/pounds spent for a commodity will match the proportion of reinforcers earned (i.e., purchases made as a result of that spending." Frequency of purchase is thus the independent variable. This avoids the problem of tautology (there are possible conditions under which this would not be true). It also avoids the problem of having varying amounts of reinforcement from each act of consumption. The predicted equilibrium point for behavioral allocation on concurrent variable ratio schedules is exclusive choice of the richest schedule, i.e., that with the lower or lowest ratio requirement (Herrnstein & Loveland, 1974; Herrnstein & Vaughan, 1980) and this is borne out empirically (Green et al., 1983). The definition captures the essence of a market transaction. We do not know, from the data on multi-brand buying, what the precise pricing schedules are. However, by assuming that functional utility is (a) the sole operative reinforcer (the *homogeneity* assumption), and (b) constant from brand to brand (the *constancy* assumption), we can ascertain which is the leaner or richer schedule from relative brand/unit prices. The aggregate data of marketing analyses are then invaluable for indicating how often consumers switch brands and how far they allocate responses between the leaner and richer schedules.

To reiterate, in consumer research, the matching law becomes the proposition that the ratio of amount of money spent for a brand to the amount spent on other brands within the product category will match the ratio of reinforcers earned (i.e., purchases made as a result of that spending) of that brand to the amount bought of other brands within the product category. The first of these, the *amount paid ratio,* was operationalized as the ratio of money spent on "Brand A," defined as the most frequently purchased brand, to money spent on "Brand B," i.e., the amount spent on the remaining brands purchased within the requisite product category: *Amount paid for Brand A / Amount paid for the remaining brands in the product category (B).* The *amount bought ratio* was calculated, in terms of the physical quantity acquired, as: *Amount bought of Brand A / Amount bought of Brand B (the remaining brands of the product category).* Logarithmic transformations were used for the analyses.

Within each of the 9 product categories, matching analysis revealed that the brands purchased were close substitutes. Measures of *s* that deviated only in the smallest degree from unity were uniformly found. The results are illustrated with data for fruit juice (see Figure 7.1: (a) shows the results for a single, typical consumer; (b) for the aggregated data set for this product.) This high degree of substitutability was found for all products and all consumers who practiced multi-brand purchasing.

Multi-brand purchasing was found extensively for all products; a small number of consumers were sole purchasers of each brand (Table 7.4). In the

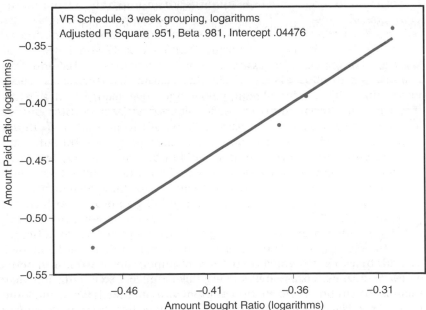

Figure 7.1(a) Matching Results for a Single Consumer

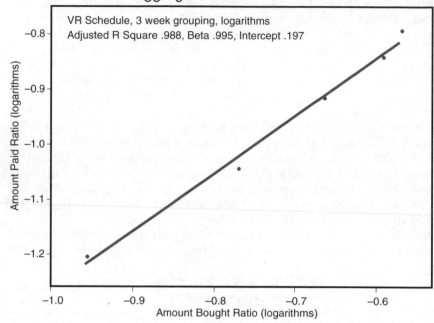

Fruit Juice: Matching Analysis
Aggregate Data

VR Schedule, 3 week grouping, logarithms
Adjusted R Square .988, Beta .995, Intercept .197

Figure 7.1(b)   Matching Results for the Aggregate Data Set for Fruit Juice

Table 7.4   Incidence of Sole Buyers

	Consumers	Sole Buyers	%
Butter	37	22	59
Coffee	58	33	57
Tea	66	35	55
Baked Beans	69	36	52
Fruit Juice	57	25	44
Margarine	73	23	32
Cereals	73	10	14
Cheese	77	7	14
Biscuits	75	9	12

case of the product category chosen to exemplify our results, fruit juice, 25 (44%) of the 57 consumers buying this item were sole purchasers; the highest proportion of sole purchasers was found for butter (59%), the lowest for cheese (9%). This result is entirely in keeping with work in marketing research on aggregate patterns of brand choice. Its degree of consistency with the prediction of behavioral economics that under the circumstances exemplified by brand choice ("ratio schedules of reinforcement") consumers would maximize by always selecting the cheapest alternative requires elaboration, and this follows the discussion of maximization.

The multi-brand buying we have seen was the case over a period of weeks. This is what the aggregate studies are picking up. But week by week we have evidence that some consumers buy the cheapest: that is what accounts for their brand switching and switching back. The price incentives to switch are there weekly, not just when a special deal is in operation.

Relative demand analysis

The sensitivity of demand (more accurately, *quantity demanded*) to price can be demonstrated by the demand curve. Madden et al., (2000) reiterate three predictions made by economic theory. First, "Increasing the unit price of a reinforcer decreases consumption of that reinforcer", i.e., demand curves plotted on logarithmic coordinates show consumption to be a positively decelerating function of unit price increases. Second, "Unit price determines consumption and response output regardless of the specific values of the cost and benefits components of the ratio". And, third, "When choosing between two qualitatively identical reinforcers available at different unit prices, ... behavior will be exclusively allocated to the alternative with the lower unit price". Foxall et al. (2004) extended Madden et al.'s use of the economics of demand in experimental situations by employing a demand analysis which presents the *relative* amounts of brands A and B as a function of their relative prices.

The relative demand analysis followed procedures employed in behavioral economics studies. In order to devise relative demand curves for the product categories, a demand analysis expressed the ratio of amount bought of the dominant brand (A) to the amount bought of the remaining brands in that category (the "amount bought ratio" described above) as a function of the ratio of the relative average prices of the dominant and the other brands (the relative price ratio). In operational terms, the relative price ratio = *Mean price of Brand A / Mean price of other brands in the repertoire.*

The expectation that logarithmically plotted demand curves would show consumption to be a positively decelerating function of unit price (Madden, et al., 2000) was generally though not universally substantiated. Relative demand curves for 6 of the 9 product categories are, as expected, downward sloping, though that for butter is approximately horizontal; three were upward sloping. Figure 7.2 illustrates with respect to fruit juice: (a) indicates the results for a single consumer; (b) for the aggregated data set.

Maximization analysis

Behavioral economists and psychologists continue to debate whether consumption is characterized by maximization of satisfactions or by some

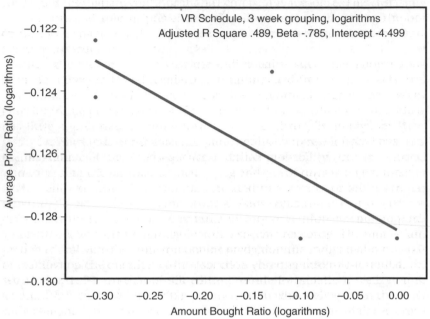

Figure 7.2(a)   Relative Demand Analysis for a Single Consumer

other principle such as satisficing or melioration (e.g., Herrnstein, 1997; Rachlin, 1989). Although most research with non-human animals has proved inconclusive (Schwartz & Reisberg, 1991), researchers have felt confident in proposing how their results apply to human consumption including the choice of products and brands in supermarkets (Green & Freed, 1993). Their assurance seems unwarranted in the absence of data specifically relevant to this facet of consumer behavior. Our basic studies have, we hope, produced evidence which allows the choices of individual consumers to be better understood and thereby to contribute meaningfully to the debate over maximization.

An analysis intended to reveal whether the observed consumer behavior was maximizing returns on price expended was undertaken, following procedures discussed by Herrnstein & Loveland (1975) and Herrnstein & Vaughan (1980). On *conc* ratio schedules, there is a fixed probability of reinforcement for each response, which can be expressed as the reciprocal of the schedule parameter. "Thus conc VR40 VR80 describes two response alternatives with reinforcement probabilities of 1/40 and 1/80, respectively." On ratio schedules, the probability of reinforcement is independent of

Fruit Juice: Relative Demand Analysis
Aggregate Data

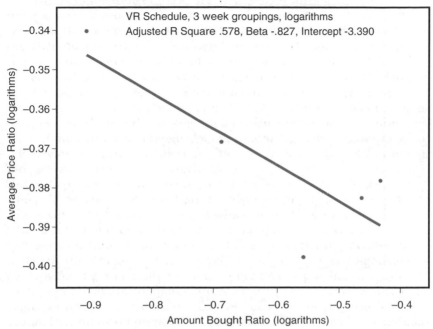

Figure 7.2(b) Relative Demand Analysis for Aggregate Data Set

response rate (something not true of VI schedules where the probability of reinforcement is inversely proportional to rate of responding). Faced with *conc* VR40 VR80 schedules, the individual's maximal probability of reinforcement is obtained by responding exclusively on the VR40 schedule. Matching theory makes the same prediction for conc VR VR schedules, claiming that maximization is under these circumstances a special case of matching (cf. Rachlin, 1982). In order to ascertain whether maximization is occurring, we plotted the amount paid ratio against probability of reinforcement where the latter is operationalized as the reciprocal of the price of brand A over the reciprocal of the price of brand A plus the reciprocal of the mean of the prices of the other brands in the consumer's consideration set (B), i.e. $1/P_A / (1/P_A + 1/P_B)$.

Maximization analysis would require that consumers purchase the cheapest option on each shopping trip among the brands they purchase. This is indeed what was found in the preliminary studies, at least where consumers were buying close substitutes, but the analysis of the current data suggest a more complicated pattern (Figure 7.3).

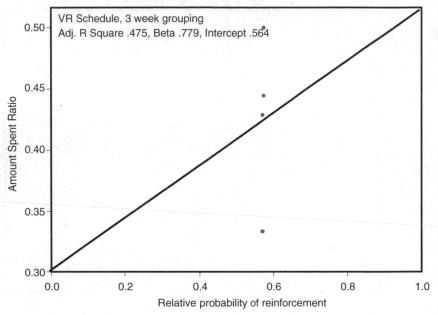

Figure 7.3(a)   Maximization Analysis for a Single Consumer

Downward-sloping demand curves do not necessarily imply maximization (Simon, 1987). The maximization analysis indicates, however, that most consumers did choose the cheapest brand on each shopping occasion regardless of product category. This is consistent with the behavioral economics approach pioneered by Herrnstein and Loveland (1975) and Herrnstein and Vaughan (1980), but close examination of the results reveals a more complicated pattern of choice than is apparent in the studies of nonhumans undertaken by those authors. First, while consumers generally selected the cheapest brand within their consideration set, these "repertoires" in many cases comprised only premium, highly differentiated brands. Many consumers did not maximize in any "absolute" sense. In each product category, own-label, or store brand, and economy versions existed which were considerably cheaper than those actually purchased. Second, while research with nonhuman subjects is typically limited to only one choice on each occasion, consumers are able to purchase more than one brand even on a single shopping trip. For 7 products, consumers in the aggregate maximized by purchasing the favorite (cheapest) brand (Brand A); for 2 products, however, (cheese and margarine), this pattern was not found. This same overall pattern was found for both the "VR" and the "FR" schedules. However, even for the 7 product categories

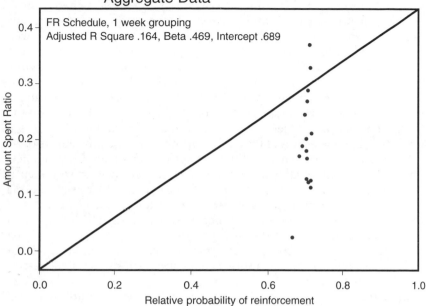

Figure 7.3(b) Maximization Analysis for the Aggregate Data Set

where consumers maximized by purchasing Brand A, there is a complication which arises from the nature of consumer choice in the marketplace and which is not encountered in laboratory research with either human or non-human animals in which choice is constrained. Although most consumers maximized in the sense that they purchased the cheapest brand within their consideration set, many also purchased a second brand priced substantially higher on the same occasion. The maximization analyses undertaken based on the behavioral economics literature was thus incapable of indicating comprehensively the pattern of consumer brand choices in relation to a simple value-for-money criterion.

These patterns of choice are consistent with findings reported in the consumer research and marketing literatures on branding which portray consumers' consideration sets as a function of the level of quality required for a variety of consumption settings.

Effects of the pattern of reinforcement on brand choice

To investigate possible effects of informational and utilitarian reinforcement values on brand choice, an attempt was made to identify different levels or magnitudes of informational and utilitarian reinforcement offered by the brands available (i.e., bought by consumers in the sample) in each product category. The set of alternative brands and product characteristics available in a supermarket within each product category can be interpreted as a set of programmed contingencies of reinforcement, which specify what responses (e.g., how much one has to pay) are followed by what consequences (e.g., product characteristics). A major part of marketing activities, according to this interpretation, is to plan and establish contingencies for the behavior of consumers (Foxall, 1999d). Not all programmed contingencies, however, have the desired or planned influences on behavior, and that is why an important issue for marketing managers and academics is to identify the actual effects of different contingencies (i.e., the effects of the price and non-price elements of the marketing mix on consumer choice). The analysis of informational and utilitarian reinforcement levels presented below follow the same logic: they refer to programmed levels of informational and utilitarian reinforcements, which may or may not influence particular instances of consumer choice. In other words, in the case of marketing activities, an event that was planned to have high reinforcement magnitude, *vis-à-vis* its aversive components (costs), can in fact have low reinforcing value for some consumers (e.g., innovations that do not attract people or are too expensive).

Since there exist no established units by which levels of utilitarian and informational reinforcement can be measured, a forced ranking system was employed whereby three informational and two utilitarian levels were ascribed to each product category. This classification allowed comparisons to be made across product categories and was in part influenced by the fact that not all brands and brand types were bought by the sample respondents during the period investigated. Levels of informational and utilitarian benefit cannot be defined absolutely – they depend ultimately on the interests of researchers – and more levels of utilitarian reinforcement, for example, might be identified for some product categories, such as cookies and cheese. However, for ease of comparison among the product categories, an equal number of levels was used in each case.

For supermarket food products like those investigated, increases in utilitarian level are obvious from the provision of extra desirable product attributes. Such attributes usually add value to the product or its consumption, are mentioned on the package or in the product name, and justify increases in price. Moreover, in most cases, several brands offer products with and without these attributes. For the product categories in question, utilitarian levels were identified based on additional attributes (e.g., plain baked beans vs. baked beans with sausage) and/or differentiated types of products (e.g., plain cookies vs. chocolate chip cookies). In the case of differentiated product types, competing companies not only usually offer their own brands of the different product types but charge different prices for them (e.g., plain cookies are cheaper than more elaborate cookies for all brands examined). The supposed utilitarian benefit levels are those apparently programmed by manufacturers, i.e., they are planned to function as benefits for the majority of consumers. Hence manufacturers usually charge higher prices for anticipated benefits of this kind. These expectations may not, of course, be justified for each and every consumer: a consumer may not, for instance, like baked beans with sausage, despite the fact that the company that markets this augmented product expects it to offer something better than plain baked beans.

Informational reinforcement, by contrast, is strongly associated with brand differentiation: the most strongly promoted and best known brands are usually associated with higher levels of prestige, social status, and trustworthiness. For the supermarket products investigated here, informational reinforcement level is closely associated with brand differentiation, which in turn is usually also related to price differentiation. Comparing the level of brand differentiation of, say, Asda Smart Price© and Heinz plain baked beans, Heinz is clearly the better known, more differentiated and, consequently, usually the more expensive brand, offering a higher level of informational reinforcement. This kind of difference among brands has been interpreted in our research as stemming from differences in informational reinforcement level. Naturally, informational reinforcement level as specified here does not exclude the possibility of there also being differences in utilitarian reinforcement between two informational magnitudes. Corporate representatives of any differentiated brand would argue strongly that their brands differ from those of other companies in terms of their "utilitarian" attributes, such as quality of raw materials and ingredients, production procedures, health control, and such like, and that their superiority and any price premium they command derive from these factors. Similarly, consumers of differentiated brands may also assert these brands' functional superiority, e.g., that they taste much better than other cheaper brands, which would imply differences in utilitarian reinforcement level. The classification adopted does not exclude such possibilities, since most consumer behavior generates both types of consequences. Nevertheless, the ranking of informational reinforcement is based on the predominant difference that one can find between products, offered by different brands, that usually have almost identical formulations (cf. Ehrenberg, 1988/1972; Foxall, 1999c) and may not even be distinguished by consumers on the basis of their physical characteristics (e.g., in blind tests).

The ranking of informational reinforcement level was based on the following general criteria: 1) increases in prices across brands for the same product type (e.g., plain baked beans, plain cookies or plain cornflakes) were considered to be indicative of differences in informational levels; 2) the cheapest store brands (e.g., Asda Smart Price©, Tesco Value©, Sainsbury Economy©) were considered to represent the lowest informational level

(Level 1); 3) store brands that do not mention good value for money or economy (e.g., Asda, Tesco, Sainsbury) and cheapest specialized brands were usually considered to represent the medium informational level (Level 2); and 4) specialized brands (e.g., Heinz, McVities, Kelloggs, Lurpak), with higher prices, were considered to represent the highest informational level (Level 3). The classification is shown in Table 7.5.

To demonstrate how individuals choose across different informational reinforcement levels, Figure 7.4 shows, again for fruit juice, the percentage of the total quantity bought at each informational level by each consumer. The black, empty, and striped bars represent the percentage bought of brands classified at informational levels 1, 2 and 3, respectively. Each vertical bar in the figure represents data for a single consumer. Data for individual consumers are plotted as a function of the average price (total amount spent divided by total quantity bought) paid by each consumer during the 16-week period. Wider or narrower bars indicate larger and smaller numbers of consumers included in the analysis of different product categories.

In general, increases in average price paid were associated with decreases in the percentage of brands bought at Level 1 of informational reinforcement and increases in the percentage of brands bought at Level 3. Considering that the average brand price was one of the criteria to classify brands at different informational levels, this may seem a trivial finding: clearly, by definition, the more the consumers buy Level-3-brands the higher should be the average price they paid. However, when one considers that the figure shows data for individual consumers, some non-trivial findings can be noted. First, it becomes clear that most consumers bought mostly brands at one particular informational level, rather than across all levels. The percentage of consumers who bought 70% or more of goods at one particular informational level is: for baked beans 92%, tea 91%, coffee 84%, margarine 84%, butter 81%, cereals 68%, fruit juice 68%, cheese 64%, and cookies 58%. This indicates that the majority of consumers make 70% or more of their purchases within one particular informational level.

A second non-trivial aspect of the data is that, when buying across informational levels, consumers tend to buy more brands at adjacent informational levels than at more distant levels (e.g., buying Levels 1 and 2, or 2 and 3, more than Levels 1 and 3). A third relevant tendency apparent

Table 7.5   Levels of Informational Reinforcement

The cheapest own (retailer) brands (Asda Smart Price ©, Tesco Value ©, Sainsbury Economy ©)	Level 1
Own (retailer) brands that do not mention good value for money or economy (Asda, Tesco, Sainsbury) and cheapest specialized brands	Level 2
Specialized brands (Heinz, McVities, Kelloggs, Lurpak) with higher prices	Level 3

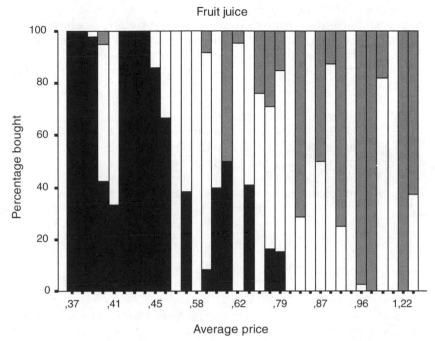

Figure 7.4 Quantity Purchases of Brands at Each Level of Informational Reinforcement (Level 1: black bars; Level 2: empty bars; Level 3: striped bars) for each consumer as a function of average price paid per consumer

from this figure is the wide difference in the average price paid across consumers, some of them buying mostly the cheapest brands while others bought mainly the most expensive ones. This finding could be deduced from the patterns of buying mostly brands at the same informational level, described above, but it is not in this case trivial, for it suggests that consumers' brand-repertoires may be influenced by economic variables such as their budget constraints. This has not been previously reported in the literature on consumers' multi-brand buying patterns. Similar analyses also indicate that, for 8 of 9 product categories, most consumers also made the large majority of their purchases within the same level of utilitarian reinforcement. The percentages of consumers who bought 70% or more of brands belonging to the same utilitarian level are, for butter 91%, baked beans 85%, coffee 84%, tea 84%, cheese 82%, fruit juice 77%, margarine 74%, cereals 66%, and cookies, 42%.

Consumer groups

The possibility arises here of comparing groups of consumers determined by their predominant buying preferences. The various groups are composed of consumers whose purchases exhibit specific patterns of informational and utilitarian reinforcement. Consumers were, therefore, classified in one or other of six groups, derived from the combination of the three levels of informational and the two levels of utilitarian reinforcement of the brands they had bought most frequently. The patterns of reinforcement defining the six groups were

Group 1 – Informational Level 1 and Utilitarian Level 1,
Group 2 – Informational Level 1 and Utilitarian Level 2,
Group 3 – Informational Level 2 and Utilitarian Level 1,
Group 4 – Informational Level 2 and Utilitarian Level 2,
Group 5 – Informational Level 3 and Utilitarian Level 1, and
Group 6 – Informational Level 3 and Utilitarian Level 2.

These groups' buying patterns were compared in terms of elasticity of demand,[1] using the equation

$$Log\ Quantity = a - b\ (Log\ Price) \tag{7.5}$$

as suggested by Kagel et al. (1995).[2]

All price elasticity coefficients were negative indicating that the quantity consumers bought tended to decrease with increases in price. Moreover, all coefficient values fell between zero and 1.0, indicating that demand was inelastic for all consumer groups. The absolute values of elasticity coefficients, shown in Figure 7.5, however, were lower for the extreme groups, Groups 1 and 6, than for the other groups, suggesting that consumers that buy predominantly intermediate-level brands showed higher price responsiveness than those buying predominantly the least- and highest-differentiated brands (split-sample reliability analyses confirm this trend).

Intra- and inter-brand elasticities

The observed decreases in the quantity bought with increases in prices, indicated by negative elasticity coefficients, may reflect different response patterns for the different groups. The tendency to buy larger quantities when prices are lower may be related to one or more of three patterns:

1) buying larger quantities of a product when its price was below its usual, average, price rather than when its price was above its average price (i.e., intra-brand or absolute elasticity);
2) buying larger quantities when buying brands belonging to cheaper, lower informational levels than when buying brands belonging to more expensive, higher informational levels (i.e., informational inter-brand or relative elasticity); and

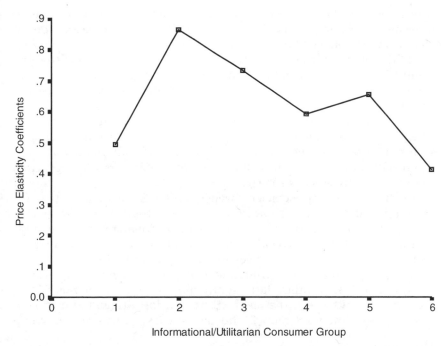

Figure 7.5 Price Elasticity Coefficients for Each Group of Consumers Classified According to the Informational and Utilitarian Level of Brands they Predominantly Purchased

3) buying larger quantities when buying brands belonging to cheaper, lower utilitarian levels than when buying brands belonging to more expensive, higher utilitarian levels (i.e., utilitarian inter-brand or relative elasticity).

One way of measuring such patterns is to decompose the global price elasticity coefficient into three different coefficients, namely, intra-brand, informational inter-brand, and utilitarian inter-brand coefficients. Such an analysis would yield an equation in which the quantity bought would be a function of intra-brand changes in price, informational reinforcement levels of the purchased brands, and the utilitarian reinforcement levels of the purchased brands, that is,

Log Quantity = a − b1 (Log Intra-Brand Price) − b2 (Log Informational Level) − b3 (Log Utilitarian Level). (7.6)

Intra-brand price was obtained by dividing the price paid for the brand by the average price for that same brand in the sample. Relative values of quantity, intra-brand price, informational level and utilitarian level with respect to their respective consumer group averages, analogous to those used to obtain global elasticity coefficients, were used. Regression coefficients were obtained for each consumer group.

All price elasticity coefficients were again negative, indicating that the quantity consumers bought tended to decrease with increases in intra-brand price variations, informational level, and utilitarian level. Moreover, with the exception of the intra-brand coefficient for Group 2 (1.51), all coefficient values were between zero and –1.0, indicating that all three types of demand tended to be inelastic for all consumer groups. Despite such similarities, the absolute values of intra-brand, informational inter-brand, and utilitarian inter-brand elasticity coefficients differed across consumer groups, as shown in Figure 7.6.

Intra-brand elasticity coefficients were lower for Groups 1 and 6 than for the intermediate groups, showing a decreasing trend from Group 2 to Group 6. This suggests that consumers buying predominantly the cheapest, least-differentiated brands (i.e., Group 1) do not change much the quantity they buy as a function of changes in brand price relative to their usual (average) price. This result suggests a tendency toward buying the cheapest brands, regardless of other, just slightly more expensive, brands. If this interpretation is correct, the observed pattern for intra-brand elasticity, which was largest for Group 2 and decreased systematically as group

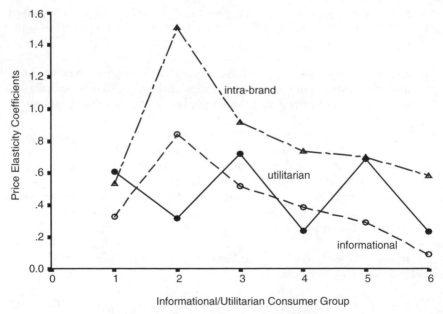

Figure 7.6   Intra-brand, Informational Inter-brand and Utilitarian Inter-brand Elasticities based on Predominant Pattern of Reinforcement

classification increased up to Group 6, suggests that responsiveness to intra-brand changes in price decreases as group classification increases. In other words, if the low intra-brand elasticity observed for Group 1 is a consequence of buying the cheapest brands most of the time, these findings point to the conclusion that as the level of differentiation of the purchased brands increases (i.e., as the price of purchased brands increases), the responsiveness of consumers to changes in prices decreases.

Informational inter-brand elasticities were smaller than intra-brand elasticities for all six groups and followed a similar pattern, with Group 1 showing a low coefficient, Group 2 showing the largest one which decreases systematically with increases in group classification up to Group 6. This suggests that consumers buying mostly the least-differentiated, cheapest brands do not change much the quantities they buy as a function of informational brand level, whereas the responsiveness to informational reinforcement of those buying intermediate-level brands decreases systematically with increases in the informational level of the predominantly purchased brands. This value is close to zero for Group 6, suggesting that consumers that already usually buy the highest informational and utilitarian level brands are not sensitive to changes in informational level (similar to a "satiation" effect, since satiated animals are not expected to be responsive to food, i.e., to do things to get food).

Utilitarian inter-brand elasticity, indicated by the filled circles, was higher for the three groups that bought predominantly low utilitarian-level brands (i.e., Groups 1, 3 and 5) than for the other three that bought high utilitarian-level brands. This finding indicates that consumers who buy predominantly brands with low utilitarian levels tend also to buy smaller quantities of higher utilitarian brands, whereas those that buy predominantly brands with high utilitarian levels do not seem to vary much the quantities they buy as a function of utilitarian brand level. Hence, the utilitarian inter-brand elasticities followed a slightly different pattern from the informational inter-brand elasticities, though like them they were mostly smaller than intra-brand elasticities. Group 1 is the only exception with·a coefficient larger than that of the intra-brand elasticities, if only marginally. Whereas the other two curves follow a similar pattern, the shape of the utilitarian curve is different in that it follows a zigzag course with Group 2 showing a lower coefficient than Group 1 and 3, and similarly Group 4 and 6 displaying a lower coefficient than their neighbor groups. The implications of this pattern are more complicated because it suggests that consumers buying mostly at utilitarian level 1, i.e. Groups 1, 3 and 5, are more sensitive to changes in utilitarian level than consumers with a preference for utilitarian level 2, independent of the informational level of the brand. For example, consumers who mostly buy the least-differentiated, cheapest brands (i.e. Group 1) are more likely to buy larger quantities than consumers who buy at but a higher utilitarian but at the same informational level (i.e. Group 2). Consumers of Group 3 however, with a lower utilitarian level than Groups 2 and 4 but a higher informational level than Group 2 and the same informational level as Group 4, is in turn more responsive to utilitarian reinforcement than both Group 2 and 4.

The dynamics of brand choice

As predicted by both matching theory and maximization theory, the empirical work confirms that choice on conc VR VR schedules exhibits both matching and maximizing. However, the examination of consumer choice in naturalistic environments raises a number of complications for behavior analysis and behavioral economics that are not evident from the experimental analysis of choice. While the realities of consumer behavior in affluent, marketing-oriented economies have implications for behavioral economics, the techniques of analysis which behavioral economics makes available to the marketing researcher also elucidate the nature of brand choice in the market place.

A common assumption in aggregate studies of consumer choice conducted by marketing scientists is that brands within a product category are functional alternatives and that consumers will include a brand within their repertoire or purchase set only if it embodies the physical and functional benefits that are common to all members of that category (Ehrenberg, 1988/1972, 1991). This proposition is seldom supported by empirical evidence. Although the discovery of matching on conc VR VR schedules is both expected and perhaps in some respects trivial, it is important for the sort of analysis we have undertaken in that it confirms that the alternative brands considered are indeed substitutes in the assumed sense. The very-nearly perfect matching that we have found is a characteristic of choices that are near-perfect substitutes (Kagel et al., 1995).

Another assumption sometimes found in the marketing literature is that price plays a relatively small part in the determination of consumer choice: brands that are highly differentiated by advertising command a premium but the consumer is generally portrayed as relatively insensitive to such differentials. Non-price elements of the marketing mix (i.e., promotional tactics, brand attributes, and distribution strategies) are thought to be more influential than price factors for affluent consumers operating within marketing-oriented economies (Foxall, 1999b). The relative demand and maximization analyses, which were intended to shed light on the sensitivity of consumer demand to price differentials among competing brands, present an equivocal impression of the relationship between market prices and quantity demanded. While the downward-sloping relative demand curves, where they were found, is supportive of this conclusion, the evidence for some product categories is mixed. The maximization analysis suggests that consumers are in some respects sensitive to price levels when making decisions about how much of a brand to buy relative to other brands in the consideration set. However, the interpretation of the data must take into account the phenomenon of multi-brand purchasing on one shopping trip. Although a consumer may exhibit economically rational price sensitivity by purchasing the cheapest brand in her consideration set, her general sensitivity to price may be confounded by her purchasing a premium-priced alternative at the same time. Hence, although the balance of probabilities (based on the relative demand and maximization analyses alone) suggest that consumer brand choice is somewhat sensitive to price, there is a concomitant need to recognize non-price elements of the marketing mix as determinants of consumer choice. The analyses of price elasticity of demand which take into consideration both the utilitarian (functional) and informational (symbolic) benefits gained by consumers from the brands they purchase and use throw more light on this.

The evidence is that consumers choose their repertoire of brands on the basis of the informational and utilitarian level of reinforcement programmed by the brands. This is likely to be related, among other things, to their budgets, which we were not able to take into consideration. However, it is also of marketing significance in that it provides opportunities for the partitioning (segmentation) of markets. There do seem to be clearly definable segments based on combinations of the utilitarian and symbolic benefits of purchase and consumption and the cost minimization. These factors encourage consumers to choose brands within a given range defined in terms of these variables. Most purchasing takes place within a fairly narrowly defined range and consumers who switch out of that range generally move only to an adjacent range.

Consumer groups defined by the informational/utilitarian level of the brands they mostly buy, show different responsiveness to changes in prices, with extreme groups showing the lowest levels of responsiveness (possibly for different reasons). Price elasticities can be decomposed into intra-brand and at least two types of inter-brand elasticities, informational and utilitarian, according to the type of reinforcing events that influence consumer choice. Intra-brand elasticity can be interpreted as a measure of responsiveness to the aversive consequences of giving up money (Alhadeff, 1982). Therefore, choice patterns can be interpreted as being determined by different combinations of the tendencies to avoid aversive consequences, maximize informational reinforcement and maximize utilitarian reinforcement. A pattern that minimizes financial loss, showing minimum responsiveness to informational attributes and some to utilitarian ones, seems to characterize choices of consumers in Group 1. The responsiveness to informational and utilitarian attributes related to changes in price seems to be an inverse function of how much of these the consumer obtains regularly. So, the results showed increasing responsiveness to informational reinforcement from Group 6 (who obtain higher levels of it) to Group 2 (who obtain lower levels of it). The same was observed for utilitarian attributes, for those groups buying lower levels of utilitarian attributes (Groups 1, 3, and 5) showed higher responsiveness to this aspect of the brands than those that buy higher levels of utilitarian attributes more regularly (Groups 2, 4, and 6).

Elasticity coefficients can be interpreted as measures of consumer "satiation" level, since the less frequently consumers purchase a given reinforcing dimension the higher their responsiveness to that dimension. In the case of intra-brand elasticity this tendency is probably related to available budget, though it was not possible to investigate this, e.g., through the construction of income-compensated demand curves (see Kagel et al., 1995). The only exceptions were obtained for consumers that buy the least differentiated brands most of the time, for whom elasticity coefficients seem to reflect a pattern of buying the cheapest products in the category.

From the point of view of the BPM, the analysis has demonstrated that relatively high and low utilitarian and informational reinforcement can be used to classify consumer behavior even within the narrow range represented by fast-moving consumer goods. In previous analyses, these variables, along with the relative openness of the consumer behavior setting, have been employed to categorize broader patterns of consumer behavior. Within that categorization, the purchase of food products is classified in terms of low utilitarian and low informational reinforcement in a relatively open setting. That categorization is meaningful when buying fast-moving consumer goods compared with buying and using other kinds of products and services (Foxall & Yani-de-Soriano, 2004). The demonstration of this paper is that these structural elements of the consumer situation also provide means of classifying consumer behavior within those broader categories.

The results for the elasticities of demand, especially those for intra-brand, inter-utilitarian and inter-informational elasticities, suggest that the explanatory variables investigated are far from the only influences on brand choice. Nevertheless, along with the results for the inter-group elasticities of demand which provide somewhat stronger evidence of a link, they indicate that utilitarian and informational reinforcement have distinct effects on brand choice and that they may form the basis of the partitioning of markets and strategies of market segmentation.

8
Context and Cognition in Consumer Choice

Attempts to predict behavior from cognitive measures have proved highly problematical unless situational influences are taken into consideration. The case has been made that the cognitive variables used to explain behavior reflect contingencies of reinforcement via surrogates of the consumer's learning history and the consumer behavior setting. Attitude researchers appear to be taking just this approach, despite their tendency to deal in respondents' perceptions or judgments of the contingencies rather than their direct influences on behavior. We have noted cognitive psychologists' tendency to think in terms of cognitive portrayals of the effects of past behavior and its situational determination, but we might argue that what they have discovered at base is the need for a behavior-based explanation of choice.

In addition, consumers' verbal and non-verbal behaviors, and perhaps their covert emotional responses, have proved predictable from measures of the structure and functions of retail and consumption situations without necessary reference to intrapersonal pre-behavioral influences. It has even proved possible to make explicit some of the situational influences that enter into attitudinal–behavioral relationships, the contingencies of reinforcement that influence both attitudes and behavior and that are responsible for any consistency between them (Newman & Foxall, 2003). Moreover, the constructs that compose the model of attitudes, situations and behavior can be extended to other areas of marketing activity, and can predict such aspects of consumer choice as preference for benefit segments and price zones (Oliveira-Castro et al., 2005a, b). Nevertheless, this chapter argues that, no matter how well situational models may predict, there remains a role for intentional constructs such as "attitude" and "belief" in the *explanation* of consumer choice. But the case for a synthesis of the behavioral and the cognitive requires closer articulation, and a framework within which to accomplish this needs more than a superficial amalgamation of their respective paradigms. Incorporating the criticisms and findings and the theoretical proposals presented in the preceding chapters into a single perspective requires new tools of intellectual analysis, ideas that encompass the intentional and contextual routes to explaining consumer choice without subjecting or reducing either to the other.

It certainly requires a more sophisticated means of demarcating social science methodologies than the PC and LPC conceptions of attitude that have served us well thus far. What is needed now is a more definitive distinction between cognitive and behavioral psychologies, a means of distinguishing them more sharply so that the contribution of each to understanding consumer behavior can be appreciated. These two basic theoretical positions can be portrayed as methodological stances each of which offers a unique means of explaining complex human behavior such as that involved in purchase and consumption. Once their contrasting avenues to understanding social and economic behavior are appreciated, then the limits to uniting them and the genuine opportunities for their synthesis may be more easily appreciated.

The intentional and contextual stances

A fundamental consideration in the case of cognitive psychology is the place of intentional idioms in the prediction and explanation of behavior. A valuable starting point in the quest to sum up the essential nature of cognitive explanation is Dennett's (1983) *intentional stance*, the attribution of pre-behavioral mental events to human and non-human animals in order to predict their behavior. In a nutshell, the intentional stance claims that *the behavior of systems such as people and computers can be predicted from the desires and beliefs, and other intentional, idioms, that can be rationally attributed to them.*

Dennett proposes several orders of intentional system, applied in his illustration, to the behavior of vervet monkeys. The assumption having been made that the behavior of the vervet can be better understood/predicted by attributing to it prebehavioral beliefs, desires and other mentalistic constructs, the question is *which* of these notions should be attributed? Given that the animal is assumed rational, the following hierarchy can be employed. *First order intention* simply incorporates beliefs, desires etc.: "*x* believes that *p*". If, however, *p* itself contains an intentional idiom, i.e., beliefs about beliefs, the elaboration of the intentional system is increased: "*x* wants *y* to *believe* that *x* is hungry" is a *second order* intentional system. And so on (see Panel A of Table 8.1): in principle, humans could presumably cope with a level of sophistication approaching infinity, but reaching beyond a handful of levels is probably impracticable (Dennett, 1987, p. 243).

The range of higher-order explanations available to us is scarcely exhausted by the intentional stance. The methodology of Skinner's operant psychology is that of an extensional science, constructed on the *contextual stance*, the view that *behavior is predictable in so far as it is assumed to be environmentally determined; specifically, in so far as it is under the control of a learning history that represents the reinforcing and punishing consequences of similar behavior previously enacted in settings similar to that currently encountered.* This is the philosophical stance that underlays the behavioral analysis presented in Chapters 5, 6 and 7, and, in particular, of the Behavioral Perspective Model.

Dennett is correct that there is a need to go beyond the zero-order level but he is too ready to limit the range of subsequent explanations by adopting a primitive understanding of behaviorism. According to Dennett, behaviorism (he is thinking particularly of Skinner's radical behaviorism) never gets beyond what he calls the killjoy level. This is strange because *radical* behaviorism has always embraced so-called private events like thoughts and feelings (this is what distinguishes it from the older, methodological behaviorism) and the inclusion of private verbal discriminative stimuli as proximal causes of behavior in the explanatory repertoire of radical behaviorists has steadily increased (though not all have employed it in practice). Moreover, since the distinction between contingency-shaped and rule-governed behavior was recognized by radical behaviorists (Skinner, 1969), the interpretation of operant behavior in terms ranging beyond the bottom of the barrel has been well and truly on the behaviorist agenda (though some more conservative experimentalists have not sought to extend their reach in this way).

While there are several forms of contextualism, some of which may be incommensurable (Hayes et al., 1993), that which characterizes behavior analysis in the radical behaviorist tradition takes "behavior-in-context" as its unit of analysis, i.e. it seeks the meaning of behavior in its relationship to its context. Such contextualist accounts of behavior are not restricted to the analysis of single stimuli and single responses but embrace the transactions between a stream of behavior and systematic relationships to its context through time. The meaning of behavior is found, therefore, not in the imputed attitude or intention of the actor but in the environmental consequences which the behavior has characteristically produced. Its meaning inheres in its function, what it does, its success in relation to its goals. Cognition itself is analyzed as contextually-bound behavior.

Panel B of Table 8.1 summarizes how this interpretive system would work. There is no implication that the stages of the operant hierarchy exactly match those of cognitive ethology. But levels of explanation ranging well beyond the purely descriptive are entirely feasible in a radical behaviorist framework and – for the record – have empirical justification that goes beyond that which Dennett would expect to adduce for his post-killjoy levels of analysis. The zero order level of analysis would be well illustrated by basic empirical regularities. It is purely descriptive and makes no demands on higher level constructs to explain it. This can be one of its major strengths, of course, given that consumer psychology so infrequently deals with this kind of descriptive analysis.

For instance, a large part of Ehrenberg's work has entailed finding empirical regularities of consumer choice from which certain laws of marketing may be derived (e.g., Ehrenberg, 1988/1972). We have already encountered aspects of this research tradition in Chapters 2 and 7. Furthermore, the work has been particularly successful in predicting aspects of repeat buying from basic descriptive measures such as brand penetration levels from measures of repeat buying rate. Two empirical generalizations, substantiated for a very wide range of consumer non-durables, may be mentioned by way of example. (i) The proportion of buyers of Brand X in one period who buy it again in a second period is $1.23w$, where w is the mean number of times these buyers of brand X purchase it in the period. (ii) The consumers who buy brand X in one period but not the next buy it in the period in question with an average frequency of 1.4 units. It does not follow that consumer psychology should be confined to this level of analysis, but it is one which is essential to the sound conduct of more theoretical and interpretive work and without it consumer and marketing research would lack foundation. In particular, the "facts" established at this level provide a program for theoretical work and also an essential test of its empirical correspondence (Ehrenberg, 1988/1972). In so far as the growth of knowledge depends upon the critical interplay of competing theories, inspiring counter-hypotheses and the generation of new empirical knowledge (Feyerabend, 1975), this level of analysis is inescapable.

Even from a radical behavioristic viewpoint, however, it is incomplete: it fails either to explain consumer choice by relating observed behavior to the environmental conditions that shape and maintain it, or even to interpret it in these terms. Even a radical behaviorist analysis requires a first-order level of explanation which achieves this. An operant consumer psychology would need to relate observed individual and aggregate buyer behaviors systematically to the patterns of reinforcement and punishment by which they can be explained and to the discriminative stimuli under whose control they might come.

But our analysis can go further still. Radical behaviorism has long proceeded beyond the analysis of contingency-shaped behavior (its first order level) by considering the (causal) role of private stimuli and the rule-governance of most if not all human behavior. Although in both cases the contingencies themselves have been held to provide ultimate control of human behavior, the interpretation of complex human behavior has in fact increasingly relied upon theoretical entities located within the individual. In contrast to the primitive radical behaviorism cited by Dennett, recent formulations deny that any but the simplest human behaviors can be considered entirely contingency-shaped – tapping one's fingers absentmindedly, for instance. The unlikelihood of operant conditioning occurring in humans without conscious awareness has long been noted (Brewer, 1974), casting doubt on whether the word "conditioning" is justified or useful. Most if not all human behavior is influenced by rules that specify setting-response-outcome contingencies which, at the most basic level, arise from the verbal behavior of others.

We saw in Chapter 5 that when the individual lacks a relevant learning history and therefore rules for performing a given behavior, decision making is required. In the cognitive depictions of this, consumer behavior is said to be preceded by "deliberative processing" or "systematic processing" or the "central route to persuasion". In a radical behaviorist interpretation, such behavior is governed by "other-rules" embodying the social pressures that give rise to the "subjective norms" of multi-attribute models. Lacking a learning history, the consumer uses other rules as a surrogate. As the consumer develops experience, a history of reinforcement and punishment prompts the generation of self-rules which take the place of others' formulations of the situation. Finally, the consumer's behavior is characterized by apparent spontaneity as the discriminative stimuli that compose the behavior setting evoke self-rule-governed responses. The higher-levels of operant analysis shown in Table 8.1, which form a sequence that was explored in Chapter 5's description of consumer decision-making in operant terms, apparently undermine Dennett's insistence that behaviorism cannot handle post-descriptive accounts of human choice.

But we have now reached an important point of difference, one that is most evident from a comparison of how the contextual stance that underpins radical behaviorism accounts for complex human behavior such as that involved in language, rule-formulation and rule-following with an account based on intentional reasoning.

Radical behaviorism provides for these higher-level phases of environment–behavior relationships in terms of stimuli and responses. The operant interpretation looks to increasingly complex contingencies to explain increasingly complex behavior. Nor is such science confined to three-term contingencies. Sidman (1994) proposes that n-term contingences can be invoked to explain increasingly complex behavior. In the three-term contingency, R the basic $R \rightarrow S^R$ relationship (performing response R produces consequence S^R which makes future enactment of R more likely) comes under the control of a discriminative stimulus, S^D such that S^R follows R only when S^D is present. If the presentation of an S^D sets the scene for reinforcement contingent upon the performance of R, then S^R will be produced only when S^D is present and R is enacted. The enactment of a response other than R (i.e., R^A) will not produce S^R even when S^D is present. When the prebehavioral stimulus is other than S^D (i.e., S^A) neither R nor not-R will produce S^R (Figure 8.1a).

The four-term contingency places this whole relationship under the control of a further stimulus, A. The discriminative stimulus, S^D, now

Table 8.1 The Stances Compared

A. COGNITIVE ETHOLOGY (based on the intentional stance)	B. OPERANT INTERPRETATION (based on the contextual stance)
Fourth order intentionality: "Tom wants Sam to recognize that Tom wants Sam to believe that there is a leopard" (p. 245)	*Rule-governed behavior III:* "Automatic" self-rule following in initiating behavior setting
Third order intentionality: "x wants y to believe that x believes he is alone" (p. 243)	*Rule-governed behavior II:* Self-rule formulation in conscious choice/to construct a learning history
Second order intentionality: "has beliefs and desires and beliefs and desires about beliefs and desires" (p. 243) "Tom want Sam to believe there is a leopard" (p. 245)	*Rule-governed behavior I:* Other-rule following (contingent on the verbal behavior of a speaker and a history of rule-following)
First order intentionality: "has beliefs and desires but no beliefs and desires about beliefs and desires" (p. 243) "Tom wants to cause Sam to run into the trees" (p. 246)	*Contingency-shaped behavior:* (relation of behavior to contingent consequences that influence its rate/other aspects of its shape)
Zero order: "the killjoy bottom of the barrel: an account that attributes no mentality, no intelligence, no communication, no intentionality at all to the [individual]" (p. 246) "Tom (like other vervet monkeys) is prone to three flavors of anxiety or arousal: leopard anxiety, eagle anxiety, and snake anxiety" (*ibid.*)	*Description:* Individual or aggregate patterns of buyer behavior. Describes behavior in the absence of any context; consumer behavior is decontextualized (not just "placeless" but lacking any systematic relationship with its context).

Sources: Panel A is derived from Dennett (1983), reprinted as Chapter 7 of Dennett's *The Intentional Stance* (1987). Page numbers in parentheses refer to this book.
Panel B is derived from Foxall (1999b).

controls the relationship between the response, R, and the reinforcing consequence, S^R, only when a further antecedent stimulus, A, is present. The presence of another antecedent stimulus (A^Δ) means that neither R nor R^Δ will produce S^R. In the presence of A, R will produce S^R only when S^D is also present (Figure 8.1b).

All of this is, according to Dennett, little higher than the killjoy or bargain basement level but when it is applied to verbal behavior its capacity to illumine a considerable range of human behavior that behaviorists have long ceded to cognitive psychologists becomes apparent. The *n*-term contingency does not have to be discussed within the confines of verbal behavior but some of its most significant implications for human behavior arise in this context. The fourth term, A or antecedent stimulus, in the four-term contingency may be considered what Michael (1982, 1993) calls an *establishing operation* (EO). An EO is a "function-altering stimulus," one, that is, which causes another stimulus to take on reinforcing functions. It could be stimulus A or A^Δ in Figure 8.1b. (EOs are clearly related to

$$S^D + R \longrightarrow S^R$$
$$S^D + R^\Delta \nrightarrow S^R$$

$$S^\Delta + R \nrightarrow S^R$$
$$S^\Delta + R^\Delta \nrightarrow S^R$$

Figure 8.1a   The Three-term Contingency

$$A +$$
$$S^D + R \longrightarrow S^R$$
$$S^D + R^\Delta \nrightarrow S^R$$

$$A^\Delta +$$
$$S^\Delta + R \nrightarrow S^R$$
$$S^\Delta + R^\Delta \nrightarrow S^R$$

Figure 8.1b   The Four-term Contingency

augmentals, rules that motivate action by pointing to the desirability of their consequences).

An advertisement for an anti-perspirant might make claims that using this product will reduce or eliminate sweating; in other words, it presents a rule for action based on the three-term contingency: the product becomes the discriminative stimulus, the proposed response repertoire involves buying and using it, and the promised consequences are a lower rate of perspiration and less social embarrassment. Advertisements of this kind often feature augmentals, e.g., strongly motivating claims that the use of the brand in question will enhance the consumer's social life. If the product is an entirely new brand, of which consumers will not have heard, they cannot by definition have established responding appropriately to these contingencies. Given the competitive nature of the anti-perspirant market, there is no reason for thinking that this product will work any better than those currently in use and thus no special reason why the rule presented in the ad should be motivating. If, however, the message is presented by a famous sports personality, his or her presence may become an establishing operation, changing the words into a motivating message by turning the rule into an augmental. The presence of this antecedent stimulus means that the rule has a greater likelihood of being acted upon.

The four-term contingency also gives rise to the analysis of *equivalence classes* and *stimulus equivalence* (Sidman, 1994). Nonhumans have proved capable of learning complex relationships if they are appropriately reinforced, but generally do not innovate by initiating relationships they have not been explicitly taught (Sidman, 1994). By contrast, even young humans display the emergent behavior of relating B to C having been trained that A is related to B and that A is related to C (that is, their selection of the appropriate response has been reinforced.) This capacity for transitivity is one of three criteria used to establish *stimulus equivalence*, a phenomenon which appears peculiar to human animals. The other criteria are symmetry (matching A to A), and reflexivity (matching B to A having learned that A relates to B.) The implication is that these stimuli (A, B and C) belong to the same *stimulus class*, since they evoke the identical response: for instance, a picture of a car (A), the written word "car" (B), and the written word "auto" (C) are all likely to evoke the oral response "car." The role of stimulus equivalence in radical behaviorist interpretation is particularly interesting as it participates in relational frame theory. According to Sidman (1994) stimulus equivalence is a basic or primitive (that is, unanalyzable) occurrence, the result of the contingencies of survival encountered in the course of phylogenic evolution rather than something acquired by learning. In this it resembles the phenomena of reinforcement and discrimination: we are just "built that way" (Sidman, 1994, p. 389).

However, Relational Frame Theory (Hayes & Hayes, 1989; Hayes et al., 2001) seeks to extend the analysis inherent in the study of stimulus equivalence. It emphasizes that the functions of a stimulus can be transferred to other stimuli, indeed that such a function can be understood only in terms of its relationships with other stimuli. A stimulus may come to reinforce behavior depending on whether it is greater than, less than or equal to another stimulus that has already received the capacity to reinforce via a training procedure. Language can be understood in this way as a symbolic process in which the functions of one stimulus are transferred to another which comes to stand for it. Because of the ubiquity of such transfers, the problem of what Chomsky (1959) called the "poverty of the stimulus," the inability of a single stimulus to account for so rich a variety of behaviors as language use entails, may be overcome. Depending on the context, a pairing of stimuli can acquire numerous meanings and functions, and an immensely wide range of linguistic abilities could be acquired in the process. Relational responding of this kind is portrayed in relational frame theory as operant behavior, an overarching response class. Relational frames such as "equal to" or "fatter than" are defined in terms of three pro- perties which partially overlap with those Sidman employed to define stim- ulus equivalence. The three properties that are peculiar to relational frames are (1) mutual entailment, (2) combinatorial entailment, and (3) the trans- formation of functions. The third of these is particularly relevant here.[1]

A transformation of stimulus functions occurs when the function of one stimulus is transferred to another stimulus which is a co-member of a rela- tional network. If a consumer has enjoyed a play by a particular author and is told that she has written a sequel, the consumer is more likely to show marked approach behavior toward the new play: reading reviews, checking out when and where it is to be performed, going to see it, and so on. As the example shows, the transfer of function is highly situation- or context- specific, depending on how concepts such as "play," and "sequel" parti- cipate in various relational frames that have become part of the consumer's operant repertoire. As a result of this kind of analysis, radical behaviorists claim that their science is able to account for socalled cognitive phenom- ena and, in particular, for the acquisition and maintenance of language (Hayes et al., 2001; see also Horne & Lowe, 1996).

In the everyday discourse of folk psychology, replete as it is with inten- tional idioms, we should say that the likelihood that one would exhibit the approach behaviors in question depends on the consumer's interests and aspirations. It is here that the point of difference between the stances becomes apparent. The kind of behavior just described could also be con- ceived as intentional, as could that of other parties to the staging of the new play. Suppose the promoter who announces the drama sequel in an advertisement which is seen by a theater-goer who enjoyed the first play. Then the promoter *wants* the consumer to *believe* that the promoter *intends* to stage as engaging a play as the previous one. This entails third-order intentionality (Allen & Bekoff, 1997; Rosenberg, 1988; Shettleworth, 1998).

It does not preclude or supersede the contextual interpretation, but the very fact that the behavior can be described in intentional idioms legitimates for many the mentalistic analysis which it permits. One might agree with Quine (1960), of course, that the non-extensional expression involved in the use of intentional idioms rules them out of a scientific analysis, but this seems an arbitrary way of overcoming the challenge presented by intentionalistic locutions. Dennett's insistence that we take intentional phenomena seriously derives from the ordinary language philosophy that requires our treating everyday discourse as indicative of underlying realities. "Our evidence that 'there really are' Intentional phenomena", he writes, "coincides with our evidence that in our ordinary language we speak as if there were, and if a science of behavior could be successfully adumbrated without speaking as if there were these 'things', the insistence that there really are Intentional phenomena would take on a hollow ring" (Dennett, 1969, p. 33).[2] But, in order to determine whether the intentional is an inevitable element in social scientific explanation, it is necessary to delve a little deeper into its essential nature.

The nature of the intentional

Dennett, we have seen, claims moreover that ascribing beliefs, attitudes, and other mentalistic thought processes to individuals is a legitimate scientific endeavor as long as it results in more accurate predictions of overt behavior than would otherwise be possible. The suspicion that our understanding of consumer choice can benefit from a more complete conceptual framework arises from social cognitive psychology's use of the contextual stance as a prelude to its using the intentional stance. The reality of situational influence on behavior – evidenced by its prediction from environmental variables regardless of cognition – also plays a part. Should we, therefore, continue to use the cognitive terminology at all? Is a conceptual framework based on some form of behaviorism, possibly radical behaviorism, more appropriate? Is there a case for combining them? And, if so, how is this to be accomplished?

These questions invite a deeper analysis of the nature of intentionality and intentional explanation. The intentionality of which Dennett and other philosophers speak is that of the philosopher and merely indicates that these processes are "about" something. In Dennett's approach (and in this he follows philosophers such as Chisholm, 1957), the intentional is entirely a linguistic phenomenon. The acute distinction to be made, he argues, is not between the physical and the mental as entities but between the physical and the mental as different kinds of sentence. The distinction derives from Brentano's rediscovery of the work of the scholastic philosophers of the middle ages and his consequent division of sentences on the basis of their containing (or not) mental terms such as *believes*, *intends*, *hopes.* In this philosophical context, all terms such as these are collectively known as *intentions* since they conform to the definition of intentionality in terms of *aboutness* (Dennett, 1996).

In other words, "intentional," in the sense in which Dennett and other philosophers use it, refers to the fact that some verbal expressions are *about* something other than themselves. We do not simply think, we think *about* something; our thoughts have content. We do not just feel; we feel *that*... All other mental expressions also have content. We do not simply want: we want *to* have or to do something; we believe *that* something is the case, we intend *that* something, and so on. What is interesting about these expressions is that it is not possible to substitute equivalent propositions in sentences containing them. We can say, using an intentional idiom, "Adele believes that that is the fourth planet from the sun." But we are not justified in saying: "Adele believes that that planet is Mars." Adele may simply not know that the fourth planet from the sun is Mars. In the jargon of philosophy, these apparently alternative codesignatives are said to be referentially opaque meaning that it is not feasible to substitute one for the other.

Although it is not often explicitly acknowledged by social cognitive psychologists (more so by philosophers of mind and psychology), the intentional stance underlies modern cognitive science. Indeed, the intentionalism encapsulated in Dennett's intentional stance is fundamental to psychological explanations predicated upon information processing. Commenting on the relationship between cognitive accounts, such as Dennett's, which employ propositional attitudes, and those such as the social cognition models, Bechtel (1988, p. 75) challenges "those working on processing accounts to attend to the intentional perspective, in which the behavior of a cognitive system is characterized in terms of its beliefs and desires about the environment. It is this intentional perspective that identifies what aspects of the behavior of a system need to be explained by the processing account." The argument, central to Dennett's entire enterprise, that the intentional stance elucidates cognitive ethology (Dennett, 1983) rests, after all, on the claim that it identifies the mental qualities and capacities of organisms and species. The intentional strategy, by identifying the propositional attitudes necessary for the organism's adaptation to its environment, provides social cognitivism, the dominant paradigm within cognitive psychology (Ostrom, 1994), with a rationale for its research program.

Not all verbal statements contain intentional idioms such as *believe* and *desire*. The language widely associated with science, for instance, does not contain intentional content. Codesignatives here are easily substitutable and are said to be referentially transparent. So, it is perfectly feasible to say – in the *extensional* language in which science usually proceeds – "That planet is Mars" *and* "That [same] planet is the fourth from the sun." Science usually adopts one or other of two additional stances that Dennett defines, each of which relies totally on extensional expression. From the *physical* stance we make predictions on the basis of the physical state or conditions of the system; it depends on knowledge we have in the form of laws of nature. Predicting that when the bough breaks the baby will fall involves using the physical stance, as does forecasting that the atmospheric conditions that are about to bring rain will also bring on my lumbago. The *design* stance is used to "make predictions solely from knowledge or assumptions about the system's functional design, irrespective of the physical constitution or condition of the innards of the particular object" (Dennett, 1978, p. 4). The information provided by this stance leads us to define what an object will do, what its function must minimally be, regardless of its form. Dennett argues that even the best chess playing computers now defy prediction by either of these stances – a claim that is far from uncontested: see, for instance, Bennett and Hacker, 2003. For such predictions, only the intentional stance suffices. In using it, "...[O]ne assumes not only (1) that the machine will function as designed, but (2) that the design is optimal as well, that the computer will 'choose' the most rational move" (Dennett, 1978, p. 5). Note that rationality here means optimal design relative to goal, and that prediction is relative to the nature and extent of the information the system has about the field of endeavor. "One predicts behavior... by ascribing to the system *the possession of certain information* and supposing it to be *directed by certain goals*, and then by working out the most reasonable or appropriate action on the basis of these ascriptions and suppositions. It is a small step to calling the information possessed the computer's *beliefs*, its goals and subgoals its *desires*." (Dennett, 1978, p. 6)

As previous chapters have argued, there is a further route to understanding behavior, one that seeks the mainsprings of human action not within the individual but in his or her environment. It is what, in this chapter, we have called the contextual stance. Consideration of the research strategies that emanate from each of these stances clarifies further the distinction between them. The use of the intentional strategy is a deductive process: it proceeds from the *a priori* ascription of rationality to the system whose behavior is to be explained. The procedure is as follows (Dennett, 1987): (1) Treat the object whose behavior is to be predicted as a rational agent, (2) figure out what beliefs that agent should have given its place in the world and its purpose do the same for its desires, and (3) predict how it will act to further its goals in the light of its beliefs. The contextual strategy is inductive: it makes no *a priori* assumption about the rationality of the system that is to be predicted but assumes that its behavior is environmentally determined. The environment is the agent. Its procedure is as follows (Foxall, 1999a): (1) Treat the behavior to be predicted as environmentally contingent, (2) figure out the past contingencies that have shaped that behavior, and (3) predict how present and future contingencies will influence the continuity of that behavior. Steps 2 and 3 require figuring out the system's learning history, including the capacity of its behavior to be contingency-shaped and rule-governed. Step 3 predicts the susceptibility of future behavior to rules and contingencies.

The essence of behaviorism

In evaluating the exploitation of this methodological perspective in practice, it is essential to recall that modern behavior analysis, no longer confined to the rat and pigeon psychology that prevailed during the heyday of behaviorism, nowadays treats subject areas that lie at the very heart of cognitive psychology, among them thinking, decision making and language (see, for example, Hayes, et al., 2001; Horne & Lowe, 1996). Its proponents claim that radical behaviorism is sufficient to deal with these phenomena, indeed with all human and animal behavior, on its own terms. That means without resort to "mentalistic" concepts such as beliefs, attitudes and intentions which are the very stuff of modern information processing views of behavioral causation. Rather, its explanations are couched within the familiar elements of the "three-term contingency."

In a nutshell, the central fact in the delineation of radical behaviorism is its conceptual avoidance of propositional content (Foxall, 1999a, 2004a). This eschewal of the *intentional stance* sets it apart not only from cognitivism but from neo-behaviorisms such as those of Tolman and Hull. Indeed, the defining characteristic of radical behaviorism is not that it avoids mediating processes *per se* but that it accounts for behavior without recourse to propositional attitudes. Based on the *contextual stance*, it provides accounts of contingency-shaped, rule-governed, verbal and private behaviors which are entirely non-intentional. Its capacity to do so is independent of any prior assumption of intentionality: it is therefore methodologically autonomous (Smith, 1994).

Given that these perspectives have proved pretty equal in the prediction of consumers' attitudes and behavior, but that each has a unique approach to explanation, what should be their relationship? They may be forever incommensurable, remote competitors; or, they may be capable of a powerful integration. That proposed here is not the first.

The ascription of intentionality

For instance, two prominent philosophies of psychology, those proposed by Staats (e.g., 1975, 1996) and Bandura (e.g., 1986, 1997), which owe much respectively to the neo-behaviorisms of Hull and Tolman, incorporate both behaviorist and cognitive elements, but each ends in some form of reductionism. These approaches to the rapprochement of cognitivism and behaviorism, known respectively as psychological behaviorism and social learning theory, prove simply inadequate to the task of retaining the autonomous positions each has been accorded in our quest to this point. Each appears to offer an integrated framework by acknowledging both environmental and personal influences on behavior, but each proceeds merely to subordinate one source of explanation to the other. In Staats's approach, cognition consists in images learned through classical conditioning, while, in Bandura's, environmental influences, when they care considered in tandem with cognitive explanations, always act through the information processing of the individual. Neither approach is to be condemned on these grounds but nor does either retain the unique characteristics of each of the underlying systems.

An approach which avoids such reductionism is Dennett's proposal that mentalistic – or "intentional" – explanatory terms be used based on a logic derived from neuro-science: the ascription of intentional terms such as *desire* and *belief* is made in a way that is consistent with the theory of evolution by natural selection. Such terms do not provide further understanding at the level of the underlying science but a "heuristic overlay" which permits more accurate explanation and prediction of behavior Dennett, 1969, 1994).[3] The argument for the retention of intentional terms is linguistic. We use language differently in describing thinking and feeling from the way in which we describe physical events. The difference between intentional and extensional language points to something that is inevitable. Can we do without intentional language? is what we are asking when we suppose that we might be able to do without cognitive variables. How then are we to ascribe intentionality (in the philosopher's sense?) (Another way of saying this is: How are we to use intentional terminology in consumer research: what does it mean?) An important proviso for materialist philosophers is the necessity of using the terminology in a way that avoids dualism, i.e., that is consistent with a materialist view of the universe, mankind's place in it and which avoids resort to the ineffable when explaining human behavior. Dennett's proposal is a method of ascribing intentional content in a way that is consistent with the demands of the logic of evolution by natural selection.

The personal and the sub-personal

Fundamental to this approach is the distinction between two levels of explanation. The personal level, which is Dennett's focus here, and which he contrasts with the subpersonal level at which physiology operates, is that of "people and their sensations and activities" rather than that of "brains and events in the nervous system" (Dennett, 1969, p. 93; cf. Elton, 2003; Foxall, 2004c). The subpersonal level provides mechanistic explanations but these are not appropriate to the explanation of socalled mental entities such as pain. Pain is known by the one in pain at the personal level, the level at which he or she can say of it that "it hurts" but cannot analyze it further. It is a level at which, as Wittgenstein (e.g., 1953) and Ryle (e.g., 1949) recognized, inquiry comes to a swift end. While there is a good understanding of the neurological basis of pain, Dennett raises the question whether the presumed evolutionarily-appropriate afferent-efferent networks underlying this understanding are sufficient (they are certainly necessary) to account for the "phenomena of pain." This resolves itself into the question whether pain is an entity that exists in addition to the physical questions that constitute this network (Dennett, 1969, p. 91).

There are no events or processes in the brain that "exhibit the characteristics of the putative 'mental phenomena' of pain" that are apparent when we speak in everyday terms about pain or pains. Such verbalizations are non-mechanical, while brain events and processes are mechanical. It is unclear for instance how an individual distinguishes a sensation of pain from a nonpainful sensation. The only distinguishing feature of pain sensations is "painfulness" which, as we have said, is an unanalyzable quality that allows of only circular definition. But people can make such distinctions and do so at the personal level, where pains are discriminated, not the subpersonal. Neurons and brains have no sensation of pains and do not discriminate them. Pains, like other mental phenomena, do not refer: our speaking of them does not pick out *any thing*; pain is simply a personal-level phenomenon that has, nevertheless, some corresponding states, events or processes at the subpersonal, physiological level.[4]

It is not permissible simply to ascribe intentional content on the basis that it is required in order to "explain" observed behavior, a procedure that would clearly be circular in its reasoning.[5] Rather, according to the procedure that Dennett (1969) proposes, it is permissible to ascribe content on the basis of evolutionarily-consistent afferent and efferent physiological occurrences that occur at the sub-personal level. The first stage is straightforward: since intentional theory assumes that the structures and events they seek to explain are appropriate to their purpose (as they would be if they had emerged in the process of evolution), an important link in this ascription is provided by hypotheses drawn from the natural selection not only of species but of brains and the nervous system. A system which through evolution has the capacity to produce appropriate efferent responses to the afferent stimulation it encounters, clearly has the ability to discriminate among the repertoire of efferent responses it might conceivably make. Its ability so to discriminate and respond to the stimulus characteristics of its complex environment means that it must be "capable of interpreting its peripheral stimulation" to engender inner states or events that co-occur with the phenomena that arise in its perceptual field. In order for us to be justified in calling the process intelligent, something must be added to this afferent analysis: the capacity to associate the outcomes of the afferent analysis with structures on the efferent portion of the brain.

In order to detect the presence of a substance *as food*, for instance, an organism must have the capacity not only to detect the substance but thereafter to stop seeking and start eating; without this capacity to associate afferent stimulation and efferent response, the organism could not be said to have detected the presence of the substance *as* that of food. Dennett uses this point to criticize behaviorists for having no answer to the question how the organism selects the appropriate response. There is a need to invest the animal which has discriminated a stimulus with the capacity to "know" what its appropriate response should be. (In fact, behaviorists have ducked this problem by designating it a part of the physiologist's assignment and drawing the conclusion that the behavioral scientists need be concerned with it no longer. The conventional behaviorist wisdom with respect to the kind of cognitive ascription to which Dennett refers is that it amounts to no more than "premature physiology.")

Ascribing content

The content of a neural state, event or structure relies on its stimulation *and* the appropriate efferent effects to which it gives rise, and in order to delineate these it is necessary to transcend the extensional description of stimulus and response. It is necessary to relate the content to the environmental conditions as perceived by the organism's sense organs in order that it can be given reference to the real-world phenomena that produced the stimulation. And it is equally important to specify what the organism "does with" the event or state so produced in order to determine what that event or state "means to" the organism. An aversive stimulus has not only to be identified along with the neural changes it engenders to signify that it means danger to the animal; in addition, the animal has to respond appropriately to the stimulus, for example, by moving away. Failure on its part to do so would mean that we were not justified in ascribing such content to the physiological processes occurring as a result of the stimulation. If we are to designate the animal's activities as "intelligent decision making" then this behavioral link must be apparent. Only events in the brain that appear appropriately linked in this way can be ascribed content, described in intentional idioms.

How are the intentional ascription and the extensionally descriptions related then? This ascribed content is not an additional characteristic of the event, state or structure to which it is allocated, some intrinsic part of it discovered within it, as its extensionally-characterized features are discovered by the physiologist. It is a matter of *additional interpretation*. The features of neural systems, extensionally-characterized in terms of physiology or physics, are describable and predictable in those terms without intentional ascription which makes reference to meaning or content. Such a scientific story, consisting in an account of behavior confined to talk of the structure and functions of neural cells and so on, is entirely extensional in character.

But such an extensional story could not, according to Dennett, provide us with an understanding of *what the organism is doing*. Only an intentional account can accomplish this, "but it is not a story about features of the world *in addition to* features of the extensional story; it just describes what happens in a different way". By contrast, an extensional theory would be confined to the description/explanation of the *motions* of the organism rather than of its *actions*.

How cognitivism and behaviorism need each other

The case has not yet been made for the explicative inadequacy of radical behaviorism that makes a synthesis of the kind this chapter proposes either attractive or inevitable. Now that the nature of intentional explanation has become clearer, however, we can pause a moment and ask what the situation would be with respect to a science of behavior based on the findings of behavior analysis. Such a science would – and does – relate environmental events systematically to the rate at which a response is performed. As a predictive device, it is successful, especially in the relatively closed settings provided by operant laboratories and filed experiments such as token economies. As earlier chapters have shown, it is increasingly successful in making accurate predictions in the relatively open settings provided by retail and consumption environments; it is also apparent that it can interpret well-known fields of consumer behavior. But such an extensional science of consumer behavior cannot provide the kind of explanation that tells us what the individual is doing or, more importantly, why. For this, it relies on some kind of ascription of intentional content, and for three reasons. Without resorting to intentional ascription, behaviorism – especially in its interpretive mode – cannot account for behavior at the personal level of explanation, nor for behavioral continuity, nor can it show how its interpretations can be feasibly delimited in the face of the equifinality of behavioral consequences.

Three problems of behaviorist explanation

The first difficulty with radical behaviorist interpretation is that it has no means of dealing with events at the personal level, which are ordinarily described only in intentional terms. This stems from the irreducibility of intentional language to extensional and is illustrated by the following examples, related by (Juarrero, 1999) of people acting contrary to their desires, beliefs and expectations in ways that cannot be entirely captured in a purely extensional description. The first is of a couple who found themselves married because, with other Jews, they went through the motions of a Jewish wedding ceremony, they with all the other participants thinking that they were engaged in an elaborate joke, only to discover that they were in fact married. No-one intended this outcome; one member of the couple fully intended to marry someone else. Another example concerns the Muslim who was acting with his real life wife in a television production who followed the script and found himself divorced from both his screen wife and his actual spouse, unable to live with her on pain of being found guilty of adultery. This, again, was contrary to the expectations the entire cast and production team held about the situation (Juarrero, 1999, pp. 53 – 55). Extensional language cannot capture the meaning inherent in the intentional sentences employed: it is not that a radical behaviorist interpretation of these behaviors is impossible but that it can never capture the entire behavior in question without resorting to intentional idioms. (For extended discussions of this point, see Chisholm, 1957, Part II, and Taylor, 1964, Part Two).

The second difficulty is that, while the plausibility of an extensional radical behaviorist interpretation depends vitally upon its capacity to account for the continuity of behavior, it is unable to do so without recourse to intentional idioms. Why should behavior that has been followed by a particular ("reinforcing") stimulus in the presence of a setting stimulus be re-enacted when a similar setting is encountered? Why should a rule that describes certain physical or social contingencies be followed at some future date when those contingencies are encountered? Why can I tell you now what I ate for lunch yesterday? The whole explanatory significance of learning history is concerned with the continuity of behavior between settings and this implies some change in the organism, some means of recording the experience of previous behavior in such a way that it will be available next time similar settings are encountered. There is no other way in which the individual can recognize the potential offered by the current behavior setting in terms of the reinforcement and punishment signaled by the discriminative stimuli that compose it. (For evidence that verbal behavior, rules, private events, and physiology are unable to provide this continuity, see Foxall, 2004a, Chapter 7). Only by the ascription of beliefs, attitudes and intentions to the individual can this continuity be achieved. Consider, for example, the radical behaviorist interpretation of consumer decision-making described in Chapter 4 where it was argued that, in the absence of a specific learning history, the consumer would rely on other-rules to formulate what to do. Of course, the consumer may have some generalized learning history that relates to situations that share some of the stimulus characteristics of the current setting; she also must have a positive history of rule-following. However, the question still arises how she integrates this history and the content of the rules presented to her: presumably, although there will doubtless be neurological correlates of this behavior, the explanatory work of the processing involved at the personal level must be done by appropriately ascribed intentional content.

The third difficulty with radical behaviorist interpretation is the delineation of its accounts, the precise determination of the consequences of an action that are responsible for its continued enactment. There is simply no means by which the learning history of an adult human can be established even approximately unless he has lived all his life in the most closed of settings. Hence, there is no unequivocal means of deciding what pattern of reinforcement is responsible for the maintenance of an observed pattern of behavior which is amenable only to an interpretive account, i.e., the complex behavior that cannot be reduced to a laboratorial analogue. The import of this problem of equifinality is that if radical behaviorist interpretation is to mean anything other than vaguely-guided speculation, on a par with any other amateur psychology, its practitioners must find a means of bringing to it some greater measure of the scientific rigor characteristic of the experimental analysis of behavior. But if the ascription of terms of contingency to the contextually-enrapt behaviors we observe seems easy, it must also be admitted that some behaviors may be neither predictable nor amenable to plausible construal within the bounds of this philosophy of psychology or, for that matter, any other single framework of conceptualization and analysis. If learning histories for the purpose of accurate – as opposed to merely plausible – operant interpretations of complex behavior are not empirically available, we ought surely to be circumspect when proffering constructions of observed activity in terminology we know only from another sphere of inquiry. The only sure way to delimit radical behaviorist interpretations is to ascribe on the basis of some systematic treatment the intentional content that can be rationally attributed to the individuals whose behavior is under interpretation.

The need for behavior analysis

We are now on the threshold of a harmonious symbiosis of two systems of thought. For, if extensional behavioral science requires the heuristic overlay provided by an additional intentional interpretation, so Dennett's approach, as it stands, requires behavioral science. In fact, we need to consider at this point two reasons why Dennett's system itself requires elaboration before it can be applied to the problem at hand. (I shall mention them briefly here in order to establish the direction that a unified consumer psychology might take, and expand upon them when the form of that new approach has been clarified and we reach the next level of detail.)

The first difficulty is that of identifying "appropriate" afferent–efferent linkages. This is the practical problem of arguing from closely demarcated and localized physiological phenomena to mental constructs that are appropriate to the personal behavior of the organism. It has proved notoriously difficult for cognitive neuropsychology to isolate the neural substrates that can be convincingly correlated with closely-defined psychological or mental events other than those involved in basic sensory activity (Uttal, 2001). This raises the strong possibility that the kinds of neurocognitive inference

Dennett wants to make may be considerably more controversial in practice than he apparently assumes.

The second difficulty concerns the kind of psychology required to comprehend human social behavior including consumption. Dennett's blueprint for psychology is that of a physiological or neurocognitive science which argues from physiology to intentionality to behavior. But there is more to the prediction and explanation of the organism's behavior than the ascription of content according to reasoning that is consistent with natural selection. Dennett (1987) claims that the behavior of an organism can be predicted only by the ascription of content relating not only to its evolution but also to its current position, those of its circumstances which signal the rewards and punishments of following a particular course of action *primed by* the organism's learning history gained in similar circumstances. It requires, in other words, the ascription of content (again to arrive at the personal level) on the basis of the theories and findings of extensional science that deals with the effects of social and physical context on the ontogenetic development of the organism, including its acquisition of a behavioral repertoire. This science is behavior analysis in which the fundamental unit of analysis is the environment–behavior contingency. Content may be legitimately attributed to the findings of this science on the basis of the principle of "selection by consequences" (Skinner, 1981) which includes not only natural selection but the process in which a behavioral repertoire is acquired in the course of operant conditioning. Behavior analysis thus provides an extensional basis for the required super-personal level of analysis.

Hence, the appropriate vehicle for the present project is, in contrast to Dennett's neurophysiologically-based psychology, a social cognitive psychology that both derives from and explains the enacted behavior of the individual. There is a possibility of overcoming these problems while retaining the advances of Dennett's system by positing *three* levels of explanatory significance – the sub-personal, the personal, and the super-personal – and by relating them in a scheme that brings behavior–environment linkages into the process of ascribing content. The resultant mutual interdependency of cognitive and behavioral explanations suggest a novel resting place for the debate that stems from their underlying antithetical, genuinely incommensurable, approaches to the explanation of behavior: "intentional behaviorism."

9
Intentional Behaviorism

Intentional behaviorism is a philosophy of psychology that derives from and extends Dennett's (1969) attempted resolution of the problem of accommodating the mental within a materialist framework of conceptualization and analysis (Foxall, 2004a). It retains Dennett's argument that the mental inheres in the necessity of describing some behavioral phenomena in intentional language, the language of propositional attitudes, which exhibits referential opacity and which are not reducible to the referentially transparent sentences that are usually employed in the natural sciences. The ascription of intentionality is appropriate at the personal level of explanation. The problem arises of using intentional idioms in a disciplined way that both avoids the tendency to proliferate mentalistic language in order to account (usually in a circular fashion) for whatever behavior is observed, and links the use of intentional language with physical reality.

We have seen that Dennett proposes that intentional content be added, as a further level of heuristic interpretation and in an evolutionarily consistent manner, to the theories and findings of extensional neuroscience, itself a sub-personal level of explanation. Intentional behaviorism is founded upon the belief that the strategy that Dennett advocates for the addition of content to physiological research may be followed in the case of operant behavioral science in order to generate a psychology of the person that takes environment–behavior relationships into consideration. The question arises: on what basis is content to be ascribed to theories and findings at the super-personal level in order to arrive at a psychology of the person that takes environment–behavior relationships into consideration? In order to find an answer to this question it is necessary to go back to Dennett's strategy of ascribing content to the sub-personal theories and findings of neuroscience, and it may be worthwhile reviewing its central themes now. At the same time, if the analogy between a subpersonal–personal level linkage and a superpersonal–personal level linkage is to be confirmed, it should be possible to show how the reasoning that develops for adding content to the extensional findings on environment–behavior relationships applies to the resolution of the problems of personal level psychology, behavioral continuity, and delimitation.

Recall that Dennett's strategy is to assume that the sequence of events that are to be intentionally explained are appropriate from an evolutionary perspective; the next step is to propose structures that will account for these appropriate sequences. The environmental significance necessary for the brain to discriminate useful from unuseful neural events is extrinsic to those neural events, the brain's necessary distinctions cannot stem solely from extensional descriptions of extrinsic stimulation and past behavior. The brain has to be able to discriminate and store fortuitously appropriate structures. Some close analogy of natural selection must be sought to provide for the capacity of the brain to do this. The necessary capacity could itself be an outcome of the evolution of species. An intentional system has to be able to discriminate and respond to the environmental factors that impinge upon it and to do this it must be able to "interpret peripheral stimulation." This entails producing within itself not representations but states or events that "co-occur" with the conditions or objects in its perceptual field. Information abstracted from the environment will nevertheless remain non-intelligent unless something else it added to it; what must be added consists in the detection of afferent and efferent links.

The association between the subpersonal–personal and superpersonal–personal levels of analysis can in each case be characterized in Skinner's (1981) term "selection by consequences," by operant conditioning through appropriate behavior–environment links, just as in Dennett's scheme this role is performed by natural selection. Dennett's proposal is dependent on an evolutionary history that produced phylogenic consequences which determine the structure of the brain and its functioning, the neural afferent–efferent relationships to which content is added in the process of intentional ascription in order to delineate the personal level of analysis. Intentional behaviorism depends also, indirectly, on this process since it is through natural selection that the organism's capacity to change as a result of contact with environmental consequences presumably came about. However, in a more direct way, this link is the result of ontogenic consequences through which behavior is shaped in the course of a lifetime.[1] Again there is a need for intentional ascription, even if (or possibly, especially if) operant behavior instantiates physiological change within the organism. Donahoe et al. (1997, p. 196) state that "In a stable context, control by consequences (as opposed to antecedents) stands as a behavioral law, but we propose (at another level of analysis) that the effects of those consequences are implemented by changes in synaptic efficacies," an idea they trace back to Watson. But this argument merely addresses the subpersonal–personal levels of linkage that Dennett proposes, and has no direct bearing on the relationship between the superpersonal–personal levels which are proposed here as a function of ontogenic development.

The super-personal level

As Gunderson (1972) summarizes Dennett's argument, humans are not simply neurophysiological organisms but also persons who exhibit complex behaviors. Dennett's case for the ascription of content rests on the understanding that because some neural events, states and structures are about other things, that is, intentional, it is possible to ascribe content to them. The basis of the contextual stance is similarly that humans are persons as well as organisms whose behavior is determined by the contingencies of reinforcement. Moreover, some of the environmental elements on which our behavior is contingent are *about* things, i.e., are such that it makes sense to attribute content to them, to add an extra layer of interpretation that is relevant to the personal level. Whereas Dennett speaks of only two levels of analysis, however, we have distinguished three. We have noted his argument for a *personal* level, at which the individual as a whole discriminates such "mental" entities as pain, and a *subpersonal* level of brains and neurons, at which level the physiological correlates of pain behavior can be detected. "..[T]he terms in our mentalistic vocabulary are nonreferring. Rather like 'sakes' or 'miles', [or centers of gravity] mentalistic terms in appropriate contexts tell us something, but succeed in doing so without thereby referring to any entities any more than the words 'sakes' or 'miles' refer to sakes or miles" (Gunderson, 1972, p. 593). At the superpersonal level we turn to the environmental contingencies that shape and maintain responding in order to find an extensional basis for the ascription of such content. Several factors distinguish this level from both the personal and the subpersonal level based on neuroscience that Dennett identifies.

First, the superpersonal level cannot capture anything of the personal level including some essential components of what it is to be human, such as being able to discriminate pain. No matter how we grimace and howl and hold our painful heads, no matter what consequences these overt actions have by way of producing sympathy or medicine or exemptions from work from others, these superlevel events are entirely separate from the discrimination of pain. Second, the superpersonal level constitutes an extensional approach to the science of behavior, one which can explain much behavior at that level but which is incapable of dealing with the things that can only be discriminated at the personal level: pain, that it is time to go home, and other intentional matters. Only by the addition of a heuristic overlay of interpretation can these personal level matters be accommodated. Third, even though neither level reduces to the other, it is incumbent upon us to show how they are linked if we are to make legitimate and convincing interpretive ascriptions. The link, moreover, must be consistent with evolutionary reasoning.[2] There are several strands to be considered here. (a) The capacity for operant reinforcement is bestowed by natural selection. What Skinner (1981) calls "selection by consequences" is the analogy/homology that links the two processes at least at the level of phylogenic and ontogenic consistency. (b) In the case of linking the personal and subpersonal levels, the links must supervene (i.e., add appropriate interpretation) between the afferent and efferent processes of the brain. The corresponding processes in operant conditioning are stimuli and responses: the heuristic overlay of intentionality must link these in ways that an extensional account cannot. There are three such ways: (i) to elucidate the personal level, (ii) to demonstrate continuity of behavior from setting to setting, (iii) to solve problems of equifinality by delimiting operant interpretations that (attempt to) proceed solely at the extensional level. These considerations bring the interpretation within the scope of an evolutionarily consistent framework of conceptualization and analysis. How? The animal that is to be successful in negotiating its environment must be able to discriminate discriminative and other setting stimuli in order to act appropriately (with behavior that will be reinforced).

There is no more reason to believe that a physiological account will eventually be available to show how this occurs any more than there is a possibility that a physiological account will be able to demonstrate an individual's discrimination of pain. The discrimination of appropriate behavior occurs at the personal level. The recognition of appropriate inaugurating stimuli is a similar process. At the very least, the intentional mode of explanation cannot be abandoned until the physiological link is demonstrated: to trust in eventual physiology is superstitious in a way in which the ascription of intentionality is not if the latter strategy results in more effective predictions of behavior. Physicists who shun the concept of center of gravity in favor of a belief in some distant more physical explanation would be showing a similar level of superstition. That physicists are not embarrassed to include centers of gravity in their predictive work should be an example to the psychologist.

The inevitability of intentional explanation

It appears then that a first alternative to an extensional system of radical behaviorist interpretation, at the level of explanation rather than description or prescription, is the amalgamation of extensional operant behavioral science and Dennett's intentional stance by which content would be ascribed to its theories and findings in order to provide a basis for radical behaviorist interpretation. The reality of this may be closer to us than we have imagined. The point is sometimes made that radical behaviorists often incorporate the language of intentionality in their popular accounts of behavior, the implication being that the extensional operant account is thereby diminished, perhaps incapable of adequately describing the events that are the subject of the accounts in question. Skinner (e.g., 1974) argues that in order to communicate to a non-specialist audience, it is useful to adopt everyday language, as does the professional astronomer who speaks of the sun "rising" and "setting" when addressing children. Many behaviorists have taken this at face value and not concerned themselves further with the charge that the use of such language necessarily invokes a theoretical stance which is inevitable in the explanation of behavior. In view of the import of the current argument, this is a serious matter that behavior analysts ought not to ignore so easily.

The accounts in question are generally interpretations rather than reports of experimental work and this suggests that at least at the level of interpretation intentional language is inevitable not only to communicate to pedestrians but to express the ideas involved in accounting for complex activity in operant terms. "Thinking" and "feeling," the very stuff of private events, are almost always spoken of in intentional language: we do not just think, we think *about* or think *that*; we do not just feel, we feel *that*; and so on. We can treat such events as stimuli and responses that do not differ in kind from those that are publicly available – though this is to make an enormous ontological leap that can never be the subject of a scientific analysis – but to insist that thoughts and feelings are simply discriminative stimuli (or establishing operations, or other source of antecedent stimulation), associating them in the process with a physiological level of extensional analysis, is to leave out entirely the personal level to which Dennett draws attention, the level without which no psychological explanation can be complete.

The suggested project is not a call for the use of mediating events or the kinds of theory that Skinner repudiated. Even less is it a regurgitation of the sometimes argued notion that the intentional and contextual stances might be conjoined or a synthesis generated that would combine "the best of each." This is not possible in practice because their respective intentional and extensional bases are incommensurable (Foxall, 1999a). But the adding of content to an extensional account is not a synthesis or amalgamation. It is not adding anything to the findings and theories derived from the experimental analysis of behavior. Rather, it is the derivation of another level of interpretation in order to facilitate understanding and prediction by taking the personal level of experience into account.

In order to advance the debate between cognitivists and behaviorists, this account takes Dennett's thesis about the relationship between extensional science and intensional psychology at face value. To do this is to share, again for the sake of argument, (a) his assessment of the (literal) shortcomings of purely extensional science as a means to understand behavior: such science simply does not go far enough in the quest to explain all behavior, and (b) his judgment that the link between the two is found in the imperatives of evolution. Extensional behavioral science is, like physiology, an autonomous approach to knowledge in its own right but it is incapable of explaining all human behavior within its own theoretical and methodological purview, nor even that it can engender plausible interpretations (that is expressed in non-convoluted language) of all behavior. It is here that an important parallel with Dennett's analysis leads to a major conclusion: the extensional science of physiology is to Dennett's intensional physical psychology what an extensional behavioral science is to the intensional psychology of social cognition. In other words, the extensional science provides the evolutionary basis for understanding behavior biologically to which intensional cognitive interpretation verbally ascribes an a–ontological, initially non-empirical dimension which yields predictions of certain behaviors that the extensional approach of itself can neither explain nor predict. What is true for the center-piece of social cognitive psychology – attitude research – is likely to be generally the case.

The strategy of ascribing optimality (rationality) to systems in order to predict their behavior is a methodological simplification that involves further ascription – of posited entities such as beliefs, attitudes and intentions which, as we have seen, have the function of fine-tuning the prediction by linking it to the system's environmental history and behavior setting. The three stages of the intentional strategy make its dependency on the prior application of the contextual strategy clear. Dennett takes pains to avoid this conclusion. He denigrates (radical) behaviorism by, first, casting it as a simplistic S-R paradigm, and, secondly, by asserting, in the absence of any adduced evidence, that it has proved unsuccessful in predicting behavior. The first of these caricatures fails to engage with the operant behavior analysis of the last thirty years, especially the analysis of behavior at the molar level, the post-Skinnerian analysis of the verbal behavior of the listener, etc. The second ignores a mass of empirical evidence. Both overlook the possibility of radical behaviorist interpretation, that is, the use of the contextual stance to account for the behavior that is not amenable to an experimental analysis.

Intentional behaviorism differs from the other systems of explanation in its comprehensive inclusion of the various elements of the contextual and intentional stances, as well as in the understanding that the ascription of intentionality reinforces rather than detracts from the prior existence of an extensional behavioral science. It follows Dennett's subtle recognition that the addition of an intentional layer of interpretation does not discover anything new but tells another story about the theories and findings produced by operant psychology. The result is not just an extra story that maps on to the original in a one on one fashion: rather it extends the scope and relevance of the interpretation. Moreover, intentional behaviorism recognizes that social cognitive psychology proceeds in a similar manner, and raises the possibility that psychology will find a platform on which it might unite.

A comprehensive framework

Radical behaviorism's need to incorporate intentional content into its explanations, and social cognitivism's reliance on the contextual stance, lead to a broadening of Dennett's framework of explanation in which content is ascribed at the personal level on the basis not only of evolutionarily consistent physiology but also that of the findings and theories of extensional behavioral science. This augmented framework of intentional behaviorism is outlined in Figure 9.1.

The strategy that Dennett advocates for the addition of content to physiological research may be followed in the case of operant behavioral science in order to generate a psychology of the person that takes environment–behavior relationships into consideration. The philosophical argument for the ascription of content in order to construct a learning history derives from the manner in which Dennett's methodology is made operational. In Dennett's original sequence, content was ascribed at the personal level on the basis of evolutionary-consistent reasoning developed from the afferent–efferent relationships discovered in physiological research. In Figure 9.1, however, two bases of explanation are portrayed. The first, on the right of the figure, is Dennett's and runs from the neural substrate of

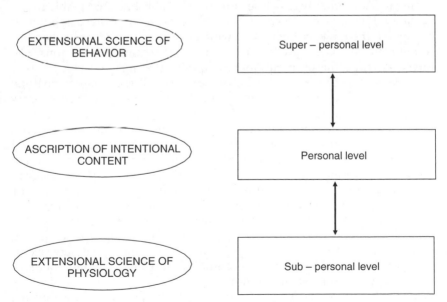

Figure 9.1   Super-personal, Personal, and Sub-personal Levels of Analysis

cognitive activity to the personal level of intentional ascription. The second, on the left of the figure, incorporates the idea of a super-personal level of analysis based on the deconstruction of operant behavior as a basis for the ascription of content at the personal level.

Dennett's account begins, we have seen, with the neural event – specifically its role in an afferent–efferent process – and ascribes content on the basis of the resulting evolutionarily consistent logic. In other words, the direction of ascription is from neurology to intentionality, from the sub-personal level to the personal level of explanation: the identification at the sub-personal level of neurophysiological afferent–efferent linkages that have evolved by natural selection justifies the attribution at the personal level of consistent intentional content. Examination of the linkages between the organism's reception of environmental stimuli relating to a predator and its emission of a response that ensures its survival (such as a fight or flight reaction), for instance, justifies the attribution to the individual of intentional propositions to the effect that it *desires* to maintain whatever physical means are necessary to maximize its biological fitness, that it *believes* that fighting or fleeing, as the case may be, will ensure this, and that it acts in accordance with this rationale. Despite the considerable ingenuity inherent in Dennett's methodology, however, and the obvious debt that the approach taken here owes him, his unique means of solving the problem of what intentional idioms can be legitimately ascribed to individual organisms in order to predict and explain their behavior has three drawbacks for a general theory of behavior.

The first is its unduly circuitous means of establishing acceptable intentionality. It is sufficient to know that an organism has evolved and how it behaves in the presence of enemies which threaten it, or of food when it is hungry, to be able to predict its behavior; the same observations lead directly to the kinds of intentional ascriptions that may be made in order to explain the behavior of the organism given that it is a product of natural selection. The detour into the sub-personal level of analysis is unnecessary in order to achieve either of these goals.

The second is the sheer impracticability of the procedure he advocates if it is to reach into the neurophysiology of behavior. Evidence of neural substrates of cognition (e.g., from fMRI scans) can show areas of the brain associated with mental activity such as thinking and emoting. However, they cannot reveal the content of these mental events. This can be done only by probing the environment–behavior superstrates of cognition (e.g., by using the contextual stance). Therefore, Dennett's strategy in *Content and Consciousness* requires the incorporation of the super-personal level of explanation through which confirmation that appropriate content is being ascribed. This requirement is doubtless implicit in his description of his strategy but, if his logical argument is to be completed, it needs to be made explicit in terms of an extensional behavioral science based on the contextual stance.[3]

The third underlines this requirement: it is the logical necessity of using observed environment–behavior linkages rather than physiology as a means of establishing the basis for intentional ascription. Bennett and Hacker (2003) make a strong case that psychological predicates are ascribed to an organism based on its behavior. Pain-ascription is warranted by a person's pain-behavior. We answer the question "How did you know he was in pain?" by reference to such behavior. Similarly we ascribe beliefs to an individual whose verbal behavior is consonant with this conclusion.[4] Moreover, behavioral indices are criterion variables that determine whether intentionality can be ascribed: sub-personal physiological findings are merely correlations of felt emotions or the behaviors that express them. While Dennett's quest appears to be for a sub-personal cognitive psychology which can be related at each point to neurophysiology in order to maintain the materialist nature of the intentional idioms (whether *abstracta* or *illata*) he finds it necessary to ascribe, ours as consumer researchers is primarily for a socio-cognitive psychology for which behavioral science performs this anchoring role.[5]

Intentional consumer choice in context

This brings us to the procedure for explaining consumer behavior in terms of intentional behaviorism. The extensional science developed by behavior analysts could equally form the basis of a social behavioral psychology through the ascription to its findings and theories of propositional content, much as Dennett proposes a physiological psychology in which content is ascribed to the findings and theories of neuroscience. Dennett's poor view of behaviorism leads him not to consider this possibility, but it is in fact both feasible and currently practiced – by social cognitive psychologists. There is already an evolutionarily consistent logic by which the ascription of intentional content to the theories and findings of behavioral science could take place: the view that "selection by consequences" is an overarching principle of causation that includes both the natural selection by which phylogenetic preservation has occurred, and the operant conditioning in which learned characteristics of behavior are preserved during the ontogeny of the individual organism (Skinner, 1981).[6]

The contextual stance leads to the contextual strategy which proceeds as follows: first, treat the behavior to be predicted as environmentally determined; second, figure out the past contingencies that have shaped that behavior; third, predict how present and future contingencies will influence the continuity of that behavior. Steps 2 and 3 require figuring out the system's learning history, including the capacity of its behavior to be contingency-shaped and rule-governed. Step 3 predicts the susceptibility of future enactments of the behavior to rules and contingencies, and thereby requires an assessment of the motivating or inhibiting nature of the behavior setting. In broad outline, the intentional behaviorism approach relies on a refinement of this: first, the assumption of rationality, then the use of the contextual strategy, followed by the use of the intentional strategy to attribute intentional content to the findings of using the contextual strategy (Figure 9.2). But the procedure can be refined through consideration of the sources of extensional knowledge that can reasonably be incorporated into the process of ascribing intentionality. For, while Figure 9.2 accords equality to the two sources of ascribed intentionality, the afferent–efferent linkages at the physiological level and the environment-behavior linkages at the behavioral, there is reason to believe that the latter is conceptually more important. The search for the basis of a social cognitive psychology of consumer choice requires further elaboration.

The role of cognitive explanation

At first glance, the intentional behaviorist strategy of attributing mental properties on the basis of behavior may appear no more than a PC approach in which strength of behavior is redescribed as strength of attitude. Intentional behaviorism is different, however, in that it is not a redescription of behavior but a means of explaining behavior: accounting for its continuity, making personal level attributions that are not only useful for scientific reasons but for legal and moral attributions. The point about these mental ascriptions in intentional behaviorism is that they are linked into a model or theory of mental causation (an attitude model for instance) that explains how the mental construct is related to antecedents and previous behavior.

Indeed, unless we ascribe at the personal level we cannot explain why information affects attitudes in the absence of direct experience: to be sure,

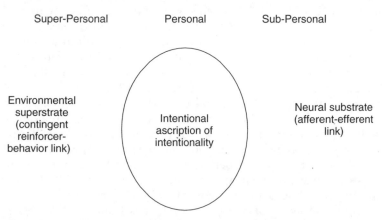

Figure 9.2   Intentional Behaviorism

there will be some general experience that allows the consumer to interpret the message (again, some kind of generalized learning history) but the only way to *explain* how a consumer interprets that message in light of that history requires an attribution at a level other than that of sub-personal or super-personal levels. These levels, the levels of extensional science, provide accounts of the mechanisms of information reception and interpretation but not of the non-mechanistic procedures by which this interpretation takes place.

This argument does not commit us ontologically to a cognitive explanation of behavior. It is the argument that the explanation of behavior cannot avoid intentional idioms, not the argument that behavior is cognitively caused (or, perhaps more accurately, explicable in cognitive terms.) This question now requires attention, not least for the practical problems inherent in the current position. It raises, for instance, an interesting problem of the technology of behavioral change in a context that is central to marketing thought and management: can behavior be modified by the prior modification of beliefs and desires, or only by the modification of the contingencies that shape and maintain it? If intentional behaviorism refuses to assign a causal capacity to the mental events which it nevertheless incorporates into its explanations, the conclusion must be that that behavior cannot be changed by prior attitude change: only changes in the contingencies can influence behavior. However, as we have seen, it remains feasible to argue that prior changes in verbal rules whether these take the form of other-rules or self-rules influence behavior. Were these constructs to be actively employed by radical behaviorists in interpretations of complex behavior – something that in practice is rare – it would be difficult to demonstrate convincingly that the idea of such rules can avoid intentional content: rules are verbal formulations that are *about* behavior and the contingencies that shape and maintain it. Attributing actively causal rather than merely passively explanatory properties to *attitude* seems inevitable. But how is intentional behaviorism to incorporate cognitive explanation? Consideration of Dennett's (1981) tripartite division of intentional psychology, provides a better understanding of both the necessity of cognitive explanation in consumer research and the nature of that cognitive account.

Dennett argues that the first kind of intentional psychology, folk psychology, provides a source of the other two: "intentional systems theory" and "sub-personal cognitive psychology." Folk psychology provides a very non-specific and unhelpful causal theory of behavior but a more systematic and useful predictive tool requires refinement. The distinction between logical constructs or *abstracta* and causally interacting *illata* provides a key. While the beliefs and desires of abstract and instrumental folk psychology are abstracta, the interactive theoretical constructs of sub-personal cognitive psychology are illata. Each of the two additional psychologies Dennett proposes rests integrally on one or other.

Intentional systems theory draws upon the notions of belief and desire but provides them with a more technical meaning than they receive in folk psychology. It is a whole-person psychology, dealing with "...the prediction and explanation from belief–desire profiles of the actions of whole systems... The *subject* of all the intentional attributions is the whole system (the person, the animal, or even the corporation or nation [see Dennett 1976] rather than any of its parts..." (Dennett, 1987, p. 58). Intentional systems theory is a performance theory in that it specifies the functional requirements of the system without going on to speculate as to what form they might take. The necessity of this general level theory is that of providing an account of intelligence, meaning, reference, or representation. Intentional systems theory is blind to the internal structure of the system. The capacity of abstracta to interrelate, predict and partly explain behavior itself suggests some underlying mechanism to which intentional systems theory does not on principle address itself. Any intentional system of interest would surely have a complex internal structure and chances are this will be found to resemble closely the instrumental intentional interpretation. Finally, *sub-personal cognitive psychology* is tasked with explaining the brain as a syntactic engine (as opposed to the task of intentional systems theory which is to explain it as a semantic engine).

Where does this leave the two main perspectives on consumer behavior with which we have been concerned – cognitive psychology and radical behaviorism? This chapter has attempted to meld them into a single overall framework of conceptualization and analysis but an important aspect of each remains to be evaluated. In the case of cognitive psychology, specifically the theories of social cognition in which attitude theory and research are currently embedded, this revolves around the capacity of this paradigm in itself to be part of a deeper cognitive–physiological synthesis; in the case of radical behaviorism, it revolves around the capacity of this paradigm to provide an extension to Dennett's framework beyond what he implicitly assumes with regard to environment–behavior linkages. Dennett's proposal with respect to the three kinds of intentional psychology, which was briefly described above, provides a useful context within which, by way of conclusion, these issues and that of future research in this avenue of consumer research can be addressed.

Dennett draws a distinction between theories that treat phenomena at an everyday, "folk," or definitional terms (a green parakeet that has a blue ancestor may produce some blue offspring even when mated with another green bird) and more reductive theories of the same phenomena (post-Mendelian genetics). Turning from biology to psychology, therefore, the questions that arise initially are "conceptual" (such as, What do all believers-in-*p* have in common?), and go on to explore the possibility that the theory that answers this question might be reduced to another level of theorizing, "neurophysiology most likely." (Note in passing that this predisposes one to seek the deeper level of theory and explanation in physiology rather than, say, in behavior science.) "The issue, then, is *what kind* of theoretical bonds can we expect – or ought we to hope – to find uniting psychological claims about beliefs, desires, and so forth with the claims of neurophysiologists and other physical scientists?" (pp. 45–6). Dennett proposes that the affinity between terms such as "offspring" and "beliefs" or "desires" – stemming from the non-technical or "folk" nature of each – means that the natural starting point for this reductive psychological theory is folk psychology.

Folk psychology

Folk psychology is what people use daily to explain and predict the behavior of others by means of the attribution to them of appropriate desires and beliefs. It is often surprisingly successful but often fails because we cannot predict all of others' behavior just by attributing desires and beliefs, etc. It is also a reasoned approach to the attribution of intentions, "a rationalistic calculus of interpretation and prediction – an idealizing, abstract, instrumentalistic interpretation method that has evolved because it works and works because we have evolved. We approach each other as *intentional systems* (Dennett, 1971), that is, as entities whose behavior can be predicted by the method of attributing beliefs, desires, and rational acumen..." (Dennett, 1987, pp. 48–9). Beliefs and desires are those the system *ought* to have... the system behaves rationally given those beliefs and desires, where "ought to have" means "would have if it were *ideally* ensconced in its environmental niche" (p. 49). The agent learns from experience (or fails to learn due to lack of experience): "so its beliefs are ... relative to its biography" (p. 49). "Folk psychology is abstract in that the beliefs and desires it attributes are not – or need not be – presumed to be intervening distinguishable states of an internal behavior-causing system" (p. 52). A belief for instance has a reality closer to that of a center of gravity or a parallelogram of forces rather than that of a system of cogs and wheels. Nevertheless, Dennett insists, "people really do have beliefs and desires just as they really have centers of gravity and the earth has an Equator" (p. 53).

Dennett now returns to the distinction between "two sorts of referents for theoretical terms: *illata* – posited theoretical entities – and *abstracta* – calculation-bound entities or logical constructs" (p. 53). Folk psychology ideally maintains this distinction by confining its pronouncements to the calculations that enable it to make predictions, but *in practice* it often falls short of this ideal by peering into the system it predicts, thereby admitting notions of the underlying structural entities that are held to be responsible for the causal relations imagined to link intentional factors like beliefs and desires. Folk psychology is in another way a source of confusion: it is committed to an underlying causal explanation but it fails to specify this in a useful way; its only value lies in its sometime predictive successes in its own terms: beliefs and desires. While ordinary folk psychology embeds the notions of illata and abstracta, it fails to provide good examples of these, partly because it is always in danger of confusing the two and thus losing the usefulness of both.

Dennett proposes to remove the confusion by defining two further kinds of intentional theory, each of which preserves the distinctive value of one or other of these concepts (1) a "strictly abstract, idealizing, holistic, instrumentalistic–pure intentional system theory," and (2) "a concrete, microtheoretical science of the actual realization of those intentional systems." (p. 57) Having done this, it should be possible to see whether reduction of any sort is feasible.

Intentional systems theory

The first, intentional systems theory, is "abstract, normative, and couched in intentional language" (p. 58) but differs from folk psychology in providing the terms "belief" and "desire" with technical meanings. It is based at the personal level of explanation. (The attitude models considered in Chapter 3 appear to fit here on this criterion. They fit also, as do decision theory and game theory which Dennett places in this category, on account of the instrumentalist, reasoned approach they take.)

Intentional systems theory is concerned with the way in which new beliefs and desires are generated through the interaction of old beliefs and desires, environmental elements, and the behavior of the system. This may give rise to the illusion of internal processing occurring naturalistically within the system but "in fact the processing is all in the manipulation of the theory and consists in updating the intentional characterization of the whole system according to the rules of attribution" (p. 58). (As Dennett points out, a parallelogram of forces would be erroneously construed by a naïve student who thought it referred to a mechanical linkage of rods and levers rather than being a graphic imagining of the effects of a pattern of forces.)

To say that intentional systems theory is a competence theory is to note that it is concerned to specify the performance required of believers, leaving the task of determining how these requirements are implemented to performance theories. This demarcation is its most useful characteristic, Dennett claims. In evolutionary theory it is the capacity of the system to acquire appropriate beliefs and desires via natural selection that is crucial to its survival: its realization, perhaps as a result of mutation, is secondary. This, Dennett argues, makes reduction of intentional systems theory to the underlying internal systemic characteristics unnecessary and undesirable.[7]

Sub-personal cognitive psychology

Useful as a competence theory is, there has to be some underlying internal structure that accounts for the capacity of the various *abstracta* that are the components of intentional systems theory to predict systemic behavior at the personal level so well. Discovering this structure and its workings is the task of the third kind of intentional psychology: sub-personal cognitive psychology, the task of which consists in "[d]iscovering the constraints on design and implementation variation, and demonstrating how particular species and individuals in fact succeed in realizing intentional systems" (p. 60).

The task of the brain, according to intentional systems theory and evolutionary biology is *semantic*: it must decipher what its stimulus inputs mean and then respond with appropriate behavior. But in fact to the physiologist the brain is no more than a *syntactic* engine: it "discriminate[s] its inputs by their structural, temporal, and physical features and let[s] its entirely mechanical activities be governed by these 'syntactic' features of its inputs" (p. 61). Hence "it is the task of sub-personal cognitive psychology to propose and test models ... of pattern recognition or stimulus generalization, concept learning, expectation, learning, goal-directed behavior, problem-solving – that not only produce a simulacrum of genuine content-sensitivity, but that do this in ways demonstrably like the way people's brains do it, exhibiting the same powers and the same vulnerabilities to deception, overload and confusion. It is here that we will find our good theoretical entities, our useful *illata*, and while some of them may well resemble the familiar entities of folk psychology – beliefs, desires, judgments, decisions – many will certainly not... The only similarity we can be sure of discovering in the *illata* of sub-personal cognitive psychology is the intentionality of their labels (see *Brainstorms* [Dennett, 1978], pp. 23–38). They will be characterized as events with content, bearing information, signaling this and ordering that" (p. 63).

"In order to give the *illata* these labels, in order to maintain any intentional interpretation of their operation at all, the theorist must always keep glancing outside the system, to see what normally produces the configuration he is describing, what effects the system's responses normally have on the environment, and what benefit normally accrues to the whole system from this activity... The alternative of ignoring the external world and its relations to the internal machinery... is not really psychology at all, but just at best abstract neurophysiology – pure internal syntax with no hope of a semantic interpretation. Psychology 'reduced' to neurophysiology in this fashion would not be psychology, for it would not be able to provide an explanation of the regularities it is psychology's particular job to explain: the reliability with which 'intelligent' organisms can cope with their environments and thus prolong their lives. Psychology can, and should, work toward an account of the physiological foundations of psychological processes, not by eliminating psychological or intentional characterizations of those processes, but by exhibiting how the brain implements the intentionally characterized performance specifications of sub-personal theories" (p. 64).[8]

Toward a super–personal cognitive psychology

The indications are that the variables employed in the attitude models we have considered (especially in Chapters 3, 4 and 6) are closer to the *abstracta* of intentional systems theory rather than the *illata* of sub-personal cognitive psychology.[9] The central concern of sub-personal cognitive psychology of anchoring *abstracta* within the explanatory basis of an extensional sub-personal science (neurophysiology), thereby translating them into *illata*, does not appear to have been accomplished by these models, whose variables remain at the personal level of analysis. While the attitude models are themselves based upon and form a part of extensional cognitive science, their theorizing is still at the level of intentional systems theory. It is evident, however, from the transformation in attitude research over the last thirty years that these variables can be construed as exhibit a reaching out toward behavioral science in order both to provide the refined measures required for the more accurate prediction of behavior and to offer a more elaborate theoretical basis for attitudinal–behavioral research. "Can be construed as" because these have not been explicit objectives of attitude researchers; nor can the faintest suggestion be made that these scientists have – something they would repudiate vociferously – embraced radical behaviorism or any other fully extensional behavioral science. Nevertheless, explicit recognition that behavioral science can provide an extensional basis of consumer research would provide the anchoring of the *abstracta* of current theory in order to produce a convincing basis for the ascription of content.

Figure 9.2 therefore serves as a rough and ready blueprint for a super-personal cognitive psychology, but on the understanding that the sub-personal–personal linkage is likely to be (a) de-emphasized on account of the impracticability of gaining empirical access to it, and because its logical place in an explanatory system is as a correlative rather than criterion variable, and thus (b) often superseded in practice in favor of the more amenable super-personal–personal linkage.

A methodologically pluralistic program for the development of the super-personal cognitive psychology that is at the heart of intentional behaviorism contains at least three research perspectives: the search for interactions between situational influences and (verbal and non-verbal) behaviors, the social cognitive approach to attitudinal–behavioral relationships, and an interpretive account of the optimal behavior of a rational system.

The behavioral perspective is the direct and extensional avenue of investigation pursued in Chapters 6 and 7 in which verbal and non-verbal behaviors are predicted on the basis of their situational determinants. As long as prediction is the singular goal of research in this tradition, the contextual stance, therefore, suffices, and radical behaviorists would claim that the identification of the environmental influences that permit the prediction and control of behavior constitutes a means of explanation. However, for reasons briefly described in this chapter, such "explanation" is deficient insofar as it has no convincing means of accounting for the continuity of behavior across situations. In order to achieve an explanation of behavior, its descriptive approach to environment–behavior relationships needs to be supplemented by an intentional account at the personal level of explanation. Figure 9.3 illustrates the domain of this strategy of super-personal cognitive psychology.

The relationship between behavior and the ascription of intentionality in Figure 9.3 requires explication. The emotions of pleasure, arousal and dominance are attributed at the personal level not simply on the basis of the consumer's verbal claim that he or she has them (or because of any other verbal or nonverbal evidence they give). They are attributed based on the situational context in which these behaviors arise: i.e., the identification of a contingency category which is plausibly related to the continued generation of such behavior over time. It is a matter of locating the super-personal–personal link that makes the behavior an operant response, i.e., one that can be systematically related to the environmental variables that control it. This is not a matter of precise one-on-one mapping: there is an element of interpretation, albeit one based on the feasibility of ascribing intentionality only in accordance with the principle of selection by consequences; hence the insistence on the behavior being operant in nature. This approach has been shown accurate at the level of aggregate consumer behavior – the same level of analysis employed in multi-attribute and other attitude modeling – though at the level of the individual consumer it may require some qualitative input in order to ascertain the influence of the person's learning history.

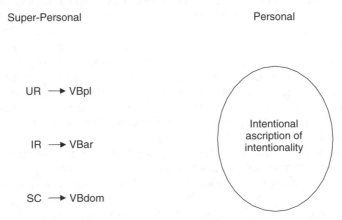

Super-Personal   Personal

UR ⟶ VBpl

IR ⟶ VBar   Intentional ascription of intentionality

SC ⟶ VBdom

Figure 9.3 Super-personal Cognitive Psychology

The judgment that PAD responses, for instance, belong to a different interpretational system from that of the underlying extensional research within which they are measured, arises from the inevitability of their being expressed in intentional language. The consumer takes pleasure *in*, is aroused *by*, and has dominion *over*, and each of the predicates which follow these prepositions exhibits intentional opacity. In using such language, we are moving beyond the extensional description of behavior in terms that exhibit transparency and adding what Dennett calls a heuristic overlay of interpretation. From an epistemological point of view, it is essential to do this in order to account for the continuity of the behavior over time, to give an account of behavior at the personal level, and to delimit the scope of the interpretation based on the findings of extensional behavioral science alone. The attribution of beliefs, attitudes, intentions and affective responses to the consumer based on, for instance, their verbal responses to the PAD scales or the questionnaires employed in attitude research generally provide a means of accounting for the continuity of behavior over a range of situations. The usual behavior analytical way of accounting for such continuity on the assumption that the discriminative stimuli encountered in subsequent situations must be similar in their behavioral effect to those that composed the situation in which the behavior was learned owes more to faith than to science. It is often not possible to indicate what elements of such stimuli are common since the persistence of behavior (which behavior analysts both describe and "explain" in terms of "stimulus and response generalization") is observed over settings which have no obvious similarities except that they generate similar patterns of behavior. Something more than the behavior analysts' convoluted analysis of memory in stimulus–response terms (Palmer, 1991; see also Donahoe & Palmer, 1994) is needed. The continuity of behavior at the personal level cannot be reduced to the operation of either subpersonal or super-personal associations of stimuli and responses, though there will undoubtedly be correlations among the variables involved. And the delimitation of environment–behavior links that can enter the analysis to those which give rise to intentional interpretations that are consistent with the selection of operant behavior by its consequences ensures that possible external contingencies are not multiplied unnecessarily in order to provide causal links that become increasingly implausible in direct proportion to the remoteness of the consequences of behavior from its enactment.[10]

The determination of the full range of attitudinal reactions that are candidates for ascription at this point is an empirical matter. Figure 8.3 illustrates the paradigm by incorporating the PAD variables which, based on the argument in Chapter 6 contend strongly to be considered the range of emotions required for this kind of analysis. But should they prove inadequate (see, for example, Bagozzi, et al., 1999), while the empirical tenor of the research program may change there is no reason to question the theoretical basis upon which it proceeds.[11]

The social cognitive perspective is essentially that discussed and evaluated in Chapters 3 and 4 and the beginning of Chapter 5. The logical sequence by which it proceeds extends from an initial intentional position (since the objective is to predict and explain behavior in cognitive terms), followed by an extensional scientific phase in which respondents' verbal behavior is sampled in a manner that takes the situational influences that shape it into consideration (and which entails a veiled but real application of the contextual stance), followed in turn by a further intentionalistic phase in which the verbal behavior of the respondents is interpreted in terms of the underlying desires and beliefs of the respondents.

This approach is essential to the overall research program of intentional consumer behaviorism insofar as it often represents the sole means of access to the individual consumer's learning history, a vital component of the BPM which has hitherto not been directly investigated. The PAD research described in Chapter 6 highlights, however, the influence of this personal variable on verbal (and presumably nonverbal) consumer behaviors. The variation around each of the mean results for each of the cognitive/affective and behavioral variables described in that chapter seems to be indicative of the influences on choice stemming from the various learning histories of the respondents, and this is borne out by consideration of the range of responses provided to the PAD questionnaire. For instance, some respondents reported higher than expected levels of pleasure for "inescapable entertainment" (CC4), "popular entertainment" (CC3), and "mandatory consumption" (CC8). If the pleasure means for the entire sample of consumers prove higher than expected, this may be put down to the fact that all consumption is likely to elicit claims of pleasantness and utility to a higher degree than other activities. But the standard deviations for these means indicate still across–subjects differences in the extent to which these activities were experienced as pleasant; and we are concerned here not with the absolute mean levels of responses but with this "anomaly" that some consumers, but not others, reported higher than expected levels of pleasure for these consumption activities. It seems likely that these differences reflect variations in learning history: consumers will have had quite different reactions to filling in the forms for a passport (CC8), for instance, some concentrating on the immediate boredom of the required bureaucracy, while others dwell on the exotic locations they will be able to visit once the desired document arrives. Similarly, watching a movie during a long-haul airplane flight (CC4), or attending a party (CC3), can be expected to evoke memories of enormous pleasure or stark dread depending on a host of personal factors including previous experience of this or similar consumption situations.

But this interpretation depends on a generalization from the experience and observation of the analyst, useful as far as it goes but crying out for a

more inter-subjective means of confirmation. The systematic verbal probing that the multi-attribute models make possible does not provide a
completely reliable means of accessing learning history but it is, first, an
improvement on the foregoing general interpretation and, second, a usual
social scientific way of understanding how the consequences of an individual's past behavior may influence his or her current and soon-to-be
enacted choices, when direct observation is precluded.

These techniques can be employed in this quest in two ways. At the level
of aggregated consumer responses, they identify the components of salient
learning histories for the consumer population under investigation while,
in the process of reconstructing a particular consumers' learning history,
they permit consumers the option of employing what Dennett refers to as
"heterophenomenology," which entails involves applying the intentional
stance to people's verbal behavior, treating it as a text to be interpreted in
terms of their beliefs and desires. Much as one examines the text of a character in a novel in terms of what he or she says, what they do and what
others say of them, plus background information about the author and his
or her other writings, so one can produce an inter-subjective account of the
text provided by another person. The heterophenomenology of the person
consists in an account of *"what it is like to be* that subject – in the subject's
own terms, given the best interpretation we can muster" (Dennett, 1991b,
p. 98). The resulting account is, like a scientific hypothesis, subject to
testing in the face of the evidence, and hence corrigible. In the case of
adult consumers, whose "objective" learning histories are lost forever, this
may be the sole means of reconstructing the consumption history on
which interpretation within the scope of intentional behaviorism relies.

The interpretive perspective is an indirect approach to understanding
the behavior of complex systems based on the a priori arguments used
by Dennett in his exposition of the intentional stance, and similarly
those used in that of the contextual stance. Where experimental analysis is
feasible, it belongs to either the cognitive or the behavioral perspective, as
does the survey research on which a hypothetico-deductive methodology
depends. However, there are complex areas of human behavior where it is
impossible to isolate the contingencies that control and permit the prediction of behavior with the precision of the laboratory. To some extent,
results can be extrapolated from the laboratory or the survey to the population as a whole or to individuals typical of it. But there are aspects of the
individual's learning history arrived at in this way that are unlikely to be
accurately assessed given the limitations of the underlying research techniques. There are aspects of susceptibility to the stimuli that compose the
behavior setting that can only be guessed at. Some a priori, albeit still
empirical, means of arriving at the required interpretation is required in the
absence of a research technique that can directly access the influence of
learning history and behavior setting on current choice.

There is need for a third strategy of interpretation, in addition to the intentional and the contextual strategies, that can operationalize the super-personal cognitive psychology framework when determinative knowledge of the contingencies of reinforcement is not available. The manner in which scientists investigate the functions of the nervous system provides a useful starting point. In contradistinction to Dennett's sub-personal-to-personal level reasoning, the procedure followed by neurophilosophy (Churchland, 1986, 2002) where the quest is for the physical substrate of behavior (including the expression of emotion which is intentional). Take, for instance, the investigation of binocular rivalry. If two different and separate visual images are presented so that each can be seen by only one eye, they do not meld into a single image but compete for visual awareness. This phenomenon, in which each eye receives different inputs, is known as *binocular rivalry*. The resulting phenomenon is *bistable perception* in which, after a short period of confusion, the brain comes to receive the stimuli in an alternating sequence: each stimulus is perceived for about one second after which the other is received for the same interval, and so on, in an alternating fashion (Churchland, 2002, pp. 136–7.) This phenomenon can be investigated only if the experimental subject is conscious and able to report which of the images is currently perceived: there is no other means, other than the behavioral, of establishing the neural correlates of the consciousness of each image.

Hence, in contemporary neurophilosophy, the logical sequence of investigation is from the super-personal level to the sub-personal – from the verbal behavior of the participant to the physiological correlate(s) of both that behavior and any personal-level ascriptions of content that may be made. And this must be also the logic of intentional behaviorism which in other words requires that the procedure embrace the super-personal level of analysis in which intentional ascription at the personal level is achieved via the observation of operant behavior (environment–behavior relationships) through extensional behavioral science. The purpose of the philosophical exercise that Dennett advances is, as he proposes, to ascertain what intentional content can be ascribed to the findings of neurological science, but the de facto procedure is more likely to entail using physiology and the logic of natural selection as a means of checking whether pre-ordained desires and beliefs can be rationally ascribed at the personal level.

The consequent methodology is thus 1. the observation of environmental–behavioral relationships (including self-reports of emotion) at the super-personal level, leading to 2. the ascription of emotional content at the personal level, leading to 3. the search for the neural correlates of emotion at the sub-personal level. Desires and beliefs, and other mental content, are thus decided upon at the super-personal level as a result of the uncovering of environment–behavior links; their appropriateness to this personal level ascription is further confirmed, where possible, by reference to the degree to which they can provide an additional heuristic overlay to the theories and findings of neurocognitive research at the sub-personal level on the basis of evolutionarily consistent reasoning.

Understanding consumer choice

Choice has several distinct connotations that go beyond the simple PC/LPC dichotomy though each has some common ground with one or other of these basic concepts of attitude. The first, consisting of *behavior-based conceptions of choice*, is concerned with the description of behavior and with the use of terminology relating to attitudes and intentions as means of referring to the continuity of behavior, its persistence over time, its duration. This approach is more closely allied to the PC conception. The second employs *attitude as an intervening variable* that mediates the influences of environmental stimuli and the emission of a response. This is essentially the LPC idea of attitude. Let us examine in each turn, before finally recapping on the notion of *choice as an intentional idiom*.

Behavior-based conceptions of choice

These conceptions differ according to whether and how consumer behavior is linked to the environmental contingencies that permit its prediction and control.

The identification of patterns of aggregated brand choice.   This is the method employed by Ehrenberg and his colleagues in which, as we have seen, buyer behavior is expressed as sequences of brand choices over time; choice is behavior, but the patterns of behavior observed by the practitioners of this method are not related generally and systematically to the broad patterns of environmental consequence to which behaviorists refer as "reinforcement." There is on occasion an attempt to relate brand purchasing to price promotions but the marketing mix is thereafter generally de-emphasized since each brand's characteristics are presumed to be those of the product category and, by and large, distribution and advertising effects are held constant. This is essentially the PC conception, whether it is applied to physical brand selections on subsequent shopping occasions or to verbal evaluations of brands. It goes beyond the PC conception of attitude or choice only insofar as it occasionally considers the effects of price promotions, which are exceptional occurrences. It is not otherwise attuned to the relationship between brand choice and the contingencies of reinforcement (and punishment) afforded by the marketing mix as a whole.

Contingency category analysis of consumer choice.   This is reminiscent of the probability conception since it refers to sequences of behavior in the context of other possible behaviors as *choice*. But it transcends the PC notion by insisting on relating these sequences to parallel sequences of reinforcement, not the schedules of reinforcement that belong to behavior analysis simple, but to the *patterns of reinforcement* that are part of the interpretive apparatus of the analysis of complex human behavior, that which is not directly amenable to laboratory experimentation. "Patterns of reinforcement" refers in turn to the combination of utilitarian and informational benefits which shape and maintain consumers' selections of products and brands. We have seen that these choices depend in two ways on the contingency categories identified in the BPM matrix. First, consumers emit verbal responses to stimuli descriptive of the situations in which they have previously had opportunity to behave or which are sufficiently similar to such consumer situations as to evoke similar verbal responses. This explanatory device goes no further than the radical behaviorist explication of the results presented in Chapter 6. It relies heavily on the descriptive behaviorisms founded upon classical and instrumental conditioning: it assumes the phenomena of stimulus and response generalization, and response discrimination without relying on an underlying explanation of when and why they occur. Its explanatory basis is the identification of the environmental elements that permit the prediction and, possibly, the influencing of behavior.

The identification of classes of consumer behavior. This approach also relies on a notion of attitude that brings the probability conception to mind but which transcends it by offering an explanation of choice that relates patterns of behavior to environmental contingencies. Choice understood in this way involves sequences of brand purchases, not simply as they are described in the analyses of aggregate buyer behavior pioneered by Ehrenberg and his colleagues, but systematically related to the reinforcing properties of utilitarian and informational aspects of the marketing mixes chosen by consumers. The results presented in Chapter 7 showed that groups of consumers whose buying behavior was characteristically reinforced by one combination or other of utilitarian and informational benefit were exhibited distinctive elasticities of demand for brands of food products. Once again, the kind of explanation of behavior provided here is that of extensional science, its expression confined to the referentially transparent language of an intellectual community that seeks the prediction and control of its subject matter. The analysis relies on the classification of consumer behavior based on the pattern of reinforcement, though the classification is at once more elaborate than that of Accomplishment, Hedonism, Accumulation, and Maintenance pursued in Chapter 5 and simpler in that it refers to the operational definition of utilitarian and informational reinforcement found in markets for consumer non-durables.

Attitude as an intervening variable

This LPC approach is essentially that of the psychological behaviorism interpretation of the research results described in Chapter 6. It is a rather more specialized framework than that adopted by attitude research in the *S-[O]-R* tradition since it makes the environmental stimuli that elicit both the intervening emotional responses of pleasure, arousal and dominance explicit in a rather detailed and systematic way based on the BPM. But it is founded upon the various underlying paradigms of Osgood, Suci, and Tannenbaum, Mehrabian and Russell, and Staats insofar as an external stimulus is held to elicit an emotional (attitudinal) response which has associated with it an internal stimulus which in turn elicits an external response. This is the familiar $S \rightarrow r \rightarrow s \rightarrow R$ sequence of explanation that derives ultimately from Hull and his contemporaries, which to all intents and purposes is nowadays indistinguishable in applied studies from the more cognitive *S-[O]-R* paradigm that can be traced to Tolman.

Choice as an intentional idiom

Intentional behaviorism is a means of ascribing intentionality at the personal level on the basis of systematic observation of environment–behavior relationships over time. This is achieved in the case of the attitude-behavior research (using the PAD variables) described in Chapter 6 by attributing emotional responses and their attendant stimuli, which may mediate behavior, on the basis of consistent verbal responses to stimuli known to elicit those emotions. In the case of the behavioral economics research described in Chapter 7, it is accomplished not simply on the basis of the continuity of behavior – as the PC conception of attitude would require – but by relating sequences of brand purchases to the pattern of reinforcement, utilitarian and informational, that maintains them. "Choice," therefore, as an intentional idiom, is a apportioned based on the observation of sustained behavioral regularities that can be traced to environmental contingencies, including the verbal behavior of the "chooser," though this must ultimately be traceable to nonverbal contingencies: since the consumer is expressing a rule for behavior, it is essential to unravel the dual contingencies that maintain his or her adherence.

We have now arrived at a means of anchoring mentalistic terms – propositional attitudes such as *believes, wants, intends* – and thereby a rule for their use in social cognitive psychology and, more pertinently, consumer research. It follows that "trust," and "choice," "dissatisfaction," and "decision-making," as well as scores of other intentional terms widely employed in consumer and marketing research need to be defined, understood and measured in strictly behavioral dimensions before they can be ascribed to consumers at the personal level. It raises also the question how far marketers seek to change "attitudes" rather than the contingencies that influence behavior, and how far changing verbal behavior can be successful strategy for subsequently modifying consumers' purchase and consumption behaviors. The model of consumer choice which emerges from the foregoing analysis has implications for the whole of marketing thought and practice, and promises not least the resolution of its attitude problems. Most of all, however, it has proved possible to establish a framework for the attribution of intentional idioms in consumer and social cognitive psychology that makes use of the capacities of both cognitive and behavioral sciences without detracting from the unique contributions of either.

Finally, it is important for two reasons that both the extensional science of operant behavior analysis and the analysis of consumer choice as a cognitive phenomenon continue their research programs both separately and in critical combination. The first is to provide an evolving and expanding base for the content ascription to which content can be ascribed in the process of interpretation. Studies of these kinds provide the behavioral science basis for the legitimate attribution of the intentional idioms which serve to explain consumer choice at the personal level by accounting for the continuity of behavior and by providing criteria for the delimitation of our interpretations of how consumer choice is related to its environmental consequences. The second is to provide alternative, competing and challenging explanations to those given by cognitive and other models of consumer behavior. Insofar as the growth of knowledge depends on "the active interplay of competing theories" (Feyerabend, 1975), it is essential to have (i) a thriving operant analysis of consumer behavior which employs both experimental and survey techniques (Foxall, 2003), (ii) operant interpretations which themselves attempt to function on an extensional level only, such as those of consumers' saving behavior, adoption of innovations, and "green" consumerism (Foxall, 1996), and (iii) operant interpretations that contain the intentional overlays necessary to provide accounts of behavior at the personal level. Their interaction is, indeed, a *sine qua non* of intellectual progress.

Hence, what characterizes the intentional behaviorist approach is the provision of a logic for incorporating both the contextual and the intentional stances into a single framework of analysis. The overarching logic is Dennett's, but its use here emphasizes that social cognitive psychologists – as opposed to the neurophysiological psychologists with whom Dennett is predominantly concerned – must reconstruct desires and beliefs in the context of the individual's rationality by considering its situation, the relationship between the rewarding and punishing environment and the behavior it produces. The contextual stance facilitates this reconstruction by *de*constructing the notion of situation in terms of (a) a learning history,

(b) the current behavior setting, and (c) their interaction. This is both consistent with and a means of operationalizing Dennett's view that the organism will have those desires and beliefs that are appropriate to it given its situation.

Notes

Preface

1. Hempel's paper was originally published in Feigl, H. and Sellars, W. (eds) (1949). *Readings in Philosophical Analysis*. New York: Appleton-Century-Crofts, pp. 373–384. Reference here is given to its republication in 1980 since this source contains revisions by the author and a brief account of how his thought has changed since the initial publication.
2. *Consumer behavior analysis* is a synthesis of behavior analysis (especially in its contribution to the behavioral economics of consumption) and consumer research in the context of marketing. The story of this development is told in the preface to *Consumer Psychology in Behavioral Perspective* (Foxall, 2004b/1990), and accounts of the nature and progression of the research program can be found in the introductory chapters of *Consumers in Context: The BPM Research Program* (Foxall, 1996) and *Consumer Behaviour Analysis: Critical Perspectives* (Foxall, 2002b).
3. See, inter alia, Foxall, 2003, 2004a; Foxall & James, 2001, 2003; Foxall & Schreženmaier, 2003; Foxall & Yani-de-Soriano, 2004; Foxall et al., 2004; Newman & Foxall, 2003; Oliveira-Castro et al., 2004, 2005a,b; Schrezenmaier et al., 2004; Yani-de-Soriano & Foxall, 2004.

2 Consumer Behavior

1. One of the earliest comprehensive models of consumer choice (Andreasen, 1965) attaches paramount significance to the influence of attitudes on purchase outcomes. Andreasen postulates that information which passes through the consumer's "filter" (i.e., screening criteria which may be described in terms of perceptual selectivity and attitudes toward the information source) impacts upon the potential customer's attitude (which is conceived as a tricomponential structure consisting of cognitive, affective and conative interactions). Attitude formation, which is influenced by personal, psychological and environmental factors as well as the processing of novel information, is followed by (i) immediate product/ brand choice or (ii) attenuated information seeking or (iii) no action. Such constraints as the availability of purchasing power, the precedence of other purchase requirements and physical capacity determine the timing of the selected item's purchase. Finally, ownership, consumption and experiential feedback to the consumer's internal "information store" (presumably long term memory) complete each repetition of the decision making sequence.

    Nicosia (1966) portrays the impact of a persuasive marketing communication for an extremely discontinuous innovation upon the consumer who is expected to "internalize" its message. If internalization, which is dependent upon the continuity of the perceptual, environmental and cognitive fields which facilitate or impede the acceptance of the message, occurs the result is the formation of an *attitude* toward the radically new item. *Motivation*, which is the assumed outcome of subsequent search behavior, determines, subject to brand availability, instore advertising and price acceptability, the purchase response. Further attitude formation is assumed to depend less on advertising than did the initial purchase since repetitive decision processes rely to some extent upon the results of experience gained by prior purchase and consumption. Consumers' *dispositions* are, nonetheless, regarded as crucial determinants of repeat buying patterns.

Howard and Sheth (1969) similarly describe the buyer's "response sequence" (attention → brand comprehension → attitude → intention → purchase) in terms of the cognition, affect and conation which are the result of 'symbolic communication'. The mental *ambiguity* arising from a marketing or social stimulus leads to the search for, and processing of information, a procedure which terminates in the formation of an *attitude* toward the product or brand on offer and the consequent establishment of a buying *intention* which causes purchase. Of all the comprehensive models of consumer decision making, that of Howard and Sheth makes the most explicit use of the $S → [O] → R$ model (see, in particular, their Chapter 9, which deals with symbolic communication).

Engel et al. (1968) advance a broadly similar model in which perceived information leads, via memory, to problem recognition, search, and the evaluation of alternatives, in a process which consists of the familiar belief → attitude → intentions sequence and, ultimately, choice. Their textbook presents an account of consumer decision making which has been painstakingly constructed through the careful integration of concepts and relationships derived from contemporary cognitive psychology: memory, selective sensory and perceptual reactions to exposure to informational stimuli, the interpretation of the meanings of stimuli, reception of the message through its comprehension and acceptance, and cognitive response as the partially processed information is admitted to long term memory.

2. The theoretical underpinnings of early consumer psychology in some ways anticipated the social cognition movement of the 1980s and 1990s (Fiske 1993; Ostrom et al., 1981; Wyer & Srull, 1986, 1989, 1994a, 1994b), including the possibility that implicit cognitive events influence social behavior (Greenwald & Banaji, 1995; Janiszewski, 1988; Schwartz & Reisberg, 1991). Prior to this development, cognitive psychology was little concerned with attitudinal and intentional outputs of information processing, while social psychology largely avoided cognitive concerns (cf. Eiser, 1980, 1986). In anticipating the advent of social cognition, consumer researchers made theoretical and methodological advances, notably in the area of attitudinal-intentional-behavioral consistency, which are contributions to social psychology as well as to consumer research. In choosing to study attitudinal–behavioral relationships, consumer psychologists recognize the import of the pivotal component of social cognitive models of consumer choice. For, if attitudes (and certain other prebehavioral elements of information processing) are not consistent with and predictive of observed consumer behavior, the whole enterprise must be called in question, as must our understanding of what marketing management is and does.

3. These considerations are relevant not only to the intellectual center ground in marketing studies which has always belonged to consumer research but to the more immediate search for managerial prescriptions. The near ubiquity of textbook recommendations for marketers makes their detailed rehearsal here superfluous, but they may be illustrated by reference to Howard's (1989) attempt to relate patterns of consumer behavior at each stage of the product life cycle to marketing strategies which traces consumer decision making and marketing response through three phases. The introduction of a new brand into a new product class at the beginning of such a cycle engenders extensive problem

solving on the part of buyers who, by definition, have no experience of the item and must establish its meaning largely on the basis of prepurchase deliberation. The introduction of subsequent product versions in the form of competing brands during the growth stage of the cycle prompts limited problem solving in which novel offerings are compared with existing choices about which much more is now known. Finally, as the product reaches its maturity, numerous brand additions require no more from the consumer than routine problem solving as additions to the range of brands are judged according to very familiar product attributes and, on the whole, brands whose characteristics are commonplace are selected on recognition.

The managerial tools available to persuade the consumer (which constitute the marketing mix of product, price, promotion and distribution) are employed at each phase to effect cognitive changes in the consumer which guide his or her decision making accordingly. Information supplied by the marketing organization influences the consumer's confidence, brand recognition and attitude; brand recognition also comes to influence confidence and attitude directly (cf. Brown & Stayman, 1992). Confidence and attitude then determine intention which in turn determines purchase. Attitude and related cognitive events and processes are clearly central to this approach, on which so much consumer analysis and marketing theory rests. As a result, it is vital to examine critically and in detail the assumption that behavior must be attitudinally consistent.

4. The story is engagingly told, with differing emphases, by Gardner (1985) as well as by Baars (1986). See also Bruner (1983). The philosophical implications of what Searle (1992) calls "the rediscovery of the mind" were soon examined by him and a host of philosophical colleagues (see for instance Bechtel & Graham, 1998; and Guttenplan, 1994, particularly his introductory *Essay on Mind*). The possibility arises that cognitivism was not dead even during the behaviorist hegemony: it was just in Europe (in the caring hands of Piaget, Broadbent and Bartlett, among others). But that is an argument for another day.

5. This program has provided one of the most widely cited contributions to the analysis of persuasive communications. Most writers on advertising and other forms of marketing communication have drawn on its conclusions without giving more than passing attention to its theoretical sources. But these conclusions cannot be fully appreciated in the absence of their conceptual context. The program actually drew on a spectrum of theoretical positions from psychoanalysis to learning theory, from field theory to reference group analysis. (A valuable overview is provided by Eagly and Chaiken, 1993). The common theme was controlled laboratory study of communications effects: source credibility, one-sided versus two-sided persuasive appeals, primacy versus recency of opposing messages, and so on (Foxall et al., 1998). The aim was to understand better how the source of a message, the message structure and content, and the characteristics of the audience influence the effectiveness of a persuasive message.

The researchers drew on reinforcement theory which is based on the finding that a response that has been rewarded or reinforced (for the importance of this distinction, see Foxall, 2004b, 1990, Chapter 2) in the past is likely to be performed more often in the future. Hence, the Yale researchers reasoned, beliefs and attitudes are verbal responses that are likely to become habitual if they are followed by positive arguments or reasons for holding them. A message ("Our popcorn is nutritious because...") is a stimulus; the extent to which the individual audience member accepts the arguments given for the advertiser's claim denotes his or her beliefs and attitudes (evaluative verbal behavior); and these are reinforced by the current or anticipated rewards of holding and repeating them. The rather eclectic methodology of the Yale group included both behavioral and intentional components: what mattered were the *anticipated* incentives promised by a communication which created or strengthened beliefs and attitudes.

6. In spite of the widespread belief that behaviorism has been superseded in the course of the "cognitive revolution," some schools of behaviorist thought are making important contributions, especially in the analysis of thinking, reasoning and decision making, areas of human endeavor widely considered to fall exclusively within the province of cognitivism. Here we are primarily concerned with *radical behaviorism*, which has given rise to behavior analysis. "The field of behavior analysis is the area of philosophy, research, and application that encompasses the experimental analysis of behavior, applied behavior analysis, operant psychology, operant conditioning, behaviorism, and Skinnerian psychology" (Vaughan, 1987, p. 97). Radical behaviorism is the philosophy of psychology which unites all of these (Skinner, 1945, 1974).

   Far from being a supplanted paradigm, radical behaviorism is a flourishing area of intellectual activity in both its neo-Skinnerian and post-Skinnerian accentuations. In particular, theoretical and empirical work on verbal behavior has transformed radical behaviorism since the fundamentals of operant conditioning were tentatively applied to marketing and promotions in the 1970s and 1980s. Much of this work has implications for consumer research (Foxall, 1987).

   First, it makes possible an interpretation of consumer behavior in terms of the situations that shape it. It can also incorporate the verbal antecedents and consequences of consumer choice, both overt and covert. Previous use of this paradigm in marketing and consumer research has generally assumed that its explanatory system can be extrapolated from the nonhuman animal laboratory, where supporting evidence has accumulated, to complex human behavior such as purchase and consumption. However, an operant analysis of complex human behavior need not rely upon principles of contingency–shaped behavior gained from laboratory research with nonhumans: it is now possible to incorporate the distinctively human capacity for language and rule-governed behavior. Consequently, operant analysis need not be restricted to simpler, routine consumer behaviors while a cognitive account is necessary for more complex behaviors based on decision making and problem solving. A behaviorist analysis may prove capable of handling both.

   Second, study of the relationship between behavior and its controlling environment promises to supply a much needed systematic understanding of the situational influences on consumer choice. As noted above, because of the emphasis in consumer research on the social-cognitive determinants of consumption, the field currently lacks an integrated model of consumer behavior in the context of its social, physical, temporal and regulatory surroundings. Radical behaviorism, a discipline concerned almost entirely with the explanation of behavior as an environmentally-determined phenomenon, can be expected to contribute importantly to the required understanding. The advent of research on consumers' verbal behavior means that this comprehension can incorporate the social influence of rule provision.

   By presenting an understanding of consumer choice as influenced by environmental considerations, behavior analysis, whether experimental or interpretational, has the potential to fill a gap in consumer research which currently lacks a coherent explication of situational control of consumer choice. However, mention of this paradigm in marketing and consumer research has usually tended to presume that its explanatory system can be extrapolated unadorned from experimental research with nonhumans to complex human interactions such as purchase and consumption. A behavior analytic account of human behavior must take full measure of the situational and speciational peculiarities of the context in which that behavior takes place. Such an exposition must be conversant with the experimental analysis of human behavior and the ramifications of radical behaviorist interpretation (Foxall, 1995a). Both require that particular attention be accorded the human capacity for verbal control of behavior.

Third, consideration of radical behaviorist explanation of consumer behavior permits discussion of a number of epistemological issues that are germane to contemporary debates about the nature of "scientific" and "interpretive" approaches to consumer research. By showing how an interpretation of consumer choice would proceed within a highly-developed behavioral science paradigm, such analysis reveals the strengths and weaknesses of a specific ontology and methodology for consumer research and facilitates comparison with other modes of inquiry and explication. For example, the divergent ways in which social cognitive and operant approaches interpret the role of previous behavior in the shaping of current responding provides insight into the varied perspectives available for comparative consumer research.

7. It is evident, however, that the intentional use of behavioral technology in marketing demands a more substantial research base than is currently available. Little is known about the reinforcing effects of rewards of varying type and magnitude. It is thirty years since Scott (1976) put forward the intriguing hypothesis that there exists a continuum of effects: "Experimental studies must include multiple levels of incentives over a broader range of magnitudes. The effects of incentives may or may not be linear, and are most likely related in some way to the price of the particular product." Related considerations to which consumer research should be addressed include the effectiveness of primary and secondary reinforcers, and of temporally immediate reinforcers compared with those which are delayed. Primary reinforcers, such as product attributes, have intrinsic utility while secondary reinforcers, such as coupons, have no intrinsic worth but must be exchanged in order to realize reinforcing benefits.

Rothschild and Gaidis (1981, p. 77) suggested a sequence of various types of reinforcement which may provide an initial hypothesis for the testing of behaviorist approaches to consumer research and marketing management. Their suggestion is that contingencies of reinforcement should be arranged so that the individual consumer is presented with the following sequence, say by a combination of product sampling, coupon offers and other deals as well as primary product attributes, in order to assess the probabilities of behavioral change: immediate primary → immediate secondary or delayed primary → delayed secondary → no (extraneous) reinforcement. More fundamental questions also present themselves for empirical test: what reinforcement contingencies are linked with initial product trial? What is their enforcing effect upon subsequent purchase? How should contingencies of reinforcement be arranged in order to increase the effectiveness of shaping and vicarious learning?

Many techniques are used in shaping whose use could be more effectively extended to the end of successive approximation. Loss leading, in-store competitions and related special offers are designed to create store loyalty. Free trials, credit terms, on approval trials, coupon offers and sampling permit the trial of products without which there can be no reinforcement. Shaping techniques carry the danger that secondary rather than primary reinforcers will be paramount and that the operant purchasing and consumption behaviors will be extinguished when the offers are withdrawn. The provision of opportunities for vicarious learning, for example, through in-store or domestic product demonstrations, assists in the education of consumers especially where innovative products are concerned, where familiar products are promoted in the context of novel uses, and where new patterns of shopping are encouraged. Connected with this may be the encouragement of the phenomena of discrimination (for example, through store logos, brand names, corporate images, with which previous positive reinforcement may become linked) and generalization (for example, through advertisements drawing attention to past product/brand use). All of these techniques are and may be further employed in order to facilitate certain responses by consumers, encouraging the seeking of buyer-dominated information, for instance, where this may usefully complement that available through marketer-dominated channels. In certain circumstances, such as a shortage of raw materials, behaviorist techniques might be employed to decrease the demand for some products or brands. Marketers, especially retailers and planners, already practice environmental design in the arrangement of displays, the use of discriminative stimuli such as piped music, store location and shopping center development. The deliberate employment of behaviorist techniques, when marketers find them reinforcing, would render such methods and approaches more effective, according to the advocates of the extension of their paradigm to marketing.

8. Contrary to general opinion, radical behaviorism provides a coherent interpretation of so-called cognitive phenomena such as thinking, reasoning and decision-making (Skinner, 1945, 1974; see Catania, 1992b). Indeed, counter to the predominant view that the behavioristic paradigm has been superseded by cognitivism largely as a result of the former's incapacity to deal with cognitive phenomena, a substantial proportion of recent work in the theoretical and experimental analysis of behavior has focused on verbal behavior (S. C. Hayes, 1989; Hayes & Chase, 1991; Hayes & Hayes, 1992; Hayes et al., 1994).

An account of private events cannot be separated from the subject of radical behaviorist interpretation in general. Radical behaviorism differs from methodological behaviorism by embracing private events as a part of its subject matter (Moore, 1994; Baum, 1994) Moreover, they are not treated as unobservables though private events such as thoughts and feelings are observed by only one person. Radical behaviorism *infers* however that other people have private events which act as verbal discriminative stimuli for their behavior (Mackenzie, 1988). But this is a far cry still from the treatment of unobservables by social cognitivists: to the radical behaviorist such "mental way stations" (Skinner, 1963) are no more than explanatory fictions that bring inquiry to a premature end by diverting attention from the ultimate causes of behavior which lie in the environment.

Some behavior analysts have cast private events as possible proximal causes of behavior, though others have argued against this (cf. *inter alia* Malott & Garcia, 1991; Hayes et al., 1986) partly on the grounds that only entities which can be manipulated in an experimental analysis of behavior should be admitted. To assume that private events are proximal causes of behavior is, nevertheless, to blur the distinction between behaviorist and cognitive modes of explanation (Foxall, 2004d/1990, 1999a; Overskeid, 1995).

9. The re-establishment of the cognitive paradigm in psychology and its displacement of behaviorism as the prevailing philosophy is now widely recognized by psychologists. Blumenthal (1978, p. viii) speaks of the "renaissance" of cognitive psychology, while Neisser (1967, p. 5) notes that "A generation ago, a book like

this one would have needed at least a chapter of self-defense against the behaviorist position. Today, happily, the climate of opinion has changed, and little or no defense is necessary." The justification for cognitive psychology is the asserted fact that "Cognitive processes exist, so it can hardly be unscientific to study them." The formal study of consumer behavior in the context of marketing, based firmly upon the behavioral sciences, proliferated at a time when behaviorism was giving way to cognitive psychology as the dominant framework of conceptualization and analysis. While behavior analysis has far from disappeared – indeed some of the most incisive accounts of behaviorism as a scientific philosophy or paradigm have been published since 1970 – by the time consumer researchers began to borrow heavily from psychology in the 1960s, it had ceased to dominate psychological explanation.

Although behavior analysis has had some effect upon the development of marketing thought and, as has been pointed out above, is implicit in much marketing practice, it has not until recently been considered an alternative framework for consumer research generally or as a source of *explanation* for consumer and marketer behaviors.

The explanations of behavior provided by cognitive psychology, and behavior analysis posit antithetical views of the acquisition of behavior and of the appropriate approach to the modification of behavior. Yet each appears to be consistent with a view of how marketing works and thus to suggest valid prescriptions for managerial action. One places the locus of behavioral control resolutely within the individual, "its proponents try to identify precisely various cognitive states, mechanisms, and processes, and to characterize attitudes and behaviors in the light of their informational determinants" (Cushman & McPhee, 1980, p. 7). The other locates the determinants of behavior equally resolutely in the external environment, both as it supposedly shaped the evolution of the species by eliciting the behavior and development upon which the survival of the species was contingent and (more importantly for a technology of behavior) as it currently controls behavior by embodying contingencies of behavioral reinforcement. Skinner (1977, p. 379) emphasizes the crucial difference between himself and both the cognitive scientists and those behaviorists who adopted intervening explicative variables in terms of the locus of control of behavior, "For me the observable operations in conditioning lay outside the organism, but Tolman put them inside, as replacements for, if not simply renditions of, mental processes, and that is where they still are in cognitive psychology today."

The common use of a given paradigm in science is evidently related to shared beliefs about what exists to be studied and the nature of the relations among its elements. But no paradigm comprehends all known facts. Rather, it is the result of selection among those facts and relations which promise to repay most abundantly further study. Paradigms are thus based upon expediency as well as current understandings of the phenomenal universe. "Radical" behaviorists such as Skinner do not deny the existence of what cognitive psychologists call mental processes but they firmly dispute their description in mental terms. Feelings are interpreted as inner, physiological processes which are the by-products of behavior but not reinforcers; attention refers not to sensory stimulation but to the contingencies upon which the process of discrimination is based; memory and recall refer to the familiarity of past experiences in the light of current environmental stimuli; problem solving is the means by which the individual develops a response which produces a 'desired' reinforcement: the problem lasts only as long as the requisite response is not available. Although 'methodological' behaviorists range from those who deny outright the existence of mental events to those who only deny their usefulness in scientific analysis and ignore them because of the inability of researchers to agree about their nature and significance, radical behaviorists reposition some alleged intrapersonal factors and reinterpret others.

As this chapter has also shown, not all behaviorists eschew assumed organocentric factors even to the extent that radical behaviorists do, and there are numerous psychologists who attempt to combine cognitive and behavioral approaches. Behavior analysis has been discussed here in radical terms. However, because this framework serves to distinguish it from cognitive approaches and it is the radical behaviorist philosophy which has been most clearly articulated of late. This book is concerned, nevertheless, with cognitive and behaviorist paradigms at their broadest.

Although it is not possible to establish or refute a scientific paradigm by direct, empirical investigation normal science proceeds within a framework which is accepted because it is generally believed to be consistent with and/or explain the available evidence. If the larger proportion of the evidence cannot be reconciled with the prevailing paradigm, then modification or replacement of that paradigm is in order. Paradigm shift may occur when (i) new results which are quite incapable of interpretation within the existing framework are incorporated in a new paradigm along with whatever previous data, theories and methodologies can be harmoniously accommodated or (ii) when novel, superior explanations reveal the inadequacies of prevailing frameworks of conception and analysis. Tracing the progress of competing paradigms is, nevertheless, an immense task and can be fully accomplished only retrospectively. The purpose of this book is more modest than this and is essentially exploratory rather than definitive.

While it draws extensively upon social psychology, it is ultimately concerned with marketing. Specifically, it is concerned with the treatment of attitudes and behavior in consumer research. The relationship between these is perhaps the most important in consumer research carried out within the cognitive information processing framework. The empirical demonstration of attitudinal–behavioral consistency is crucial to the continued acceptance of the cognitive paradigm. Unless actual or hypothetical intrapersonal states procure and determine behavior the edifice of contemporary marketing theory must begin to crumble. If additional concepts and empirical data have to be taken into consideration in an alternative explanation of behavior, the obvious conclusion is that the cognitive paradigm has been modified or replaced. The following chapter examines critically the prevailing view of the nature of marketing (especially marketing communication) as a persuasive force which acts upon consumer behavior through the antecedent modification of their attitudes, and contrasts this with the view that any influence on behavior effected by marketing and advertising is relatively weak and occurs by reinforcing experience rather than by the alteration of mental states.

The appropriate paradigm within which to undertake consumer research and the marketing management which relies upon it will, among other things, provide an interpretation of attitudinal–behavioral dynamics which is consistent with psychological and marketing theory that is derived from the available empirical evidence. How can we discover which paradigm is the more adequate for the explanation of actual attitudinal–behavioral relationships? As Jacoby (1978, p. 337) put it in a landmark assessment of consumer research of its time, "No other single psychological construct has permeated consumer research as has the construct of attitude." The answer to this question is thus of immense paradigmatic significance in consumer research and marketing theory.

3 The Behavior of Consumers' Attitudes

1. Hardly surprisingly, therefore, numerous competing theories of attitude have been advanced during the past several decades, a fact which confirms the impression that this field of social psychology is even now at a critical stage of development. At an earlier stage, cognitive consistency theories appeared in several versions, for example the dissonance theory of Festinger (1957) and the affective-consistency approach of Rosenberg (1960) which challenged the even earlier balance theory of Heider (1946) and the congruity theory of Osgood and Tannenbaum (1955). Learning theories and, in particular the behavioristic self-perception theory of Bem (1967), have provided distinctive explanations of observed events (cf. Bandura, 1986; Staats, 1975, 1996). Social judgment theories, attribution theory, and functional theory have also been devised to account for the same phenomena (Sherif et al., 1965; Kelley, 1967; Katz, 1960; Kelman, 1958) and some of these have found echoes in the marketing literature. The reference to Kuhn's description of a science in crisis is justified further by the proliferation of *ad hoc* empirical investigations of attitudes and behavior. The critical state of attitude research is only too clear from the various arguments adduced in flavour of definitions and general notions of the structure of attitudes–from the representation of attitudes as tricomponential amalgams of cognition, affect and conation, to their consideration in terms of just cognition and affect, to the restriction of the term to refer to affect alone (Eagly & Chaiken, 1993).

2. Cohen's (1964, p. 138) expectation that attitudes constitute "precursors of behavior, ... determinants of how person will actually behave in his daily affairs" is over forty years old but it remains strong, as the prevalence of latent process conceptions attests. Even the vivid demonstration by LaPiere (1934) that verbal statements of intention to act in a given way, in this case with regard to the accommodation of a Chinese couple in an American hotel or restaurant, can fail dramatically to vary with actual behavior has not expunged this expectation. LaPiere obtained statements that most restaurateurs and hoteliers were unwilling to accommodate such a couple, *after* they had experienced overwhelming success in being so received): his findings still haunt sociologists and social psychologists but have done nothing to arrest the growth of empirical research directed toward the practical demonstration of attitudinal–behavioral consistency. The success of this venture depends in large part on the definition of attitude adopted by researchers.

   The idea of causality implies that one variable produces another or that a change in one variable can produce consistent change in another in the absence of extraneous changes in contextual factors. There are four possible causal relationships between attitudes and behavior: (i) attitudes cause behaviors, (ii) behaviors cause attitudes, (iii) attitudes and behaviors are reciprocally causative, or (iv) attitudes and behaviors are unrelated. Each of these propositions is supported by at least one eminent psychologist who adduces empirical evidence and theoretical explanation in favor of his stance (Kahle & Berman, 1979). Any pattern of association is compatible with definitions derived from the probability conception of attitude since causality is ascribed to environmental factors rather than internal, mediating states. Definitions derived from the latent process conception are, however, compatible with the proposition that there is a causal relationship between attitudes and behavior which is uni-directional from attitudes to behavior and is not altered by environmental factors.

   This would, however, be a very stringent criterion by which to judge the data on attitudinal–behavioral relationships. The problem of establishing the direction of any causation beyond doubt is immense given the deficiencies of current methodologies (cf. Bentler & Speckart, 1981). Fortunately, it is possible to compare latent process and probability conceptions in terms of the evidence without formulating a definition that is either untestable or simplistic. While correlational evidence of attitudinal behavioral consistency "irrespective of situations" is not sufficient to demonstrate a causal relationship, it is certainly necessary to that demonstration. If the latent process conception is valid, therefore, variance in attitudinal measures will explain statistically all the variance in corresponding behavioral measures: at the very least, given the noise surrounding the data, very high correlations between attitudes (verbal statements or opinions) and corresponding behavior should be found since the assumption is that both are mediated by the same underlying, "true" attitude or latent process. But the more necessary it becomes to add explanatory variables in regressions of behavior on attitude, the less satisfactory the explanation prompted by the latent process conception of attitudinal–behavioral relations must be adjudged. The increasing need to employ contextual variables to account for behavior patterns would render the probability conception more and more appropriate as an explicative device.

3. Factors not explicitly included in the theory which have been found to improve the predictability of behavior include (in general, see Eagly & Chaiken, 1993; for full list of references, see Foxall, 1997b): personal norm, self-identity, self-schemas, size and content of consideration set, availability of relevant skills, resources and cooperation, action control, past behavior/habit, amount of reasoning during intention formation, perceived control/confidence, and attitude functions.

4 Prior Behavior

1. Note, however, that this is not universally the case and depends to some extent on the measure of past behavior employed. Hence, self-reported past behavior is a poor guide to future behavior in the case of a socially-desirable act such as waste recycling (e.g., Davies, et al. 2002).

2. This is precisely the kind of behavior which, according to Catania (1992a) is contingency-shaped rather than rule-governed; see the discussion of instructed behavior in Chapter 5. See also Note 15 below.

3. Bagozzi's (2004) paper contains the most up-to-date source of references in this field at the time of writing, and exemplifies well what I have called the "reaching out toward behavior" of contemporary social cognitive research.

4. Cf. Eagly & Chaiken, 1993, p. 204, who argue that these approaches cannot properly be considered alternatives.

5 The Situated Consumer

1. The significance of the consumer situation construct requires its distinction from that of consumer behavior setting scope. *A consumer behavior setting* comprises the discriminative stimuli which signal the likely consequences of emitting a particular response, i.e. the probable levels of utilitarian and informational reinforcement, and that of aversive outcome. In other words, it provides a summary of the reinforcement and punishment contingent upon the performance of the requisite response. This is an abstract definition, general and theoretical, because it is

dependent on other variables (the consumer's learning and evolutionary histories, for instance) in order to have a concrete influence on behavior.

Consumer behavior setting scope is the extent to which the consumer's current behavior is narrowly determined by elements of the behavior setting in which it is located. It is determined not only by the elements of the behavior setting (social and physical surroundings, temporal frame, regulatory frame) but by the consumer's history of behaving in similar settings and the consequences of having done so. Consumer behavior settings of varying scope may be arrayed on a continuum of closed-open consumer behavior settings, the most closed setting controlling the nature of the consumer's responses entirely and predictably; the most open, having minimal external control over behavior which is accordingly much more difficult to predict.

This is a somewhat more operational idea of the immediate determinant of consumer response: consumer behavior setting *scope* comprehends both the setting and the consumer's learning history which "activates" the setting elements, converting some of them from neutral stimuli into discriminative stimuli which bring behavior under stimulus control. However, this is still a rather abstract depiction of environment-behavior relationships. To that extent and, since these concepts are not unobservables posited at some other realm than observed behavior, both consumer behavior setting and consumer behavior setting scope may be considered examples of the kinds of descriptive theoretical entity which can organize collections of facts, for which Skinner (1947) called. Note that the contingency analysis involved in deciding upon the scope of a consumer behavior setting is of a macro-level: strictly speaking, from it we can predict the operant class to which the consumer's response belongs.

However, a *consumer situation* is a particular (concrete, real world) consumer behavior setting and a learning history. It is delineated by the synomorphic presence of a given individual (who embodies a behavioral learning history and an evolutionary history) and a specific consumer behavior setting, e.g. John Smith at the barber's. This is a more empirically available entity, not in the sense that it comprises data while the preceding notions of consumer behavior setting and consumer behavior setting scope were hypothetical constructs, but in as much as it is amenable to direct observation in and of itself rather than a précis of empirical relationships at a disaggregated level. It is a description of a situation which has potential for influencing/ determining behavior or making it more predictable.

2. While the operant behavior of nonhumans is shaped entirely by direct contact with the contingencies (Lowe, 1989), that of humans frequently comes under an additional source of control. That control is verbal, as when the actions of a new student are modified as a result of the instructions given by the university authorities irrespective of the student's direct experience of the contingencies to which those instructions refer. The analysis of rule-governed, as contrasted with contingency-shaped behavior is a longstanding theme in operant psychology, as is that of verbal behavior in general (Skinner, 1945, 1957, 1969). Nor need this analysis exclude any of the behaviors portrayed in many cognitive accounts as "information processing." As Richelle (1993, p. 144) defines the scope of the study of verbal behavior: "Rule-governed behavior is more on the side of the intellect as opposed to emotion, of logical argument as opposed to intuition, of deliberation as opposed to impulse, of knowledge as opposed to know-how, of word as opposed to deed, of reason as opposed to faith, of truth as opposed to belief, of

rationality as opposed to passion, of consciousness as opposed to unconsciousness, of culture as opposed to nature."

Skinner (1957) defined verbal behavior as behavior that is reinforced through the mediation of other persons: it impinges upon the social, rather than the physical environment (Moore, 1994). Since verbal responding is a behavioral phenomenon, it is defined functionally, not logically, and the style of its analysis does not differ from that of any other operant behavior (Moore, 1994, p. 289; Skinner, 1957). Consonant with the metatheoretical stance of radical behaviorism (Skinner, 1945), such functional analysis diverges fundamentally from the formalism preferred by most linguists, including the formal standpoint from which Chomsky (1959) launched his critical review of Skinner's *Verbal behavior* (MacCorquodale, 1969,1970; Richelle, 1993, pp. 120–128).

Verbal behavior initially inspired little empirical work by behavior analysts and some segments of the recent upsurge in research on verbal responding are critical of Skinner, not least for his alleged concentration on the verbal behavior of the speaker and his apparent disregard of that of the listener (Hayes & Hayes, 1989; cf. Skinner, 1989), but also for his failure to consider reference and postulation (Parrott, 1986), and for the "unwarranted dominance" of Skinner's book in its acceptance as the sole behavior theoretic approach to verbal responding and its consequent overshadowing of other theoretical approaches including relational frame analysis (S. C. Hayes, 1994; cf. Hayes & Hayes, 1992).

3. The reason for the difficulty of defining plying and tracking exclusively is that a single rule often embodies elements of both (Poppen, 1989): sometimes both elements of such a rule require the same behavior to be performed (in which case the rule is a *congruent*); sometimes there is conflict (when the rule is known as a *contrant*).

4. The usual functional distinction made of reinforcers is between primary and secondary. *Primary reinforcers* such as sexual satisfaction, water and food are effective from birth and for almost all species. Their effectiveness is not contingent upon their relationship with other reinforcers; the apparent biological determination of these inherent reinforcers has led to their being known as *natural*. *Secondary reinforcers* acquire their capacity to influence the rate of behavior in the course of the individual's experience; their power to do so depends upon their being repeatedly paired with primary reinforcers. An example is money, with which many primary reinforcers can be obtained. Some authors also speak of *social reinforcers*, including praise, affection and attention, which are a combination of primary and secondary reinforcers.

A more useful functional distinction in the present context is between *contingency-derived reinforcers* and *rule-derived reinforcers*. Contingency-derived reinforcers are both primary and secondary. Their effect is apparent in the contingency-shaping of behavior; it derives from the impact which behavior has directly upon its environment. These reinforcers are generally associated with pleasurable effects for the individual who is in a state of reinforcer deprivation (though behavior analysts usually avoid the notion that something is reinforcing because it is pleasant). But evolution has required that most acts whose rate is influenced by primary reinforcers have pleasant outcomes: eating sugar and avoiding pain, for instance. Secondary reinforcers such as foods, furniture, housing, and music usually also have a utilitarian effect. Contingency-derived reinforcers are, therefore, *utilitarian* reinforcers. (Though, in human contexts, rules may be implicated in the pairing of primary and secondary stimuli).

Rule-derived reinforcers have their effect only by virtue of being specified in rules – e.g., that money is a measure of individual prestige as well as a medium of exchange; other tokens, university degrees, etc. None of these derives its reinforcing power from "nature"; none is a reinforcer from the organism's birth. They are only useful/reinforcing in so far as they are symbols, i.e., as they point to something else – a level of performance, success, access to a job, etc. Rule-derived reinforcers are social and verbal; their effect is on behavior that is mediated by others (where the "other" may be the individual him/herself). Such instructed behavior, the verbal behavior of the listener, is reinforced by the individual's level of achievement of socially- (or personally-) prescribed goals; the behavior consists of pliance or tracking. In the case of pliance, the informational reinforcement derives from the praise, recognition, acknowledgement extended by the mediating individual(s) to the rule-follower. (Informational punishment would be the result of noncompliance or counter-compliance). In the case of tracking, the informational reinforcement derives from consonance between the physical environment as it is experienced and as it was described by the mediating individual (who may be the behaver). (Informational punishment would result from a lack of such consonance). These reinforcers are always secondary. They derive power from the social status and/or self-esteem conferred as a result of the behaviors they maintain. Rule-derived reinforcers are, therefore, *informational* reinforcers.

It may be worth emphasizing here that no one-to-one mapping of primary/ secondary reinforcement on to utilitarian/ informational reinforcement is implied by this reasoning. Primary reinforcement emphasizes utilitarian but may, in humans at least, have an informational component. Human awareness and competitiveness can, for instance, make success in survival a matter of status. Secondary reinforcement involves both utilitarian and informational reinforcers: by definition, the required pairing requires both; by demonstration, consumer operants comprise elements of each. Social/verbal reinforcement emphasizes informational but entails the emergent utilitarian consequences included in social status and self-esteem.

Sources of reinforcement

Contingency-derived	Primary reinforcement	Utilitarian (plus Informational)
Contingency-derived (may be rule-assisted)	Secondary	Utilitarian and Informational
Rule-derived	Social/Verbal	Informational (plus Utilitarian)

Hence the most that we can deduce with respect to the distinction between contingency-shaped and rule-governed behavior is this: the former is shaped and maintained *predominantly* by utilitarian reinforcement; the latter, *predominantly*, by informational reinforcement.

Nor should the impression be given that we are speaking here of utilitarian and informational reinforcers as inalienably distinct entities as though there were some things or events that always and invariably reinforce via utility while others always and invariably reinforcer informationally. We are speaking of the functions of reinforcers. Function is always determined by the situation. Most things or events which are consequences of behavior have both utilitarian and informational functions: jewelry is mainly informational but also performs a utilitarian function; air conditioners are principally utilitarian but may add to one's social status (especially in a West European country where they are relatively scarce as compared with the US. Even in North America, an air-conditioned car may confer some status; it certainly does in Britain).

Primary and secondary reinforces are often differentiated on the basis of the speed with which they cease to reinforce. Primary reinforcers are permanent and universal in their effectiveness; but there is no logical reason why secondary reinforcers should be either: money may give way to bartered goods as a means of exchange in some circumstances; horse-drawn carriages are seldom as functionally useful in industrial societies today as they were in the rural societies of a century ago. Informational reinforcers are more contingent still upon social usages: fashions, forms of address, fad products, etc. quickly cease to reinforce and may punish when they no longer confer membership of a group. Powdered wigs may, alas, be gone forever.

Moreover, the effects of utilitarian and informational reinforcers may be mutually-strengthening. Since informational reinforcement is socially-contrived and symbolic, its power stems ultimately from its pairing with contingency-derived or utilitarian reinforcement. It reinforces only in so far as it is linked with the reinforcers provided by the contingencies themselves, only in so far as the rules it reflects are consonant with those environmental contingencies. Hence the behaviors that confer informational reinforcement lead ultimately to pleasure just as surely as do the utilitarian reinforcers with which they are associated. Where those utilitarian reinforcers are secondary, they are effective only in so far as they are related to primary reinforcers. This is only to say that the ultimate reinforces are always primary – natural, non-contingent, biological. The BPM classification of consumer operants reflects this: all four operant classes of consumer behavior are reinforced by a combination of utilitarian and informational reinforcement rather than by one or other of these.

Since this is a functional classification of reinforcers, any particular item such as money might have both utilitarian and informational effects. Money has generally been regarded as a secondary reinforcer which derives its power from the primary reinforcers which can be acquired with it. But it can also play the role of an informational reinforcer: social status and self-esteem both stem from the performance feedback provided by a high salary or bank balance. Operationally, therefore, the interpretation of the meaning of money will depend upon the situation under investigation. Furthermore, operational measures of utilitarian and informational reinforcement (whether these are being used in a quantitative analysis or qualitative interpretation of consumer behavior) must reflect the pleasurable/utilitarian and social/personal functions of reinforcers respectively. That is, we should look for expressions (verbal and nonverbal) of pleasure or usefulness in order to identify utilitarian reinforcers; and for considerations of status/self-esteem in order to identify informational reinforcers.

5. An *operant class* of consumer behavior consists of a set of responses which, irrespective of their topographical (dis)similarities, correspond in terms of the pattern of reinforcement which maintains them, i.e., the configuration of relatively high/relatively low utilitarian reinforcement and relatively high/relatively low informational reinforcement associated with their continuance.

The actual procedure by which these four classes of behavior were initially derived is as follows (Foxall, 2004d/1990). On the basis of the BPM reinforcer variables, four theoretical classes were known to be possible: high, high; high, low; low, high; and low, low. Broad kinds of consumer behavior were allocated to each of these on the basis of the definitions of utilitarian and informational reinforcement and the responses maintained by "incentives" and "feedback" in the applied behavior analysis of environmental conservation. Only when this had been done satisfactorily were labels attached to the operant classes.

The first operant class suggests behaviors which supply high levels of incentive and high levels of status/esteem. Activities leading to personal accomplishment seem to belong here: cultural achievements which bring more than the pleasure of listening to a performance or reading a classic novel for the joy of the story. Consumer behaviors maintained by a high level of utilitarian reinforcement but, relatively speaking, a low level of informational reinforcement suggest entertainments, pleasures, the amelioration of one's own suffering; in short the hedonistic activities involved in increasing one's pleasure and/or decreasing one's pain. Where informational reinforcement is high but utilitarian relatively low, the characteristic behaviors indicate saving and collecting. Incremental acquisition is not without its satisfactions from day to day or week to week and ultimately such behavior depends upon the utilitarian benefits of having the products in questions. But the behaviors of gradually saving and collecting are maintained from week to week or whatever by feedback on performance: how much interest has my saving attracted? how many more points do I need for the bonus gift? how soon do these magazines transform themselves into an encyclopedia? Finally, there are behaviors maintained by relatively low levels of both utilitarian and informational reinforcement. These ought to include activities which are routine or mandatory, the minimal consumer responses one needs to effect to stay alive or duties one must perform to continue to exist as a citizen. These four operant classes of consumer behavior are described, respectively, as Accomplishment, Hedonism, Accumulation and Maintenance.

An understanding of the probable consequences of current consumer behavior, which have through prior generation presumably brought the consumer to the current behavior setting, is intended as a response to the problem of equifinality. Each of these classes is an operant equifinality class in the sense that it is one of a series of topographically distinct behaviors that are severally maintained by the same pattern of reinforcement: placing the behavior in question in one or other of these constitutes an important stage in locating that behavior. Only by isolating these consequences, an act which partly supplements and partly acts as a surrogate for a full reconstruction of the consumer's learning history, can we propose an answer to Lee's (1988) second question of operant interpretation, "What has been done?" In other words, "What ends have been achieved?" and "How is the action effective?" Chapter 8 will propose that only by the use of intentional terms (i.e., understandings of what the individual desires and believes), can a specific behavioral component of an equifinality class be effectively demarcated (see also Foxall, 2004a).

6. A *contingency category* summarizes the contingencies of reinforcement pertaining to a set of consumer situations. It thus presents in outline the pattern of reinforcement which typically maintains the response in question, and the scope of the consumer behavior setting in which it occurs. Since pattern of reinforcement is defined by the relative levels of two sources of reinforcer, utilitarian and informational, there are eight contingency categories (shown in the BPM contingency matrix, Figure 5.3).

The BPM contingency matrix suggests a *functional* typology of consumer situations: the placing of any particular consumer behavior within this scheme depends on the pattern of utilitarian and informational reinforcement which maintains it. Saving up belongs in CC5 because it is primarily maintained by expressive reinforcement, secondarily by instrumental. The behavior is best regarded as Accumulation. But collecting antiques would be CC1 or 2 because it is Accomplishment: behavior maintained by high levels of both instrumental and expressive reinforcement.

The consumer situations and behaviors assigned to each of these eight contingency categories are defined functionally rather than morphologically and topographically identical behaviors may be assigned at different times to difference operant classes and contingency categories depending on the interpretation of the combination of contingencies maintaining them. The labels employed in Figure 5.3 are, therefore, ultimately arbitrary, though they have proved useful in the interpretation of consumer behavior (Foxall 1994a). Some topographically similar behaviors can be allocated to more than one contingency category depending on the particular environmental determinants which are to be emphasized. Status consumption involves both aspects of expressive reinforcement: status and/or self-esteem. Collecting, for instance, may not be a public affair: personal (private) reinforcement may be to the fore as the joy of acquisition and ownership etc.

7. Radical behaviorist interpretation is a matter of locating behavior; that is, of reconstructing the contingencies that produced it, without the direct aid of experimental method. This might easily be misunderstood as imposing external order on observed actions of sentient beings and, indeed, operant accounts of contingency-shaped behavior are often criticized for omitting the actor's "subjective" experience of situations. In fact, behaviorists have tackled this question of individual reaction by accounting for a person's behavior within the situation; the account includes consideration of the individual's verbal behavior, the rule-governance of his or her earlier activities, and the continuity of behavior over time. This is achieved by reference to the individual's environmental history (Skinner, 1974, p. 77), for the meaning of an operant response is to be found in what has preceded it. According to Skinner – note that the concept of meaning expounded later differs from his – the meaning of an act is not found in the current setting: neither in the discriminative stimuli that compose the setting, nor in the responses that take place there, nor in their outcomes. Rather, it is located solely in the history of exposure to similar contingencies which have brought behavior under the control of the current situation (p. 91).

Meaning is thus defined in terms of the function of a response, not – as the structuralists would have it – in its topography. And function is determined by the individual's learning history. The meaning of a response is found in the past contingencies that control the topography of current behavior and empower current discriminative stimuli (Skinner, 1974, p. 91). Thus topographies of behavior may resemble one another closely but the meanings of the behaviors may differ markedly. Two customers may buy ties from the same assistant, one right after the other, but the meaning of doing so can be quite different if the first tie is bought as a present (and therefore controlled by a history of gift giving) while the second is bought for personal use (and controlled by a history of wearing "ordinary" ties to the office). The meanings do not depend on the reinforcer (the type of tie) but on these histories of buying, giving, wearing, and their outcomes.

Consumer behavior is located at the meeting place of the consumer's learning history and the current consumer behavior setting. This intersection is the consumer situation. Both of its components are necessary to the operant reconstruction of the meaning of a particular response or behavior pattern to the consumer.

The consumer's learning history determines what can act as a discriminative stimulus of current behavior; that learning history thereby also determines what is a potential reinforcer or punisher. But that learning history, which shapes the individuality, the unique response potential, of the consumer, is activated by the consumer behavior setting. It has no meaning in itself and can confer no significance on the current behavior of the consumer unless an opportunity to act presents itself: that opportunity is afforded by the current setting which primes the learning history's capacity to shape current consumer choice. When this has occurred, whatever consumer behavior takes place is a function of the interaction of historical and current environments: it can be located in time and space.

In practice, this detailed level of analysis relates particular consumer responses – browsing, evaluating, buying, using – to the elements of the consumer situation in which they arise. In accounting for the approach, avoidance and escape responses of consumers, this micro-level interpretation involves identifying the discriminative stimuli that compose the setting, the consequences to which they point, and, as far as is feasible, the learning history of the individual. Ultimately, the purpose is to understand the meaning of the observed pattern of behavior for the individual consumer.

Since direct empirical access to the consumer's learning history is denied the observer, an operant interpretation often necessarily concentrates on those environmental factors that can be observed or inferred, notably elements of the behavior setting. The assumption is – and all interpretive systems rest upon an act of faith – that the reinforcing consequences these setting elements prefigure are broadly those which have shaped and maintained similar behavior in the past; such (setting) elements and (behavioral) consequences can thus be used as a guide to the predisposing/ inhibiting nature of the consumer's learning history. But there is no reason why the resulting account cannot be checked, corroborated, and amended by the individual's own recollection of that history; no reason why the consumer's verbal account cannot provide the interpretation; no reason why the operant interpretation cannot be "thick" rather than "thin" in Ryle's (1968) terms (see also Geertz, 1973). The sole criterion is our resulting understanding of "how the action of interest makes a difference to the person's life. That is, what does the action produce or present that would not be produced or presented otherwise?" (Lee, 1988, p. 137). The framework could easily accommodate a fourth interpretive level to embrace the detailed, self-described and analyzed experience of an individual consumer related to the organizing environment.

8. Some clarification of the meaning of "hedonic consumption" within the present research program may be in order. It has always been a cardinal point of the BPM approach that *all* products, services, situations contain elements of *both* utilitarian reinforcement and informational reinforcement. The fourfold classification of consumer behaviors (accomplishment, pleasure, accumulation and maintenance) emphasizes this, and empirical research (summarized in Chapters 6 and 7) has confirmed it. However, it is natural to ask whether there are any products/services that are entirely utilitarian in terms of the reinforcement they offer, any that are entirely informational? An air conditioning unit appears entirely functional, wholly utilitarian in the benefits it provides. It is a means of keeping cool and fresh on a hot day, of remaining warm when it is cold outside. A wedding ring, by contrast, seems an entirely informational product, the purpose of which is to signal the marital status of a man or woman, to deter suitors, to avoid confusing and embarrassing social incidents. It apparently has no utilitarian benefit at all. In fact, jewelry in general, and certainly that of the more expensive kind, seems

to have little or no utilitarian function, its purpose being apparently to display and reflect the wealth of its owner. Somehow, though, this leaves air conditioners and wedding rings under-analyzed.

This is partly because "culture" impinges on and enters into the definition of the pattern of reinforcement provided by any particular product or service. An air conditioning unit might, in many parts of the US where they are ubiquitous, be thought of as entirely utilitarian; but, in many other parts of the world where such a product would be a relative novelty, there might well be some informational reinforcement to be gained from owning and conspicuously using an air conditioner. In addition to its capacity to confer status and self-esteem, a wedding ring and other jewelry can have a more utilitarian purpose: the adornment of the body, the enhancement its wearer's looks (including the attractiveness of the hands).

The required further analysis recognizes that utilitarian reinforcement and informational reinforcement can each be subdivided into an instrumental element and a hedonic element (see figure). Instrumental utilitarian reinforcement is avoidance behavior in the context of deprivation of some physical product or service, e.g. drinking water when thirsty. This is negatively reinforced behavior. Hedonic utilitarian reinforcement would be eating ice cream, positively reinforced behavior that involves pleasure. Instrumental informational reinforcement would be avoidance behavior in the context of social belonging (again, negatively reinforced); e.g., buying a motor bike in order to gain entrance to a motor biking club, wearing a suit in order to conform to the minimal requirement of membership of one's occupational group. Hedonic informational reinforcement is positively reinforced behavior that leads to status/self-esteem enhancement in social situations, e.g., being the most immaculately dressed person in one's occupational group. These correspond in some ways to how we measured utilitarian reinforcement and informational reinforcement in the brand choice work but they could also be operationalised in a further survey/experiment. (In the interests of terminological clarity, it seems useful to retain the term "reinforcement" for utilitarian reinforcement and informational reinforcement (as before) and use the term "benefit" in relation to instrumental and hedonic outcomes.)

This has implications for the way in which we ascribe utilitarian reinforcement or informational reinforcement to products/services or environments which emphasize the interaction of apparently inherent features of the product or service and the situational, often socially- or culturally-defined determination of the predominance of utilitarian or informational reward it embodies. There is, especially, a link with what has become known as "hedonic consumption."

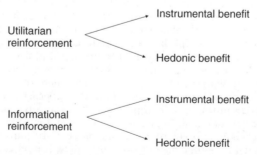

Figure Subdivision of Utilitarian reinforcement and Informational reinforcement

These products fit the specifications of two of the four classes of consumer behavior: maintenance and pleasure: utilitarian reinforcement that is *predominantly* instrumental (maintenance) (water, basic food); utilitarian reinforcement that is *predominantly* hedonic (pleasure) (ice cream); informational reinforcement that is *predominantly* instrumental (maintenance) (group membership qualification); informational reinforcement that is *predominantly* hedonic (pleasure) (excelling within the group).

What of the other two classes of consumer behavior (accomplishment and accumulation)? Accomplishment is high utilitarian reinforcement, high informational reinforcement. Accumulation is high informational reinforcement, low utilitarian reinforcement. It is important to bear in mind that utilitarian reinforcement ≠ instrumental benefit; informational reinforcement ≠ hedonic benefit (see table.) Accumulation, typified by saving up, is largely a matter of informational reinforcement, secondarily of utilitarian reinforcement: but it seems predominantly instrumental, secondarily hedonic. Accomplishment is a matter of high utilitarian reinforcement and high informational reinforcement: but it seems predominantly hedonic, secondarily instrumental.

The emerging pattern seems to be as follows:

High instrumental + low hedonic = Maintenance (low utilitarian reinforcement, low informational reinforcement) and Accumulation (low utilitarian reinforcement and high informational reinforcement).

High hedonic + low instrumental = Pleasure (low utilitarian reinforcement, high informational reinforcement) and Accomplishment (high utilitarian reinforcement, high informational reinforcement).

Hence, high instrumental benefit is associated with low utilitarian reinforcement regardless of whether the attendant informational reinforcement is high or low. Low hedonic is similarly associated with low utilitarian reinforcement and *either* high or low informational reinforcement. High hedonic benefit is associated with high informational reinforcement regardless of whether the attendant utilitarian reinforcement is high or low. Low instrumental benefit is similarly associated with high informational reinforcement and with *either* high or low utilitarian reinforcement.

The Relationship of Consumption Benefit to Patterns of Reinforcement

	Instrumental	Hedonic
High	Low UTILITARIAN REINFORCEMENT, *either* high *or* low INFORMATIONAL REINFORCEMENT	High INFORMATIONAL REINFORCEMENT, *either* high *or* low UTILITARIAN REINFORCEMENT
Low	High INFORMATIONAL REINFORCEMENT, *either* high *or* low UTILITARIAN REINFORCEMENT	Low UTILITARIAN REINFORCEMENT, *either* high *or* low INFORMATIONAL REINFORCEMENT

Whence this pattern? We need to distinguish carefully utilitarian reinforcement and informational reinforcement on the one hand and instrumental benefit and hedonic benefit on the other. The OED definitions of the latter are: *Instrumental* 'serving as a means', and as we have noted in the examples given above this seems to be generally negatively reinforced. *Hedonic* 'of or characterized by pleasure', and apparently positively reinforced. These are not to be confused with the definitions inherent in our dichotomisation of reinforcement:

> *Utilitarian* = functional, mediated by the product, positively reinforced (which suggests that the hedonic element must generally be the stronger). If so, this explains why we got higher pleasure scores for the behaviors that led to utilitarian reinforcement in the PAD research.

Note the implication that instrumental and hedonic benefits are not separate from each other, not necessarily mutually exclusive. Obviously the hedonic value of doing something can result from its high level of instrumentality. Sometimes, for cultural/economic reasons it was necessary in the PAD research (see Chapter 6) to increase the instrumental value of a reward so much that the hedonic element is also very high. For example, in the Venezuelan research, because interest rates were so high in that country, we had to propose very high rewards for saving (CC5); as a result, we also obtained higher than expected pleasure scores (hedonic benefits) in that case.

> *Informational* = symbolic, mediated by others, more likely to be positively reinforced in the case of Accomplishment and Hedonism rather than Accumulation and Maintenance. We would expect accumulation to be a more closed setting than say CC1 or 3 since getting interest on savings, for instance, depends on being locked in to the scheme; CC7 also rather closed (e.g. grocery shopping) since it is a necessity. CC1 and 3, by contrast, are 'luxuries': we should expect different e_Ds for behaviors in different settings.

While we are on the theme of negative reinforcement: In the case of (relatively) closed settings, the hypothesis has always been that behavior tends to be negatively reinforced (especially in CC4, 6 and 8) as compared with that which takes place in open settings. Presumably this is because behavior in closed settings is largely instrumental: you have to be there to get the goodies but might not want to be there otherwise. CC8, although open has a tendency to promote negatively reinforced behavior too (being in a supermarket to get the weekly shopping). (All these are based on gross generalizations regarding what people experience in these settings, of course: some people actually enjoy being prisoners in airplanes!)

We have briefly touched on the implications of this conceptual refinement for the PAD research. Let us say a few words about the more recent research on brand choice (see Chapter 7). Our operational measures of utilitarian reinforcement and informational reinforcement were as follows:

Utilitarian reinforcement: as brands increase in this, they offer something more, an additional source of consumer benefit (baked beans with sausage, cars with air conditioning). This is on the face of it an increase in instrumental benefit, though it also heralds a contingent increase in hedonic benefit. (We would expect consumers faced with low utilitarian reinforcement brand versions to score lower on pleasure than those faced with high utilitarian reinforcement versions).

Informational reinforcement: this adds predominantly hedonic benefit, though manufacturers would claim it also involved instrumental benefits. (We would expect similarly increasing pleasure scores with increasing informational reinforcement). [Incidentally, we would expect lower pleasure scores for closed as opposed to open settings: this is what we found].

Hence, "hedonic consumption" is that which leads principally to hedonic benefits (as we have defined it) and is further analyzable by reference to the pattern of reinforcement within which it occurs.

9. Behavior analytic consumer research portrays consumer behavior as the outcome of environmental consequences, acting either directly or through verbal descriptions (rules). Behavior is contingency-shaped when the person has much experience of the outcomes of this or similar behavior. When this is not the case, behavior is usually preceded by review of the contingencies described by other-rules (instructions provided by other people). In this process, and through direct behavioral experience, the individual forms personal self-rules about how the contingencies operate. As behavior comes under the control of self-rules, it appears spontaneous and routine, though it has a long history in which it was shaped by successive approximations to what it has become. Most human behavior is rule-governed to some extent but ultimately the contingencies themselves determine what people actually do. Adherents of this viewpoint interpret pre-behavioral deliberation not as mental processing but as a behavior in its own right in which the consequences of acting are reviewed and evaluated.

As this chapter has argued, the BPM proposes that consumer behavior is a function of the interaction of the scope of the current consumer behavior setting and the individual's learning history. This interaction motivates a specific behavior by prefiguring the utilitarian and informational consequences it is likely to produce. A relatively closed behavior setting involves mainly other-rules which describe not only the contingencies but the social reinforcements and punishments of compliance or noncompliance. Compliant behavior in these settings is negatively reinforced while noncompliance is punished.

Relatively open settings involve mainly self-rules. Personal learning history encapsulates an individual's disposition toward complying with the instructions of others (which is activated by the discriminative stimuli that compose a closed setting) as well as the basis for derivation of self-rules (which are activated by the elements of an open setting). Utilitarian reinforcement consists in the utilitarian benefits of purchase and consumption: the behavior that produces it is contingency-shaped. Informational reinforcement consists in social standing and the achievement of personal norms: the behavior that produces it is rule-governed. Self-rules appear to refer to the attitudes formed through deliberation; other-rules, to subjective norms; when self-rules have been employed frequently, the behavior appears to come under the automatic stimulus control of the behavior setting.

Behavior analysts have surmised that behavior is rule-governed only on its initial emission; thereafter, it comes under contingency control. The analysis undertaken in this chapter suggests a more elongated process.

At first the consumer has no specific learning history with respect to the consumption behavior in question. Perhaps presented with a new brand in a new product class, there is no accumulated experience or knowledge of buying and using the item and the consequences of doing so. However, in proportion to the consumer's having a learning history for rule-following, other-rules may be sought out for guidance and action. These might take the form of the advertising claims which first created awareness of the innovation; alternatively, they might come from significant others, acquaintances and opinion leaders. Whatever their source, these rules are not passively accepted by the consumer but used as the basis of a sequence of deliberation and evaluation, first of the claims themselves, and their comparison with similar claims for other products and brands, then of accumulated consumption experience. The consumer's actions involved in the trial and repeat purchase/consumption of the product develops a learning history. Moreover, reasoning with respect to personal experience of the item, and the evaluation of this experience, will lead to the formation of self-rules which henceforth guide action without constant deliberation. The consumer has moved from the central route to the peripheral, from deliberation to spontaneity, from systematic reasoning to the application of heuristics. The initial lack of a relevant learning history prompted a search for other-rules; the acquisition of such a history means that self-rules can be extracted from experience. Only the acquisition of such an extensive history can transform the behavior finally from rule-governed to contingency-shaped and even then the distinction between self-rule governance and contingency shaping is not empirically available.

The import of this analysis lies not in its superficially reiterating the sequence of consumer decision making found in cognitive models of initial and subsequent information processing but in its capacity to account for these phenomena without extensive reliance on theoretical entities posited at a metabehavioral level.

6   Attitudes, Situations, and Behavior

1. Mehrabian and Russell's (1974a) concept of *arousal* distinguishes the appropriate emotional response for environments rich in informational reinforcement. *Arousal* is determined by both the environment and by intrapersonal factors such as anxiety-proneness. The environmental input to *arousal* is measured in terms of the "information rate", a concept by which Mehrabian and Russell take account such aspects of the intensity of stimuli as their complexity, novelty, crowding and harmony. The rationale for this concept is that most environments include not one single stimulus such as hue, loudness, pitch of sound or temperature, but simultaneously include stimulation in various sense modalities and multiple stimulus dimensions within each modality. For example, a setting may include many colors, and various combinations of sounds and temperatures. Information rate stems not only from the colors themselves but from their variety and tone; from the loudness of noises, the speed of visual stimulation, and the pungency of smells. Many of these stimuli also vary in time. The combination of all these variations offers different levels of information, and these determine responses. Responses are also affected by how they relate to those previously encountered in other settings. They are thus dependent on the familiarity the consumer has with settings of a particular type and thus with his or her reinforcement history.
2. Mehrabian has undertaken substantial refinement of the PAD scales so that three sets can be distinguished. The original "PAD$_{74}$" scales dating from the work with Russell (Mehrabian & Russell, 1974a) were revised by Mehrabian (1978) and Mehrabian (1995). The first of these remain in the public domain and are the most widely used. Although the post-1974 scales exhibit increasing psychometric usefulness, the original scales correlate sufficiently highly with them to ensure their continuing validity and reliability. (PAD$_{74}$ scales correlate .64 (P), .40 (A)

and .60 (D) with the PAD$_{78}$ scales. (Mehrabian 1978, 1980, p. 51). PAD$_{78}$ scales correlate .96 (p < .01), .67 (p < .01) and .86)p < .01) respectively with the PAD$_{95}$ scales. (Mehrabian 1995, p. 356). Although the latest scales are undoubtedly higher in construct validity and reliability than the earlier ones, there is sufficient consistency to make it worthwhile to draw conclusions based on the almost universally used 1974 scales.

3. The connection between informational reinforcement and *arousal* is not so obvious as that between utilitarian reinforcement and *pleasure*, and requires further elaboration. Mehrabian and Russell use information theory to account for the overall effect of a variety of components of stimulation in a given setting along a single dimension, e.g., complexity, diversity, unity, congruity, artificiality, crowding, symmetry, meaningfulness, harmony, novelty, surprising, rare, unexpected, and changing. The concept of information rate can be used to characterize complex spatial and temporal combinations of stimuli within and across settings. Significant in the present context is the fact that information rate depends on differences, variations and contrasts within the environment that signal among other things performance feedback. A physical example is provided by the yellow lines sometimes painted across roads to indicate to drivers how fast they are traveling, especially at road junctions and other places where it is necessary to reduce speed. A social example is the degree of crowding indicated by the closeness of other consumers in a retail environment which is related to arousal and possibly avoidance or escape reactions. Again, the comments of friends and family members, both verbal and nonverbal on the clothes one has bought or where one has vacationed yield social performance feedback on a consumer's performance as an economic and social agent and this has direct influence on his or her social status, self-image and self-esteem. Information rate is measured by 14 semantic differential scales on which the respondent describes situations as, for example, *simple...complex, novel...familiar, dense...sparse* (Mehrabian and Russell, 1974a). Since information rate correlates consistently with *arousal* and its rationale and components are, therefore, germane to the argument that *arousal* provides a suitable measure of informational reinforcement (especially insofar as this is conceived as performance feedback).

4. The approach relies on an assiduous reading of the failings of early attitude theory and research which demonstrated only weak relationships between measures of attitudes and measures of behavior but which gained markedly in predictive value once two kinds of environmental influence were taken into account. The success of the Theories of Reasoned Action and Planned Behavior stem from their inclusion of close situational correspondence in the cognitive and behavioral measures they employ and the behavioral history of the respondent, i.e., the consequences which similar behavior has had for them in the past. The BPM is a formalization of these developments. Through the adoption of Mehrabian and Russell's work in the testing of this model, a psychometrically sound instrument has been employed to show how consumers' emotional responses to the environments they confront are distributed.

Without any of these elements, the research program described would have been unconvincing. Careful attention to the deficiencies of attitude research, especially in the form of Wicker's milestone review, indicated not only the sources of deficiency but also the need for a suitable model of situational influences on choice. The BPM has provided such a model and its taxonomy of situations in terms of pattern of reinforcement and behavior setting scope has proved a successful testing ground for Mehrabian and Russell's framework for the conceptualization and analysis of emotional response to environments. The consequent framing of attitude as a classically-conditioned affective response provided a means of framing hypotheses by means of which both the BPM and Mehrabian and Russell's approach could be empirically examined with positive consequences for attitude–behavior research in marketing and psychological research.

5. Research on human verbal responding has flourished during the last several years. In particular, differences between humans' and animals' susceptibility to the contingencies programmed in experiments have raised considerable theoretical debate over the role of language in controlling behavior. Human responding has been described in several studies as conforming to what is known as the Matching Law (Herrnstein, 1997). Essentially, this proposes that in a situation of choice between two responses that lead on differing schedules of reinforcement to the same reinforcer, the subject allocates responses between the choices in proportion to the amount of reinforcement actually obtained from each. We shall return to this in greater detail in Chapter 7.

For now, it is important to recognize that some researchers (notably Lowe, 1983) have argued that human responding frequently deviates substantially from the matching relationships found for other animals. Horne and Lowe (1993, p. 53) summarize six experiments involving human performances on concurrent VI schedules: "In our studies, ... less than half the subjects' performances resembled those typically found in animal choice studies. For many of the remaining subjects, there were not mere 'deviations' from the matching typically observed in nonhumans; rather their performance was qualitatively different and could not be described by the matching equations." Departures from the matching law have been reported by several other researchers (e.g., Silberberg et al., 1991). Horne and Lowe (1993, p. 54) comment that "Together with the data from our six experiments, these findings clearly demonstrate that human subjects showing ideal matching, or even a close approximation to it, are the exception rather than the rule in the literature."

Departures such as these are apparently explained by humans' capacity for verbalizing the contingencies of reinforcement which they believe to be in operation, formulating their own ideas about the nature of the rules by which rewards are delivered. Information, accurate or otherwise, about the contingencies operating in experimental settings is provided in the instructions given by the experimenter: use of such information may account for the digressions shown in human behavior from patterns found in experiments with nonhumans. Verbal behavior may thus be invoked in the search for the causes of both the relatively simple behaviors emitted in experimental settings and the more complex patterns of response found in the situations of purchase and consumption.

7 Patterns of Brand Choice

1. Price elasticity of demand (e_D) is a measure of the extent to which a (percentage) change in the price of a commodity is associated with a (percentage) change in the quantity demanded of that commodity:

$$\varepsilon_D = \frac{\% \text{ change in quantity demanded}}{\% \text{ change in price.}}$$

If $e_D = 0$, there is no change in the quantity demanded when price changes and elasticity is said to be "perfect" or "complete." If $0 < e_D < 1$, the quantity demanded changes as price changes but not to the same percentage extent, and demand is said to be "inelastic." If $1 < e_D < \infty$, quantity demanded changes by a greater percentage than does price, and demand is said to be "elastic."

2. Some modifications of the measures of quantity and price were necessary for the following reasons. First, price variation throughout the 16-week period was not very wide and can be expected to be even less so within each consumer group, since the classification of individuals in such groups was dependent upon the informational level of the brands they bought most frequently, which in turn were classified in part based on their average price. Therefore, each consumer group can be expected to have a different price average within a relatively restricted range of prices. Second, the analysis of purchases of brands by a particular consumer group for each product category would reduce dramatically the number of data points available to calculate price elasticities. For example, in the case of baked beans, there was no consumer classified in consumer Group 2, which would restrict the analysis for the product category. One possible solution for this problem would be to aggregate all the data obtained from all the products and then calculate price elasticities for each consumer group. This solution would pose another type of measurement problem. Considering that the measurement scales (and even units) of quantity and price varied greatly among product categories, it would be difficult to calculate one single regression line using data from different products.

One way of overcoming all such problems would be to use measures of quantity and price relative to the average of each consumer group (e.g., Bell et al., 1999; see also Oliveira-Castro et al., 2005a, b). These relative measures can be calculated by dividing the quantities bought (and prices paid) on each purchase by the average quantity bought (and average price paid) of each product within each consumer group. The resulting data would provide an estimate of price elasticity relative to the consumer group mean, that is, it would provide an estimate of changes in quantities as a function of changes in prices above and below the mean of each consumer group. Data from each product would be "standardized" to the product mean for each group, yielding unitless ratio values above and below 1.0. Data from all products and groups would become comparable in terms of responsiveness around the mean.

This procedure was adopted in the analyses described next. Each quantity data point for the regression was calculated by dividing the quantity bought on a shopping occasion by the average quantity for that specific consumer group for that specific product. Analogously, each price data point for the regression consisted of the price paid on a given shopping occasion divided by the average price paid by that specific group when buying that specific product. Then, for example, the quantity bought of Tesco Value© instant coffee by a specific consumer on a given shopping trip was divided by the average quantity of instant coffee bought by all consumers in Group 1 (Informational and Utilitarian Level 1). This same procedure was used to calculate the correspondent measures of price. A regression analysis was then conducted with all data points obtained for all consumers classified in Group 1, including data points from all product categories. The same was done with the data for the other five consumer groups (the number of paired data points, N, for the six groups ranged from 179 to 897).

8 Context and Cognition in Consumer Choice

1. *Mutual entailment* is the symmetry of stimulus equivalence: the derived bidirectionality of stimulus relations. The relationship A → B entails the relationship B → A. *Combinatorial entailment* is the transitivity and the equivalence of stimulus equivalence: when in a particular context A → B and B → C, and also a relation is entailed between A and C and another between C and A. E.g., if A is harder than B and B is harder than C, then a harder-than relation is entailed between A and C and a softer-than relation between C and A.

2. In *Content and Consciousness*, Dennett employs the device of capitalizing the initial letter of intentional when it refers to the philosophical concept, thereby distinguishing it from everyday intentionality. Although he did not retain this usage in later writings, he maintained it in the second edition of *Content and Consciousness* and it is thus retained in the quotations from that source.

3. The reasons for selecting Dennett from among the philosophers who have considered intentionality and behavior range from the accessibility of his work to the wide spectrum of concerns with which he has dealt (and is dealing) that are relevant to the quest for a viable basis for understanding social cognition. But the most important is that Dennett is the living philosopher who has done most to explore the philosophical consequences of cognitive psychology. Given the impossibility of exploring the entire corpus of philosophical cognitive science and that Dennett's work is used here as a template rather than a doctrine – indeed even a template which will come under criticism and from which my final offering will deviate importantly – this concentration on one source of cognitive philosophy seems justified. For critical review of Dennett's work, see, *inter alia*, Stich (1981, 1983), Churchland (1981), and the peer commentary on "Intentional systems in cognitive ethology" (Dennett, 1983). More general peer commentary can be found in Dahlbom (1993); *Philosophical Topics* (1994); Ross et al. (2000), and Brook and Ross (2002). Alternative accounts of intentionality are presented by Anscombe (1957), Chisholm (1957), and Searle (1983).

4. This is not an identity theory: Dennett does not identify the experience of pain with some physical happening; he maintains two separate levels of explanation: one in which the experience of pain, while felt, does not refer, and one in which the descriptions of neural occurrences refer to actual neural structures, events and states in which the extensionally-characterized science deals. Cf. Dennett, 1969, 1978).

5. Attitude researchers' early attempts to predict (and thereby partly explain) specific behaviors based on global cognitive measures – predicting behavior toward the object from attitude toward the object – provide an example of what Dennett called "pure phenomenology:" the explanation is in fact stated in terms derived essentially from the behavior it is purported to predict/explain. It failed in part because of the circularity of its underlying methodology: attitudes were those entities that would predict behavior, they were in themselves predispositions to act in the prescribed manner. That there should be such precursors of behavior, that they should be measurable and that they should lead to the prediction and explanation of the specific behaviors in which researchers were interested amounted to a circularity of reasoning in which intentional terms were ascribed to respondents' verbal behavior, taken to refer to some deeper mental structure or event or process which in turn was assumed to cause or explain nonverbal behaviors. The difficulty with this latent process view of attitude is that it relies on the ascription of content based on the observation of one kind of behavior which is

then assumed to correlate with another; the ascription derived from the first ought therefore to provide a means of predicting and explaining the second. There is no reason however, for these separate behaviors to be correlated unless the environmental circumstances that shape and maintain them are similar, unless they lead to similar consequences in terms of rewards and sanctions. Pure phenomenology is baseless to predict and explain because it is founded upon a closed system of intentional attribution.

One way of reacting to this would be to abandon the idea of intentionality altogether, to turn to a strict descriptive behaviorism which embodied a probability construct of "attitude," in fact an approach to behavior that simply counted how often a particular response (buying product A or brand B, or whatever) was performed and calling this probability the buyer's attitude or tendency or disposition. This is essentially Ehrenberg's approach which was discussed earlier. Another behavior-based approach goes further than this by seeking the causes of such a response in the system of utilitarian and informational rewards made available by the marketing system. This research program, which has resulted in an explanatory, not purely descriptive, approach based on the BPM, is an example of an extensional science approach to consumer choice which, although it does not incorporate intentionalistic terminology, is consistent with a probability conception of attitude. Its predictive capacity, like that of the situational approach to attitudinal–behavioral consistency developed in the last chapter, appears to predict with at least the same accuracy as the cognitive approaches more prevalent in consumer research. However, there are reasons to believe that at the level of *explanation* further elaboration is required and that this can be achieved by the inclusion – within a strict framework of attribution – of intentional terminology. The initial phases of this process are akin to those proposed and followed by Dennett, which are outlined in the text. However, I have considerably expanded on his approach in making it relevant to the explanation of consumer choice, and in the comprehensive analysis indicated by the empirical research on attitudinal-behavioral consistency considered in earlier chapters.

9   Intentional Behaviorism

1. An essential rationale of Skinner's explanatory system is "selection by consequences," (Skinner, 1981) which links operant conditioning with evolutionary biology on one hand and cultural evolution on the other. Indeed, one way in which behavior analysis seeks to establish the plausibility of its accounts of both animal and human behaviors is by employing the evolution of biological species through natural selection as an analogue for the procedure in which operant behavior is selected by the environment (Smith, 1994). The essence of evolutionary explanation lies in the inferred action of a selective environment on the continuity of the form, function and behavior of an organism or organization and the species to which it belongs. Operant conditioning has also been portrayed by its adherents as an evolutionary process in its own right, one whose causal mode is selection through consequences.

   Evolutionary biology deals with the selection of organisms that are adapted to living and reproducing in a specific local environment. Such an organism, its form, function and behavior, constitutes the phenotype which is the result of the organism's genetic composition (genotype) and the action of the environment on that organism during the course of its development (ontogeny). Although the environment acts directly upon the phenotype, the fundamental unit of selection is the gene since it alone is capable of self-replication and of thereby ensuring the continuity of selected features through their manifestation in the inheriting phenotype through successive generations (Dawkins, 1982). Genes contain both genotype and phenotype information.

Variation in the phenotype is closely related to variation in the genotype: though phenotypic variation may be modified by the environment, characteristics becoming statistically dominant during this process are not – in Darwin's (1859) account – heritable through sexual reproduction except through mutation of genotype or phenotype information. The action of the environment on the phenotype determines the extent to which the genotype potential is expressed. Variation between individuals means that some are better suited (adapted) to a particular immediate environment than are others, and this has implications for (but is not identical with) their genotypic fitness, i.e. their capacity to reproduce successfully. "Survival of the fittest" refers to the selective action of the environment in which more adapted or adaptable individuals are able to survive and reproduce their advantageous characteristics. (See also Sober, 1993).

The metaprinciple of "selection by consequences" is used by Skinner (1981) to describe and relate natural selection, which is shaped and maintained by "contingencies of survival," and the selection and persistence of instrumental human behavior in operant conditioning, in which behavior is shaped and maintained by "contingencies of reinforcement." A subset of the latter is cultural evolution, in which behaviors that are of utility to the survival and welfare of social groups and organizations are selected and transmitted, according to their consequences, from generation to generation.

It is not only in behavioral psychology that the evolutionary analogy is apparent as a means of conceptualizing behavior. *In biology*, Dawkins (1988, p. 33) points out that in natural selection, "the replicators are the genes, and the consequences by which they are selected are their phenotypic effects, that is, mostly their effects on the embryonic development of the body in which they sit." However, in operant conditioning, "the replicators are the habits in the animal's repertoire, originally spontaneously produced (the equivalent of mutation). The consequences are reinforcement, positive and negative [and punishment]. The habits can be seen as replicators because their frequency of emergence from the animal's motor system increases, or decreases, as a result of their reinforcement [or punishing] consequences." The principal causal agency is the environment which acts to select the consequences of some behaviors but not others and thereby ensures the continuity of that which is selected. Biologist Maynard Smith (1986, p. 75) also mentions the similarity of the processes: "There is an obvious analogy between operant conditioning and evolution by natural selection. Behavior becomes adapted to the environment by the reinforcement of spontaneous acts, just as morphological structure is adapted by the natural selection of spontaneous mutations." *In the philosophy of social science*, Van Parijs (1981) identifies the evolutionary process, as it occurs in the social and economic spheres, as that of operant conditioning. He designates this mechanism, which relies on behavioral reinforcement, as "R-evolution" in contrast to the "NS-evolution" which characterizes the survival of the fittest that occurs in natural selection. Richelle, who, unlike Dawkins and Van Parijs is a behaviorist, has also written of the compatibility of natural selection and the environmental selection of behavior:

> There is nothing implausible in the idea that one basic process is at work throughout numerous levels of complexity or in a wide variety of living species. The same fundamental mechanism is called upon in evolutionary biology to account for the simplest and for the most complex living forms. The same is true of the basic principles governing the genetic code. One basic principle is acceptable if it provides for structural diversification. This is exactly what the variation-selection process does in biological evolution. But the observed diversity must not hide the basic process that produces it. The same might be true of behavior... Viewed in this perspective, operant behavior has little to do with the repetition of stereotyped responses which has become the popular representation of it. It is a highly dynamic process grounded in behavioral variation. Novel and creative behavior, and problem-solving do not raise particular difficulties in this view... (Richelle (1987, pp. 135–6, p. 134).

In evolutionary economics, Dosi and Orsenigo (1988, p. 13), refer to the evolutionary process as that in which "individual and organizational behaviors, to different degrees and through different processes, are selected, penalized or rewarded." In contrast to the presumption of conditions of static equilibrium which pervades neoclassical economics, evolutionary economics emphasizes "discovery, learning, selection, evolution and complexity" (Dosi & Orsenigo, 1988, p. 15).

2. Hence what Goldsmith refers to as the dual nature of causation. As important as the homology of natural selection and operant conditioning is the dual nature of causation in psychology as well as biology. Goldsmith (1991, p. 6) observes that "Virtually every question that one can pose in biology has two very different kinds of answers:" proximate and ultimate, which supply complementary explanation. The following table shows how this extends to the three levels at which Skinner claims that selection by consequences takes place.

Proximate and ultimate causation in natural selection and operant learning

	PROXIMATE CAUSATION	ULTIMATE CAUSATION
Natural selection	Biochemical, physiological predisposition, phenotype	Function in adaptation and fitness, genetic predisposition, genotype
Operant behavior	Discriminative stimuli, especially in humans verbal, rules	Learning history
Cultural evolution	Ditto as provided by group artifacts, group-specific objects, rules, mores, etc.	Social history

All these types of behavior are the result of contingencies (of survival or rein-forcement). But the contingencies are not the cause; they are a description of the behavior in the environment, i.e., of the functional relationship between the two. The causes of operant behavior are (i) the (susceptibility to/meaning of) dis-criminative stimuli acquired in a learning history, and (ii) the learning history itself.

The dual nature of biological contingency is mirrored in the case of operant learning. Proximate causation is the realm of the consumer behavior setting, consisting of the usually visible instigators of behavior. Ultimate causation is found in a history of reinforcement and punishment. The distinction has methodological implications. Experimentation is concerned with the manipula-tion of proximate causes, especially discriminative stimuli in the operant chamber. Of course, the subject has a learning history which determines its response to the discriminative stimuli, and in the case of laboratory animals, this learning history is known to the experimenter. Interpretation is concerned with ultimate causation where the learning history is not known (at least not in detail). The gaps must, therefore, be filled in with plausible guesses. The question to which radical behaviorists have given scant regard is what procedure to follow in doing this. However, the associations between proximate causation and experimental manipulation and between ultimate causation and interpreta-tion are not absolute. Where the proximate discriminative stimulus consist in verbal responses, interpretation is inevitable; experimentation, impossible.

Goldsmith (1991, p. 7) points out that proximate cause in biology "has to do with the characteristics that one can see – characteristics that are the final expression of the genetic program (the genotype) that is present in the fertilized egg from which the organism grew. Explanations of proximate causation are often couched in the language of physiology and biochemistry and are fre-quently the subject of experimental manipulation." In operant psychology, proximate cause concerns visible behavior whose characteristics are the final expression of the individual's learning history. Explanations at this level are often couched in the language of discriminative stimuli including verbal dis-criminative stimuli and private events such as thoughts. Proximate causation is amenable to experimental manipulation when the factors responsible for stimu-lus control are publicly available. But when they are inferred private events, interpretation is inevitable – behavior analysts sometimes refuse to admit them. Much of the behavior studied is rule-governed (ultimately contingency-shaped). Emphasis on proximate causation, to the exclusion of consideration of ultimate causation leads to folk psychology and cognitivism.

Ultimate cause, Goldsmith notes, is the "province of the evolutionary bio-logist who is interested in the historical origins of genotypes. Explanations of ultimate cause invoke the concept of adaptation of organisms to their environ-ments as well as evolutionary inferences based on comparative studies of dif-ferent kinds of organisms. Direct experimental manipulation is not unknown but is usually more difficult to achieve." Ultimate cause is the domain of the operant psychologist interested in the environmental shaping of a learning history. It too involves consideration of the adaptation of behavior to its envi-ronment, but it is that of the operant class rather than the individual response. Ultimate causation involves interpretation in terms of what is known of operant behavior in accessible, manipulable settings. This dimension is often subsumed under the general rubric of "experience", the contingency-shaping of which is ignored.

Evolution, is "in a fundamental sense, ... the sifting of genotypes; however, differential survival and reproduction occur among phenotypes. In the world of interacting organisms, phenotypes are the agents of the genotypes, and it is the phenotypes – the organisms themselves – that compete and whose performance determines reproductive success. Obviously, natural selection can act only if the basis for differential survival and reproduction is heritable. Phenotypic differences that are not the result of underlying genotypic differences therefore cannot serve as the basis for evolutionary change... It is for this central reason that we must be concerned with how the genotype becomes translated into the phenotype and with the effects of the environment on this process" (Goldsmith, 1991, p. 25). Current behavioral responses are the expression of the individual's learning history. It is responses that compete and survive (are reinforced) or die out (extinguish). A major difference between natural selection and operant behavior is that whereas the former is Darwinian, the latter is Lamarckian: acquired characteristics can be "inherited" (preserved) as small changes in responses are repeated. Learning during the history of the individual is related to the probability of a current response being maintained as a result of elements of environmental continuity (leading to generalization) but also through verbal behavior (rules which describe past and current contingencies).

Learning histories "replicate" in the sense that they prime the responses that are their expressions. But responses "reproduce" in the sense that they recur. Both processes require appropriate environmental conditions, the discriminative stimuli and reinforcers that make replication and reproduction more probable. Cultural evolution is therefore the continuation of a social learning history; operant conditioning, the reproduction of a response.

3. Strictly speaking the contextual stance need not be restricted to operant psychology: it is simply a means of suggesting environment–behavior relationships that are consistent with selection-by-consequences, and which can, therefore, act as indicators of the intentional content to be ascribed at the personal level. Radical behaviorism has the advantage from an analytical point of view that it strives to accomplish an entirely extensional account of behavior, i.e., one free of intentional content. In view of the thesis of Chapter 8 that intentional ascription takes place based on the findings and theories of an extensional behavioral science, behavior analysis appears the best contender on which to found the current argument. This does not imply uncritical acceptance of radical behaviorism – indeed, if that were the case, Chapter 8 would be impossible!

4. This is not to deny that individuals can have personal level access to their pain, a source of information about it that is unavailable to the observer of their external behavior (Bennett & Hacker, 2003; Foxall, 2004a; Malcolm, 1977). By contrast, for teleological behaviorists such as Rachlin (1994) and Stout (1996), there is no reason to believe that a person who does not emit behavior that an observer can interpret as constituting pain is in pain.

5. There is controversy among philosophers over the significance of Dennett's distinction between personal and sub-personal levels of explanation, and the uses to which it may be put (cf. Bermúdez, 2000; Elton, 2000; Hornsby, 2000).The disagreement is occasioned in some degree by the different emphases Dennett himself has accorded the meanings and usages of these levels since he introduced the distinction in 1969, and by the different criteria he has emphasized over the years as appropriate to justify the ascription of content. Difficulties include the number of intentional explanations suggested by Dennett's successive analyses, the relationships among them, and the legitimacy of ascribing

content at more than one level. While Dennett's initial distinction apparently precluded the ascription of content at the sub-personal level, which was identified with neuroscientific theory and research, his later tendency casts the personal/sub-personal distinction as that between the whole and its parts, with the results that the personal level as a source of explanation in its own right has been relatively ignored. The later thinking which permitted the ascription of content to sub-personal components via the pragmatic use of the intentional stance helped blur the original distinction between explanatory levels. Dennett's associated attempt to formulate the philosophical basis of "sub-personal cognitive psychology" in contradistinction to the intentional systems theory that inhered in the personal level of explanation, increased confusion.

The grounds on which the ascription of content may be made have become vaguer insofar as they have become detached from the logic of evolutionarily-consistent reasoning that originally underpinned the distinction. Admittedly, the rules for ascribing beliefs and desires to a rational system include consideration of what beliefs and desires it "ought" to have given its position and circumstances, and this is bound to include considerations that stem from its phylogenetic history as well as its current setting. But this is a less detailed and less logically constructed version of the procedure for allocation content than that given in *Content and Consciousness* (Dennett, 1969). This procedure involves the ascription of content to the theories and findings of the extensional sciences that proceed at the sub-personal level, but it leaves them intact in the process. It is an additional level of interpretation; it does not take place in the terms of the extensional science on which it is built and is thus not a contribution to neuroscience; rather, it comprises a heuristic device that is composed of intentional idioms which do not belong in an extensional science. It exists on a level other than the sub-personal which characterizes science: the personal level, the only level at which it is legitimate to ascribe content, according to the early Dennett. This is the process in which the ascription of intentional idioms takes place and the process produces the personal level by prescribing in a way that is highly circumscribed by the logic of evolution by natural selection the content that an evolved entity "ought" to have by virtue of its phylogeny.

The presupposition Dennett makes about sub-personal cognitive psychology to the effect that elements of sub-personal physiology such as the brain and the remainder of the nervous system can be treated as intentional systems in themselves in order to predict their behavior certainly comes under considerable criticism from Bennett and Hacker (2003) on the grounds that it is intelligible to ascribe intentionality only to systems that are known to bear beliefs and desires.

Bennett and Hacker (2003, p. 73) specifically criticize Dennett on the grounds that he has committed the "mereological fallacy." Mereology refers to the logical relations of parts and wholes. The mereological principle says that psychological predicates that properly apply only to human beings cannot be meaningfully attributed to parts of the human being such as the brain. Hence, the ascription to a part of an organism the attributes that properly belong only to the whole organism is the mereological fallacy: "Human beings, but not their brains, can be said to be thoughtful or thoughtless; animals, but not their brains, let alone the hemispheres of their brains, can be said to see, hear, smell and taste things; people, but not their brains, can be said to make decisions or to be indecisive." (ibid). This fallacy is widespread among neurophysiologists they claim, citing scientists who argue that "the brain *has experiences, believes, thinks, interprets* clues *on the basis of information* made available to it, and *makes guesses... cate-*

gorizes... and *conceptually manipulates rules...* [T]he brain *knows* things, *reasons* inductively, and *constructs hypotheses* on the basis of arguments, and its constituent neurons are *intelligent*, can *estimate probabilities*, and *present arguments*. [T]he brain *poses questions, searches for answers*, and *constructs hypotheses...* [B]rains *decide*, or at least 'decide', and *initiate voluntary action*. [T]here are *symbols in the brain*, and the brain *uses*, and presumably *understands*, symbols... [T]he brain *makes classifications, comparisons*, and *decisions"* (pp. 68–70). However, these authors contend that we simply do not know what it is for brains to do these things: we only know what it is for a person to do them. Whether psychological behavior can be imputed to the brain is, however, they further point out, a philosophical matter rather than an empirical one.

The mereological principle is non-empirical: it is not subject to confirmation or disconfirmation by experimentation or other empirical means. It is a convention and could be overturned but only at the cost of changing a great deal else, changing the meaning of words and a host of familiar concept (p. 81). These authors are, therefore, adamant that intentionality cannot be ascribed to artifacts like computers, thermostats, molecules, brains. "Not only is it a subclass of psychological *attributes* that are the appropriate bearers of intentionality and not animals or things, but, further, only animals, and fairly sophisticated animals at that, and not parts of animals, let alone molecules, thermostats or computers, are the subject of such attributes" (p. 423).

This seems equivalent to saying that there has to be an ontological basis for a being/entity's believing in order to ascribe rational beliefs to it. The problem with Dennett's levels arises when he switches from the sub-personal as a means of working out what intentional idioms can be ascribed at the personal level to the idea that the raison d'être of intentional idioms is their capacity to predict behavior. He then gets involved in how to predict sub-personal events, characterizes them as (parts of) intentional systems and applies the intentional stance.

"Given Dennett's conception of the intentional stance, it is unclear what precisely he means by claiming that the brain gathers information, anticipates things, interprets the information it receives, arrives at conclusions, etc. Presumably *he* is "adopting the intentional stance" towards the brain, and its treating it as if it were a rational agent that believes what it ought to believe and desires what it ought to desire and acts on its beliefs and desires. But this is not coherent. We know what it is to treat a young child as if it were an adult, rational human being, but do we have any idea what it would be like to treat a *brain* as if it were a rational being? The brain... is not a possible subject of beliefs and desires; there is no such thing as a brain acting on beliefs and desires, and there is nothing that the brain does that can be predicted on the basis of its beliefs and desires" (Bennett & Hacker, 2003, p. 426). This is precisely what Dennett does in his later work: treating the subsystem of the brain as an intentional system. The answer is to restrict (a) the ascription of intentionality to the personal level *of people*, (b) to use the intentional stance again only for persons and (c) to use the intentional stance as a device for explanation rather than prediction (cf. Elton, 2003).

6. Operant conditioning is theoretical in itself: it is something not observed by the researcher but attributed: what the observer sees is that in a given environment (defined in terms of establishing operations and discriminative stimuli) the behavior of an organism that receives particular consequences is more likely to be repeated than when those consequences are absent. What the observer

claims is that these consequences that alter the frequency of a response have a reinforcing effect on its occurrence.

7. Theories that prompt evocations of "action at a distance," sometimes made by radical behaviorists to account for the continuity of behavior that cannot be linked to current stimulation (e.g., Lee, 1988) properly belong in this category of competence theories: they must for the sake of the principles of scientific explanation (Mallot, 1989) acknowledge that a sub-personal explanation is ultimately achievable.

8. It could be argued therefore that intentional behaviorism is already inherent in all three of Dennett's intentional psychologies. He clearly does not leave out the environment–behavior link, nor did he in *Content and Consciousness* (1969). However, intentional behaviorism is making more explicit what he leaves implicit: the systematic role of environmental consequences in learning and, what he overlooks, behavior analysis as an extensional science that can play a similar role in the ascription of content to that he proposes for neurophysiology. Dennett shows an ambivalent approach to behaviorism: on one hand he repudiates it as unable even to predict behavior (which is patently false) and on the other he acknowledges that "the law of effect will not go away" (Dennett 1978, Chapter 5). Moreover, given the difficulties apparently inherent in making the afferent–efferent → personal level ascriptions, the environment-behavior linkages which are more amenable to this ascription come into their own in a way that Dennett apparently did not contemplate.

9. It is surely difficult to maintain a sharp dichotomy between *abstracta* and *illata*.

10. I have covered the points made in this paragraph in greater detail in *Content and Cognition: Interpreting Complex Behavior* (Foxall, 2004a).

11. There is certainly no suggestion that the BPM variables account for the detailed framework of emotional responses precisely as formulated by Mehrabian in the way suggested in this table:

BPM Accommodation of Mehrabian's Taxonomy of Affective Responses

	Closed setting scope	Open setting scope
Accomplishment	*CC2* +P +A –D Amazed, infatuated, surprised, impressed, loved	*CC1* +P +A +D Bold, creative, vigorous, powerful, admired
Hedonism	*CC4* +P –A –D Consoled, sleepy, tranquilized, sheltered, protected	*CC3* +P –A +D Unperturbed, untroubled, quiet, relaxed, leisurely
Accumulation	*CC6* –P +A –D Humiliated, pain, puzzled, unsafe, embarrassed	*CC5* –P +A +D Cruel, hate, scornful, disgusted, hostile
Maintenance	*CC8* –P –A –D Lonely, unhappy, bored, sad, depressed	*CC7* –P –A + D Uninterested, uncaring, unconcerned, uninterested, selfish, proud

References

Abelson, R. P. (1972). Are attitudes necessary? In King, B. T. & McGinnies, E. (eds), *Attitudes, Conflict and Social Change*. New York: Academic Press.

Abelson, R. P. (1981). Psychological status of the script concept, *American Psychologist*, 36, 715–29.

Ajzen, I. (1985). From intentions to actions: a Theory of Planned Behavior. In: Kuhl, J. & Beckman, J. (eds) *Action Control: From Cognition to Behavior*. Berlin: Springer–Verlag. pp. 11–39.

Ajzen, I. (1987). Attitudes, traits, and actions: dispositional prediction of behavior in personality and social psychology, *Advances in Experimental Social Psychology*, 20, (Ed. L. Berkovitz). San Diego: Academic Press. pp. 1–63.

Ajzen, I. (1988). *Attitudes, Personality and Behavior*. Milton Keynes: Open University Press.

Ajzen, I. (1991). The Theory of Planned Behavior, *Organizational Behavior and Human Decision Processes*, 50, 179–211.

Ajzen, I. & M. Fishbein, M. (1972). Attitudes and normative beliefs as factors influencing behavioral intentions, *Journal of Personality and Social Psychology*, 21, 1–9.

Ajzen, I. & Fishbein, M. (1977). Attitude-behavior relations: A theoretical analysis and review of empirical research, *Psychological Bulletin*, 84, 888–918.

Ajzen, I. & Fishbein, M. (1980). *Understanding Attitudes and Predicting Social Behavior*, Englewood Cliffs, NJ: Prentice Hall.

Ajzen, I. & Madden, T. J. (1986). Prediction of goal-directed behavior: attitudes, intentions, and perceived behavioral control, *Journal of Experimental Social Psychology*, 22, 453–74.

Alba, J. W., Hutchinson, J. W. & Lynch, J. G. (1991). Memory and decision making. In: Robertson, T. S. & Kassarjian, H. H. (eds) *Handbook of Consumer Behavior*. Englewood Cliffs, NJ: Prentice-Hall. pp. 1–49.

Albanese, P. J. (2002). *The Personality Continuum and Consumer Behavior*. Westport CT: Quorum Books.

Alexander, C. N. (1966). Attitude as a scientific concept, *Social Forces*, 45, 278–281.

Alhadeff, D. A. (1982). *Microeconomics and Human Behavior: Toward a New Synthesis of Economics and Psychology*. Berkeley, CA: University of California Press.

Allen, C. & Bekoff, M. (1997). *Species of Mind: The Philosophy and Biology of Cognitive Ethology*. Cambridge, MA: MIT Press.

Allen, C. T., Machleit, K. A. & Kleine, S. S. (1992). A comparison of attitudes and emotions as predictors of behavior at diverse levels of behavioral experience, *Journal of Consumer Research*, 18, 493–504.

Allport, G. W. (1935). Attitudes. In: Murchison, C. (ed) *Handbook of Social Psychology*. Worcester, MA: Clark University Press. pp. 798–844.

Amsel, A. & Rashotte, M. E. (1984). *Mechanisms of Adaptive Behavior: Clark L. Hull's Theoretical Papers, with Commentary*. New York: Columbia University Press.

Anderson, A. S., Campbell, D. M. & Shepherd, R. (1995). The influence of dietary advice on nutrient intake during pregnancy, *British Journal of Nutrition*, 73, 163–77.

Andreasen, A. (1965). Attitudes and customer behavior: a decision model. In: Preston, L. E. (ed.) *New Research in Marketing*. Berkeley, CA: University of California Press.

Anscombe, G. E. M. (1957). *Intention*. Oxford: Blackwell.

Armitage, C. J. & Connor, M. (1999a). The Theory of Planned Behaviour: Assessment of predictive validity and "perceived control," *British Journal of Social Psychology*, 38, 35–54.

Armitage, C. J. & Connor, M. (1999b). Predictive validity of the Theory of Planned Behavior: The role of questionnaire format and social desirability, *Journal of Community & Applied Social Psychology*, 9, 262–272.

Atkinson, R. C. & Shiffrin, R. M. (1971). The control of short-term memory, *Scientific American*, 225, 82–90.

Baars, B. J. (1986). *The Cognitive Revolution in Psychology*. New York: The Guilford Press.

Bagozzi, R. P. (1981). Attitudes, intentions, and behavior: a test of some key hypotheses, *Journal of Personality and Social Psychology*, 41, 607–27.

Bagozzi, R. P. (1986). Attitude formation under the Theory of Reasoned Action and a purposeful behaviour reformulation, *British Journal of Social Psychology*, 25, 95–107.

Bagozzi, R. P. (1991). Enactment processes in the Theory of Reasoned Action. Unpublished manuscript. University of Michigan.

Bagozzi, R. P. (1992). The self-regulation of attitudes, intentions, and behavior, *Social Psychology Quarterly*, 55, 178–204.

Bagozzi, R. P. (1993). On the neglect of volition in consumer research: a critique and proposal, *Psychology and Marketing*, 10, 215–37.

Bagozzi, R. P. (2004). Consumer action: The role of intentionality, emotion, sociality, and agency. In: Griffin, A. & Otnes, C. (eds) *The 16th Converse Symposium*. Chicago: American Marketing Association.

Bagozzi, R. P. & Edwards, E. A. (1998). Goal setting and goal pursuit in the regulation of body weight, *Psychology and Health*, 13, 593–621.

Bagozzi, R. P. & Edwards, E. A. (2000). Goal-striving and the implementation of goal intentions in the regulation of body weight, *Psychology and Health*, 15, 255–270.

Bagozzi, R. P. & Kimmel, S. K. (1995). A comparison of leading theories for the prediction of goal-directed behaviours, *British Journal of Social Psychology*, 34, 472–61.

Bagozzi, R. P. & Van Loo, M. F. (1991). Motivational and reasoned processes in the theory of consumer choice. In: Frantz, R., Singh, H. & Gerber, J. (eds) *Handbook of Behavioral Economics. Vol. 2B: Behavioral Decision Making*. Greenwich, CT: JAI. pp. 401–437.

Bagozzi, R. P. & Warshaw, P. R. (1990). Trying to consume, *Journal of Consumer Research*, 17, 127–140.

Bagozzi, R. P. & Warshaw, P. R. (1992). An examination of the etiology of the attitude-behavior relation for goal-directed behaviors, *Multivariate Behavioral Research*, 27, 601–634.

Bagozzi, R. P., Baumgartner, H. & Pieters, R. (1998). Goal-directed emotions, *Cognition and Emotion*, 12, 1–26.

Bagozzi, R. P., Baumgartner, H. & Yi, Y. (1992a). Appraisal processes in the enactment of intentions to use coupons, *Psychology and Marketing*, 9, 469–486.

Bagozzi, R. P., Baumgartner, H. & Yi, Y. (1992b). State versus action orientation and the Theory of Reasoned Action: an application to coupon usage, *Journal of Consumer Research*, 18, 505–518.

Bagozzi, R. P., Gopinath, M. & Nyer, P. U. (1999). The role of emotions in marketing, *Journal of the Academy of Marketing Science*, 27, 184–206.

Bagozzi, R. P. & Yi, Y. (1989). The degree of intention formation as a moderator of the attitude-behavior relationship, *Social Psychology Quarterly*, 52, 266–79.

Bagozzi, R. P., Yi, Y. & Baumgartner, H. (1990). The level of effort required for behavior as a moderator of the attitude-behavior relation, *European Journal of Social Psychology*, 20, 45–59.

Ball, D., Lamb, C. & Brodie, R. v (1992). Segmentation and market structure when both consumer and situational characteristics are explanatory, *Psychology and Marketing*, 9, 395–408.

Bandura, A. (1986). *Social Foundations of Thought and Action: A Social Cognitive Theory*. Englewood Cliffs, NJ: Prentice Hall.

Bandura, A. (1997). *Self-Efficacy: The Exercise of Control*. New York: W. H. Freeman.

Bargh, J. A. (1994). The four horsemen of automaticity: awareness, intention, efficiency, and control in social cognition. In: Wyer, R. S. & Srull, T. K. (eds) *Handbook of Social Cognition. Volume 1: Basic Processes*. Second edition. Hillsdale, NJ: Erlbaum. pp. 1–40.

Bargh, J. A., Chaiken, S., Govender, R. & Pratto, F. (1992). The generality of the automatic attitude activation effect, *Journal of Personality and Social Psychology*, 62, 893–912.

Barker, R. G.(1968). *Ecological Psychology: Concepts and Methods for Studying the Environment of Human Behavior*. Stanford, CA: Stanford University Press.

Baudrillard, J. 1970. *La Société de Consommation*. Paris: Gallimard.

Baum, W. M. (1974). On two types of deviation from the matching law, *Journal of he Experimental Analysis of Behaviour*, 22, 231–42.

Baum, W. M. (1979). Matching, undermatching and overmatching in studies of choice, *Journal of the Experimental Analysis of Behavior*, 32, 269–81.

Baum, W. M. (1994). *Understanding Behaviorism: Science, Behavior and Culture*. New York: HarperCollins.

Baum, W. (2004). Molar and molecular views of choice, *Behavioural Processes*, 66. 349–359.

Beale, D. A. & Manstead, A. S. R. (1991). Predicting mothers' intentions to limit frequency of infants' sugar intake: testing the Theory of Planned Behavior, *Journal of Applied Social Psychology*, 21, 409–31.

Bechtel, W. (1988). *Philosophy of Mind: An Outline for Cognitive Science*. Hillsdale, NJ: Lawrence Erlbaum Associates.

Bechtel, W. & Graham, G. (1998). (eds) *A Companion to Cognitive Science*. Oxford: Blackwell.

Bell, D. R., Chiang, J. & Padmanabhan, V. (1999). The decomposition of promotional response: An empirical generalization, *Marketing Science, 18*, 504–526.

Bem, D. J. (1967). Self-perception: an alternative interpretation of cognitive dissonance phenomena, *Psychological Review*, 74, 183–200.

Bem, D. (1972). Self-perception theory. In: Berkovitz, L. (ed.) *Advances in Experimental Social Psychology*, 6, San Diego, CA: Academic Press. pp. 1–62.

Bennett, M. R. & Hacker, P. M. S. (2003). *Philosophical Foundations of Neuroscience*. Oxford: Blackwell.

Bentler, P. M. & Speckart, G. (1979). Models of attitude-behavior relations, *Psychological Review*, 86, 452–64.

Bentler, P. M. & Speckart, G. (1981). Attitudes "cause" behaviors: A structural equation analysis, *Journal of Personality and Social Psychology*, 40, 226–38.

Berger, I. E. (1992). The nature of attitude accessibility and attitude confidence: a triangulated experiment, *Journal of Consumer Psychology*, 1, 103–24.

Bermúdez, J. L. (2000). Personal and sub-personal: A difference without a distinction, *Philosophical Explorations*, 3, 63–82.

Black, R. D. Collison (1987). Utility. In Eatwell, J., Milgate, M. & Newman, P. (eds) *The New Palgrave: A dictionary of Economics*. London: Macmillan. pp. 776–779.

Blascovich, J., Ernst, J. M., Tomaka, J., Kelsey, R. M., Salomon, K. L. & Fazio, R. H. (1993). Attitude accessibility as a moderator of automatic reactivity during decision making, *Journal of Personality and Social Psychology*, 64, 165–76.

Blumenthal , A. L. (1977). *The Process of Cognition*. Englewood Cliffs: Prentice-Hall.

Bogardus, E. S. (1925). Measuring social distances, *Journal of Applied Sociology*, 9, 299–308.

Bohner, G., Moskowitz, G. B. & Chaiken, S. (1995). The interplay of heuristic and systematic processing of social information. In: Stroebe, W. and Hewstone, M. (eds) *European Review of Social Psychology*, Volume 6, Chichester: Wiley. pp. 33–68.

Bourdieu, P. (1984). *Distinction: A Social Critique of the Judgement of Taste*. Trans. Nice, R. Cambridge, MA: Harvard University Press.

Bower, G. R. (1972). A selective review of organizational factors in memory. In Tulving, E. & Donaldson, W. (eds), *Organization of Memory*. New York: Academic Press.

Brewer, W. F. (1974). There is no convincing evidence for operant or classical conditioning in adult humans. In W. B. Weimer, & D. S. Palermo (eds) *Cognition and the symbolic processes* (pp. 1–42). Hillsdale, NJ: Erldaum.

Briñol, P., Rucker, D. D., Tormala, Z. & Petty, R. E. (2004). Individual differences in resistance to persuasion: The role of beliefs and meta-beliefs. In Knowles, E. & Linn, J. A. (eds) *Resistance to Persuasion*. Mahwah, NJ: Lawrence Erlbaum Associates. pp. 83–104.

Britt, S. H. (1978). *Psychological Principles of Marketing and Consumer Behavior* Lexington, MA: D. C. Heath.

Brook, A. & Ross, D. (eds) (2002). *Daniel Dennett*. Cambridge: Cambridge University Press.

Brown, S. P. & Stayman, D. M. (1992). Antecedents and consequences of attitude toward the ad: a meta-analysis, *Journal of Consumer Research*, 19, 34–51.

Bruner, J. S. (1983). *In Search of Mind*. New York: Harper.

Budd, R. J., North, D. & Spencer, C. (1984). Understanding seat-belt use: a test of Bentler and Speckart's extension of the "Theory of Reasoned Action", *European Journal of Social psychology*, 14, 69–78.

Catania, A. C. (1992a) *Learning*. Third edition. Prentice-Hall, Englewood Cliffs, NJ.

Catania, A. C. (1992b). B. F. Skinner, organism, *American Psychologist*, **47**, 1521–1530.

Catania, A. C., Matthews, B. A. & Shimoff, E. H. (1990). Properties of rule-governed behaviour and their implications. In: Blackman, D. E. & Lejeune, H. (eds) *Behaviour Analysis in Theory and Practice: Contributions and Controversies*.London: Erlbaum, pp. 215–230.

Catania, A. C., Shimoff, E. & Matthews, B. A. (1989). An experimental analysis of rule-governed behavior. In: Hayes, S. C. (ed.) *Rule-Governed Behavior: Cognition, Contingencies, and Instructional Control*. New York: Plenum. pp. 119–150.

Chaiken, S. (1980). Heuristic versus systematic information processing and the use of source versus message cues in persuasion, *Journal of Personality and Social Psychology*, 39, 752–66.

Charng, H., Piliavin, J. A. & Callero, P. L. (1988). Role identity and reasoned action in the prediction of repeated behavior, *Social Psychology Quarterly*, 51, 133–51.

Chase, P. N. & Danforth, J. S. (1991). The role of rules in concept formation. In: Hayes, L. J. & Chase, P. N. (eds) *Dialogues on Verbal Behavior*. Reno, NV: Context Press. pp. 205–25.

Chase, P. N. & Bjamadottir, G. S. (1992) 'Instructing variability: some features of a problem-solving repertoire'. In: Hayes, S. C. & Hayes, L. J. (eds) *Understanding Verbal Relations*. Reno, NV: Context Press. pp. 181–196.

Chisholm, R. M. (1957). *Perceiving: A Philosophical Study*. Ithaca, NY: Cornell University Press.

Chomsky, N. (1957). *Syntactic Structures*. The Hague: Mouton.

Chomsky, N. (1959). Review of B. F. Skinner's *Verbal Behavior*. *Language*, 35, 26–58.

Churchland, P. M. (1981). Eliminative materialism and the propositional attitudes. *Journal of Philosophy*, 78, 67–90.

Churchland, P. S. (1986). *Neurophilosophy: Toward a Unified Science of the Mind/Brain*. Cambridge, MA: MIT Press.

Churchland, P. S. (2002). *Brain-Wise: Studies in Neurophilosophy*. Cambridge, MA: MIT Press.

Cialdini, R. B. (1984). *The Psychology of Persuasion*. New York: Quill.

Cohen, A. (1964) *Attitude Change and Social Influence*. New York: Basic Books.

Cohen, J. (1992). A power primer, *Psychological Bulletin*, 112, 155–159.

Colley, R. H. (1961). *Defining Advertising Goals for Measured Results*. New York: Association of National Advertisers.

Crick, F. (1988). *What Mad Pursuit*. London: Weidenfeld and Nicholson.

Cushman, D. P. & McPhee, R. D. (1980). (eds) *Message–Attitude–Behavior Relationship: Theory, Methodology, and Application*. New York: Academic Press.

Dabholkar, P. A. (1994). Incorporating choice into an attitudinal framework: analyzing models of mental comparison processes, *Journal of Consumer Research*, 21, 100–118.

Dahlbom, B. (1993). *Dennett and his critics: Demystifying mind*. Oxford, UK and Cambridge, MA: Blackwell.

Dall'Olmo Riley, F., Ehrenberg, A. S. C., Castleberry, S. B., Barwise, T. P. & Barnard, N. (1997). The variability of attitude repeat rates, *International Journal of Research in Marketing*, 14, 437–550.

Davies, J., Foxall, G. R. & Pallister, J. G. (2002). Beyond the intention–behaviour mythology: an integrated model of recycling, *Marketing Theory*, 2, 29–113.

Davison, M. & McCarthy, D. (eds) (1988). *The Matching Law: A Research Review*. Hillsdale, NJ: Erlbaum.

Dawkins, R. (1982). *The Extended Phenotype: The Long Reach of the Gene*. Oxford: Oxford University Press.

Dawkins, R. (1988). Replicators, consequences, and displacement activities. In Catania, A. C. & Harnad, S. (eds) *The Selection of Behavior. The Operant Behaviorism of B. F. Skinner: Comments and Consequences*. New York: Cambridge University Press. pp. 33–35.

Day, G. S. (1973). Attitudes and attitude change. In H. H. Kassarjian & T. S. Robertson, *Perspectives in Consumer Behavior* (London: Scott Foresman, 1973) pp. 188–209.

DeFleur, M. L. & Westie, F. R. (1963). Attitude as a Scientific Concept, *Social Forces*, vol. 42, 17–31.

Dennett, D. C. (1969). *Content and Consciousness*. London: Routledge.

Dennett, D. C. (1971). Intentional systems, *Journal of Philosophy*, LXVIII, 87–106. (Reprinted in Dennett (1978).

Dennett, D. C. (1976). Conditions of personhood. In: Rorty, A. (ed.) *The Identities of Persons*. Berkeley, CA: University of California Press.

Dennett, D. C. (1978). *Brainstorms*. Montgomery, VT: Bradford.

Dennett, D. C. (1981). Three kinds of intentional psychology. In R. Healy (ed), *Reduction, Time and Reality*. Cambridge: Cambridge University Press. (Reprinted in Dennett, 1987).

Dennett, D. C. (1983). Intentional systems in cognitive ethology: The "Panglossian paradigm" defended. *The Behavioral and Brain Sciences*, 6, 343–390.

Dennett, D. C. (1987). *The Intentional Stance*. Cambridge, MA: MIT Press.

Dennett, D. C. (1991a). Real patterns. *Journal of Psychology*, 88, 27–51.

Dennett, D. C. (1991b). *Consciousness explained*. New York: Little, Brown and Co.

Dennett, D. C. (1994). Dennett, Daniel C. In S. Guttenplan (ed), *A Companion to the Philosophy of Mind* (pp. 236–244). Oxford: Blackwell.

Dennett, D. C. (1995). *Darwin's Dangerous Idea: Evolution and the Meanings of Life*. New York: Simon and Shuster.

Dennett, D. C. (1996). *Kinds of Minds: Toward an Understanding of Consciousness*. London: Weidenfeld and Nicolson.

de Villiers, P. A. & Herrnstein, R. J. (1976). Toward a law of response strength, *Psychological Bulletin*, 83, 1131–1153.

Donahoe, J. W. & Palmer, D. C. (1994). *Learning and complex behavior*. Boston, MA: Allyn and Bacon.

Donahoe, J. W., Palmer, D. C., & Burgos, J. E. (1997). The S-R issue: Its status in behavior analysis and in Donahoe and Palmer's *Learning and complex behavior*. *Journal of the Experimental Analysis of Behavior*, 67, 193–211.

Donovan, R. J. & Rossier, J. R. (1982). Store atmosphere: an experimental psychology approach, *Journal of Retailing*, 58, 34–57.

Donovan, R. J., Rossier, J. R., Marcoolyn, G. & Nesdale, A. (1994). Store Atmosphere and Purchasing Behavior, *Journal of Retailing*, 70, 283-94.

Doob L. W. (1947). The behavior of attitudes, *Psychological Review*, 54, 135–56.

Dosi, G. & Orsenigo, L. (1988). Coordination and transformation: an overview of structures, behaviours and change in evolutionary environments In Dosi, G., Freeman, C., Nelson, R. Silverberg, G. & Soete, L. (eds) *Technical Change and Economic Theory*. London: Pinter. pp. 13–37.

Downing, J. W., Judd, C. M. & Brauer, M. (1992). Effects of repeated expressions on attitude extremity, *Journal of Personality and Social Psychology*, 62, 17–29.

Dulany, D. E. (1968). Awareness, rules and propositional control. In Horton, D. and Dixon, T. (eds) *Verbal Behaviour and S-R Behavior Theory*. Englewood Cliffs: Prentice-Hall. pp. 340–87.

Eagly, A. H. & Chaiken, S. (1993). *The Psychology of Attitudes*. Fort Worth, TX: Harcourt Brace Jovanovich.

East, R. (1990). *Changing Consumer Behaviour*. Cassell, London.

East, R. (1992) 'The effect of experience on the decision making of expert and novice buyers', *Journal of Marketing Management*, 8, 167–176.

East, R. (1993). Investment decisions and the theory of planned behavior, *Journal of Economic Psychology*, 14, 337–375.

East, R. (1997) *Consumer Behaviour: Advances and Applications in Marketing*. London: Prentice-Hall.

Echabe, A. E., Rovira, D. P. & Garate, J. F. V. (1988) 'Testing Ajzen and Fishbein's attitude model: the prediction of voting, *European Journal of Social Psychology*, 18, 181–9.

Ehrenberg, A. S. C. (1988/1972). *Repeat Buying*. London: Griffin.

Ehrenberg, A. S. C. (1991). New brands and the existing market. *Journal of the Market Research Society*, 33, 285–299.

Ehrenberg, A. S. C. (1993). Theory or well-based results: Which comes first? In: Laurent, G., Lilien, G. & Pras, B. (eds) *Research Traditions in Marketing* (pp. 79–108). Dordrecht: Kluwer Academic Publishing.

Ehrenberg, A. S. C. & Goodhardt, G. J. (1979–1981). *Essays on Understanding Buyer Behavior*. New York: Market Research Corporation of America/J. Walter Thompson.

Ehrenberg, A. S. C. & Uncles, M. D. (1995) *Dirichlet-type Markets: A Review*. London: South Bank Business School.

Ehrenberg, A. S. C. & Uncles, M. D. (1999). *Understanding Dirichlet-type Markets.* London: South Bank Business School.

Ehrenberg, A. S. C., Goodhardt, G. J. & Barwise, P. (1990). Double jeopardy revisited, *Journal of Marketing,* 54, 82–91.

Eiser, J. R. (1980). *Cognitive Social Psychology: A Guide to Theory and Research.* London: McGraw-Hill.

Eiser, J. R. (1986). *Social Psychology: Attitudes, Cognition and Social Behaviour.* Cambridge: Cambridge University Press.

Eiser, J. R. (1987) *The Expression of Attitude.* New York: Springer-Verlag.

Eiser, J. R. & van der Pligt, J. (1988) *Attitudes and Decisions.* London: Routledge.

Elton, M. (2000). Consciousness: Only at the personal level, *Philosophical Explorations,* 3, 25–41.

Elton, M. (2003). *Daniel Dennett: Reconciling Science and Our Self-Conception.* Cambridge: Polity.

Engel, J. F., Blackwell, R. D. & Kollat, D. T. (1978). *Consumer behavior,* 3rd edn Hindsdale, IL: Dryden.

Engel, J. F., Blackwell, R. D. & Miniard, P. W. (1995) *Consumer Behavior.* Eighth edition. Fort Worth, TX: Dryden.

Engel, J. F., Kollat, D. T. & Blackwell, R. D. (1968) *Consumer Behavior.* New York: Holt, Rinehart and Winston.

Ericsson, K. A. & Simon, H. A. (1993) *Protocol Analysis: Verbal Reports as Data.* Cambridge, MA: MIT Press.

Ewen, S. 1990. Marketing dreams: the political elements of style, in Tomlinson, A. (ed) *Consumption, Identity and Style.* London: Routledge. pp. 41–56.

Fantino, E. (2004). Behavior-analytic approaches to decision-making, *Behavioural Processes,* 66, 279–288.

Fazio, R. H. (1986). How do attitudes guide behavior? In: Sorrentino, R. M. & Higgins, E. T. (eds) *Handbook of Motivation and Cognition: Foundations of Social Behavior.* Chichester: Wiley. pp. 204–243.

Fazio, R. H. (1989). On the power and functionality of attitudes: the role of attitude accessibility. In Pratkanis, A. R., Breckler, A. J. & Greenwald, A. G. (eds) *Attitude Structure and Function.* Hillsdale, NJ: Erlbaum. pp. 153–180.

Fazio, R. H. (1990). Multiple processes by which attitudes guide behavior: the MODE model as an integrative framework. In: Zanna, M. P. (ed.) *Advances in Experimental Social Psychology,* Volume 23. San Diego, CA: Academic Press. pp. 75–109.

Fazio, R. H. (1994), Attitudes as object-evaluation associations: determinants, consequences, and correlates of attitude accessibility. In: Petty, R. E. & Krosnick, J. A. (eds) *Attitude Strength: Antecedents and Consequences.* Hillsdale, NJ: Erlbaum. pp. 247–282.

Fazio, R. H. & Zanna, M. P. (1978a). Attitudinal qualities relating to the strength of the attitude-behavior relationship, *Journal of Experimental Social Psychology,* 14, 398–408.

Fazio, R. H. & Zanna, M. P. (1978b). On the predictive validity of attitudes: the roles of direct experience and confidence, *Journal of Personality,* 46, 228–43.

Fazio, R. H. & Zanna, M. P. (1981). Direct experience and attitude-behavior consistency, *Advances in Experimental Social Psychology,* 14, 161–202.

Fazio, R. H., Powell, M. C. & Williams, C. J. (1989). The role of attitude accessibility in the attitude-to-behavior process, *Journal of Consumer Research,* 16, 280–88.

Fazio, R. H., Chen, J., McDonel, E. C. & Sherman, S. J. (1982). Attitude accessibility, attitude-behavior consistency, and the strength of the object-evaluation association, *Journal of Experimental Social Psychology,* 18, 339–57.

Featherstone, M. (1991). *Consumer Culture and Postmodernism*. London: Sage.
Ferster, C. B. & Skinner, B. F. (1957). Schedules of Reinforcement. New York: Prentice-Hall.
Festinger, L. (1957). *A Theory of Cognitive Dissonance*. Palo Alto, CA: Stanford University Press.
Feyerabend, P. (1970). Consolations for the specialist. In: Lakatos, I. & Musgrave, A. (eds) *Criticism and the Growth of Knowledge*. Cambridge: Cambridge University Press.
Feyerabend, P. (1975). *Against Method*. NLB, London.
Fishbein, M. (1967a). (ed) *Readings in Attitude Theory and Measurement*, New York: Wiley.
Fishbein, M. (1967b). Attitude and the prediction of behavior. In M. Fishbein (ed) *Readings in Attitude Theory and Measurement*. New York: Wiley. pp. 377-92
Fishbein, M. (1972). The search for attitudinal-behavioral consistency. In: Cohen, J. S. (ed) *Behavioral Science Foundations of Consumer Behavior*. New York: Free Press.
Fishbein, M. (1973). The prediction of behavior from attitudinal variables. In C. D. Mortensen & K. K. Sereno (eds), *Advances in Communications Research*. New York: Harper & Row. pp. 3-31.
Fishbein, M. & Ajzen, I. (1975). *Belief, Attitude, Intention and Behavior*. Reading, MA: Addison-Wesley.
Fiske, S. T. (1993). Social cognition and social perception, *Annual Review of Psychology*, 44, 155–94.
Foxall, G. R. (1980). Marketing models of buyer behaviour, *European Research*, 8, 192-206
Foxall, G. R. (1983) *Consumer Choice*. London: St. Martin's, New York: Macmillan.
Foxall, G. R. (1984). Consumers' intentions and behavior: A note on research and a challenge to researchers, *Journal of the Market Research Society*, 26, 231–41.
Foxall, G. R. (1986). The role of radical behaviorism in the explanation of consumer choice, *Advances in Consumer Research*, 13, 195–206.
Foxall, G. R. (1987). Radical behaviorism and consumer research: theoretical promise and empirical problems, *International Journal of Research in Marketing*, 4, 111–129.
Foxall, G. R. (1988). Critical relativism and active interplay: the role of the experimental analysis of behaviour in consumer research, In: Psychology of Micro and Macro Economics. (ed.) Vanden Abeele, P. *Proceedings of the 13th Annual Colloquium of the International Association for Research in Economic Psychology*, Leuven, September, 1–36. Reprinted in Foxall (1996).
Foxall, G. R. (1992a). The consumer situation: an integrative model for research in marketing, *Journal of Marketing Management*, 8, 392–404.
Foxall, G. R. (1992b). The Behavioral Perspective Model of purchase and consumption: From consumer theory to marketing management, *Journal of the Academy of Marketing Science*, 20, 189–98.
Foxall, G. R. (1993a). Consumer behavior as an evolutionary process, *European Journal of Marketing*, 27(8), 46–57.
Foxall, G. R. (1993b). Situated consumer behavior: a behavioral interpretation of purchase and consumption. In: Costa, J. A. & Belk, R. W. (eds) *Research in Consumer Behavior*, 6, Greenwich, CT: JAI. pp. 113–52.
Foxall, G. R. (1994). Behaviour analysis and consumer psychology, *Journal of Economic Psychology*, 15, 5–91.
Foxall, G. R. (1995a). Science and interpretation in consumer research: a radical behaviorist perspective, *European Journal of Marketing*, 29(9), 3–99.
Foxall, G. R. (1995b). The psychological basis of marketing. In Baker, M. J. ed. *The Companion Encyclopedia of Marketing*. London: Routledge.

Foxall, G. R. (1996) *Consumers in Context: The BPM Research Program*, London and New York: ITP.

Foxall, G. R. (1997a). *Marketing Psychology: The Paradigm in the Wings*. London: Macmillan.

Foxall, G. R. (1997b). The explanation of consumer behavior: from social cognition to environmental control, *International Review of Industrial and Organizational Psychology*, eds. Cooper, C. L. & Robertson, I. Chichester: Wiley.

Foxall, G. R. (1997c). The emotional texture of consumer environments: a systematic approach to atmospherics, *Journal of Economic Psychology*, 18, 505–523.

Foxall, G. R. (1997d). Affective responses to consumer situations, *International Review of Retail, Distribution and Consumer Research*, 7, 191–225.

Foxall, G. R. (1998a). Radical behaviorist interpretation: Generating and Evaluating an account of consumer behavior, *The Behavior Analyst*, 21, 321–354.

Foxall, G. R. (1998b). Intention versus context in consumer psychology, *Journal of Marketing Management*, 14, 29–62.

Foxall, G. R. (1999a). The contextual stance. *Philosophical Psychology*, 12, 25–52.

Foxall, G. R. (1999b). The Behavioural Perspective Model: consensibility and consensuality, *European Journal of Marketing*, 33, 570–596.

Foxall, G. R. (1999c). The substitutability of brands, *Managerial and Decision Economics*, 20, 241–57.

Foxall, G. R. (1999d). The marketing firm, *Journal of Economic Psychology*, 20, 207–234.

Foxall, G. R. (2001). Foundations of consumer behaviour analysis, *Marketing Theory*, 1, 165–199.

Foxall, G. R. (2002a) (ed). *Consumer Behavior Analysis: Critical Perspectives*. 3 Vols. London and New York: Routledge.

Foxall, G. R. (2002b). Marketing's attitude problem – and how to solve it, *Journal of Customer Behaviour*, 1, 19–48.

Foxall, G. R. (2003). The behaviour analysis of consumer choice, *Journal of Economic Psychology*, 24, 581–588.

Foxall, G. R. (2004a). *Context and Cognition: Interpreting Complex Behavior*. Reno, NV: Context Press.

Foxall, G. R. (2004b/1990), *Consumer Psychology in Behavioral Perspective*. Frederick, MD: Beard Books.

Foxall, G. R. (2004c). *The Sources of Intentional Psychology*. Unpublished working paper.

Foxall, G. R. (2004d). Beyond the marketing philosophy: context and intention in the explanation of consumer choice. *Philosophy of Management*, 4, 67–85.

Foxall, G. R. & Goldsmith, R. E. (1994). *Consumer Psychology for Marketing*. London and New York: Routledge.

Foxall, G. R. & Greenley, G. E. (1998). The affective structure of consumer situations, *Environment and Behavior*, 30, 781–798.

Foxall, G. R. & Greenley, G. E. (1999). Consumers' emotional responses to service environments, *Journal of Business Research*, 46, 149–58.

Foxall, G. R. & Greenley, G. E. (2000). Predicting and explaining responses to consumer environments: An empirical test and theoretical extension of the Behavioural Perspective Model, *The Service Industries Journal*, 20, 39–63.

Foxall, G. R. & James, V. K. (2001). Behavior analysis of consumer brand choice: a preliminary analysis, *European Journal of Behavior Analysis*, 2, 209–220.

Foxall, G. R. & James, V. (2003). The behavioral ecology of brand choice: how and what do consumers maximize? *Psychology and Marketing*, 20, 811–836.

Foxall, G. R., Goldsmith, R. E. & Brown, S. (1998). *Consumer Psychology for Marketing*. Second edition. London and New York: Thomson.

Foxall, G. R. & Schrezenmaier, T. C. (2003). The behavioral economics of consumer brand choice: establishing a methodology, *Journal of Economic Psychology*, 24, 675–695.

Foxall, G. R. & Yani-de-Soriano, M. M. (2004). Situational influences on consumers' attitudes and behavior, *Journal of Business Research*, in press.

Foxall, G. R., Oliveira-Castro, J. M. & Schrezenmaier, T. C. (2004). The behavioral economics of consumer brand choice: Patterns of reinforcement and utility maximization, *Behavioural Processes*, 66, 235–260.

Fredericks, A. J. & Dossett, D. L. (1983). Attitude-behavior relations: a comparison of the Fishbein-Ajzen and Bentler-Speckart models, *Journal of Personality and Social Psychology*, 45, 501–12.

Galbraith, J. K. (1967). *The New Industrial State*. London: Penguin Books.

Gardner, H. (1985). *The Mind's New Science: A History of the Cognitive Revolution*. New York: Basic Books.

Geertz, C. (1973). *The Interpretation of Cultures*. New York: Basic Books.

Giles, M. & Cairns, E. (1995). Blood donation and Ajzen's theory of planned behaviour: an examination of perceived behavioral control, *British Journal of Social Psychology*, 34, 173–88.

Goffman, E. (1968). *Asylums*. London: Penguin Books. (First published by New York: Anchor Books, Doubleday, 1961.)

Goldsmith, T. H. (1991). *The Biological Roots of Human Behavior*. New York: Oxford University Press.

Gordon, W. C. (1989). *Learning and Memory*. Pacific Grove, CA: Brook/Cole.

Gould, J. & Kolb, W. L. (eds) (1964) *A Dictionary of the Social Sciences*. London: Tavistock.

Green, L. & Freed, D., E. (1993). The substitutability of reinforcers, *Journal of the Experimental Analysis of Behavior*, 60, 141–158.

Green, L., Rachlin, H. & Hanson, J. (1983). Matching and maximizing with concurrent ratio-interval schedules, *Journal of the Experimental Analysis of Behavior*, 40, 217–224.

Greenwald, A. G. & Banaji, M. R. (1995). Implicit social cognition: attitudes, self-esteem, and stereotypes, *Psychological Review*, 102, 4–27.

Greenwald, A. G & Levitt, C. (1984). Audience involvement in advertising: four levels, *Journal of Consumer Research*, 11, 581–592.

Griffin, J. & Parfitt, D. (1987). Hedonism. In: Eatwell, J., Milgate, M. & Newman, P. (eds) *The New Palgrave: A Dictionary of Economics*. London: Macmillan.

Guerin, B. (1994a) *Analyzing Social Behavior: Behavior Analysis and the Social Sciences*. Reno, NV: Context Press.

Guerin, B. (1994b). Attitudes and beliefs as verbal behavior, *The Behavior Analyst*, 17.

Gunderson, K. (1972). *Content and consciousness* and the mind-body problem. *Journal of Philosophy*, 69, 591–604.

Guttenplan, S. (1994) (ed). *A Companion to the Philosophy of Mind*. Oxford: Blackwell.

Hackenberg, T. D. & Joker, V. R. (1994). Instructional versus schedule control of humans' choices in situations of diminishing returns, *Journal of the Experimental Analysis of Behavior*, 62, 367–83.

Hansen, F. (1976). Psychological theories of consumer choice, *Journal of Consumer Research*, 3, 117–136.

Hantula, D. A., DiClemente, D. F. & Rajala, A. K. (2001). Outside the box: The analysis of consumer behavior. In Hayes, L., Austin, J. & Flemming. R. (eds) *Organizational Change*. Reno, NV: Context Press. pp. 203–233.

Haugtvedt, C. P. & Petty, R. E. (1992). Personality and persuasion: need for cognition moderates the persistence and resistance of attitudes, *Journal of Personality and Social psychology*, 62, 308–19.

Havlena, W. J. & Holbrook, M. B. (1986). The varieties of consumption experience: Comparing two typologies of emotion in consumer behavior, *Journal of Consumer Research*, 13, 394–404.

Havlena, W. J., Holbrook, M. B. & Lehmann, D. R. (1989). Assessing the validity of emotional typologies, *Psychology and Marketing*, 6, 97–112.

Hawkins, S. A. & Hoch, S. J. (1992) 'Low-involvement learning: memory without evaluation', *Journal of Consumer Research*, 19, 212–25.

Hayes, S. C. (1986). The case of the silent dog – Verbal reports and the analysis of rules: A review of Ericsson and Simon's *Protocol analysis: Verbal reports as data*. *Journal of the Experimental Analysis of Behavior*, 45, 351–363.

Hayes, S. C. (1989). (ed.) *Rule-Governed Behavior: Cognition, Contingencies, and Instructional Control*. New York: Plenum.

Hayes, L. J. and Chase, P. N. (eds) (1991). *Dialogues on Verbal Behavior*. Reno, NV: Context Press.

Hayes, S. C. & Hayes, L. J. (1989). The verbal action of the listener as a basis for rule-governance. In: Hayes, S. C. (ed) *Rule-Governed Behavior: Cognition, Contingencies, and Instructional Control*. New York: Plenum. pp. 153–90.

Hayes, S. C. & Hayes, L. J. (eds) (1992). *Understanding Verbal Relations*. Reno, NV: Context Press.

Hayes, S. C., Hayes, L. J., Reese, H. W. & Sarbin, T. R. (eds) (1993). *Varieties of Scientific Contextualism*. Reno, NV: Context Press.

Hayes, S. C., Brownstein, A. J., Haas, J. R. & Greenway, D. E. (1986). Instructions, multiple schedules, and extinction: distinguishing rule-governed from schedule-controlled behavior, *Journal of the Experimental Analysis of Behavior*, 46, 137–47.

Hayes, S. C., Barnes-Holmes, D. & Roche, B. (2001). *Relational Frame Theory: A Post-Skinnerian Account of Human Language and Cognition*. New York: Kluwer.

Hayes, S. C., Hayes, L. J., Sato, M. & Ono, K. (eds) (1994) *Behavior Analysis of Language and Cognition*. Reno, NV: Context Press.

Hayes, S. C., Strosahl, K. D., & Wilson, K. G. (1999). *Acceptance and Commitment Therapy: An Experiential Approach to Behavior Change*. New York: The Guilford Press.

Heider, F. (1946). Attitudes and cognitive organization, *Journal of Psychology*, 21, 107–12.

Hempel, C. G. (1980). The logical analysis of psychology. In Block, N. (ed) *Readings in Philosophical Psychology*. Vol. I. London: Methuen. pp. 14–23.

Herrnstein, R. J. (1961). Relative and absolute strength of response as a function of frequency of reinforcement, *Journal of the Experimental Analysis of Behavior*, 4, 267–72.

Herrnstein, R. J. (1970). On the law of effect, *Journal of the Experimental Analysis of Behavior*, 13, 243–66.

Herrnstein, R. J. (1979). Derivatives of matching, *Psychological Review*, 86, 486–95.

Herrnstein, R. J. (1997). *The Matching Law: Papers in Psychology and Economics*. Edited by H. Rachlin & D. I. Laibson. New York: Russell Sage Foundation/Cambridge, MA: Harvard University Press.

Herrnstein, R. J. & Loveland, D. H. (1974). Hunger and constraint in a multiple schedule. *Journal of the Experimental Analysis of Behavior*, 24, 107–116.

Herrnstein, R. J. & Loveland, D. H. (1975). Maximizing and matching on concurrent ratio schedules. *Journal of the Experimental Analysis of Behavior*, 24, 107–116.

Herrnstein, R. J. & Vaughan, W. (1980). Melioration and behavioral allocation. In J. E. R. Staddon (ed), *Limits to Action: The Allocation of Individual Behavior* (pp. 143–176). New York: Academic Press.

Hirsch, F. (1976). *Social Limits to Growth*. Cambridge, MA: Harvard University Press.

Holbrook, M. B. & Batra, R. (1987). Assessing the role of emotions as mediators of consumer responses to advertising, *Journal of Consumer Research*, 14, 404–419.

Homans, G. C. (1974). *Social Behavior: Its Elementary Forms*. New York: Harcourt Brace Jovanovich.

Horne, P. J. & Lowe, C. F. (1993). Determinants of human performance on concurrent schedules, *Journal of the Experimental Analysis of Behavior*, 59, 29–60.

Horne, P. J. & Lowe, C. F. (1996). On the origins of naming and other symbolic behavior, *Journal of the Experimental Analysis of Behavior*, 65, 185–241.

Hornsby, J. (2000). Personal and sub-personal: A defence of Dennett's early distinction, *Philosophical Explorations*, 3, 6–24.

Hovland, C. L., Janis, I. L. & Kelley, H. H. (1953). *Communication and Persuasion*. New Haven, CT: Yale University Press.

Howard, J. (1965). *Marketing Theory*. Boston, Mass.: Ally & Bacon.

Howard, J. A. (1989) *Consumer Behavior in Marketing Strategy*. Englewood Cliffs, NJ: Prentice-Hall.

Howard, J. A. & Sheth, J. N. (1969). *The Theory of Buyer Behavior*. New York: Wiley.

Huang, H. M. (2001). The theory of emotions in marketing, *Journal of Business and Psychology*, 16, 239–247.

Hull, C. L. (1935). The conflicting psychologies of learning – a way out, *Psychological Review*, 42, 491–516.

Hull, C. L. (1952). *A Behavior System*. New Haven: Yale University Press.

Hyten, C. M. & Burns, R. (1986). Social relations and social behavior. In: Reese, H. W. & Parrott, L. J. (eds) *Behavior Science: Philosophical, Methodological, and Empirical Advances*. Hillsdale, NJ: Erlbaum. pp. 163–83.

Hyten, C. M. & Chase, P. N. (1991). An analysis of self-editing: method and preliminary findings. In: Hayes, L. J. & Chase, P. N. (eds) *Dialogues on Verbal Behavior*. Reno, NV: Context Press. pp. 67–81.

Ito, Y. (1994). Models and problem solving: effects and use of the "views of probability." In: Hayes, S. C., Hayes, L. J., Sato, M. & Ono, K. (eds) *Behavior Analysis of Language and Cognition*. Reno, NV: Context Press. pp. 259–80.

Jacoby, J. (1978). Consumer research: A state of the art review, *Journal of Marketing*, 42, 87–96.

Jones, E. E. & Gerard, H. B. (1967). *Foundations of Social Psychology*. New York: Wiley.

Janiszewski, C. (1988). Preconscious processing effects: the independence of attitude formation and conscious thought, *Journal of Consumer Research*, 15, 199–209.

Juarrero, A. (1999). *Dynamics in Action: Intentional Behavior as a Complex System*. Cambridge, MA: MIT Press.

Kagel, J. H., Battalio, R. C. & Green, L. (1995). *Economic Choice Theory: An Experimental Analysis of Animal Behavior*. Cambridge: Cambridge University Press.

Kahle, L. R. & Berman, J. J. (1979). Attitudes cause behavior: A cross-lagged panel analysis', *Journal of Personality and Social Psychology*, 37, 315–21.

Kardes, F. R. (1988). Spontaneous inference processes in advertising: the effects of conclusion omission and involvement on persuasion, *Journal of Consumer Research*, 15, 225–33.

Katona, G. (1960). *The Powerful Consumer*. New York: McGraw-Hill.

Katz, D. (1960). The functional approach to the study of attitudes, *Public Opinion Quarterly*, 24, 163–204.

Kelley, H. H. (1967). Attribution theory in social psychology, *Nebraska Symposium on Motivation*. Vol. 15. pp. 192–238.

Kelman, H. C. (1958). Compliance, identification and internalisation', *Journal of Conflict Resolution*, 2, 51–60.

Keynes, J. M. (1936). *The General Theory of Employment, Interest and Money*. London: Macmillan.

Knowles, E. S. & Linn, J. A. (eds) (2004). *Resistance and Persuasion*. Mahwah, NJ: Lawrence Erlbaum Associates.

Knox, S. & de Chernatony, L. (1994). Attitude, personal norms and intentions. In: Jenkins, M. & Knox, S. (eds) *Advances in Consumer Marketing*. Kogan Page, London. pp. 85–98.

Koffka, K. (1935). *Principles of Gestalt Psychology*. New York: Harcourt, Brace and World.

Kuhn, T. S. (1970) *The Structure of Scientific Revolutions*. Second edition. Chicago, IL: Chicago University Press.

Lalljee, M., Brown, L. B. & Ginsburg, G. P. (1984). Attitudes: disposition, behaviour or evaluation? *British Journal of Social Psychology*, 23, 233–244.

Langer, E. J. (1989a) *Mindfulness*. Reading, MA: Addison-Wesley.

Langer, E. J. (1989b). Minding matters: the consequences of mindlessness-mindfulness. In: Berkowitz, L. (ed.) *Advances in Experimental Social Psychology*, 22, San Diego, CA: Academic Press. pp. 137–73.

LaPiere, R. T. (1934). Attitudes vs. actions, *Social Forces*, 13, 230–37.

Lavidge, R. J. & Steiner, J. A. (1961). A model for predictive measurement of advertising effectiveness, *Journal of Marketing*, 25, 59–62

Lea, S. E. G., Tarpy, R. M. & Webley, P. (1987). *The Individual in the Economy*. Cambridge: Cambridge University Press.

Lee, V. L. (1988) *Beyond Behaviorism*. London: Erlbaum.

Lewis, A., Webley, P. & Furnham, A. (1995). *The New Economic Mind*. Hemel Hempstead: Harvester/Wheatsheaf.

Likert, R. (1932). A technique for the measurement of attitudes, *Archives of Psychology*, 140, 5–53.

Lionberger, H. F. (1960). *Adoption of New Ideas and Practices*. Ames, Iowa: State University Press.

Liska, A. E. (1984). A critical examination of the causal structure of the Fishbein/Ajzen attitude-behavior model, *Social Psychology Quarterly*, 47, 621–74.

Lott, A. J. & Lott, B. E. (1968). A learning approach to interpersonal attitudes. In Greenwald, A. G., Brock, T. C. & Ostrom, T. M. (eds) *Psychological Foundations of Attitudes*. San Diego, CA: Academic Press. pp. 67–88.

Lowe, C. F. (1983). Radical behaviorism and human psychology. In Davey, G. C. L. (ed.) *Animal Models of Human Behavior: Conceptual, Evolutionary and Neurobiological Perspectives*. Chichester: Wiley. pp. 71–93.

Lowe, C. F. (1989). *From Conditioning to Consciousness: The Cultural Origins of Mind*. Bangor: University College of North Wales.

Lunn, J. A. (1971). A review of consumer decision process models. Amsterdam: ESOMAR Conference Papers.

Mackenzie, B. (1988). The challenge to Skinner's theory of behavior. In Catania, A. C. & Harnad, S. (eds) *The Selection of Behavior. The Operant Behaviorism of B. F. Skinner: Comments and Consequences*. New York: Cambridge University Press. pp. 111–113.

MacCorquodale, K. (1969). B. F. Skinner's *Verbal Behavior*: a retrospective appreciation, *Journal of the Experimental Analysis of Behavior*, 12, 831–41.

MacCorquodale, K. (1970). On Chomsky's review of Skinner's *Verbal Behavior*, *Journal of the Experimental Analysis of Behavior*, 13, 85–99.

Madden, G. W., Bickel, W. K. & Jacobs, E. A. (2000). Three predictions of the economic concept of unit price in a choice context, *Journal of the Experimental Analysis of Behavior*, 73, 45–64.

Madden, T. J. & Sprott, J. (1995). A comparison of theoretical extensions to the Theory of Reasoned Action, *Proceedings of the Society of Consumer Psychology*, 1995 Annual Convention, La Jolla, CA. pp. 1–9.

Madden, T. J., Ellen, P. S. & Ajzen, I. (1992). A comparison of the Theory of Planned Behavior and the Theory of Reasoned Action, *Personality and Social Psychology Bulletin*, 18, 3–9.

Malcolm, N. (1977). Behaviorism as a philosophy of psychology. In N. Malcolm, *Thought and knowledge.* (pp. 85–103.) Ithaca, NY: Cornell University Press. First published in T. W. Wann (ed) (1964). *Behaviorism and phenomenology: Contrasting bases for modern psychology* (pp. 141–162). Chicago: University of Chicago Press.

Malott R. W. (1989). The achievement of evasive goals: control by rules describing contingencies that are not direct acting. In: Hayes, S. C. (ed) *Rule-Governed Behavior: Cognition, Contingencies, and Instructional Control.* New York: Plenum. pp. 269–324.

Malott, R. W. & Garcia, M. E. (1991). Role of private events in rule-governed behavior. In: Hayes, L. J. & Chase, P. N. (eds) *Dialogues on Verbal Behavior.* Reno, NV: Context Press. pp. 237–254.

Mano, H. & Oliver, R, L. (1993). Assessing the dimensionality and structure of the consumption experience: Evaluation, feeling, and satisfaction, *Journal of Consumer Research*, 20, 451–466.

Manstead, A. S. R. & Parker, D. (1995). 'Evaluating and extending the Theory of Planned Behavior. In: Stroebe, W. & Hewstone, M. (eds) *European Review of Social Psychology*, Volume 6. Chichester: Wiley. pp. 69–95.

Marsh, A. & Matheson, J. (1983). *Smoking Attitudes and Behaviour.* London: HMSO.

Mason, R. (1984). Conspicuous consumption: a literature review, *European Journal of Marketing*, 18(3), 26–39.

Mason, R. (1998). *The Economics of Conspicuous Consumption: Theory and Thought since 1700.* Cheltenham: Edward Elgar.

Maynard Smith, J. (1986). *The Problems of Biology.* Oxford: Oxford University Press.

McGuire, W. J. (1969). An information-processing model of advertising effectiveness, *Symposium on behavior and Management Science in Marketing.* Chicago, IL: Chicago University.

McGuire, W. J. (1976). Some internal psychological factors influencing consumer choice, *Journal of Consumer Research*, 2, 302–19.

Mehrabian, A. (1978). Measures of individual differences in stimulus screening and arousability, *Educational and Psychological Measurement*, 38, 1105-1117.

Mehrabian, A. (1979). Effect of emotional state on alcohol consumption, *Psychological Reports*, 44, 271–82.

Mehrabian, A. (1980). *Basic Dimensions for a General Psychological Theory.* Cambridge, MA: Oelgeschlager, Gunn & Hain.

Mehrabian, A. (1995). Framework for a comprehensive description and measurement of emotional scales, *Genetic, Social, and General Psychology Monographs* , 2, 341–361.

Mehrabian, A. & Riccioni, M. (1986). Measures of eating-related characteristics for the general population: relationships with temperament, *Journal of Personality Assessment*, 50, 610–29.

Mehrabian, A. & Russell, J. A. (1974a). *An Approach to Environmental Psychology*, Cambridge, MA: MIT Press.

Mehrabian, A. & Russell, J. A. (1974b). The basic emotional impact of environments, *Perceptual and Motor Skills*, 38, 283–301.

Mehrabian, A. & Russell, J. A. (1975). Environmental effects on affiliation among strangers, *Humanitas*, 11, 219–30.

Mehrabian, A. & de Wetter, R. (1987). Experimental test of an emotion-based approach to fitting brand names to products, *Journal of Applied Psychology*, 72, 125–30.

Menger, C. (1956). *Gruendste der Volkwirtschaftslehre*, trans. Dingwall, J. and Hoselitz, B. F. Glencoe, IL: Free Press.

Michael, J. (1982). Distinguishing between discriminative and motivational functions of stimuli. *Journal of the Experimental Analysis of Behavior*, 37, 149–155.

Michael, J. (1993). Establishing operations. *The Behavior Analyst*, 16, 191–206.

Miller, G. A. (1956). The magical number seven plus or minus two: Some limits on our capacity for processing information, *Psychological Review*, 63, 81–96.

Miller, G. A. (1962). *Psychology*. Harmondsworth: Penguin.

Miller, G. A., Galanter, E. & Pribram, K. H. (1960). *Plans and the Structure of Behavior*. New York: Holt, Rinehart and Winston.

Mittal, B. (1988). Achieving higher seat belt usage: the role of habit in bridging the attitude-behavior gap, *Journal of Applied Social Psychology*, 18, 993–1016.

Moore, J. (1981). On mentalism, methodological behaviorism and radical behaviorism, *Behaviorism*, 9, 59–67.

Moore, J. (1994). On introspection and verbal reports. In: Hayes, S. C., Hayes, L. J., Sato, M. & Ono K. (eds) *Behavior Analysis of Language and Cognition*. Context Press, Reno, NV. pp. 281–99.

Moore, J. (1999). The basic principles of behaviorism. In Thyer, B. A. (ed) *The Philosophical Legacy of Behaviorism*. Dordrecht: Kluwer. pp. 41–68.

Morgan, R. L. & Heise, D. (1988). Structure of emotions, *Social Psychology Quarterly*, 51, 19–31.

Morojele, N .K. & Stephenson, G. M. (1992). The Minnesota model in the treatment of addiction: a social psychological assessment of changes in beliefs and attributions, *Journal of Community and Applied Social Psychology*, 2, 25–41.

Morwitz, V. G., Johnson, E. & Schmittlein, D. (1993). Does measuring intent change behavior? *Journal of Consumer Research*, 20, 46–61.

Mostyn, B. (1978). *The Attitude–Behaviour Relationship*. Bradford: MCB Publications.

Murphy, C. D. (1914). What makes men buy. In *Advertising*. New York: A. W. Shaw.

Myers-Levy, J. (1991). Elaborating on elaboration: the distinction between relational and item-specific elaboration, *Journal of Consumer Research*, 18, 358–67.

Neisser, V. (1967). *Cognitive Psychology*. Englewood Cliffs, NJ: Prentice-Hall.

Netemeyer, R. G., Burton, S. & Johnston, M. (1991). A comparison of two models for the prediction of volitional and goal-directed behaviors: a confirmatory analysis approach, *Social Psychology Quarterly*, 54, 87–100.

Newcomb, T. N., Turner, R. H. & Converse, P. E. (1965). *Social Psychology*. New York: Holt.

Newell, A. & Simon, H. A. (1956). The logic theory machine: A complex information processing system, *IRE Transactions on Information Theory*, IT-2(3), 61–79.

Newell, A., Shaw, J. C. & Simon, H. A. (1958). Elements of a theory of human problem solving, *Psychological Review*, 65, 151–66.

Newman, A. & Foxall, G. R. (2003). In-store customer behaviour in the fashion sector: some emerging methodological and theoretical direction, *International Journal of Retail and Distribution Management*, 31, 591–600.

Nicosia, F. M. (1966) *Consumer Decision Processes*, Englewood Cliffs, NJ: Prentice-Hall.

Nord, W. R. & Peter, J. P. (1980). A behavior modification perspective on marketing, *Journal of Marketing*, 44, 36–7.

Oliveira-Castro, J. M., Foxall, G. R. & Schrezenmaier, T. C. (2005a). Patterns of consumer response to retail price differentials. *Service Industries Journal*, in press.

Oliveira-Castro, J. M., Foxall, G. R. & Schrezenmaier, T. C. (2005b). Consumer brand choice: individual and group analyses of demand elasticity. *Journal of the Experimental Analysis of Behavior*. In press.

Olson, J. M. & Zanna, M. P. (1993). Attitudes and attitude change, *Annual Review of Psychology*, 44, 117–54.

Osgood, C. E. & Tannenbaum, P. H. (1955). The principle of congruity in the prediction of attitude change, *Psychological Review*, 62, 42–55.

Osgood, C. E., Suci, G. J. & Tannenbaum, P. H. (1957). *The Measurement of Meaning* Urbana, IL: University of Illinois Press.

Osgood, C. E., May, W. H. & Miron, M. S. (1975).*Cross-cultural Universals of Affective Meaning*. Urbana, IL: University of Illinois Press.

O'Shaughnessy, J. & O'Shaughnessy, N. J. (2003). *The Marketing Power of Emotion*. Oxford: Oxford University Press.

Ostrom, T. M. (1994). Foreword. In: Wyer, R. S. & Srull, T. K. (eds) *Handbook of Social Cognition. Volume 1: Basic Processes*. Hillsdale, NJ: Erlbaum. pp. vii–xii.

Ostrom, T. M., Prior, J. B. & Simpson, D. D. (1981). The organization of social information. In: Higgins, E. T., Herman, C. P. & Zanna, M. P. (eds) *Social Cognition: The Ontario Symposium*. Hillsdale, NJ: Erlbaum. pp. 3–38.

Overskeid, G. (1995). Cognitive or behaviorist – who can tell the difference? The case of implicit and explicit knowledge, *British Journal of Psychology*, 46, 312–19.

Palmer, D. C. (1991). A behavioral interpretation of memory. In Hayes, L. J. & Chase, P. N. (eds) *Dialogues on Verbal Behavior*. Reno, NV: Context Press. pp. 259–279.

Parrott, L. J. (1986). The role of postulation in the analysis of inapparent events. In Reese, H. W. & Parrott, L. J. (eds) *Behavior Science: Philosophical, Methodological, and Empirical Advances*. Hillsdale, NJ: Erlbaum. pp. 35–60.

Pavlov, I. (1927). *Conditioned Reflexes*. London: Oxford University Press.

Petty, R. E. & Cacioppo, J. T. (1986a) *Communication and Persuasion: Central and Peripheral Routes to Attitude Change*. New York: Springer-Verlag.

Petty, R. E. & Cacioppo, J. T. (1986b). The elaboration likelihood model of persuasion. In: Berkowitz, L. (ed) *Advances in Experimental Social Psychology*, 19, 123–205.

Petty, R. E., Unnava, R. & Strathman, A. J. (1991). Theories of attitude change. In: Robertson, T. S. & Kassarjian, H. H. (eds) *Handbook of Consumer Behavior*. Englewood Cliffs, NJ: Prentice-Hall. pp. 241–280.

Petty, R. E., Priester, J. R. & Wegener, D. T. (1994). Cognitive processes in attitude change. In: Wyer, R. S. & Srull, T. K. (eds) (1994) *Handbook of Social Cognition. Volume 2: Application*. Second edition. Hillsdale, NJ: Erlbaum.

Philosophical Topics (1994). The Philosophy of Daniel Dennett. *Philosophical Topics* 22(1&2), 1–568.

Pierce, W. D. & Epling, W. F. (1983). Choice, matching, and human behavior, *The Behavior Analyst*, 6, 57–76.

Poppen, R. L. (1989). Some clinical implications of rule-governed behavior. In: Hayes, S. C. (ed.) *Rule-governed Behavior*. New York: Plenum. pp. 325–57.

Popper, K. (1992). *Unended Quest: An Intellectual Autobiography*. London: Routledge.

Quine, W. V. O. (1960). *Word and object*. Cambridge, MA: MIT Press.

Raats, M. N., Shepherd, R. & Sparks, P. (1995). Including moral dimensions of choice within the structure of the Theory of Planned Behavior, *Journal of Applied Social Psychology*, 25, 484–94.

Rachlin, H. (1982). Economics of the matching law. In Commons, M. L., Herrnstein, R. J. & Rachlin, H. (eds) *Quantitative Analysis of Behavior. Volume II: Matching and Maximizing Accounts*. Cambridge, MA: Ballinger. pp. 347–374.

Rachlin, H. (1989). *Judgment, Decision, and Choice: A Cognitive/Behavioral Synthesis*. New York: Freeman.

Rachlin, H. (1994) *Behavior and Mind: The Roots of Modern Psychology*, New York: Oxford University Press.

Rajala, A. K., & Hantula, D. A. (2000). Towards a behavioral ecology of consumption: Delay-reduction effects on foraging in a simulated internet mall. *Managerial and Decision Economics*, 21, 145–158.

Rajecki, D. W. (1982) *Attitudes: Themes and Advances*. Sunderland, MA: Sinauer.

Ramsey, S. L., Lord, C. G., Wallace, D. S. & Pugh, M. A. (1994). The role of subtypes in attitudes toward superordinate social categories, *British Journal of Social Psychology*, 33, 387–403.

Randall, D. M. & Wolff, J. A. (1994). The time interval in the intention-behaviour relationship, *British Journal of Social Psychology*, 33, 405–18.

Rao, A. R. & Monroe, K. B. (1988). The moderating effect of prior knowledge on cue utilization in product evaluations, *Journal of Consumer Research*, 15, 253–63.

Rao, A. R. & Sieben, W. A. (1992). 'The effects of prior knowledge on price acceptability and the type of information examined', *Journal of Consumer Research*, 19, 256–70.

Reese, H. W. (1992a). Rules as nonverbal entities. In: Hayes, S. C. & Hayes, L. J. (eds) *Understanding Verbal Relations*. Reno, NV: Context Press. pp. 121–34.

Reese, H. W. (1992b). Problem solving by algorithms and heuristics. In: Hayes, S. C. & Hayes, L. J. (eds) *Understanding Verbal Relations*. Reno, NV: Context Press. pp. 153–80.

Reese, II. W. (1994). Cognitive and behavioral approaches to problem-solving. In: Hayes, S. C., Hayes, L. J., Sato, M. & Ono, K. (eds) *Behavior Analysis of Language and Cognition*. Reno, NV: Context Press. pp. 197–258.

Reich, B. & Adcock, C. (1976). *Values, Attitudes and Behaviour Change*. London: Methuen.

Ribes, E. (1991). Language as contingency-substitution behavior. In: Hayes, L. J. & Chase, P. N. (eds) *Dialogues on Verbal Behavior*. Reno, NV: Context Press. pp. 47–58.

Ribes, E. (1992). An analysis of thinking. In: Hayes, S. C. & Hayes, L. J. (eds) *Understanding Verbal Relations*. Reno, NV: Context Press. pp. 209–24.

Richard, R. (1994) *Regret is what you get: the impact of anticipated feelings and emotions on human behaviour*. Unpublished doctoral dissertation. University of Amsterdam.

Richelle, M. N. (1993) *B. F. Skinner: A Reappraisal*. London: Erlbaum.

Rogers, E. M. (1962). *Diffusion of Innovation*. New York: Free Press.

Rogers, E. M. & Shoemaker, F. F. (1971). *Communication of Innovations*. New York: Free Press.

Ronis, D. L., Yates, J. F. & Kirscht, J. P. (1989) 'Attitudes, decisions and habits as determinants of repeated behavior'. In: Pratkanis, A. R., Breckler, S. J. & Greenwald, A. G. (eds) *Attitude Structure and Function*. Erlbaum, Hillsdale, NJ. pp. 213–40.

Rosenberg, M. J. (1960). An analysis of affective cognitive consistency. In Hovland, C. I., & Rosenberg, M. J. (eds), *Attitude Organization and Change*. New Haven, CT: Yale University Press. pp. 15–64.

Rosenberg, A. (1988). *Philosophy of Social Science*. Oxford: Clarendon.

Ross, D., Brook, A., & Thompson, D. (eds) (2000). *Dennett's philosophy: A comprehensive assessment*. Cambridge, MA: MIT Press.

Rossiter, J. R. & Percy, L. (1997). *Advertising Communications & Promotion Management*. Second edition. Boston, MA: Irwin McGraw-Hill.

Rothschild, M. L. & Gaidis, W. C. (1981). Behavioral learning theory: Its relevance to marketing and promotions, *Journal of Marketing*, 45, 70–78.

Russell, J. A. (1980). A circumplex model of affect, *Journal of Personality and Social Psychology*, 39, 345–356.

Russell, J. A. & Mehrabian, A. (1976). Environmental variables in consumer research, *Journal of Consumer Research*, 3, 62–3.

Russell, J. A. & Mehrabian, A. (1977). Evidence for a three-factor theory of emotions. *Journal of Research in Personality*, 11, 273–294.

Russell, J. A. & Mehrabian, A. (1978). Approach-avoidance and affiliation as functions of the emotion-eliciting quality of an environment, *Environment and Behavior*, 10, 355–87.

Russell, J. A. & Pratt, G. (1980) A description of the affective quality attributed to environments, *Journal of Personality and Social Psychology*, 38, 311–22.

Ryle, G. (1949). *The Concept of Mind*. London: Hutchinson.

Ryle, G. (1968). Thinking and reflecting. In *The Human Agent: Royal Institute of Philosophy Lectures. Volume 1 – 1966–1967*. London: Macmillan. pp. 210–226.

Sartre, J.-P. (1973). *Being and Nothingness*. Trans. H. E. Barnes. New York: Washington Square Press.

Sarver, V. T. (1983). Ajzen and Fishbein's Theory of Reasoned Action: a critical assessment, *Journal for the Theory of Social Behaviour*, 13, 155–63.

Schoggen, P. (1989). *Behavior Settings*. Stanford, CA: Stanford University Press.

Schuman, H. & Johnson, M. P. (1976). Attitudes and behavior, *Annual Review of Sociology*, 2, 161–207.

Schrezenmaier, T. C., Oliveira-Castro, J. M. & Foxall, G. R. (2004). *Consumer Choice in Behavioral Perspective*. Unpublished working paper.

Schwartz, S. H. (1978). Temporal instability as a moderator of the attitude-behavior relationship, *Journal of Personality and Social Psychology*, 36, 715–24.

Schwartz, B. & Reisberg, D. (1991). *Learning and Memory*. New York: W. W. Norton.

Scott, C. A. (1976). Effects of trial and incentives on repeat purchase behavior, *Journal of Marketing Research*, 13, 260–270.

Searle, J. (1983). *Intentionality: An essay in the philosophy of mind*. Cambridge: Cambridge University Press.

Searle, J. (1992). *The Rediscovery of the Mind*. Cambridge, MA and London: The MIT Press.

Seibold, D. (1980). Attitude-verbal report-behavior relationships as causal processes: formulation, test, and communication implications. In: Cushman, D. P. and McPhee, R. D. (eds) *Message-Attitude-Behavior Relationship*. New York: Academic Press. pp. 195–244.

Shaver, P., Schwartz, J., Kirson, D. & O'Connor, C. (1987). Emotion knowledge: Further exploration of a prototype approach, *Journal of Personality and Social Psychology*, 52, 1061–1086.

Shavitt, S. (1989). Operationalizing functional theories of attitude. In: Pratkanis, A. R., Breckler, S. J. & Greenwald, A. G. (eds) *Attitude Structure and Function*. Hillsdale, NJ: Erlbaum. pp. 311–37.

Sheeran, P. (2002). Intention–behavior relations: A conceptual and empirical review. In Stroebe, W. & Hewstone, M. (eds) *European Review of Social Psychology*, 23, 1–36.

Sheppard, B. H., Hartwick, J. & Warshaw, P. R. (1988). The Theory of Reasoned Action: A meta-analysis of past research with recommendations for modifications and future research, *Journal of Consumer Research*, 15, 325–343.

Sherif, C. W., Sherif, M. & Nebergall, R. E. (1965). *Attitude and Attitude Change*, Philadelphia: Saunders.

Sherman, E., Mathur, A. & Smith, R. B. (1997). Store environment and consumer purchase behavior: Mediating role of consumer emotions, *Psychology and Marketing*, 14, 361–378.

Shettleworth, S. J. (1998). *Cognition, Evolution, and Behavior*. Oxford: Oxford University Press.

Sidman, M. (1994). *Equivalence Relations and Behavior: A Research Story*. Boston, MA: Authors Cooperative.

Silberberg, A., Thomas, J. R. & Berendzen, N. (1991). Human choice on concurrent variable interval variable ration schedules, *Journal of the Experimental Analysis of Behavior*, 56, 575–584.

Simon, H. A. (1987). Rational decision making in business organizations. (Nobel Prize Acceptance Speech). In: Green, L. & Kagel, J. H. (eds). *Advances in Behavioral Economics*. Volume 1. Norwood, NJ: Ablex. pp. 18–47.

Skinner, B. F. (1938) *The Behavior of Organisms*. Century, New York.

Skinner, B. F. (1945). The operational analysis of psychological terms, *Psychological Review*, 52, 270–77, 291–4.

Skinner, B. F. (1947). Experimental psychology. In Denis, W. (ed) *Current Trends in Psychology*. Pittsburgh, PA: University of Pittsburgh Press.

Skinner, B. F. (1950). Are theories of learning necessary? *Psychological Review*, 57, 193–216.

Skinner, B. F. (1953) *Science and Human Behavior*. New York: Macmillan.

Skinner, B. F. (1957) *Verbal Behavior*. New York: Century.

Skinner, B. F. (1963). Behaviorism at fifty, *Science*, 140, 951–8.

Skinner, B. F. (1969) *Contingencies of Reinforcement: A Theoretical Analysis*, Englewood Cliffs, NJ: Prentice-Hall.

Skinner, B. F. (1971) *Beyond Freedom and Dignity*. New York: Knopf.

Skinner, B. F. (1974) *About Behaviorism*. New York: Knopf.

Skinner, B. F. (1977). Why I am not a cognitive psychologist, *Behaviorism*, 5, 1–10.

Skinner, B. F. (1978). *Reflection on Behaviorism and Society*. Englewood Cliffs: Prentice Hall.

Skinner, B. F. (1981). Selection by consequences. *Science, 213* (31 July), 501–504.

Skinner, B. F. (1989). The behavior of the listener. In: Hayes, S. C. (ed.) *Rule-governed Behavior: Cognition, Contingencies, and Instructional Control*. New York: Plenum. pp. 85–96.

Skinner, B. F. (1990) 'Can psychology be a science of mind?' *American Psychologist*, 45, 1206–10.

Smith, L. D. (1986) *Behaviorism and Logical Positivism: A Reassessment of the Alliance*, Stanford, CA: Stanford University Press.

Smith, S. M., Haugtvedt, C. P. & Petty, R. E. (1994) 'Need for cognition and the effects of repeated expression on attitude accessibility and extremity', *Advances in Consumer Research*, 21, 234–7.

Smith, T. L. (1994). *Behavior and its Causes*. Dordrecht: Kluwer.

Sober, E. (1993) *Philosophy of Biology*, New York: Oxford University Press.

Solso, R. L. (1973). (ed.) *Contemporary Issues in Cognitive Psychology: The Loyola Symposium*. Washington, DC: V. H . Winston and Sons.

Soriano, M. Y., Foxall, G. R. & Pearson, G. (2002). Emotional Responses to consumers' environments: An empirical examination of the behavioural perspective model in a Latin American context. *Journal of Consumer Behaviour*, 2, 138–154.

Sparks, P. & Shepherd, R. (1995). 'Self-identity and the Theory of Planned Behavior: assessing the role of identification with "green consumerism"', *Social Psychology Quarterly*, 55, 388–99.

Sparks, P., Hedderley, D. & Shepherd, R. (1991). Expectancy-value models of attitudes: a note on the relationsip between theory and methodology, *European Journal of Social Psychology*, 21, 261–271.

Sparks, P., Shepherd, R. & Frewer, L. J. (1995). Assessing and structuring attitudes toward the use of gene technology in food production: the role of perceived ethical obligation, *Basic and Applied Social Psychology*, 16, 267–85.

Staats, A. W. (1975). *Social Behaviorism*. Homewood, IL: The Dorsey Press.

Staats, A. W. (1996). *Behavior and Personality: Psychological Behaviorism*. New York: Springer.

Staats, A. W. & Staats, C. K. (1958). Attitudes established by classical conditioning, *Journal of Abnormal and Social Psychology*, 57, 37–40.

Staats, A. W. & Staats, C. K. (1963). *Complex Human Behavior*. New York: Holt.

Staddon, J. E. R. (1997). Why behaviorism needs internal states. In Hayes, L. J. & Ghezzi, P. M. (eds) *Investigations in Behavioral Epistemology*. Reno, NV: Context Press. pp. 107–119.

Starch, D. (1923). *Principles of Advertising*. New York: A. W. Shaw.

Stayman, D. M. & Kardes, F. R. (1992). Spontaneous inference processes in advertising: effects of need for cognition and self-monitoring on inference generation and utilization, *Journal of Consumer Psychology*, 1, 125–42.

Stich, S. P. (1981). Dennett on intentional systems. *Philosophical Topics*, 12, 39–62.

Stich, S. P. (1983). *From Folk Psychology to Cognitive Science*. Cambridge, MA: MIT Press.

Stout, R. (1996). *Things that Happen because they Should: A Teleological Approach to Action*. Oxford: Clarendon Press.

Strong, (1925). *Principles of Selling*. New York: McGraw-Hill.

Sutton, S. (1998). Predicting and explaining intentions and behavior: How well are we doing? *Journal of Applied Social Psychology*, 28, 1317–1338.

Sutton, S. A. & Hallett, R. (1989). Understanding seat belt intentions and behavior: a decision making approach, *Journal of Applied Social Psychology*, 19, 1310–25.

Sutton, S. A., Marsh, A. & Matheson, J. (1987). Explaining smokers' decisions to stop. Test of an expectancy-value model, *Social Behavior*, 2, 35–50.

Tajfel, H. & Fraser, C. (1978). (eds) *Introducing Social Psychology*. Harmondsworth: Penguin.

Taylor, C. (1964). *The Explanation of Behaviour*. London: Routledge and Kegan Paul.

Taylor, S. D., Bagozzi, R. P. & Gaither, C. A. (2001). Gender differences in the self-regulation of hypertension, *Journal of Behavioral Medicine*, 24, 469–487.

Tesser, A. & Shaffer, D. (1990) 'Attitudes and attitude change', *Annual Review of Psychology*, 41, 479–524.

Tesser, A., Martin, L. L. & Mendolia, M. (1994). The role of thought in changing attitude strength. In: Petty, R. E. & Krosnick, J. A. (eds) *Attitude Strength: Antecedents and Consequences*. Hillsdale, NJ: Erlbaum. pp. 73–92.

Thelen, H. & Withal, J. (1949). Three frames of reference, *Human Relations*, April.

Thomas, K. (1971). (ed) *Attitudes and Behaviour*. Harmondsworth: Penguin.

Thompson, K. E., Haziris, N. & Alekos, P. J. (1994). Attitudes and food choice behavior, *British Food Journal*, 96(11), 9–13.

Thompson, K. E., Thompson, N. J. & Hill, R. W. (1995) *The role of attitude, normative and control beliefs in drink choice behaviour*, Unpublished paper. Cranfield University.

Thurstone, L. L. (1931). The measurement of social attitudes, *Journal of Abnormal and Social Psychology*, 26, 249–69.

Tolman, E. C. (1932). *Purposive Behavior*. New York: Century.

Tormala, Z. L.& Petty, R. E. (2004). Resisting persuasion and attitude certainty: A meta-cognitive analysis. In Knowles, E. & Linn, J. A. (eds) *Resistance to Persuasion*. Mahwah, NJ: Lawrence Erlbaum Associates. pp. 65–82.

Trafimow, D. & Fishbein, M. (1995). Do people really distinguish between behavioral and normative beliefs? *British Journal of Social Psychology*, 34, 257–66.

Triandis, H. (1980). Values, attitudes and interpersonal behavior. In: Howe, H. E. & Page, M. M. (eds) *Nebraska Symposium on Motivation 1979*, **27**, Lincoln: University of Nebraska Press. pp. 195–259.

Tripp, C., Jensen, T. D. & Carlson, L. (1994). The effects of multiple product endorsements by celebrities on consumers' attitudes and intentions, *Journal of Consumer Research*, 20, 535–47.

Tversky, A. & Kahneman, D. (1974). Judgment under uncertainty: heuristics and biases, *Science*, 185, 1124–31.

Uncles, M. & Ehrenberg, A. S. C. (1990). The buying of packaged goods at US retail chains, *Journal of Retailing*, 66, 278–294.

Upmeyer, A. (1989). (ed) *Attitudes and Behavioral Decisions*. New York: Springer–Verlag.

Uttal, W. R. (2001). *The New Phrenology: The Limits of Localizing Cognitive Processes in the Brain*. Cambridge, MA: MIT Press.

Vaughan, M. (1987). Rule-governed behavior and higher mental processes. In Modgil, S. and Modgil, C. (eds). *B. F. Skinner: Consensus and Controversy*. Brighton: Falmer Press. pp. 257–264.

Valentine, E. R. (1992). *Conceptual Issues in Psychology*. London: Routledge.

Van Parijs, P. (1981). *Evolutionary Explanation in the Social Sciences*. Totowa, NJ: Rowman and Littlefield.

Van den Putte, B. (1993) *On the Theory of Reasoned Action*. Unpublished doctoral dissertation. University of Amsterdam.

van Knippenberg, D., Lossie, N. & Wilke, H. (1994). In-group prototypicality and persuasion: determinants of heuristic and systematic message processing, *British Journal of Social Psychology*, 33, 289–300.

Vaughan, M. (1987). Rule-governed behavior and higher mental processes. In Modgil, S. and Modgil, C. (eds) *B. F. Skinner: Consensus and Controversy*. Brighton: Falmer Press. pp. 257–264.

Vaughan, M. E. (1991). Toward a methodology for studying verbal behavior'. In: Hayes, L. J. & Chase, P. N. (eds) *Dialogues on Verbal Behavior*. Reno, NV: Context Press. pp. 82–4.

Veblen, T. 1899. *The Theory of the Leisure Class*. New York: Macmillan.

Viner, J. (1925). The utility concept in value theory and its critics, *Journal of Political Economy*, 33, 369–87.

Vuchinich, R. E. & Tucker, J. A. (1996). The molar context of alcohol abuse. In Green, L. & Kagel, J. H. (eds) *Advances in Behavioral Economics*. Volume 3. Norwood, NJ: Ablex. pp. 133–162.

Walters, C. (1978). *Consumer Behavior*. Homewood, Illinois: Irwin.

Watson, J. B. (1914). *Behavior*. New York: Holt.

Watson, J. B. (1924). *Behaviorism*. New York: People's Institute Publishing Co.

Wearden, J. (1988). Some neglected problems in the analysis of human operant behavior. In: Davey, G. C. L. & Cullen, C. (eds) *Human Operant Conditioning and Behaviour Modification*. Chichester: Wiley.

Webster, R. (1996). *Why Freud was Wrong: Sin, Science and Psychoanalysis*, London: HarperCollins.

White, K. M., Terry, D. J. & Hogg, M. A. (1994) 'Safer sex behavior: the role of attitudes, norms and control factors', *Journal of Applied Social Psychology*, **24**, 2164–92.

Wicker, A. W. (1969). Attitude versus actions: the relationship of verbal and overt behavioral responses to attitude objects, *Social Issues*, 25, 41–78.

Wicker, A. W. (1971). An examination of the "other variables" explanation of attitude-behavior inconsistency, *Journal of Personality and Social Psychology*, 19, 18–30.

Wicker, A. W. (1979). *An Introduction to Ecological Psychology*. Monterey, CA: Brooks/Cole.

Wilson, D. T., Matthews, H. L. & Harvey, J. W. (1975). An empirical test of the Fishbein Behavioral Intention Model, *Journal of Consumer Research*, 1.

Wittgenstein, L. (1953). *Philosophical Investigations*. (ed. Anscombe, G. E. M. & Rhees, R., trans. Anscombe, G. E. M.). Oxford: Blackwell.

Wittenbraker, J., Gibbs, B. L. & Khale, L. R. (1983). Seat belt attitudes, habits, and behaviors: an adaptive amendment to the Fishbein model, *Journal of Applied Social Psychology*, 13, 406–21.

Woolley, E. M. (1914). Finding the point of contact. In *Advertising*. vol. VI of the Library of Business Practice. New York: A. W. Shaw.

Wyer, R. S. & Srull, T. K. (1986). Human cognition in its social context, *Psychological Review*, 93, 322–59.

Wyer, R. S. & Srull, T. K. (1989). *Memory and Cognition in its Social Context*. Hillsdale, NJ: Erlbaum.

Wyer, R. S. & Srull, T. K. (1994a). (eds) *Handbook of Social Cognition. Volume 1: Basic Processes*. Second edition. Hillsdale, NJ: Erlbaum.

Wyer, R. S. & Srull, T. K. (1994b). (eds) *Handbook of Social Cognition. Volume 2: Application*. Second edition. Hillsdale, NJ: Erlbaum.

Yani-de-Soriano, M. & Foxall, G. R. (2004). *The Dominance Dimension in Consumer Behavior and Retail Marketing*. Unpublished working paper.

Zettle, R. D. & Hayes, S. C. (1982). Rule-governed behavior: a potential framework for cognitive-behavioral therapy. In: Kendall, P. C. (ed.) *Advances in Cognitive – behavioral Research and Therapy*. New York: Academic Press. pp. 73–117.

Zimbardo, P. & Ebbesen, E. B. (1970). *Influencing Attitudes and Changing Behavior*. Reading, MA: Addison-Wesley.

Zuriff, G. E. (1985) *Behaviorism: A Conceptual Reconstruction*. New York: Columbia University Press.

Index